The New Catholic Geography Series

NORTH AMERICAN NEIGHBORS

AUTHORS

Sister Marion, S.C.H.

George H. McVey

Sister M. Juliana, O.P.

EDUCATIONAL CONSULTANTS

John W. Conoyer

Richard W. Ward

Sister M. Paschal, C.S.J.

Don Sharkey

Sister Julia Bertrand, O.P.

W. H. Sadlier, Inc.

New York, Chicago

CONTENTS

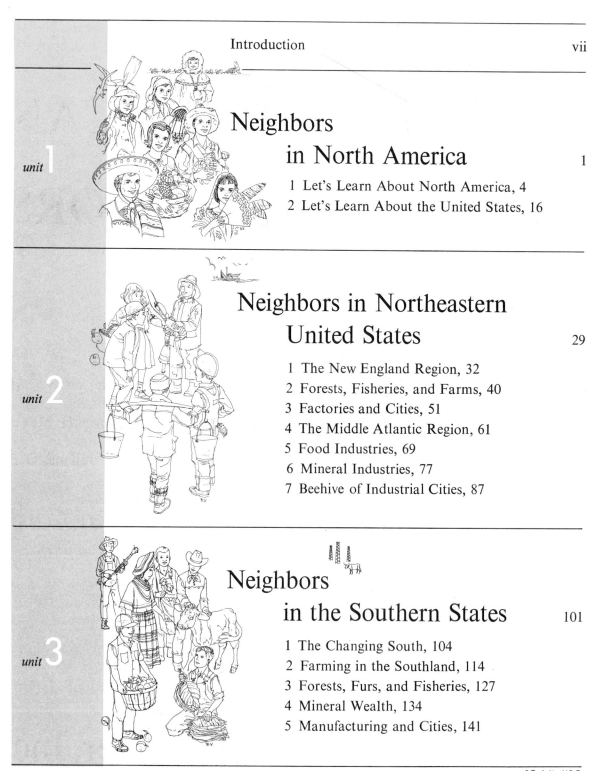

PO 1-65 VRC

COPYRIGHT 1960 • WILLIAM H. SADLIER, INC.

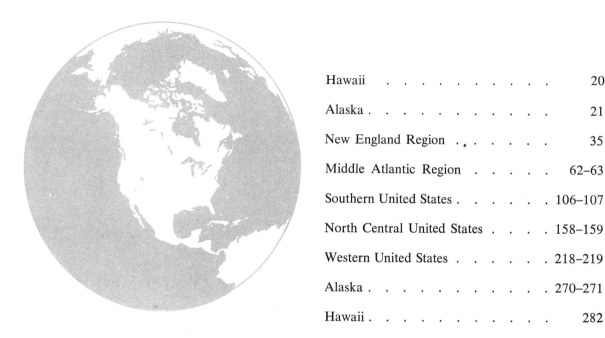

MAPS

Global Maps · Page

Product Maps · Page

Physical-Political Maps

Political Maps (atlas) · Plate

Thinking About Geography

Now you are a year older. You now have your first geography *text book*. Of course, you will still be interested in traveling to different places, and there will be many new and exciting things for you to see. But this year you will find that you also have to study important facts and learn important ideas, just as you do in history and in arithmetic.

Your geography book is divided into Units. At the beginning of each Unit you will find a short preview of the things you are going to learn in that Unit. You will then find colorful and interesting maps of the region you are going to study. Little by little, you will become used to working with maps, and you will learn why they are one of the most important tools in the study of geography.

You will also find interesting pictures of people and places. These will help you to understand the country you are studying.

Your most important duty as a Christian is to save your soul, and you must do it in this world that God has provided for us all to live in. Geography is the study of this world. Work hard, so that you will be better able to save your soul by knowing all there is to know of God's world.

How well do you remember your study of geography from last year? Perhaps you recall that you studied from a book that was written very much like a story book. It was all about traveling from one country to another around the world.

Thinking About Geography. *Geography* means the study of the earth and its people. Last year you read about many different kinds of people in different parts of the world. This year, you will be studying the geography of North America. This means that you will be studying your own region. In order to study geography correctly, you must follow certain principles. Plan to use these as you study.

Location. By location, we mean the position occupied by a continent, a country, a region, or a city—where it is situated, or placed. The location of a region tells much about the region. Look for details such as nearness to the equator, boundaries, and trade routes. For each region you study, make yourself familiar with its location by using your classroom globe, the maps in this book, and other aids.

Climate. Climate is the kind of weather a place has over a long period of time. In the same way that the weather affects you, climate affects people all over the world. It has an influence on people's choice of a place to live, how they make their living, and how they clothe and house themselves and their families. You can learn a great deal about people by studying the ways in which they adjust to different, and sometimes unpleasant, climate conditions.

Surface Features. A very important principle to keep in mind as you study each new country is the appearance of its surface. Mountains, hills, plains, valleys, grasslands, and plateaus are some of the kinds of surface features you will find. Notice the way in which each of these has a strong effect on the way people live and work, and on the climate which they enjoy.

Natural Resources. By natural resources we mean anything of use or value placed within a region by God. Wherever these gifts are plentiful, and man uses them wisely, people are better off. Not all countries, however, have equal amounts of these blessings. The United States has been generously supplied with these gifts; other countries are not so fortunate.

Trade and Transportation. In many places, people have learned to make up for a lack of resources by trading with other countries. In this way, the family of men around the world share the blessings of God upon the earth. Transportation includes all the means which people have for moving goods back and forth in trade, and for moving themselves from place to place. You will learn, for example, that the airplane is fast becoming important in the transportation of goods and people throughout the world.

Occupations and Cities. The work which men choose often depends upon the natural resources, transportation, location, and climate of their region. Knowing the occupations of people in other lands helps us understand them. Many people are occupied in farming. They grow the food which people need to live. More and more, however, people's work is bringing them together in cities. You will be interested to see the kinds of cities in which your neighbors live.

The People. You must always keep in mind that your study of geography is a study of people in different parts of the world. Understanding the geography of a country is only important when it helps us understand the people. How the people govern themselves, how they worship God, how they educate their children, how they amuse themselves and express themselves in literature and art are also important. Your study of geography this year will be successful if you have learned more about the people who are your neighbors close to home and far away.

Neighbors in North America

North America is a continent; that is, it is a great mass of land on the surface of the earth. There are seven of these continents altogether. North America is the most important one to us, because most of the people of our country live in North America.

The land area of North America is mostly taken up by three large countries—the United States, Canada, and Mexico. In addition, there are several smaller countries and some small islands which are also included in our study of the geography of North America.

This year, you will be studying all about the lands and people of North America. You will recognize some of the places because they are near your home or because you might have visited them. Many of the places will be quite new to you.

You will see that people have different ways of living, working, and playing. But you will also learn a very important fact: that people are very much the same wherever they happen to be living. God has blessed everybody with the gift of life, and to some He has given different means of using that gift. All people owe thanks to God, however, and depend upon Him. We show our thanks in one way by helping and understanding our neighbors in other parts of the world.

When you turn this page, you will see a picture of our continent as it might look from far up in the air.

In this Unit you will learn that:

1 North America is one of the seven *continents,* or land masses, on the surface of the earth.

2 North America is bounded on the east by the Atlantic Ocean, the Gulf of Mexico, and the Caribbean Sea. To the south, a narrow neck of land connects North America with South America. To the west lies the Pacific Ocean, and to the north is the Arctic Ocean.

3 The continent of North America includes Canada, Mexico, and our own country, the United States of America. There is also a number of smaller nations in the southern part of our continent, called Central America, and some islands which are considered part of North America.

4 The United States occupies the central part of North America. It stretches from the Atlantic Ocean to the Pacific, and is bounded on the north by Canada and on the south by Mexico. In addition, the states of Alaska and Hawaii are separated from the forty-eight states. Alaska is far to the north, and Hawaii is a group of islands located to the west in the Pacific Ocean.

NORTH AMERICA

If you were able to look at the earth from a point high in space, this is how North America might appear. Notice first the shape of the continent. It is wide at the top, or north, and narrows to a point in the south, where it is joined to South America.

The Atlantic Ocean lies along most of the eastern part of North America. The north Atlantic separates North America from Europe. The Pacific Ocean washes the entire western coast. It separates North America from Asia. In the north is the ice-covered Arctic Ocean. Other bodies of water, called gulfs and bays, appear to take bites out of the coast, especially in the east. Inland are the five Great Lakes and many rivers carrying water back to the sea.

The most outstanding surface feature of North America is the spiny backbone of mountains which runs from north to south all along the western coast. The Rocky Mountains are the most important group in this chain. In the center of the continent you see the wide level area of the Great Central Plain. Farther east is another, but lower, group of mountains and a narrow plain along the Atlantic coast.

Extending across the middle of the continent are forty-eight of the fifty United States of America. Canada is in the north. Projecting outward from the northwest corner of the continent is Alaska, our forty-ninth state. A group of islands far out in the Pacific make up Hawaii, our fiftieth state. South of the United States are Mexico and the other countries located in Central America and the island chain of the West Indies.

Pacific Ocean

Arctic Ocean

EUROPE

Hudson Bay

Rocky Mountains

Central Plain

Atlantic Ocean

Gulf of Mexico

West Indies

SOUTH AMERICA

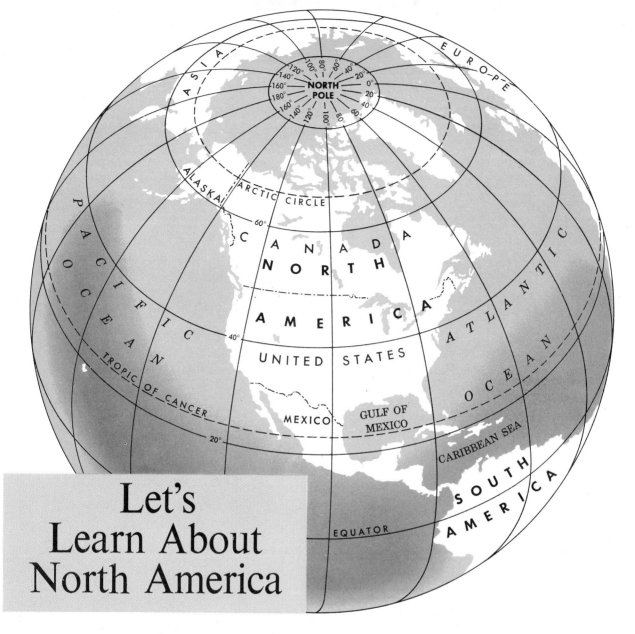

The globe shows labels including: NORTH POLE, with longitude markings 120°, 100°, 80°, 60°, 40°, 20°, 0°, 20°, 40°, 60°, 80°, 100°, 120°, 140°, 160°, 180°, 160°, 140°; ASIA, EUROPE, ALASKA, ARCTIC CIRCLE, CANADA, NORTH AMERICA, UNITED STATES, MEXICO, GULF OF MEXICO, PACIFIC OCEAN, TROPIC OF CANCER, ATLANTIC OCEAN, CARIBBEAN SEA, SOUTH AMERICA, EQUATOR; latitude markings 60°, 40°, 20°.

Let's Learn About North America

North America is a continent. This means that it is a large mass of land on the earth's surface. The continent is almost completely surrounded by oceans, and there are other smaller bodies of water inland. To learn about North America, we must first study the earth, the planet on which North America is located. When we have learned where North America is on the surface of the earth, we shall be ready to learn about North America itself.

The Earth We Live On. Our earth is a huge ball whirling through space. It makes one complete trip, or *revolution*, around the sun each year. It follows an almost circular path, called its *orbit*. While it is making this trip around the sun, it is also spinning like a top. Try to imagine a long stick pushed through this ball. The earth, or ball, spins around on this stick. It makes one spin, or *rotation*, every 24 hours.

We call the imaginary stick the *axis*. The two ends of the axis are called the *poles*. Look at the globe in your classroom.

You can see the North Pole and the South Pole. These imaginary poles will be of great help to us in our study of geography because they will help us find directions.

Directions. When someone travels toward the North Pole, he is traveling in a direction called *north*. Behind him is the direction called *south*. If he points with his right hand, he is pointing in the direction called *east,* and if he points with his left hand, he is pointing in the direction called *west*.

If you know where the North Pole is, you now can find four directions, in the shape of a cross: facing the North Pole, north; to the right, east; behind you, south; to the left, west. Of course, you must be facing toward the North Pole for these directions to be correct.

There are also many combinations of these directions. Between your right hand and the direction you are facing is another direction, called northeast — halfway between north and east. Between your left hand and the direction behind you is another — southwest. These in-between directions can be found also between west and north and between east and south.

There are lines drawn on globes and on maps. These lines can also be of help in finding directions. Some lines run from north to south; others from east to west. The north-to-south lines are called *meridians*. There is a line drawn around the surface of the earth midway between the poles. Because it seems to cut the earth in two *equal* halves, this imaginary east-to-west line is called the *equator*. In addition to the equator, other imaginary lines also circle the earth in an east-to-west direction. They are called *parallels*. Parallel means that these lines run in the same direction, and are the same distance apart.

The poles, the equator, the meridians, and the parallels will become very important to us as we study geography. Try to find each of these on your classroom globe. Remember that the poles, the parallels, and the meridians are imaginary—they do not really appear on the surface of the earth. In the diagram below, you can see some of them. Notice that one half of the earth is called a *hemisphere*.

Looking at Our Earth. The globes are cut to show the divisions of the earth into hemispheres. They are: northern and southern, eastern and western.

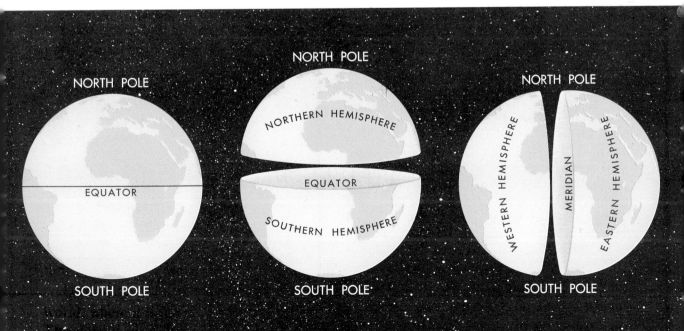

Studying the Map

A. North America is a continent in the northern hemisphere. It is wide at the north and narrows to a point in the south. It is surrounded by several different bodies of water. **1.** What are the names of the bodies of water which touch the eastern coast of North America? **2.** Which body of water washes the entire western coast of North America? **3.** Which body of water is to the north of North America? **4.** What is the name of the continent to the south, to which North America is connected at the Isthmus of Panama? **5.** What is the name of the continent which is close to the northwest corner of North America?

B. 1. Using your scale of miles, measure the north-to-south extent of North America. Measure this distance along the meridian which is labeled 80°. **2.** What is the distance from east to west across the United States, measured along the parallel labeled 40°? **3.** Name the range of mountains which extends throughout most of the western section of North America. **4.** How do these mountains compare in height with the mountain range located near the eastern coast? **5.** A great lowland area extends throughout the central part of the continent. What is its name? **6.** Does the eastern part or the western part of the Great Central Plain have the higher elevation? **7.** Find and name the lowland area along the Atlantic coast. along the coast of the Gulf of Mexico. **8.** Is the surface of Central America mostly lowland or highland? How can you tell?

C. 1. Name four large bays or gulfs which indent the coast of North America. **2.** Name the five Great Lakes. **3.** Which is the largest? **4.** Locate and name the chief river system in the central part of North America. **5.** Name three tributaries, or rivers which flow into this system. **6.** Name the river which forms the boundary between the United States and Mexico. **7.** Into which body of water does it empty? **8.** Locate the Mackenzie River in the northern part of North America. Into which body of water does it flow? **9.** Find and name the river which flows from the Great Lakes to the Atlantic Ocean. **10.** Locate the island group called the West Indies. Which are the largest of these islands? **11.** Locate and name the chain of islands which extends from the northwestern corner of North America.

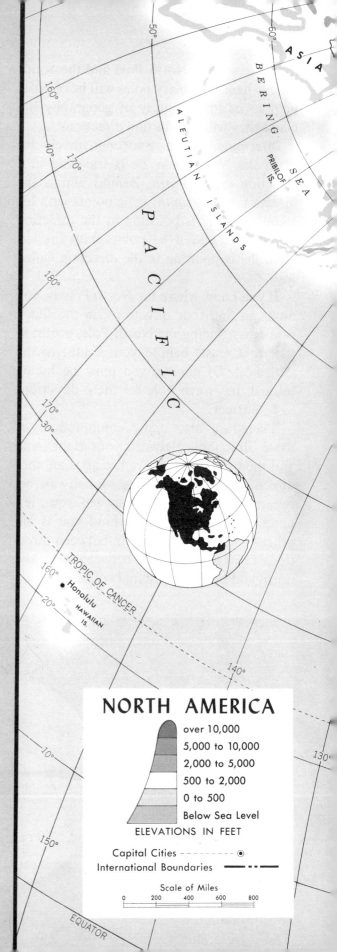

NORTH AMERICA

	over 10,000
	5,000 to 10,000
	2,000 to 5,000
	500 to 2,000
	0 to 500
	Below Sea Level

ELEVATIONS IN FEET

Capital Cities ------- ◉
International Boundaries ▬ ▬ ▪ ▬

Scale of Miles

0   200   400   600   800

Direction and the Compass. It is easy to find the direction north on the globe. North is in the direction of the North Pole. To find north on the earth, you must face the North Pole also. But how can you face the North Pole if you cannot see it?

To locate the North Pole, we use the *compass.* This is a tiny magnet, shaped like a needle. When it is allowed to turn freely, one end will point to the North Pole. This is because the earth is really a huge magnet also. Once we know the direction of the North Pole, all the other directions can be found.

The compass has always been a very important instrument for travelers. Sailors, airplane pilots, explorers, and all who must find their directions without any signs to guide them, use the compass. Perhaps you have used a compass on some trip.

Finding Directions. A group of Boy Scouts hiking in the mountains uses a map and compass to find their way home. This prevents becoming lost.

Finding Our Place on the Globe. The best way to see our continent of North America is on the classroom globe. The globe gives the only true picture of the whole earth, because the earth is round like a ball, or a globe. The whole earth can never be drawn correctly on a flat piece of paper. A flat map is only correct for small parts of the earth.

As you look at the globe, you will see that most of the earth is covered with water. As you turn the globe, you will find our continent of North America. It is a huge continent, stretching almost from the North Pole to the equator. The continent is so wide in the north that it almost touches Asia. In the south the continent is so narrow that men have dug a canal across it. This is the Panama Canal. It is in the country named Panama, the southernmost country in North America.

Now find the Atlantic Ocean, and look at North America from that direction. You will see that the Atlantic touches North America along most of its eastern side. To the south, where North America becomes narrow, a part of the Atlantic Ocean called the Gulf of Mexico cuts deep into North America. Further south, the Caribbean Sea also touches the east side of North America. This sea is separated from the Atlantic Ocean by a chain of islands sticking out from North America.

Turn your globe a little, and find the Pacific Ocean. It touches the entire western side, or *coast,* of North America. On this coast, there are fewer openings and broken places along the shoreline than on the east coast. Now find the Arctic Ocean, which is to the north. Where it touches the northern part of North America the coast is broken up into many large and small islands. You can also see where Hudson Bay extends into the northern part of North America.

ARCTIC OCEAN

ARCTIC CIRCLE

NORTH
AMERICA

EUROPE

ASIA

PACIFIC
OCEAN

ATLANTIC
OCEAN

AFRICA

PACIFIC

OCEAN

SOUTH
AMERICA

EQUATOR

INDIAN
OCEAN

AUSTRALIA

ANTARCTIC CIRCLE

ANTARCTICA

The Other Continents. Spin the globe slowly and look at all the large land masses on the surface of the earth. These large land masses are called *continents,* and there are seven continents altogether. Some of them are near our continent of North America; some are very far away. The closest one is called South America. It is connected to North America by a narrow strip of land, which is called an *isthmus.* This is the Isthmus of Panama. The Panama Canal, dug across this isthmus, links the Atlantic and Pacific Oceans. Notice that South America is shaped somewhat like North America, although it is smaller. Both are wide in the north and narrow in the south.

In the northwest corner, North America comes very close to the continent of Asia. These two giant continents are separated by a very narrow stretch of water called the Bering Strait. Australia, the smallest con-

The Continents of the Earth. Here you see the major land masses of the earth. A flat map like this does not show true sizes, as a globe would do.

tinent in the world, is very far away from North America, to the southwest. It is nearly half-way around the world. Antarctica, far to the south, is almost as far away.

To the east of North America, across the Atlantic Ocean, is the continent of Europe. You will see that Europe has had a very strong effect on North America, even though it is far away. South of Europe is the large continent called Africa.

The Size of North America. North America is the third largest of the seven continents. Only Asia and Africa are greater in area. North America covers more than nine million square miles of the earth's surface. A square mile is an area which is bounded by four equal sides, each side measuring a mile in length.

The Surface of North America. What is North America made of? Like all the other continents, it is made up of land and water. Let us examine some of the different areas of land and water in North America. We shall be studying the *surface* of our continent. The surface of a continent is important because of its effect upon the way people live and work.

Turn to the map on pages 2 and 3. It is called a *global* map of North America, because it gives us a picture of the continent very much like the picture we would see on a globe. On this map, you can see that the surface of North America takes many different shapes and forms.

Near the western edge of North America, notice the wrinkled, jagged appearance of

the surface. This indicates a long chain of *mountains*. A mountain is land that stands high above the surrounding land. These North American mountains run in a single group from north to south almost the entire length of the continent. Although they have different names in different parts of North America, we know them best as the Rocky Mountains.

In the east there is another group of mountains. This group does not appear as high or rugged as the western group. These lower, rounded, mountains are known as the Appalachians.

Between the two groups of mountains there is a long, wide, level stretch of land. Such a surface is called a *plain*. All over the world, we find most people make their homes on plains. You will be interested to discover, as you continue to study geography, why this is so.

Typical Land Forms. This is a picture of an imaginary countryside. Notice that more houses and buildings appear on the plain. Do you know why?

MOUNTAINS

HILLS

VALLEY

PLATEAU

PLAIN

Rivers are Important. The river in this picture has its *source*, or beginning, in the distant mountains. It provides water and transportation.

The plain in the middle of the continent of North America is called the Central Plain. This plain extends from the Gulf of Mexico in the south to the Arctic Ocean in the north. Near the Rocky Mountains, in the west, it becomes slightly higher ground and is called the Great Plains.

The Rivers and Lakes. In the middle of North America, running from north to south, is a long body of water called a *river*. A river is a body of water which flows from a high place across the land to a larger body of water. Often smaller rivers join together and become bigger and bigger as they head for the sea. Rivers pouring down from mountain heights move quickly and powerfully. Across level land, rivers spread out and move more slowly.

The river you see in the middle of North America is really a group of rivers. The most important ones are the Missouri, the Mississippi, and the Ohio. In the west there are many smaller rivers pouring into the Pacific Ocean. On the east coast also, many rivers pour into the Atlantic Ocean. We shall learn more about all of them in the chapters to come. We shall see how the rivers continue to serve mankind by providing fresh water, a quick and easy way to travel, and a source of great power to turn the wheels of factories.

The Great Lakes in Perspective. In this artist's view of the Great Lakes, notice the different heights above sea level. Canals allow ships to descend.

On the map you can see another large body of water in the center of North America. More exactly, it is five oddly shaped bodies of water, lying close to each other. These five bodies of water are called the Great Lakes. In addition, there are many smaller lakes dotting the surface of North America. They are useful to man in many ways. Most of our important rivers start in lakes as they begin their journey to the ocean. A large number of lakes have been formed behind man-made dams.

On the map you will also notice several bodies of water in North America which are much larger than lakes. In the north, there is Hudson Bay. It is like a long arm of the Arctic Ocean cutting into the land. Farther south, the Gulf of Mexico seems to take a large bite out of North America. It is an extension of the Atlantic Ocean. There are also many smaller bays all around the shores of North America. You will soon learn the important uses these have.

Climate of North America. Everyone knows what weather is; at least everyone complains about it often enough. *Climate* is a word which describes the kind of weather a place usually has over long periods of time.

Climate is very important if we want to understand how men live and work in any part of the world. Certain kinds of climate affect people in certain ways. There are some jobs which would be pleasant in cool weather, but unpleasant in hot weather. Other jobs can only be done in hot weather, like growing cotton or tobacco. The houses we live in are built according to the kind of weather we usually have. The kind of clothes we wear and the games we play all depend upon the climate.

In North America, the weather changes often. This is not true in some parts of the world, where it is the same all year around. Throughout most parts of North America, there are four different seasons, each with different kinds of weather.

There are several reasons for our changing climate. North America lies between the equator, where it is mostly very hot, and the North Pole, where it is mostly very cold. Its climate goes mostly from warm to cool. Many parts of the continent of North America are located near large bodies of water. This location helps keep land warmer in the winter and cooler in the summer. The winds which blow over North America move most often from west to east. These winds bring frequent weather changes, often causing the weather to change each day.

Natural Resources. *Natural resources* are the gifts which God has placed in nature for man's use. They require that man use his strength and his wisdom to change them into useful forms. They also require that man use them carefully, and not waste them. In the future, men will still have need for them. If we waste them, future Americans will suffer the loss.

Natural resources include the soil in which we grow our food, the forests which give us wood and paper, the ground which gives us oil, coal, iron, aluminum and so many other metals. Other natural resources are the rivers and lakes which give us ways to carry ourselves and our goods from place to place, and the sea which gives us fish to eat and makes our climate pleasant.

In these and many, many other ways, North America has been plentifully blessed by God. This continent, blessed in its resources and its climate, in location and beauty, is truly a wonderful place for us to live and work and play.

Forest Wealth. Wood is a very important natural resource. The timber floating down this stream will go to make houses, furniture, and paper.

THE PEOPLE OF NORTH AMERICA

To learn geography, we study the location, surface, and climate of a country, as well as its natural resources, cities, farms, and other facts. Learning these facts is important, but not so important as learning about the people who live there. Geographic facts are important only because they influence the way people live, work, and play.

There are many people in North America — about 256 million of them. The special map below shows the areas where the largest numbers of North Americans live. You can see in the pictures on these pages that in different parts of North America, people look and dress according to the climate and customs of their surroundings.

You should always keep in mind, however, that no matter how different people may look, they are all, like us, children of the same Heavenly Father. The more you learn about our neighbors in North America, the more you will come to understand and appreciate them as members of this great family.

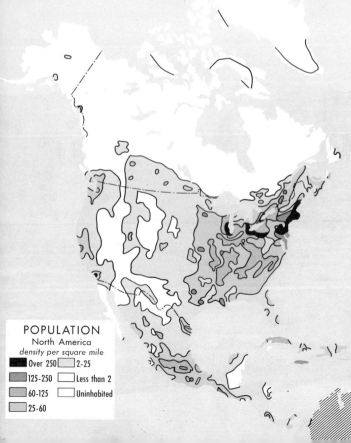

POPULATION
North America
density per square mile

- Over 250
- 125-250
- 60-125
- 25-60
- 2-25
- Less than 2
- Uninhabited

Facts *to remember*

1. North America, the third largest continent, is located in the Northern Hemisphere. It is bounded on the east by the Atlantic Ocean, the Gulf of Mexico, and the Caribbean Sea; by the Pacific Ocean to the west; and by the Arctic Ocean to the north. In the south it is connected to South America.

2. The Rocky Mountains in the west and the Appalachian Highlands in the east are major mountain groups. Between them lies the Central Plain. In North America there are many major rivers, five Great Lakes and many smaller lakes, and numerous coastal bays and inlets.

3. The climate of North America is generally temperate, with four seasons. However, in the southern part the climate is more nearly tropical —wet and hot—and in the north it is very cold. On the coast and near large bodies of water the climate does not have the extremes of temperature found farther inland.

4. Natural resources include all the gifts which God has placed in nature for man's use. The natural resources of North America are many— soil, forests, minerals, water supply, and fish are some of them.

What *have I learned?*

Answer each question in a complete sentence.

1. What is the name of the imaginary stick around which the earth spins?

2. What are the north-to-south lines on a map called?

3. Which is the most exact picture of the earth— a map or a globe?

4. What is the name of the ocean which touches North America along its eastern side?

5. What do we call the large land masses on the surface of the earth?

6. How many continents are there?

7. How does North America compare with the other continents in size?

8. Why are certain maps called *global* maps?

9. Name the three important rivers that are located in the middle of North America.

10. What word indicates the kind of weather a place is used to having over a long period of time?

2 Let's Learn About the United States

Our Nation's Capital. Washington, D. C., is the home of the Government of the United States. Many citizens visit their capital city every year.

What should you learn about your own country? The answer is, of course—everything. As you go through school, you will be studying about people and places in many different parts of the world, like those you read about last year. It is important first, though, that you know all you can about the people and places of your own country.

If you live in the northern part of the United States, you may know very little about how people live and work in the south. If you live on the coast, you may never have seen a prairie; if you live in the city, you may never have seen a field of wheat. Yet all of these things are part of the United States. In the chapters ahead you will learn about them, and many more.

A Good Location. Turn back to pages 2 and 3 and look again at the global map of North America. What are some physical features you see on the map which people might find very useful? First of all, notice the wide, green central lowland, or plains area, of North America. People living in a country in which these plains are located would use the good farm land to produce much of their food. Second, notice the east and west coasts of North America. A country which included both of these would have an excellent means for trading with other countries of the world. Certainly the long river systems and the lakes in the center of the continent would be desirable features for a country to have, also.

There are other desirable qualities not showing so clearly on the map. Which part of North America has the best climate? Remember that the continent extends a very long way from north to south. A country which is located in the middle of North America would avoid a climate that is either very hot or very cold. A country located in this part of the continent could be expected to enjoy a fairly moderate climate, with few extremes of hot or cold.

The map does not show the vast areas of valuable woodland covering the slopes of the Appalachian Mountains, or the coal deposits lying under the ground. Nor does it show the areas where valuable iron ore is found near the Great Lakes, the areas around the Gulf of Mexico where precious oil waits to be pumped, the numbers of fish which abound in all the coastal waters, or the many ideal locations for cities.

This Is Your Country. The United States of America is the nation, blessed by God, which occupies the most desirable area on the continent of North America. All the desirable features just listed are found in this fortunate land. Look at the physical-political map of the United States on pages 18 and 19. The U. S. stretches across the middle of North America, from the Atlantic Ocean to the Pacific. Two other parts of North America are also included as part of the United States—Alaska, in the very northern part of the continent, and Hawaii, a group of islands in the Pacific Ocean. Look at the maps of Alaska and Hawaii on pages 20 and 21.

Favored by location, climate, natural resources, and an energetic and courageous population, the United States has risen to its present position of world leadership. In the following pages you will learn more about the many gifts which God has showered on this land. Always remember the obligation that is upon all men to use God's gifts according to His plan, sharing them in justice. This obligation is especially binding upon us, as citizens of the United States. We have received so much.

Size and Location. The United States occupies an area of more than 3 million square miles. When the two separated states of Alaska and Hawaii are considered, the total is more than 3½ million square miles of the earth's surface. The United States is the fourth largest country in the world; only Soviet Russia (the largest), China, and Canada have greater areas.

In the picture below, you can compare the area of the United States with the area of Russia. Notice that the maps of each country have been placed over each other.

The United States and the Soviet Union. A comparison map shows the difference in size between these giants. How else do the countries differ?

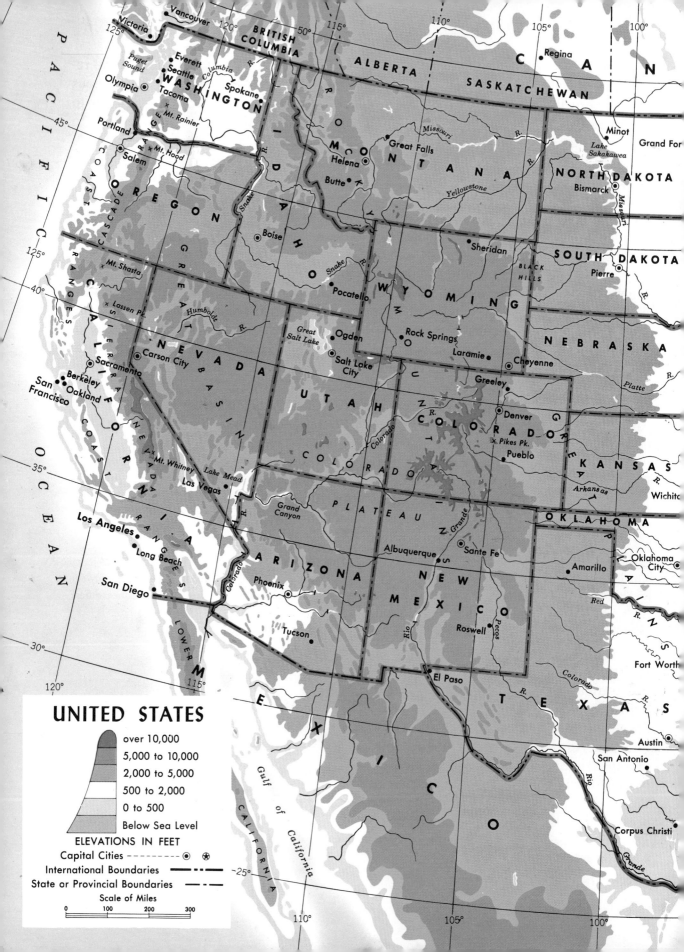

Studying the Map

On pages 18 and 19 the Physical-Political map of the United States appears. This map includes the forty-eight states which lie together in the central part of the continent of North America. On these pages the Physical-Political maps of Hawaii and Alaska, our forty-ninth and fiftieth states, appear. The key in each map shows how color tints are used to indicate elevation above sea level.

A. On pages 18 and 19 the Rocky Mountains can be seen located in the western section of the United States. **1.** Which states are crossed by this great mountain range? **2.** What other mountain groups appear in the western section of the United States? **3.** How do they compare in height with the Rocky Mountains? **4.** What central highland area can be found in the states of Missouri and Arkansas? **5.** What is the major mountain group in the eastern section of the United States? **6.** How do the mountains of the East compare in height with the Rocky Mountains? in extent?

B. 1. What name is given to the lowland region of central United States? **2.** What is the western part of this region called? **3.** What is the name of the plain located along the eastern coast of the United States? **4.** What is the name of the plain located along the southern coast of the United States?

C. 1. How does the shape and outline of the eastern coast of the United States compare with that of the western coast? **2.** What are the names of the five Great Lakes? **3.** Name and trace the direction of flow of five major rivers of the United States.

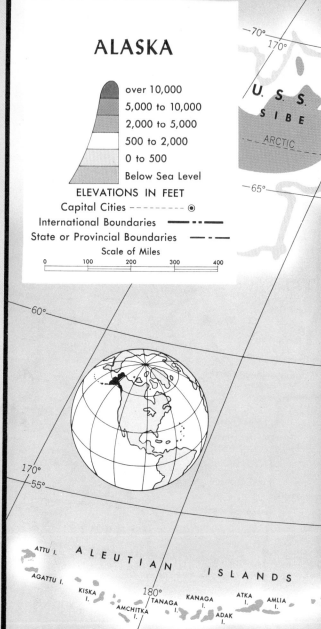

Studying the Map of Hawaii

1. Name the major islands of the Hawaiian Island group, from southeast to northwest. **2.** On which island do you find the greatest elevation above sea level? **3.** On which islands do you find lowland areas? **4.** What city is the capital of the state of Hawaii? **5.** On which island is it located? **6.** Between what degrees of latitude are the main islands of Hawaii located? **7.** What does this indicate about the climate of our fiftieth state?

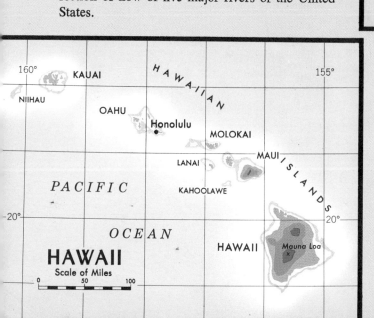

Studying the Map of Alaska

A. Alaska is the largest of the fifty United States. It extends as a peninsula from the northwest corner of North America, and includes a chain of islands to the southwest, and a strip of coastline and coastal islands to the southeast. **1.** What is the point of highest elevation in the state of Alaska? **2.** How does this compare with the point of highest elevation on the map of the forty-eight states on pages 18-19? **3.** Using the scale of miles, determine the distance which separates Alaska from Asia. **4.** What is the name of the narrow body of water between Alaska and Asia? **5.** Name three large rivers of Alaska. **6.** Name three major cities of Alaska. **7.** What is the name of the capital of Alaska? **8.** What is the name of the group of islands which extends like a chain from southwestern Alaska into the Pacific Ocean? **9.** What country is along the eastern border of Alaska? **10.** What country occupies that part of Asia which is closest to Alaska? **11.** What is the northernmost place in Alaska? **12.** What is the southernmost city of Alaska? **13.** Approximately how many miles separate the two places?

Western Wilderness. The Yellowstone River plunges on its course through a steep-sided gorge. This is in the rugged Rocky Mountain section of our land.

The northern border of the United States extends from the Atlantic Ocean to the Pacific Ocean. Across this border to the north is the country of Canada. To the east, along its entire coast, the United States faces the Atlantic Ocean. In the south, the waters of the Gulf of Mexico wash our shores. From the Gulf of Mexico to the Pacific Ocean runs the border between the United States and the country of Mexico. Along the western shore, the United States faces the broad Pacific Ocean. The United States extends like a wide belt across the entire middle of the continent of North America.

Roughly one thousand miles to the north of this belt the huge state of Alaska bulges out from the northwestern corner of North America. It is the largest state of the United States, occupying more than one half million square miles. It is bounded by Canada in the east, the Pacific Ocean to the south, and the Arctic Ocean to the north. West of Alaska, across the narrow Bering Strait, lies Asia.

Our fiftieth state, Hawaii, is situated in the Pacific Ocean, two thousand miles from our western shore. This island group occupies 6,423 square miles, and is completely surrounded by the warm waters of the Pacific Ocean.

Surface of the United States. Most of the major surface features which you read about in North America are found within the borders of the United States as well. The vast Central Plain of North America is perhaps our outstanding surface feature, taking up almost the entire middle of the United States. In the west, the Rocky Mountains run in a north-to-south direction. Mount Whitney is the highest mountain in California—14,495 feet above sea level. However, Mount McKinley in Alaska is the highest mountain in the United States—20,320 feet. In the east, a lower range of mountains called the Appalachians runs from north to south.

Between the Appalachians and the Atlantic Ocean is the Atlantic Coastal Plain. This lowland runs the entire length of the coast, extending inland several hundred miles. In the south, the Gulf Coastal Plain faces the Gulf of Mexico. Farther west, the Colorado Plateau is a high, flat-topped area rising above the Great Plains. On the west coast, there is no wide coastal plain as in the east or the south. Between the low mountains along the Pacific coast, however, and the higher mountains further inland there are long, fertile valleys. Like the Atlantic and Gulf Coastal Plains, these valleys are good farm lands.

Rivers and Lakes. The one most important river in the United States is really a system made up of several rivers. It is called the Mississippi-Missouri River system. Find it on the map on pages 18 and 19. Notice that this system has branches extending into widely separated areas of central, western, and eastern United States. We say that it *drains* this vast area. The soil and mud which it carries along in its course to the Gulf of Mexico are deposited where the Mississippi reaches the southern coast. This pileup of soil and mud is called a *delta*. Notice how the Mississippi Delta extends out into the waters of the Gulf.

Other important rivers are the Arkansas, the Red River, the Ohio, and the Allegheny, which pour into the Mississippi-Missouri from different directions; the Columbia in the northwest, and the Snake River which joins it; the Rio Grande which forms the boundary between the United States and Mexico in the south, and pours into the Gulf of Mexico; and the Yukon in Alaska, which empties into the Bering Sea.

We have already learned about the five large lakes of central North America, called the Great Lakes. They lie between the United States and Canada. See the map on pages 18 and 19. Reading from west to east, their names are Superior (the largest), Michigan, Huron, Erie, and Ontario. There are many other lakes scattered throughout the United States. Some of them are large, man-made lakes which have grown where dams were built across rivers.

Forests of the United States. One of the most important natural resources of the United States is its large area of forest land. At one time, nearly the entire Atlantic Coastal Plain was covered with trees. They gradually thinned out because the people needed to clear the trees for farming, and also because of wasteful ways of lumbering.

Today we realize that forests are valuable in many ways. They are valuable for the wood and wood products which they can supply. They must be saved so that they will continue to provide these products in the future, and not be entirely used up in the present. In addition, forests are of great help in protecting good cropland. We shall learn about all this as we go on with our study of different regions of the United States of America.

Croplands of the United States. *Cropland* means land that is suitable for raising food. *Growing season* means the amount of time each year in which crops and vegetables can be raised—the number of months of suitable weather. We are very fortunate in the United States because we have both a large area of very good cropland, and generally a long growing season. As a result, we are able to provide more than enough food to supply the needs of every man, woman, and child in the country. In fact, each year we have a *surplus* of food; that is, a quantity of food left over after everybody's needs have been filled. This surplus

America's Cropland. Rich soil is a valuable resource for any nation. Here a tractor is cultivating a field, turning over the rich, fertile soil.

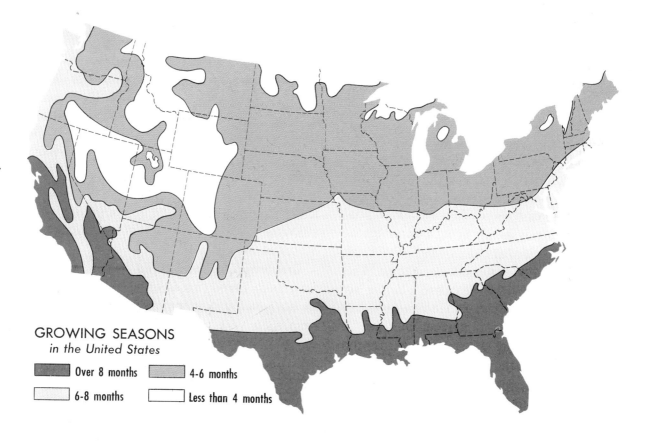

GROWING SEASONS
in the United States

■ Over 8 months	▨ 4-6 months
▫ 6-8 months	□ Less than 4 months

is usually sold or given to areas of the world where cropland and growing season are not so favorable. In this way we share with others the gifts God has given us.

YEARLY RAINFALL
in the United States

■ Over 60 inches	□ 10-20 inches
▨ 40-60 inches	□ Less than 10 inches
▫ 20-40 inches	

There are millions of square miles of rich cropland in our Great Plains area in the central part of the country. In the western section, where there is less rain, the land is used for grazing cattle to provide meat for our tables. In addition, every state in the United States has land that is suitable for growing certain crops. Only in Alaska will you find conditions which do not favor farming so well, as we shall see.

Climate of the United States. Although the climate is quite different from one part of the United States to another, we can say that it is generally a moderate climate throughout. Regions along the coasts, for example, enjoy a mild climate brought about by the steady ocean winds, while the interior sections have a climate that is quite changeable, with frequent extremes of hot and cold. The southern section has a warmer climate than the northern section.

The maps on page 24 help to show the climate of the United States. They show the length of the growing season and the amounts of rainfall received in different parts of the country.

Our Mineral Wealth. Another of our very valuable natural resources, and one which people often think of first, is our mineral wealth. By mineral wealth we mean all the metal, fuel and chemical products which are dug, scraped, or pumped up out of the earth. Some examples of our mineral wealth are oil, coal, iron, copper, salt, lead, sulfur, and many others.

With minerals as with cropland, almost every region of the United States abounds in one or more of these valuable gifts of God. Because these minerals are all used in making other things, or making machinery run, the United States has become the greatest industrial nation in the world. Like our other resources, minerals must be used wisely, with thought taken for the needs of future Americans.

Underground Wealth. Coal is one of the many minerals which a modern, industrial nation like ours has to have. Miners have a hard, but important, job.

THE PEOPLE OF
THE UNITED STATES

The very first people to live in our country were the Indians. Men who have studied history very carefully think that the Indians may have come from Asia. It is possible that, very long ago, the Indians might have come across the narrow Bering Strait into Alaska. Some may have sailed across the Pacific Ocean. Nobody knows for sure. But the Indians were here for a very long time before anybody else came to North America. They lived simply—hunting and fishing, and doing some farming. They gathered together in tribes, or nations, and in each part of the continent a certain group of Indians made their homes.

The first settlement of people from Europe was made on the eastern coast of North America. Remember, at that time there was no country called the United States. These European people sailed across the Atlantic with their families and made their homes in a land that was still wild and unsettled except for the Indians. They came from England, France, Spain, Sweden, Holland, Germany, and many other places in Europe. Often the countries of Europe which sent these settlers quarreled and warred over the ownership of land in America. Gradually, the settlers forgot their homelands in Europe and decided to make their own country in America. Thirteen small *colonies,* or settlements, on the east coast joined together. As you know, they fought a war against England, their "mother country." When they won the war, they established the United States of America.

More and more people came from Europe to the new country. They were attracted by the freedom which Americans enjoyed— freedom to practice their religion peacefully, freedom to choose their own government, freedom to choose their own way of life. Often these freedoms did not exist in the countries of Europe. The new settlers joined the older settlers in working and planning to maintain these freedoms in the United States of America.

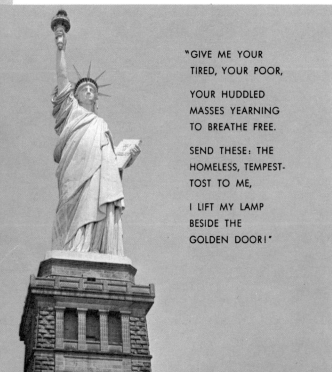

"GIVE ME YOUR TIRED, YOUR POOR,

YOUR HUDDLED MASSES YEARNING TO BREATHE FREE.

SEND THESE: THE HOMELESS, TEMPEST-TOST TO ME,

I LIFT MY LAMP BESIDE THE GOLDEN DOOR!"

Facts *to remember*

1. The United States occupies the most desirable part of the North American continent. God has blessed our country with favorable location, mild climate, many natural resources, and an energetic and courageous population. As members of this privileged nation, we are obliged to use these gifts according to God's plan, sharing them in justice.

2. The United States consists of 50 states occupying an area of more than three million square miles. It is the third largest country in the world. The Atlantic Ocean is along its eastern border and the broad Pacific Ocean washes its western shore. Canada lies to the north. To the south is the Gulf of Mexico and our neighbor, Mexico.

3. The major surface features of North America are found within the borders of the United States. Besides the Rocky Mountains and the Appalachian Mountains, there are fertile plains and valleys. The most important river system is the Mississippi-Missouri system which drains the entire central part of the country. Lakes Superior, Michigan, Huron, Erie, and Ontario, called the Great Lakes, lie between the United States and Canada.

4. The United States has valuable forests which supply wood and wood products as well as help in protecting the farmlands. Our nation has a large area of good cropland, and generally a long growing season, two things which enable us to produce more than enough food for our population. Because of the abundance of minerals, the United States has become the greatest industrial nation in the world.

Facts *to understand*

Answer each of the following in a complete sentence.

1. What are some physical features of the United States which people can make good use of?

2. Why do we say that the United States of America is especially blessed by God?

3. How can forests be of value to a nation?

4. What conditions of surface and climate favor farming in the United States?

5. What natural resources have helped most to make the United States the greatest industrial nation in the world?

Unit One Review

Questions for Discussion and Review

1. Explain why most people make their homes on plains. 2. Give reasons for our making use of imaginary lines when describing the earth. 3. When looking at a map, how can you tell whether a city is east or west of your home? 4. How would you define a continent? 5. Why did the people of Europe want to settle in America? 6. Account for the fact that most of North America has a temperate or moderate climate. 7. Give reasons for the United States having a surplus of food. 8. In what ways has God blessed the United States? 9. Why are forests considered so valuable to a country? 10. What reason may be given for the United States having become the greatest industrial nation in the world? 11. Name three oceans which touch the shores of North America. 12. Who were the first people to live in North America?

Using the maps and globe

1. Use the wall map to indicate the various directions on a map: north, east, southeast, etc.
2. Locate the seven continents on the globe.
3. Compare the area and the surface features of North America with those of Africa by using the wall map or the globe.
4. On an outline map of the United States, label the land and water bodies that border our country.
5. Locate the Great Lakes, the Mississippi-Missouri system, the Ohio River, the Columbia River, the Rio Grande, the Rocky Mountains, the Appalachian Mountains, the Atlantic Coastal Plain, the Great Plains, Hawaii, Alaska, and the Colorado Plateau.

Using Geography Words

Here is a list of special words that have been used in this Unit. Write a sentence using each word, to prove you know its meaning in geography.

surface	prairie	region
surplus	cropland	mountain
delta	natural	growing season
mineral	resources	colonies

Getting Information from Books

Read reference books such as *Compton's Pictured Encyclopedia* and other works on the following topics. Prepare to give a report on one.

North Pole	Isthmus of Panama	Alaska
The compass	Bering Strait	

Final Test

Write each sentence on your paper, choosing the correct word or words from the parenthesis.
1. The earth makes one complete rotation (once a year, every 24 hours, once a month).
2. The imaginary east-to-west line around the center of the earth is the (equator, meridian, axis).
3. The Atlantic Ocean touches the (northern, eastern, western) side of North America.
4. (East, south, north) is usually shown at the top of a map.
5. There are (five, eleven, seven) continents.
6. A (delta, river, lake) is a long body of water.
7. North America has mostly a (temperate, tropic, polar) climate.
8. A good food-producing area is a (mountain, desert, plain).
9. (The United States, Alaska, Russia) stretches across the middle of North America.
10. (Colorado, New York, Alaska) is the largest state in the United States.

Applying Christian Principles

Write these sentences on another paper. Choose the ending that makes the sentence correct.
1. The people of the United States are obliged to make use of God's gifts by a. carefully protecting them for the use of our nation only b. sharing them with others c. using them for war purposes only.
2. Immigrants who came to our country from Europe helped us to preserve our freedom by a. insisting upon keeping their own customs b. working and planning to maintain freedom c. making others live according to their standards.
3. We share our gifts with others a. when we burn our surplus crops b. when we sell or give our surplus crops to areas of the world where they are needed c. when we put our surplus crops into reserve in case we should have a shortage of food at some future time.

Neighbors in Northeastern United States

THE NEW ENGLAND REGION

THE MIDDLE ATLANTIC REGION

The first official flag of the United States that was ever flown contained just thirteen stars, arranged in a circle. They stood for the thirteen states which made up our country when it was founded. There are thirteen states in the section you are now going to study. They are: Maine, New Hampshire, Vermont, Massachusetts, Rhode Island, Connecticut, New York, New Jersey, Pennsylvania, Delaware, Maryland, Virginia, and West Virginia. Ten of them were among the thirteen original states of the United States of America.

As we study the geography of the Northeastern States, we shall divide them into two regions. New England includes the six northernmost states, and the Middle Atlantic Region includes the seven states which lie along the middle section of our country's Atlantic coast line.

These two regions were settled very early in our country's history. Then, during the last century, waves of immigrants came to the United States, and large numbers of them settled in the Northeastern States. Today, the cities of the Northeastern States have a huge population. The people of this tiny, crowded area are proud of their busy cities and historic states. Most of all, however, like their neighbors throughout the country, they are proud to be Americans.

In this Unit
you will learn that:

1 The Northeastern States are divided into two regions — The New England Region and the Middle Atlantic Region.

2 The surface is mostly hilly. Lowland areas extend inland along the rivers which flow to the Atlantic. A coastal plain also extends inland, as far as the foothills of the Appalachian Highlands.

3 Nearness to the ocean is one reason for the generally moderate climate. In New England, the growing season is shorter, and the northern winters are very cold.

4 Great amounts of food are required to feed the large city populations. There are many dairy farms, poultry farms, fruit and vegetable farms, and fisheries.

5 A great amount of manufacturing is done in New England, although there are few mineral resources. Mostly small manufactured items are produced. In the Middle Atlantic States, the mineral industries are most important. The many large cities produce coal, iron and steel, cement, and oil products, as well as clothing, chemicals and canned foods.

29

THE NORTHEASTERN STATES

Perched on the edge of the wide Atlantic Ocean, thirteen of the fifty United States of America fit into the northeastern part of our country. Although some of them extend inland as far as the Great Lakes, all except two have an Atlantic coast. Across the ocean is Europe. From that continent came the various peoples who first settled here and who have continued to add to the region's huge population.

Notice the rugged outline of the coast in this region. Some of the finest harbors and fishing grounds of the world are found along this coast. Densely populated industrial cities also crowd the coast and the narrow plain separating it from the Appalachian Highlands.

New England Countryside. The old, covered wooden bridge, the swift stream, and the bright autumn leaves form a typical New England scene.

The New England Region

Five tiny states and one larger state, fitting together like the pieces of a jigsaw puzzle, form the northeast corner of the United States. The larger one is Maine, in the north. Two other states, Vermont and New Hampshire, lie just west of Maine. To the south lie three other states—Massachusetts, Connecticut, and Rhode Island. These six states are called New England.

Location and Size. Look at the map on page 35. To the north of New England lies part of our neighbor nation, Canada. To the west of New England is the state of New York. On the south and the east, New England is bounded by the sea. The Atlantic Ocean is to the east, and the calmer waters of Long Island Sound are to the south. Of the six states, only Vermont has no coast line. We shall soon see how the people of New England, so close to the sea, and nearer to Europe than any other part of the United States, have played an important part in the history of our country.

The total area of New England is 66,600 square miles. These six states form a really tiny part of our country. For example, all six states would fit into the state of Washington, even though it is the smallest of the Western States. In spite of their size, however, the New England States were important in colonial days and are still a busy section of our country.

Irregular Coast. As you look at the map of New England, notice that the coast is broken up, or irregular. In some places arms of the sea extend into the land, forming many bays and inlets. Rocky islands dot the coast of Maine. In other places, parts of the land stick out into the water as *capes* and *peninsulas*. In winter, severe storms lash this rugged shore. In summer, cool breezes make it very pleasant for the many vacationists who come to Cape Cod and the other stretches of sandy beach along the New England coast.

Highlands and Lowlands. The surface of much of New England is rugged land with a rough, uneven surface. It is made up mostly of highland areas, with some lowland areas near the coast and in the river valleys. Those who have studied the surface of New England tell us an interesting story of something that happened there many thousand years ago. At that time a thick mass of slowly-moving ice covered almost all of this area. A large sheet of moving ice is called a *glacier*.

This glacier moved southward over New England from Canada where it had formed. It did many things to the land it moved across. In the north, the rugged highlands have had their peaks rounded by the glacier so that they are not nearly so high as they once were. Like a giant bulldozer, the glacier scraped away the soil from the surface of the land. It cut valleys, changed the direction of rivers, and formed huge piles of gravel and rocks. As the ice melted, huge rocks and boulders it had been carrying were left behind. New England, like other parts of northern United States, shows clearly today the effects of this glacier.

Mountain areas cover the northern part of New England—the Green Mountains running from north to south through the state of Vermont, and the White Mountains in northern New Hampshire. In the White Mountains is located Mount Washington, the highest peak in the northeastern part of the United States. The Berkshire Hills in Massachusetts are really worn-down mountains and are also part of the New England highlands.

The more important lowland areas of New England are located in the three southern states, mostly along the coast or in the river valleys. These river valleys extend from the highlands of the north southward to the coast.

The Rivers. The longest river in New England is the Connecticut River. Like almost all the rivers in New England, it runs from north to south. The Connecticut has its *source,* or beginning, near the Canadian border in the White Mountains of New Hampshire. It flows south, forming the border between Vermont and New Hampshire, through Massachusetts and Connecticut to the Long Island Sound. The point where it pours out into the Sound is called its *mouth.* Along the Connecticut River, especially in the south, lies a green fertile lowland, called the Connecticut Valley. This valley is of great importance to the people of New England.

The Connecticut River. Looking across the river, from Vermont to New Hampshire, you can see the foothills of New Hampshire's White Mountains.

Now look at the map and find other rivers flowing from the highlands south to the coastal lowlands. In Maine they are the Penobscot, the Kennebec, and the Androscoggin. The strange-sounding names of these Maine rivers are all Indian words.

In New Hampshire, the Merrimac River flows southward into Massachusetts and then eastward into the Atlantic Ocean. Three smaller rivers, the Charles, the Mystic, and the Neponset, flow into Boston Harbor. Throughout the other states of New England, you will find many other smaller rivers. Most of these rivers flow swiftly, and they have great importance. They produce electric power to turn the wheels of mills and factories. Their mouths form excellent harbors for the ships which carry products to and from New England.

The Climate of New England. As you have learned, climate is the kind of weather a place has over a long period of time. In general, New England has long, cold winters with short, warm summers. Spring and fall are shorter seasons in New England than in sections of the country farther south.

In the three northern states of New England the growing season is only about 100 days. In Massachusetts, Connecticut, and Rhode Island, the growing season is longer. This means that in southern New England, farmers can raise crops which require a long time to ripen.

New England receives a moderate amount of rainfall, with the areas near the coast getting more than places inland. The amount does not vary much from season to season. Snow covers the mountainsides almost all winter long, and skiing is a popular sport. The mountains of the northern states are famous for the winter sports which they provide. Tourists are also attracted by the beauty and splendor of New England during the short autumn season.

Studying the Map

A. The New England States occupy the northeastern corner of the United States. 1. How are boundary lines between states shown? Trace the boundary line between Maine and New Hampshire. 2. Name the New England States in order of their area. 3. Which state lies farthest north? farthest south? 4. Which state extends farthest east? 5. Name the New England States which touch the Atlantic coast. Which state does not touch the ocean? 6. Which state lies directly west of New England? Name the lake that forms part of the boundary between this state and New England. 7. What country is north of the New England States? Name the three New England States which border this country. 8. What name is given to the part of the Massachusetts coast which extends way out into the Atlantic Ocean? Name the two large islands that lie south of it.

B. 1. How is elevation above sea level shown on this kind of map? 2. Which color tint shows the lowest land areas? the highest land areas? 3. Are the highest areas inland or along the coast? 4. The highest point in New England is Mt. Washington in New Hampshire. In which mountain group is it located? What does the map tell you about its height above sea level? 5. Name the mountains in Vermont. How do they compare in height with the White Mountains? 6. The Berkshire Hills in Massachusetts are mountains, too. How do they compare in height with the Green and the White Mountains? 7. New England's longest river is the Connecticut. For which two states does the river form the boundary? Through which other New England states does it flow? Into what body of water does the Connecticut River empty? 8. Many New England rivers flow into the Atlantic Ocean. Locate and name four of these rivers. 9. Many summer vacationers come to New England lakes. Locate and name the three largest lakes of New England.

C. Most of New England's almost ten million people live in the larger cities and towns. 1. How are the capital cities shown on the map? List the New England States and their capitals. 2. On what river is the capital of Maine? the capital of New Hampshire? the capital of Connecticut? 3. Name three bays along the coast on which large cities are located. Name each city.

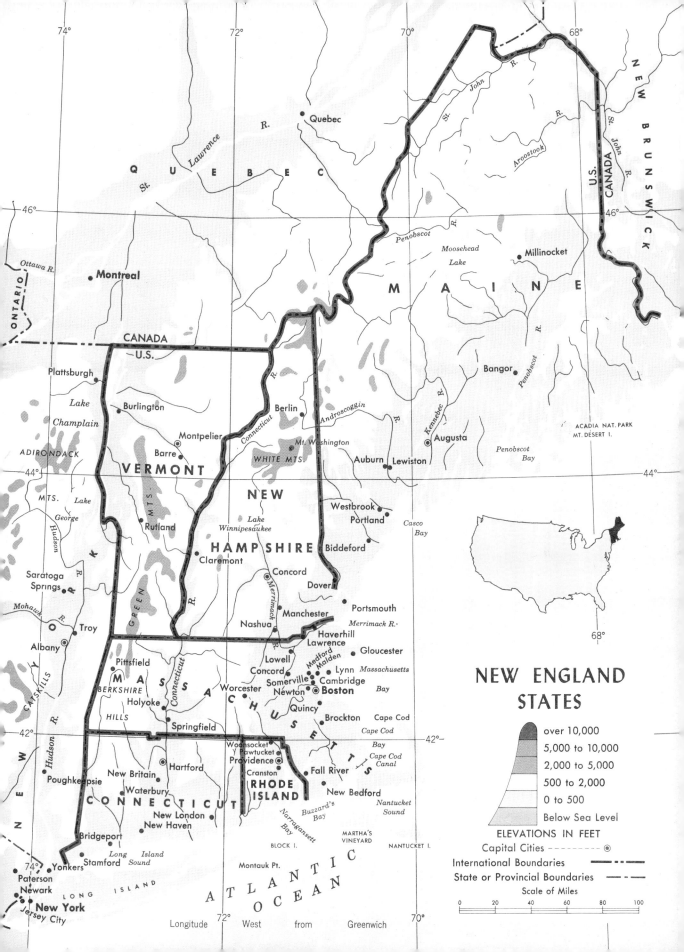

NEW ENGLAND STATES

74°   72°   70°   68°

Quebec

St. Lawrence R.

QUEBEC

NEW BRUNSWICK

ONTARIO

Ottawa R.

Montreal

46°

Penobscot R.

St. John R.

Aroostook R.

St. John R.

U.S. CANADA

46°

CANADA
U.S.

Plattsburgh

MAINE

Moosehead Lake

Millinocket

Lake Champlain

Burlington

Berlin

Androscoggin

Bangor

Penobscot R.

ADIRONDACK

Montpelier

Barre

VERMONT

WHITE MTS.

Mt. Washington

Penobscot R.

Kennebec R.

Augusta

ACADIA NAT. PARK
MT. DESERT I.

MTS.

Lake George

NEW

Auburn Lewiston

44°

44°

Rutland

HAMPSHIRE

Lake Winnipesaukee

Westbrook
Portland

Casco Bay

Penobscot Bay

Saratoga Springs

Hudson R.

Claremont

Biddeford

GREEN MTS.

Concord

Connecticut R.

Merrimack R.

Dover

Mohawk R.

Troy

Portsmouth

Albany

Manchester

Nashua

Merrimack R.

Haverhill
Lawrence

Pittsfield

Lowell

Gloucester

BERKSHIRE

MASSACHUSETTS

Concord

Medford Malden

Lynn Massachusetts Bay

Holyoke

Worcester

Somerville Cambridge
Newton **Boston**

HILLS

Springfield

Quincy

Brockton

Cape Cod

42°

Hudson R.

Woonsocket
Pawtucket

Cape Cod Bay

42°

Poughkeepsie

New Britain

Hartford

Providence
Cranston

Fall River

Cape Cod Canal

NEW YORK

Waterbury

RHODE ISLAND

New Bedford

Nantucket Sound

CONNECTICUT

New London

Buzzard's Bay

Catskills

Bridgeport

New Haven

Narragansett Bay

MARTHA'S VINEYARD

NANTUCKET I.

Yonkers

Stamford

Long Island Sound

BLOCK I.

74°

Paterson

Montauk Pt.

Newark

LONG

ISLAND

A T L A N T I C

New York

O C E A N

Jersey City

72° West

70°

Longitude   West   from   Greenwich

NEW ENGLAND STATES

Elevation
over 10,000
5,000 to 10,000
2,000 to 5,000
500 to 2,000
0 to 500
Below Sea Level

ELEVATIONS IN FEET

Capital Cities --------- ◉

International Boundaries ▬▬▬

State or Provincial Boundaries ▬ ▪ ▬

Scale of Miles

0   20   40   60   80   100

Self-Reliant New Englanders. Using tools made by the local blacksmith, the hardy settlers cleared the land and cut down trees for their houses.

Early Days in New England. Because of its closeness to Europe, some of the first settlements in North America were in New England. A group of people called the Puritans were among the first to come. They could not practice their religion in England, so they came to find peace and freedom in North America. They named the section they settled New England, in honor of their mother country which they still loved and remembered fondly.

Living conditions were not easy in early days. The settlers had to make many of the things they needed by hand, or else do without them. In spite of advice from friendly Indians, the early farmers of New England found the thin and stony soil very difficult to work for producing food crops. The long, cold winters added to their difficulties because many of the crops did not ripen during the short growing season. Many settlers died of sickness and starvation. Many others pushed farther south, or west into New York, to find better farming conditions.

The settlers who built towns along the coast turned to ocean trade and fishing for a living. During the Revolutionary War, the colonists of New England united with colonists of settlements all along the Atlantic coast. Together, thirteen colonies became the United States of America. As a result, the people of New England became independent of England in several ways. First, they became independent in government. Just as important, they later became independent in trade and commerce.

SEAMEN'S MUSEUM AT MYSTIC, CONNECTICUT

Dedicated to the memory of the thousands of New England seamen who have gone "down to the sea in ships," the seaside town of Mystic, Connecticut, has been rebuilt to look exactly as it did 200 years ago. Old-time sailing vessels are tied up at its piers, and visitors find this museum a fascinating glimpse into the past.

At one time, hundreds of whaling ships from the ports of Nantucket, New Bedford, and others made New England the whaling center of the world. Their brave crews spent three years at a time at sea hunting the dangerous and valuable whales. This has all changed today, but the memory of greater days lives on in the old whalers docked at Mystic.

Many New England seamen also served in the sailing vessels which once handled so much of this country's foreign trade. Some of these old-time freighters and clippers, kept in good condition, are moored at Mystic. One can be seen in the photograph below.

Old Whaling Ship. This three-masted whaling ship is now a floating museum. The last of its kind, it is docked at a pier in Mystic, Connecticut.

Historic Waterfront. This dockside street in Mystic, Connecticut, has been rebuilt to show the old wharves and houses as they once looked.

Using the Swift Streams. At first, New England factories like this iron works in Massachusetts used water wheels to harness the river's power.

New England Grows. Factories soon sprang up along the banks of swift-flowing streams. Using the abundant water power, New England factories started to turn out all sorts of goods and articles. The people of New England no longer had to buy manufactured goods from the mother country. New England ships, sailing from its many excellent harbors, carried a large amount of the young country's trade with other countries throughout the world. Tobacco from farms in Connecticut became famous. Today New England still engages in manufacturing and trade.

Main Street, New England. Worcester, Massachusetts, is a typical New England industrial city. Now electricity powers the wheels of its mills.

New England Today. New England's people at one time were mostly English and Protestant. Today, this is no longer so. A large part of the population is now made up of immigrants and children of immigrants. These are people who came to our country during the last 100 years from different countries of Europe. Those who settled in New England came mostly from Ireland and Italy, and were almost all Catholic. There are also many French-speaking people from Canada, as well as Portuguese fishermen from Europe. Each of these groups has played its share in the development of present-day New England.

The population of New England is now close to 10 million. Most of these people live in the southern states of Rhode Island, Connecticut, and Massachusetts. Most of them live in or near the large cities. In these cities the people engage in various industries and manufacturing jobs, clerical jobs in the offices of the large insurance companies and banks, and in the important fishing business. Outside the cities and in northern New England, the people work mostly on farms or in the forests. In the next few chapters, we shall find out more about how the people from different parts of New England live and work.

Facts *to remember*

1. The five small states of Vermont, New Hampshire, Massachusetts, Connecticut, and Rhode Island, together with Maine, are located in the northeast corner of the United States. They are called the New England States. In area they are no larger than the state of Washington.
2. The New England region has a short growing season with long, cold winters.
3. Because they lie closer to Europe than any other part of the United States, these states have played an important part in the history of our nation. The first settlers were mostly Protestant, but today, because of later Irish and Italian immigrants, the population is mostly Catholic.

4. Many swift-flowing rivers furnish abundant water-power for New England's many factories. Early settlers, finding the thin, stony soil difficult to cultivate, turned to making articles needed in their homes. Thus, manufacturing began at an early date.

What *have I learned?*

In each of the following sentences, the word in capital letters makes the sentence right or wrong. Write all the sentences correctly on a piece of paper. Change the wrong words to correct words.
1. The people of New England are FARTHER from Europe than any other part of the United States.
2. The coast line of New England is IRREGULAR.
3. A glacier once moved over this land leaving a SMOOTH surface.
4. The PENOBSCOT River is the longest river in New England.
5. The more important LOWLAND areas of New England are located in the three southern states.
6. Most of New England has a SHORT growing season.
7. Early farmers found the soil of this region very PRODUCTIVE.
8. The first way in which the thirteen colonies became independent of England was in TRADE.
9. New England was able to import and export goods through its POOR harbors.
10. Most of New England's population live in the SOUTHERN states of Rhode Island, Connecticut, and Massachusetts.

Facts *to understand*

Answer each of the following in a complete sentence.
1. Why do the three northern states of New England have a shorter growing season than the three southern states?
2. Why should New Englanders look upon their swift-flowing rivers as helpful?
3. Account for the fact that today many of the people of New England are Catholic.
4. Why were the early settlers of New England willing to endure hardship, sickness, and suffering in a strange land?
5. Why are the New England States a busy section of our country today?

2
Forests, Fisheries, and Farms

New England Fishermen. Aboard a small boat called a "dragger", these fishermen of Gloucester prepare their net. Note their heavy clothing.

In order to study the way people live and work outside the cities and towns of New England, we shall study three different kinds of work. Many New Englanders make their living by working in the forests, or in some part of the fishing industry, or as farmers. We shall find out how each of these different kinds of work is carried on in New England.

New England Forests. At one time, New England was almost completely covered by trees. The Puritans found that a forest extended inland from the coast as far as the peaks of the highest mountains. However, the early settlers needed farm land, not forests. In order to till the soil and plant crops, trees had to be cut down to make room for farms.

When shipbuilding became an important industry along the coast, more and more trees were cut down to provide lumber for the wooden ships. The great New England forest began to disappear, especially in the southern part.

In later years, many farmers gave up the hard work of trying to farm the bare stony earth which did not yield good crops. They deserted their farms. In many places forests began to grow again on land that was once used as farmland. Today you can see places in New England where stone walls marking the old boundaries of deserted farms run right through the forest.

Large areas of New England are still forested, and others that once were forests are again covered with growths of young trees.

These young trees are called *brush*. In other places where trees have grown larger, we call the growth *woodland*. In time, these brush and woodland sections will again become forests.

Forest to Pulp Mill. Let us see what kind of work is being done in New England forests today. Trees that are too small for lumber can be used in making wood pulp.

The paper you are holding in your hand is made from wood pulp. So is the paper used to print other books, to make bags, tissues, cartons, signs, and so many other things we see everyday.

Strange as it seems, most of our paper is made from wood. Some of the wood for making paper in the United States comes from New England. That is one important use for the forests of New England. In the northern New England states there are large areas of spruce and hemlock trees. They make the best wood pulp for paper.

In winter, the woodcutters saw down the trees. The logs are hauled by tractor-drawn sleds over snow-covered ground to the banks of frozen streams. In spring, melting snow from the mountains floods all the streams and floats the logs down to the saw-mills. Here big power saws cut the logs into smaller pieces to be sent to the mills where the paper is made.

First, the bark is peeled off, and the wood is ground into small chips by a sharp machine. The chips are mixed with water, and certain chemicals are added. The whole mixture is heated in large tanks until it becomes the sticky pulp from which paper is made. Much more water is added to the sticky mixture to make it quite thin. When it is allowed to flow onto a moving belt, it hardens into paper.

The cities of Holyoke and Haverhill in Massachusetts, Berlin in New Hampshire, and Millinocket in Maine are important paper-making centers. Near each of these cities are forests, fresh water, and swift streams which provide power for the mills.

Springtime on the Kennebec. Melting snow floods the streams in spring, and logs from the forests of Maine float down the stream to the sawmills.

Making Paper. The wet pulp mixture has dried into paper which is being wound onto huge rolls. These rolls will be split into various sizes.

The United States uses more paper than any other country in the world. Huge amounts of wood pulp are needed to make our newspapers, books, magazines, writing

paper, towels, and the many other paper products we use. The forests of New England do not provide enough pulp to fill the needs of the busy northeastern United States. Much more pulp must come from other parts of our country and even from other countries, such as Canada.

Recreation Areas. Forest areas in New England are fine places for recreation both summer and winter. In summer good highways bring vacationers to the woodlands and lakes for camping, fishing, and swimming. A national park, Acadia, is on Mount Desert Island off the coast of Maine. Its granite peaks and wooded hills are enjoyed by many summer visitors. New England is becoming more and more important as a winter vacationland. The snowy slopes of the highlands are ideal for skiing. Frozen lakes and streams are excellent for ice skating. There are many resorts and hotels that are open both winter and summer.

A Sportsman's Paradise. The hunter is drawing aim on a deer in the wintry forests of Vermont. Why does he wear such a bright red jacket?

Collecting Maple Syrup. From holes drilled into the tree, sap oozes into the buckets. Then the clear liquid is boiled to make syrup or sugar.

Maple Syrup. Another forest product of New England is maple syrup. Early New England farmers learned from the Indians how to tap the sugar maple trees in the spring. Today it is still an important forest occupation.

A hole is drilled into the tree, and the sap that drips from it is collected in buckets. The buckets of sap are carried to a sugar house where the sap is boiled down to make thick maple syrup. By boiling it even longer, it becomes a hard sugar with a delicious flavor. Pure maple syrup and maple sugar candy are often bought by vacationers who come to New England. The maple syrup is also sold to companies that use it in making pancake syrups.

The northeastern United States and Canada are the only places in the world where the sugar maple grows. Vermont and the neighboring state of New York are the leading producers.

Saving Our Forests. In New England, as in many other parts of the United States, the forests are a very noticeable example of the natural resources with which our country has been blessed. In the past, greedy men cut the forests down thoughtlessly, ignoring the needs of the future.

Today we realize that we must be very careful in the way we use natural resources like our forests. Great care is taken to prevent wasteful forest fires. Every time trees are cut down in a certain area, other trees are planted to replace them. *Conservation* is the name we give to this careful use of natural resources.

Forests, Fisheries, and Farms **43**

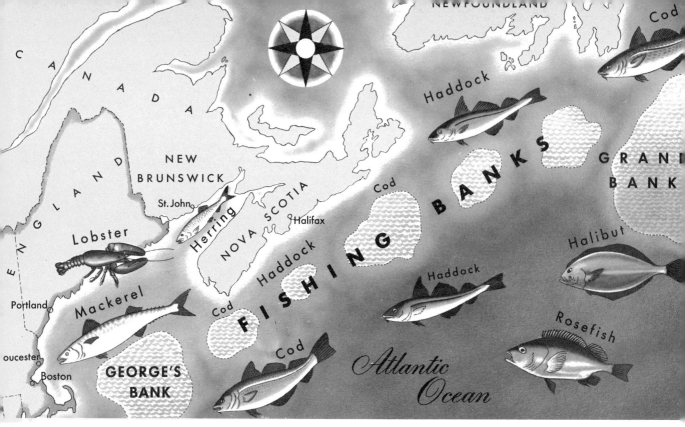

An Old Industry. Some of the first people who came to New England did not come to farm. They expected to make their living by fishing. Others turned to the sea when they were unsuccessful at farming. All the while New England was growing up, fishing and whaling boats put out from Boston, Gloucester, and other towns along the New England coast.

They found large quantities of fish in the waters near New England. The good harbors along the coast became fine fishing ports. More than enough fish were caught to supply the colonists. A large amount was shipped to Europe in exchange for goods that were so badly needed in the New World, such as machinery and shoes.

Fishing, one of America's oldest industries, is still important in New England.

Fishing Banks. Off the coast of New England lie some of the world's best fishing banks. The map seen above shows their location. Fishing banks are shallow parts of the ocean where fish come in great numbers to feed. The banks are on the *continental shelf*. This is part of the land that extends out from the coast for some distance under the sea. The end of the shelf drops off into deep water.

The shallow waters of the fishing banks contain plankton, tiny floating plant-like life upon which small fish feed. The small fish, in turn, bring the large fish who feed upon them. Hence, more fish can be caught at fishing banks than elsewhere.

Fishing is easier at the fishing banks. Nets can be dragged along the bottom of the shallow water where the fish are feeding. Long lines are not needed.

Great catches of cod, rosefish, halibut, haddock, mackerel, and herring are taken each year at the fishing banks and along the coast of New England.

Dangerous Industry. New England's fishermen face many dangers. They must fight for their lives when a storm lashes the ocean into huge waves. In the winter when the ocean spray falls on the decks of the boats, they become coated with ice. There is always danger of sliding off the slippery open decks into the cold sea. The fishing banks are often covered with fog. They are located near the point where the warm air over the Gulf Stream Current meets cold air over the Labrador Current and produces fog. Ocean liners have been known to run down fishing vessels that could not be seen in the dense fog.

In the last hundred years, over 5000 New England fishermen have been lost at sea. Once each year, at the start of the fishing season, the people of Gloucester gather on the beach. They cast flowers into the ocean in memory of the fishermen who lost their lives at sea during the past year.

Fishing boats have been made safer in recent years. Large, power-operated boats took the place of sailing schooners and small fishing boats. The radio warns of storms and other weather changes. Radar and other direction-finding devices help prevent collisions in the fogs.

Processing Fish. At one time all fish caught in New England waters were packed in ice to be sold fresh just as soon as the fishing vessel reached port. Some are still handled this way to be carried by rapid transportation to inland areas.

Today, many fish are cleaned, "quick frozen," and stored in freezers for future sale. In this way they can be kept for a long time and carried to wherever they are in demand. You have seen and probably eaten frozen fish sticks and fillets from time to time.

Some fish, especially, cod, are salted and dried. This is not done so much anymore as it was in the early days of the industry. Today more people prefer fresh or frozen fish. American sardines, which are really baby herring, are canned.

When fish are processed, parts that cannot be eaten are not wasted. They are used to make many products including glue, fertilizer, animal feed, insect sprays, oil for paints and varnish, and even medicine. Cod liver oil is one well-known example.

Fishing Ports. The chief New England fishing ports are Boston, Gloucester, and New Bedford in Massachusetts, and Portland on the coast of Maine. The Boston fish pier is one of the largest in the world. All along the pier are processing plants from which fish are shipped to many parts of the world. Gloucester was an important fishing port from colonial times and is still the most important fishing center in New England. New Bedford, the old whaling port, now freezes and stores most of the nation's catch of sea scallops.

A fishing craft called a *dragger* (left, above) pulls an open-mouthed net along the bottom of the sea. The two other pictures above show men fishing for mackerel with a *purse seine*. Our Lady of Good Voyage (right) is regarded by the New England fishermen as their patroness and protector.

New England Dairy Farm. The red brick color of the barns stands out against the green of the trees. The stream provides clear, fresh water.

Early Farms. When the first colonists came to New England, they found the land covered by forest. They knew only one way to survive in this new land, and that was by tilling the soil to provide their food. To do so, they had to clear away the forest. When they did clear it in places, they found the soil underneath poor and stony. In addition, the farmers had only a short growing season because of the long severe winters. This limited the kind of crops they could produce.

Many New England farmers left their farms as soon as there were other kinds of work they could do: shipbuilding, trade, manufacturing, or fishing. Others went farther west or south in the New World to find better conditions for farming. To this day, New England has less farming than any other part of the United States. Some farming is carried on, however. In fact, there are some special crops for which New England is famous.

In many other parts of the world, conditions are not ideal for farming. Unfortunately, many people in other countries do not receive enough food because they cannot raise enough. Our country's leaders are helping these people to develop their natural resources, so that they can trade other goods for food.

Dairy Farms. Throughout much of New England, conditions are excellent for raising dairy cows. The cool weather and regular rainfall encourage the growth of rich grass on hillsides and on ground that is too stony for other crops. One of the effects of the passing of the glacier thousands of years ago was the creation of many lakes and streams. These furnish clear cool water for cows to drink. Trees offer shade for the cows in summer.

Most of the milk from New England dairy farms is sold daily as fresh milk in the nearby towns and cities. Because it sours quickly, milk cannot be shipped long distances. That is why most of the dairy farms are located within a short distance of the larger cities and towns.

New England dairy farmers also grow some crops as winter *fodder,* or feed, for their animals. Hay, oats, and corn are grown. They also raise vegetables for their own use and keep a few fruit trees.

Working Together on a Dairy Farm. The farmer's son is helping his father take care of the cows. He checks figures on the growth of the calves.

Nearly every farmer has his chicken houses. Chickens do not take up much of the farmer's time, but they help him to add to his income by selling eggs and poultry.

From Farm to City. The truck takes on fresh milk from the barn into its refrigerated tank. Next step is the local pasteurizing-bottling plant.

Drying Tobacco Leaves. These broad leaves are hung on racks to dry in the sun. Tobacco grown in the Connecticut Valley is of very high grade.

The Connecticut Valley. The best farming land in all of New England is in the Connecticut Valley. This valley runs north and south on both sides of the Connecticut

Tobacco Farming. These tobacco plants are protected from direct sunlight and harmful insects by a thin cotton cloth stretched over the fields.

River. It is a wide fertile valley, about half of which is used as farmland. In the narrow northern part, the valley farmers engage mostly in dairy and poultry farming, and in maple sugar production. Toward the south, the valley widens where it passes through Massachusetts and Connecticut. Here tobacco, potatoes, onions, vegetables, fruits, and poultry are raised.

Connecticut Valley tobacco requires a great amount of careful attention and hard labor. The plants begin to grow in glasshouses, where they receive sunlight, but are protected from the cold outside air. When they become bigger, they are set out in the fields. A thin cotton cloth is stretched over them to shade them and keep off insects. The leaves are cut when fully grown and dried slowly while hanging in sheds. Connecticut Valley tobacco is of high quality and is used mostly in making cigars. Because it is grown in the shade, tobacco from the Connecticut Valley has a very light color. This is especially desirable in making the outside wrapper of a cigar. For the filler, or inside of a cigar, a darker tobacco from the South or from Cuba is most often used.

Potatoes. One of the very best areas of the United States for raising potatoes is the state of Maine. Potatoes require a certain kind of soil, and the fertile sandy soil of Maine is just right. They also do best where the summer is cool with regular rainfall as it is in Maine—not too little or too much at any one time.

Maine potato farmers plant their crop in late May and harvest it in early September. In this way, they take full advantage of the short growing season. Potatoes are grown throughout the state of Maine, and in the Connecticut Valley as well, but one county in northeastern Maine is best known for this crop. Aroostook County ranks with the best areas in the United States as a producer of large quantities of top-grade potatoes.

Cranberry Bogs. Cranberries were the "first fruit of America." The berries grew wild on the swampy, sandy soil of Cape Cod in Massachusetts. The Indians brought the cranberries with wild turkey as a gift to the Puritans. It is still the custom to eat cranberry sauce with turkey.

Today cranberries are carefully cultivated. Those you had for your last Thanksgiving dinner probably grew on vines that had been planted in wet, sandy areas called *bogs.* The enemies of the plant are frost, weeds, and insects. When there is danger of frost, the farmer floods the bog, and the water keeps the plants from freezing. Sometimes he does the same thing during the summer to kill the weeds and insects by drowning them under the water.

The berries ripen under the summer sun and are picked in the early fall before the first frost. Picking cranberries is hard work. The picker works on his hands and knees and uses a tool called a rocker scoop. It has teeth like a comb and removes the berries from the vine. The berries are poured on screens which sort them.

Forests, Fisheries, and Farms 49

Packing Cranberries. Thousands of crates of these red, shiny berries are shipped from Cape Cod each year. Many are made into juice or sauce.

Sorted cranberries are packed in boxes and barrels according to grade. They are then sent to markets or to a cannery. Cranberries are grown on Cape Cod in Massachusetts. This region, along with swampy areas in New Jersey, Washington, and Wisconsin, raises practically all the cranberries used in the United States.

Other Crops. Four fifths of the people of New England live in cities. They require large amounts of fresh vegetables. To meet this need, there are many small vegetable farms located near the bigger towns and cities. These small farms raise string beans, squash, carrots, beets, tomatoes, and many other vegetables.

The farmers who raise these vegetables ship them into the city by truck early in the morning. Around the cities of the south especially, there are many apple and peach orchards. Strawberries, raspberries, and other small fruits also grow well in the soil and climate of southern New England.

Facts *to remember*

1. Forests, fresh water, and swift streams which provide power make the cities of Holyoke and Haverhill in Massachusetts, Berlin in New Hampshire, and Millinocket in Maine important paper-making centers. Maple sugar is another product obtained from the New England forests.
2. Good coastal harbors make excellent fishing ports. Off the coast of New England lie some of the world's best fishing banks. Great catches of fish are taken annually from the waters of this region. Processing fish is a major industry. Boston, Gloucester, and New Bedford, in Massachusetts, and Portland, in Maine, are the chief New England fishing ports.
3. New England is an outstanding dairy region. Aroostock County, in Maine, is best known for large quantities of top-grade potatoes. The wide fertile valley of the Connecticut River is the best farming land of all New England. Here high quality tobacco and other crops are raised.
4. Many vegetable farmers and fruit growers help to supply food for the large city population of New England. Cape Cod in Massachusetts is noted for its fine cranberries.

What *have I learned?*

Answer each question in a complete sentence.
1. Which country is the greatest user of paper in the world?
2. Give a reason for New England being considered a good fishing area.
3. Why is there less farming in New England today than elsewhere in the United States?
4. Where is the best farming land in all of New England?
5. Why is there such a demand for large amounts of fresh vegetables in New England?

Facts *to understand*

In a complete sentence give a reason for each of the following statements.
1. The United States uses more paper than any other country in the world.
2. Fish were shipped to Europe in exchange for badly-needed goods.
3. More fish can be caught at fishing banks than elsewhere.

3
Factories and Cities

End of the Day. Their shift over, thousands of workers pour out of this modern factory. New England is famous for its many skilled workers.

I n the last chapter you learned that the early people of New England did not do well with farming. Many turned to other kinds of work. Some became shipbuilders, others became fishermen. There was still another way to make a living which had an appeal for many of the early settlers.

The slow ocean voyage from England meant that people had to wait a very long time for glass, needles, shoes, guns, and the many other things that are made, not grown. In addition, these items were very expensive when they arrived from the mother country. It was not surprising that many early New Englanders thought of starting to make these things right at home.

Making Things. The art of making things by hand or machine is called *manufacturing*. At first, it may seem a little difficult to think of items being manufactured in New England. As a rule, factories are located where there is coal, oil, or some other fuel nearby for running machinery. New England has none of these. Usually, factories for making things of steel are located near a supply of iron. There is very little of this metal in the ground of New England. There is no cotton for making cloth, because growing cotton requires a warm climate. There is very little leather for making shoes because New England is not a cattle country. In spite of these difficulties, New England soon became an important manufacturing region of the United States, and manufactured goods are New England's most important products today.

Two Valuable Resources. This section of the country had the advantage of two things which made up for its lack of fuel and mineral resources. First, the people who planned the factories and mills and worked in them were energetic and ambitious. They worked hard at their task. Skilled workers and intelligent managers like these are needed for successful manufacturing. Second, the large number of small, swiftly-flowing streams gave the factories a cheap source of power to turn their wheels and produce electricity. This helped to make up for the lack of fuels.

Cloth and Clothing. The first factory built in New England was a textile factory. A *textile* is any woven cloth. Factories which make textiles are often called *mills*.

For a long time, most of the cotton cloth made in the United States came from the mills of New England. The two sections of New England which were most important in producing cotton cloth were mainly in Massachusetts. The first was around the cities of Fall River and New Bedford in Massachusetts, and Pawtucket and Woonsocket in Rhode Island. The other was in the Merrimac Valley, around the cities of Lowell and Lawrence in Massachusetts, and Manchester and Nashua in New Hampshire.

Today, many of the mills have gone. In some places, new industries such as plastics and electronics have taken their place. Some mills that once made cotton cloth are now making nylon and other new textiles. In many places, however, towns that were once busy and prosperous have become deserted. Most of our cotton cloth is now made in the southern states of our country. Later you will learn why this change took place when you study the Southern States.

Modern Spinning Machines. Automatic spindles and looms make it possible for modern textile mills to produce great amounts of materials.

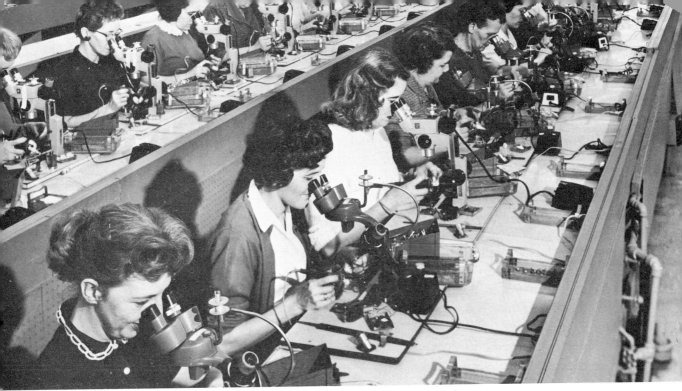

Parts for Pocket Radios. The all-important transistors are so tiny that the women who work at assembling them in this plant use microscopes.

Shoemaking. At first, shoes and boots were made by skilled workers, called *craftsmen*. They worked in their homes or in small workshops. Later, large factories grew up around Lynn, Brockton, and Boston in Massachusetts, and in other towns. In the factories each man does only one small part of the whole job. He learns to do this with such great skill that the shoes are made at greater speed. Power-driven machines operated by these skilled workers now do most of the work. Unlike the cotton cloth business, shoemaking has remained important in New England.

Metal Manufactures. New England has no deposits of iron in the ground from which to make metal. There are no deposits of any other metals, such as copper or lead, either. They have to be shipped in from other areas. In spite of this, the value of the manufactured metal products in New England is greater than the value of any of its other manufactures. New England factories can make everything from a simple safety pin to a typewriter.

Machine tools are a good example of the kind of metal manufacturing done here. These tools are small. They require a great deal of labor and care by a highly skilled worker. Machine tools are then used in other factories where different items are

Machine Shop. The automatic machine which this man is operating cuts teeth into gear drums. In the foreground, gleaming drums wait to be cut.

Factories and Cities **53**

made. They cut, drill, bore, grind, and shape. Manufacturing done in many other parts of the United States depends upon the excellent machine tools from New England.

Watches, airplane instruments, rocket parts, jewelry, and silverware are among the other metal products of New England's factories. Waltham, Massachusetts, and Waterbury, Connecticut, are especially famous for watches and clocks. New Britain, Connecticut, leads in the production of hardware. Airplane parts and rocket engine parts are made in Hartford and Stamford, Connecticut. Brassware is produced in Bridgeport and New Haven, Connecticut. Jewelry is made in Providence, Rhode Island.

The kinds of products made in New England's factories require smaller amounts of raw materials and more skilled labor.

A Jeweler at Work. Making jewelry is another occupation which requires skill and patience. Notice the special eyepiece which this man uses.

AT WORK IN NEW ENGLAND'S FACTORIES

In a modern industrial nation such as the United States, all sections of the country do a certain amount of manufacturing. You will learn soon that the Southern States are becoming a textile-manufacturing region and that the Middle Atlantic States produce great quantities of iron and steel. The Midwest is famous for the manufacture of automobiles and trucks, while the Western States make airplanes and aluminum.

Most of the articles produced in the New England factories, however, are not large or heavy and do not require great amounts of raw material. In this region, there is a lack of space and of nearby raw materials, but there is an abundance of highly skilled labor. Therefore, its factories turn out mostly the small, intricate items which require great attention and care, but not great amounts of raw materials.

Electronic tubes, watches, silverware, instruments, jewelry, needles and pins, engine parts, plastics, shoes, and tools are among the hundreds of manufactured goods which the skilled craftsmen of New England make.

An Old Industry. This shoemaker is stitching a shoe, using modern, automatic machinery. Massachusetts leads in making shoes.

Where TV Sets Are Made. Women in this electronics plant are assembling the many tiny parts in complicated patterns.

High-Speed Production. With this *drill press,* the worker can stamp out a large number of metal parts in a short time.

Quarrying Granite. Fine stone used in monuments and buildings comes from this Vermont quarry. Huge blocks, cut by power tools, are moved by crane.

Stone From the Earth. You have just read that New England has almost no metal at all. Nor has it any oil or gas to be taken from the ground. In the ground of New England, however, there is one very valuable natural resource. This is building stone. The place where stone is taken from the ground is called a *quarry,* just as the place where coal is taken is called a *mine.* There are many quarries in New England.

Some of the kinds of building stone for which New England is famous are granite, marble, and slate. Granite is used for building construction, and in the design of monuments and memorials. In some places it is also used for street paving. The cities of Barre, in Vermont, and Quincy, in Massachusetts, are noted as centers of granite quarrying.

Marble is well known for its beautiful appearance. It is used for altars, statues, ornaments, and monuments. Marble is a hard stone, with fine coloring and grain marking, and it takes a high polish. More marble is taken from quarries in Vermont than from any other state.

Slate is a building stone that is quarried mostly in Vermont and Maine. It has a hard, very smooth surface, and may be gray, blue, purple, or green. At one time, slate had many more uses than it has today. Sidewalks, blackboards, tombstones, and many other items were made from it. Today it is used chiefly for roofs, because it can be split into thin sheets.

QUEBEC

St. Lawrence R.

CANADA
UNITED STATES

NEW BRUNSWICK

ONTARIO

Lake

CANADA
UNITED STATES

WINTER
SPORTS &
RECREATION

M A I N E

Moosehead
Lake

Penobscot R.

Millinocket

MAPLE SYRUP

MARBLE

Berlin

MACHINERY

Bangor

FISH PROCESSING
FREEZING

FOOD
PROCESSING

Champlain

Montpelier

Barre

N E W

Augusta

CEMENT

BUILDING
STONE

COMMERCIAL
FISHING

VERMONT

MTS.

MTS.

Lake
Winnepesaukee

Bath

Portland

BUILDING
STONE

Rutland

H A M P S H I R E

Concord

PETROLEUM

WHEAT
FLOUR

COMMERCIAL
FISHING

MACHINE
TOOLS

GREEN

WHITE

Connecticut R.

Manchester

Haverhill

ATLANTIC
OCEAN

Lowell

ELECTRONICS

Gloucester

RAW WOOL
HIDES & SKINS

BERKSHIRE

M A S S A C H U S E T T S

Worcester

Boston

TEXTILES MACHINERY
SHOES PAPER

Holyoke

HILLS

Hartford

AIRPLANE
ENGINES

Providence

Cape Cod

Waterbury

C O N N E C T I C U T

MACHINE TOOLS
New London

RHODE
ISLAND

New
Bedford

CRANBERRIES

Danbury

New Haven

Bridgeport

Long Island
Sound

BLOCK
I.

MARTHA'S
VINEYARD

NANTUCKET I.

COMMERCIAL
FISHING

NEW
JERSEY

N E W   Y O R K

ATLANTIC OCEAN

Capital Cities ⊙   Canal ⊢⊣

International Boundaries ▬ ▪ ▬

State or Provincial Boundaries ▬ ▬ ▬

Scale of Miles

0   20   40   60   80   100

Boston From the Air. Looking north over the city, you see the downtown section and the Charles River (center). Boston Common is to the left.

New England's Largest City.

Boston is the largest city in New England, and one of the ten largest cities in the United States. Throughout Massachusetts and the rest of New England, Boston is often called "The Hub," because it is the center of transportation and trade for the entire area. Railroads, highways, airplane routes, and shipping lanes cross at Boston. It is linked closely with the rest of the United States and the world.

One fourth of all the people in New England live in or near Boston. In this Atlantic coast city there are a great many industries. It is a center for wool manufacturing, and receives raw wool for weaving from many parts of the world. It imports hides and skins for the leather industries of New England. To *import* means to bring in from other places raw materials and food which cannot be produced at home.

Boston also exports goods. This means just the opposite of import. Woven textiles, machinery, shoes, and paper products are shipped out from Boston. The excellent harbor at Boston is always busy with ships coming and going. It has deep water, and over fifty miles of docks are available.

Boston is also famous for its many fine

schools, colleges, and universities. There are some world-famous hospitals here, where doctors are studying the causes and seeking the cure of dreaded diseases. About three fourths of the people of Boston are Catholic, and there are a great many beautiful churches and fine Catholic grammar schools, high schools, and colleges.

The Port of Boston. This seaport has about 120 miles of waterfront and 260 piers. Here a freighter is being unloaded at a pier in South Boston.

Richard Cardinal Cushing, Archbishop of Boston, is one of the four Americans who are Cardinals—Princes of the Church.

Boston Skyline. Harvard students at Cambridge can see Memorial Drive, a new superhighway, and the city of Boston just across the Charles River.

"The British Are Coming!" A monument to the memory of Paul Revere shows him on his famous ride. Signal lanterns hung in the Old North Church.

Historic Boston. Tourists from all over the United States come to Boston to see the many places of historic interest. They want to see Boston Common and Faneuil Hall, where the early patriots first organized to free the colonies from the mother country. The old North Church is interesting, because in its tower the lantern was hung to tell Paul Revere to begin his famous ride. A monument marks the place where the battle of Bunker Hill was won, and in Boston Harbor the famous old Navy ship "Old Ironsides" rides at anchor.

Facts *to remember*

1. New Englanders began to manufacture their own goods because of the distance from the mother country and because English goods were expensive.
2. Energetic and ambitious people harnessed the cheap power in many swiftly-flowing streams and made New England a manufacturing center. Shoemaking has remained an important industry, while the cotton cloth business had declined.
3. In spite of the fact that New England has no iron, copper, or lead, it ranks high in metal manufactures. Other parts of the United States depend upon the excellent machine tools which come

from this area. Waltham, Massachusetts, and Waterbury, Connecticut, are famous for watches and clocks; New Britain, Connecticut, leads in hardware production; Hartford and Stamford, Connecticut, make airplane parts and rocket engine parts.
4. New England is famous for its granite, marble, and slate. More marble is quarried in Vermont than in any other state.
5. Boston is the largest city in New England and one of the ten largest cities in the United States. It is closely linked with the rest of the United States and the world, for it is the center of transportation and trade for the entire area. It is a great import and export center. Much wool manufacturing is done here. Boston is famous for its fine schools, colleges, and universities.

What *have I learned?*

Copy the names in column A. Opposite each name, write the item in column B that best fits it.

A	B
1. Boston	a. producer of brassware
2. Brockton	b. makes airplane and rocket engine parts
3. Quincy	c. large shoemaking center
4. Woonsocket	d. "The Hub"
5. Waterbury	e. cotton cloth manufacture
6. Hartford	f. makes jewelry
7. New Britain	g. leading hardware producer
8. Providence	h. famous for watches and clocks
9. New Haven	i. granite quarrying center

Facts *to understand*

Give reasons for each statement.
1. New England has no fuel or mineral resources, and yet it is an important manufacturing region.
2. Although New England has no metal deposits, the value of the manufactured metal products is greater than the value of any of its other manufactures.
3. Boston is called "The Hub."
4. Tourists come to Boston to see the places of historic interest.
5. Building stone is New England's valuable natural resource.

4

The Middle Atlantic Region

New York City from the Air. The port of New York, at the mouth of the Hudson, handles more freight and passengers than any other port in the world.

Like the New England region, the Middle Atlantic region was also a landing place for the early English settlers. In fact, the first permanent English settlement was at Jamestown, Virginia, in the southern part of the Middle Atlantic region. The states we will study in this region are New York, New Jersey, Pennsylvania, Maryland, Delaware, Virginia, and West Virginia. All but Pennsylvania and West Virginia touch the Atlantic Ocean. Also in this region is the District of Columbia, where Washington, our nation's capital, is located.

Location. Turn to the map of the Middle Atlantic region on pages 62 and 63. Find the New England region which you have just studied. Now run your finger south along the coast line. You will touch the coasts of New York, New Jersey, Delaware, Maryland, and Virginia. Note the irregular coast line. Later you will discover the great importance of this irregular coast line in providing excellent harbors.

Some of the coastal states extend very far inland as well. The northernmost of the Middle Atlantic States is New York. On the east, New York touches Connecticut, Massachusetts, and Vermont. Canada lies to the north and west, across the St. Lawrence River and Lake Ontario.

The Middle Atlantic Region **61**

Studying the Map

A. The seven Middle Atlantic States lie along or near the eastern coast of the United States between the New England and the Southern States. **1.** List the Middle Atlantic States in order of their size. (Check your list with the areas shown on the map on pp. 18-19.) **2.** Which state lies farthest north? farthest south? **3.** Which of the Middle Atlantic States borders New England? **4.** Which two of the Great Lakes border New York? Which one borders Pennsylvania? **5.** Name the river that forms part of the boundary between New York State and Canada. **6.** Name the Middle Atlantic States that border the Atlantic Coast. Which two of the states do not touch the ocean? **7.** Which part of New York State extends out into the Atlantic Ocean?

B. **1.** Locate the lowland along the Atlantic Coast. Why is it colored green? **2.** Find the Appalachian Highlands. Over which Middle Atlantic States do they extend? **3.** Name two mountain areas in New York State. Which of these has peaks higher than 5000 feet? **4.** Find the Hudson River in New York State. Where does it rise? Into what body of water does it flow? **5.** What river forms the boundary between New Jersey and Pennsylvania? Where does it rise? Into what body of water does it flow? **6.** Find the Susquehanna River. Into what body of water does it flow? **7.** Locate and name three important bays along the Middle Atlantic Coast.

C. Just as in New England, most of the people of the Middle Atlantic States live in the larger cities and towns. **1.** List the seven Middle Atlantic States. Next to each state write the name of its capital. **2.** Which great city lies on the Atlantic Coast at the mouth of the Hudson River? **3.** Find the New York State Barge Canal. What bodies of water are joined by this canal? **4.** On what river are Philadelphia and Trenton located? Washington, D.C.? **5.** On what bay is Baltimore located? Wilmington? **6.** Name the three cities located on Hampton Roads, Virginia. **7.** Which city is located in western Pennsylvania at the junction of the Allegheny, Monongahela, and Ohio Rivers? **8.** After studying this map of the Middle Atlantic States what can you say about the location of important cities?

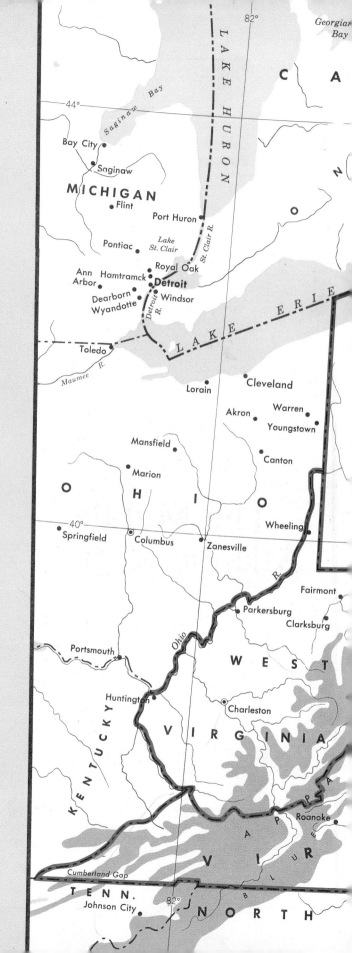

MIDDLE ATLANTIC STATES

CANADA

L. Simcoe

Toronto

LAKE ONTARIO

Niagara Falls
Welland Canal
Buffalo
Niagara R.
Erie

Watertown
THOUSAND IS.
Oswego

St. Lawrence Seaway
St. Lawrence R.
Lawrence

Plattsburgh
Lake Champlain
ADIRONDACK MTS.
Burlington
Montpelier

VERMONT

Lake George
Rutland
GREEN MTS.

MT. Washington
WHITE MTS.
Androscoggin R.

NEW HAMPSHIRE

Claremont
Concord
Manchester
Nashua
Lowell
Concord
Somerville
Boston
Quincy
Woonsocket

44°

New York State Barge Canal
Rochester
Oneida L.
Rome
Utica
Syracuse
Auburn
Genesee R.
Finger Lakes

NEW YORK

Saratoga Springs
Amsterdam
Schenectady
Albany
Troy

Pittsfield
BERKSHIRE HILLS
Holyoke
Springfield
Worcester
Hartford

MASS.

Pawtucket
Providence
Cranston
Fall River
RHODE ISLAND

Elmira
Binghamton
CATSKILLS

Hudson R.

New Britain
Waterbury
New Haven

CONNECTICUT

Poughkeepsie
Newburgh

Allegheny R.

Susquehanna R.

Scranton
Wilkes-Barre

HIGHLAND

Delaware R.

White Plains
Paterson
Jersey City
Newark
Elizabeth

Yonkers
New York
Bayonne

Bridgeport

Long Island Sound
LONG ISLAND
BLOCK I.
Montauk Pt.

OCEAN

PENNSYLVANIA

Pittsburgh
Johnstown
Altoona

ALLEGHENY MTS.

Easton
Allentown
Bethlehem

Reading

New York Bay
Sandy Hook

Harrisburg
Susquehanna R.
Lancaster
York

Trenton

NEW JERSEY

Atlantic City

74°

Chester
Camden
Wilmington

Cumberland

Hagerstown
Potomac R.
Baltimore
Annapolis
Washington D.C.
Alexandria

BLUE RIDGE MTS.

SHENANDOAH NATIONAL PARK
Shenandoah R.

Charlottesville
James R.
Lynchburg
Richmond

VIRGINIA

DELAWARE
Dover
Cape May
Delaware Bay

COASTAL PLAIN

Chesapeake Bay

ATLANTIC

OCEAN

40°

Cape Charles
Newport News
Portsmouth
Norfolk
Hampton Roads
Dismal Swamp
Kerr L.
Roanoke R.

78°

CAROLINA

ELEVATIONS IN FEET

- over 10,000
- 5,000 to 10,000
- 2,000 to 5,000
- 500 to 2,000
- 0 to 500
- Below Sea Level

Capital Cities -------- ⊙
International Boundaries ——
State or Provincial Boundaries —·—·—

Scale of Miles

0   20   40   60   80   100

Delaware Water Gap. The Delaware River flows through this scenic mountain gorge. Here it forms the border between New Jersey and Pennsylvania.

South of New York State is Pennsylvania. It is one of the two Middle Atlantic States without a coast line. To the east of Pennsylvania is New Jersey. To the south and west of New Jersey is the tiny state of Delaware, and still farther south and west, Maryland. Virginia lies south of Maryland. The small District of Columbia is on the border between these two states. West Virginia is inland from Virginia. Like Pennsylvania, it has no coast. Virginia is the southernmost of the Middle Atlantic States. To the south lies the state of North Carolina.

The Lowland Regions. The map on pages 62 and 63 shows the principal surface features of the Middle Atlantic Region. First, find the two main lowland areas. One is the Atlantic Coastal Plain, which runs from north to south through this region and extends for some distance in from the coast. The coastal plain was once part of the ocean floor, but it was lifted up by forces within the earth. That is why it is sandy and quite level throughout.

The other lowland area is the Hudson-Mohawk Valley, which occupies a large part of the interior of New York State. This valley was once the principal lowland route from the Atlantic coast to the interior of North America. It is still a very important transportation route, with New York City at one end and Buffalo on Lake Erie at the other end. Notice that both lowland areas are shaded dark green on the map.

Just west of the Atlantic Coastal Plain, the land becomes somewhat higher. This area is known as the Piedmont Plateau. The word *piedmont* means "foot of the mountains." West of the Piedmont Plateau, the land becomes much higher. This high section is called the Appalachian Highlands.

Many rivers and streams plunge down from the hills. They bring water to farms, fields, and forests, and they supply the power for plants which make electricity.

Appalachian Highlands. The Appalachian Highlands extend from north to south through the states of New York, Pennsylvania, West Virginia, and Virginia. Some parts are so high they are called mountains. The Blue Ridge Mountains in Virginia, for example, and the Catskill Mountains in New York, are parts of the Appalachian Highlands. The western part of the Appalachian Highlands is a rugged plateau.

In the highest parts of the Appalachians, evergreen forests cover most of the land. Farms are rare because of the steep, stony hills, and the air is cool even in summer. Vacationers find these highland areas pleasant as an escape from the city heat.

In the Appalachian Highlands there is a series of ridges and wide, fertile valleys. These extend more than one thousand miles from New York in the north to Alabama in the south. The sheltered valleys of the Appalachians are areas of rich farmland with good soil.

Waterways. In the early days of our country most travel was by water or overland routes because of the lack of other means of traveling. Today, these means are still used because they are cheaper and better suited for many purposes than air travel.

The Middle Atlantic region has an excellent system of waterways. First of all, there is the Atlantic Ocean. The irregular coast line provides a number of good harbors where ships can load and unload protected from the ocean winds. Ships sail in and out of these harbors to all parts of the world. Around these harbors have grown great world-trading cities like New York, Philadelphia, and Baltimore.

To the north and west of the Middle Atlantic Region are the Great Lakes. The Great Lakes can be used to transport goods to and from Midwestern United States and Canada. The St. Lawrence River connects the lakes to the Atlantic Ocean. The New York State Barge Canal connects the Great Lakes with the Hudson River. The Hudson then leads south to New York Harbor and the Atlantic Ocean. Find each of these waterways on the map on pages 62-63.

In addition to the Hudson and the St. Lawrence, there are other important rivers in the Middle Atlantic region. At the city of Pittsburgh, in western Pennsylvania, two rivers join to form the Ohio River. The Ohio flows into the mighty Mississippi, main waterway of the Southern States. Ships can go all the way to the Gulf of Mexico by this route. In addition, there are many other smaller rivers which carry goods and people throughout the region.

Milder Climate than New England. In many parts of the Middle Atlantic region, the climate is influenced somewhat by the presence of large bodies of water. The Atlantic Coastal Plain lies near the ocean, and Lake Erie and Lake Ontario influence the climate of the interior areas. Let us see

Rip Van Winkle's Country. The Hudson River Valley and Catskill Mountains of New York are the scene of many of Washington Irving's stories.

what effect a large body of water has on climate.

Water does not heat so quickly as land, nor does it cool off so quickly. Large bodies of water are cooler than near-by land in summer and warmer in winter. Places near water, therefore, are cooled by breezes from the water in summer and warmed in the winter. As a result, places like the Atlantic Coast Plain near the ocean and areas near the Great Lakes have milder climates—summers not too hot, winters not too cold.

In the spring, when the land is beginning to be warmed by the sun, the air over the water is still cool. Winds blowing from the water to the land really delay the warm weather because they are cool. Right into the summer, winds blowing from the water have a cooling effect on the land. In winter, the land becomes cool more quickly than the water. Winds blowing from the water carry air that is still warm, and this helps keep the winter weather moderate.

In general, then, throughout the Middle Atlantic region, the climate is more moderate than it is in New England. There are short, mild winters, with a long growing season for crops in the spring, summer, and fall. The amount of rain which falls is fairly even in all seasons, and plentiful enough for all kinds of crops. Later, you will read more about climate conditions which favor certain kinds of crops in certain parts of the Middle Atlantic region.

Why the People Came. From the earliest days, people came from all parts of Europe to this region. The excellent harbors and locations for cities along the coast attracted settlers from England, Scotland, Ireland, Sweden, the Netherlands, Germany, and other countries. To the north, in New England, the settlers were almost all English. To the south also, the settlers were almost all English. Only in this middle section of the Atlantic Seaboard were there so many settlers from so many different countries.

After the Revolutionary War, the people of this region joined those of the North and those of the South in setting up the United States of America. The old colonies became the new states. Only West Virginia was not one of the first thirteen new states.

The Earliest Settlers. The first settlements in this region were on the very edge of the Atlantic Ocean. The early colonists had their farms near the ocean or along the rivers which ran to the ocean. They were close to ports that received supplies from Europe. The rivers which cross the Atlantic Coastal Plain have their sources in the Appalachian Highlands. At the edge of the Piedmont Plateau, these rivers fall to the level of the coastal plain. Ocean ships could only sail up the rivers as far as the falls.

The border between the coastal plain and the Piedmont came to be known as the *fall line*. Beyond it, few people would venture, because it meant being cut off from supplies. Many towns and villages sprang up along the fall line. Some of these later became important cities.

In time, most of the good farmland along the coast was claimed. New settlers gradually began to move beyond the fall line. Daniel Boone and other great explorers led people across the Appalachian Highlands. This was the beginning of the great westward movement that was to continue all the way to the Pacific Ocean.

The Immigrants Arrive. Waves of immigrants began to pour into the United States from the crowded countries of Europe after 1865. They entered through the great port cities of the eastern coast. You have already learned how many of them came to the cities of New England. Large numbers traveled far inland to settle on the farms of the middle west.

THE MIDDLE ATLANTIC COLONIES

The names of the various Middle Atlantic States are the old names which applied to the original colonies. Maryland and Virginia were given their names to honor two different queens of England. Pennsylvania, meaning "Penn's Woods," was the name given to the settlement established by William Penn and his followers.

The first permanent establishment in this region was made by a group of Englishmen at Jamestown, Virginia. It was not long, however, before thousands of people from many countries of Europe followed the English settlers to the New World. They soon built up a fast growing string of busy cities along the Atlantic Coast.

Many more, however, stayed in the cities of the Middle Atlantic region where it was easy to find work in the many industries. Their numbers swelled the population of coastal cities like New York, Philadelphia, Baltimore, and Newark, as well as the large factory cities like Pittsburgh in the interior.

The People Today. The population of the Middle Atlantic Seaboard is made up of the descendants of people from all over the world. There are those whose ancestors settled here hundreds of years ago. There are descendants of the immigrants you have just read about.

There are also two other groups of people who make up a large part of the population. When the Negro slaves were set free in this country, many came from the Southern States to settle in cities of the Middle Atlantic Region. Their descendants form a sizeable part of the population of the larger cities like New York, Philadelphia, Boston, and Washington. More recently, thousands of people from the island of Puerto Rico have arrived in this section. They come to the cities of the Middle Atlantic region looking for work and better living conditions.

Most of the people of this region live in cities and work in manufacturing industries. More and more people come to live and work in these cities each year, swelling the already large populations. There are, of course, still many farmers and fishermen.

Facts *to remember*

1. In the Middle Atlantic States, all but Pennsylvania and West Virginia touch the Atlantic Ocean.
2. This group of states has two main lowland areas. One is the Atlantic Coastal Plain, the other is the Hudson-Mohawk Valley. West of the Atlantic Coastal Plain is the Piedmont Plateau. Just west of the plateau is a higher section known as the Appalachian Highlands. The valleys of the Appalachian Highlands are areas of rich farmland.

3. Excellent waterways provide good harbors, cheap transportation, and easy communication with other parts of the United States. The outstanding waterways of this region are the Atlantic Ocean, the Great Lakes, the St. Lawrence River, the Hudson River, and the Ohio River.
4. The climate is more moderate than it is in New England. There is a long growing season.
5. Excellent harbors and locations for cities along the coast attracted settlers from other countries.
6. Many nationalities are to be found in the Middle Atlantic States.

What *have I learned?*

Answer each question in a complete sentence.
1. What inland waterway is used to transport goods to and from the United States and Canada?
2. Name the higher land just west of the Piedmont Plateau.
3. Which two Middle Atlantic States have no coast line?
4. What valley is today an important transportation route between New York City and Buffalo?
5. What term is given to the boundary between the coastal plain and the Piedmont?
6. Name two groups of mountains located within the Appalachian Highlands.
7. Name three important rivers located in the Middle Atlantic States.
8. Name three countries from which the early settlers of the Middle Atlantic region came.
9. Which one of the Middle Atlantic States was not one of the thirteen original states?
10. What is one advantage of waterways over other means of transportation?

Facts *to understand*

Answer each of the following questions in a sentence or two.
1. Of what importance is the irregular coast line of the Middle Atlantic States?
2. Why is the Hudson-Mohawk Valley an important transportation route?
3. Tell why there are not many farms in the higher parts of the Appalachian Highlands.
4. Tell how bodies of water moderate climate.
5. Why are so many people from all parts of Europe attracted to the Middle Atlantic region?

Fulton Fish Market. Cargoes of fresh fish and seafood for New York City's tables are delivered daily to this busy market along the East River.

5
Middle Atlantic Food Industries

The busy towns and cities of the Middle Atlantic States have a large population. More than one fourth of the people of the United States live in this region. Large quantities of food are required to feed all these people. Much of it comes from nearby farms. Large catches of fish are taken in the coastal waters and help supply the food needs of the Middle Atlantic region. A great amount of food is also imported.

Outside the cities and towns are many different kinds of farms which supply food and food products. Among them are dairy farms, which sell fresh milk for the children in the cities. Vegetable farmers send their products to city markets or to freezing plants and canneries. Poultry farms provide eggs and meat. Orchards supply apples and other kinds of fruit.

Along the Middle Atlantic coast, from Long Island's shores to the waters off Virginia, fishermen are busy. In the bays and inlets along the coast, oysters and other shellfish are a large part of the catch.

In addition to the many foods which are produced in this region, many more have to be brought in by truck, railroad, and boat. Some of them are: meats, such as beef and lamb, flour, citrus fruits, and sugar.

Dairying in New York and Pennsylvania. Most of us know that milk is our most nearly perfect food. It is especially important for growing children to drink plenty of fresh milk.

The hilly uplands of the Appalachian region in northern Pennsylvania and southern New York are a great dairying region. The grass-covered lower slopes and the valleys are well suited for summer grazing. Dairy farmers raise hay, corn, and other crops. Hay and corn are the chief winter feed for the dairy cows.

Bottling Pasteurized Milk. Fresh milk is inspected and pasteurized, then sealed by sterilized machines into spotless waxed-paper containers.

From the Farm to Your Home. Let us see what happens to the milk from the time the cow is milked until the fresh milk reaches your table. On the dairy farm we find a barn, a silo, and a milk house. When the cows are not in the pasture, they are kept in a barn and fed corn which has been stored in a silo. Cows are milked in the barn early in the morning and again at night. Some cows are still milked by hand, but on the larger dairy farms electric milking machines are used. The fresh milk is kept cool in large cans or tanks in the milk house. This "house" is really a large icebox.

The large cities of the Middle Atlantic region are ready markets for the fresh milk. In addition, some of the milk is used to make butter, cheese, and ice cream, or is made into evaporated or powdered milk by removing part or all of the water it contains. These are called *milk products*.

Some of the farmers send their milk to nearby cities in large cans. Those who are farther away use stainless steel tank trucks. A tank truck keeps milk cool in the same way as a thermos bottle keeps liquids cool. Railroads which carry milk have electrically-cooled tank cars. This careful handling keeps the milk from spoiling.

A Dairy Farm in New Jersey. The Middle Atlantic area resembles New England, with many dairy farms to meet the needs of large city populations.

When milk reaches the city milk plant, it must be tested for quality and cleanliness. In addition, the milk must be made safe to drink. This is done by heating it to a high

Working in a Frozen Food Plant. This woman operates a machine that packages frozen strawberries. A great amount of farm produce is now frozen.

temperature for thirty minutes and then allowing it to cool slowly. The process is called *pasteurization*. Great care must be taken to keep the milk clean. Automatic washing machines are used at the bottling plant to clean the milk bottles. Dairies also use sanitary waxed-paper containers. The bottles or containers are not touched by human hands until another machine fills them with milk and seals them. All this is done to be sure that city people have a safe supply of milk. This is the product that you have delivered to your door or that you buy at the market.

The Atlantic Coastal Plain extends from Cape Cod to Florida. Part of this coastal plain is in the Middle Atlantic States. There are many farms on this coastal plain. The chief areas are Long Island, western New Jersey, and a region called "Delmarva." Delmarva is the peninsula that lies between Chesapeake Bay and the Atlantic Ocean. It includes parts of Delaware, Maryland, and Virginia, combining all three state names.

Most of the farms on the coastal plain are

truck farms. Cauliflower, potatoes, cabbage, tomatoes, snap beans, and leafy green vegetables are the chief crops. Coastal plain farmers plant several crops a year. They use fertilizers regularly to keep the soil rich and very productive.

Hauling Farm Produce to Market. Workers on this New York farm are picking baskets of ripe tomatoes and loading them on a city-bound truck.

These farmers employ a great many laborers for planting, cultivating, and harvesting their crops. As a result, they can obtain large crops from a small amount of land. This is called *intensive farming*.

Every day during the long growing season, railroads and trucks carry the baskets of fresh-picked vegetables to markets in nearby cities. Much of the produce is quick-frozen and packaged at plants near the farms. In Baltimore and other cities there are canneries to which vegetables and fruits are sent.

Piedmont Farms. Just west of the coastal plain is the Piedmont. This region has a higher elevation than the coastal plain. The part of the Piedmont in the Middle Atlantic States extends from New Jersey to Virginia.

It does not extend into New York State. Tobacco is grown on the Piedmont Plateau in Virginia, Maryland, and Pennsylvania. The German farmers near Lancaster, Pennsylvania, raise more tobacco on an acre of ground than any other tobacco growers.

Farmers call tobacco a "soil robber" because it removes so many minerals from the soil. The minerals are foods for growing plants. If you were to grow tobacco year after year on the same soil, each acre of ground would yield less and less. Therefore, farmers in this region plant the tobacco in different fields each year. In the other fields they plant crops like wheat and corn. One field is always planted in clover, which helps to make the soil fertile again. This method of using different fields each year is called *crop rotation*. It is an example of the many different ways in which man makes wise use of the earth.

Tobacco Farm in Maryland. This state is one of the leading producers of tobacco and tobacco products. The leaves here are drying in the sun.

In other parts of the Piedmont, farmers carry on *mixed farming*. They plant several kinds of crops, keep farm animals, and raise poultry. Corn, wheat, and hay are raised and fed to the livestock. The farmer makes his money by selling meat, milk, and eggs to markets in nearby cities.

During the spring in the Middle Atlantic States, the fruit trees in the orchards are beautiful with their colorful blossoms. Later in the year these same trees are loaded down with fruit.

Apples grow well on the hillsides and ridges of the Appalachians. On the hillsides there is less danger of frost than in the valleys. At night the cold, heavy air sinks to the bottom of the valley. This movement of cold air to the valley keeps the hillsides warmer. It is called *frost drainage*. Frost drainage is very helpful to fruit growers because it keeps frost off the hillside trees. A single frost can ruin an entire crop.

So many apples grow on one ridge in Virginia that the people call it "Apple Pie Ridge." There are many apple-packing houses and storage plants in this part of Virginia. Some of the apples are even shipped to Norfolk to be exported to Europe.

Fruit is also grown along the coastal plain. The sandy soil is good for strawberries, blackberries, blueberries, and raspberries. There are plenty of apple and peach orchards in Delaware and southern New Jersey. Those fruit orchards are near water, so there is less danger from frost.

New York is a leading fruit-producing state. There are large orchards on the plain just south of Lake Ontario, as well as in the Finger Lakes region and in the Hudson Valley. Large amounts of apples, peaches, and pears are canned and preserved in local canneries. In western New York, near Lake Erie, there are many grape vineyards. Wine-making is important here.

Picking Peaches. Throughout the Middle Atlantic region, fruit-growers employ young college students in the summers to help in the harvest.

Middle Atlantic Fisheries. Just as in New England, fishing is an important task for many people along the Middle Atlantic coast. From Long Island Sound southward, the many bays and river mouths, as well as the ocean waters off the coast, provide good fishing. Oysters, clams, crabs, and other shellfish make up a large part of the catch. Cod, halibut, haddock, and mackerel are caught offshore in the Atlantic. Shad fishing is especially good in Delaware Bay. The eggs of the shad, called the *roe,* are delicious and bring in a high price in the markets of the coastal cities.

Tremendous catches of menhaden are caught in the Atlantic. In fact more of this fish are caught than any other fish or shellfish. Menhaden are too oily to be used as human food. They can, however, be used in making fertilizer, hog and poultry feed, paint, linoleum, printing inks, and soap.

Oyster Beds. Oysters are popular and are good food because they contain minerals and vitamins. Oysters are found in many waters along the Atlantic coast, especially

A Bucket of Tasty Oysters. Fishermen in Chesapeake Bay bring in a large catch. Many fishermen work at gathering this popular shellfish.

in Delaware Bay, Chesapeake Bay, and Long Island Sound.

Oysters grow best in shallow waters along the coast. They attach themselves to clean rocks, gravel, and shells at the bottom of bays and inlets. Places like these are called *oyster beds*. Here the oysters feed upon material they obtain from sea water.

Today baby oysters are placed in beds. They are allowed to feed and grow on the bottom of a bay or inlet. In one or two years when they are large enough to use, the oysters are gathered by pulling dredges over the beds. This method of planting baby oysters in beds is called *oyster farming*.

Along the shores of Chesapeake Bay and other bays, we find buildings called *oyster houses*. Here the oysters are sorted according to their size. Then they are packed in ice or in special refrigerator cars and sent to cities all over the United States. Oystermen often remove the meat from the shell. This is called *shucking,* and the workers are called *shuckers*. The oyster meat is packed in containers and sent to markets. Some of it is canned.

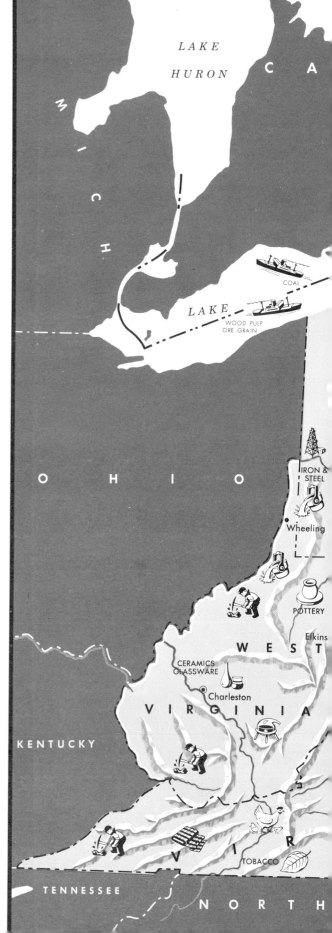

CANADA

MAINE

VERMONT

NEW HAMPSHIRE

• Massena

LAKE ONTARIO

• Watertown

MASSACHUSETTS

Niagara Falls

Buffalo

WHEAT
IRON ORE

LAKE ERIE

Erie

ELECTRONICS

Rochester

FLOUR

NEW YORK

• Corning

Syracuse

BRASSWARE

Utica

FURS

Schenectady

Albany

MILK

COMPUTERS

Kingston

CONNECTICUT

RHODE ISLAND

LOCOMOTIVES

CARBON

FURS

BARLEY

MEDICINES

PENNSYLVANIA

Wilkes-Barre

Scranton

CEMENT

NEW

Yonkers

New York

Newark

OCEAN

PETROLEUM
SUGAR COFFEE

CORK

Altoona

Pittsburgh

Harrisburg

Easton

Allentown

Bethlehem

POTTERY

Bayonne

JERSEY

Trenton

IRON, STEEL,
VEHICLES
ELECTRICAL MACHINERY

SUGAR REFINING

Philadelphia

Camden

Wilmington

COD HALIBUT
HADDOCK MENHADEN

MARYLAND

Baltimore

Washington D.C.

DEL.

Salisbury

SHAD

HIDES WOOL SUGAR
WOOD PULP COAL
IRON ORE PETROLEUM

CANNED TOMATOES

VIRGINIA

R.R. LOCOMOTIVES
(SHIPBUILDING)
TEXTILES IRON
AND STEEL GOODS

Lynchburg

Richmond

ATLANTIC

G

Newport News

Norfolk

• Danville

Capital Cities ⊙   Canal +—+—+

International Boundaries ·—·—·

State or Provincial Boundaries — — —

Scale of Miles

0   20   40   60   80   100

FUEL OIL
GYPSUM POTASH
NITROGEN

TOBACCO
COAL COTTON
LUMBER

CAROLINA

Facts *to remember*

1. More than one fourth of the people of the United States live in the Middle Atlantic States. These people require large quantities of food.

2. The hilly uplands of the Appalachian region in northern Pennsylvania and southern New York form a great dairying region. The grass-covered lower slopes and valleys of these areas are suited for grazing, and hay and corn can be raised for feeding the stock.

3. Milk is sent to the cities by stainless-steel tank trucks or in electrically-cooled tank cars. Milk must be tested for quality, pasteurized for cleanliness, and placed in sterilized bottles or containers.

4. Long Island, western New Jersey, and the Delmarva region are the chief farming areas. The Delmarva region is between the Chesapeake Bay and the Atlantic Ocean. Most of the farms on the coastal plain are truck farms in which intensive farming is used to obtain large crops from a small plot of land.

5. The German farmers near Lancaster, Pennsylvania raise more tobacco on an acre of ground than any other tobacco growers in the United States. Since tobacco removes many minerals from the soil as it grows, the farmers must rotate their crops. Apples grow on the hillsides of the Appalachians. New York is a leading fruit-producing state.

6. Large catches of fish taken from the coastal waters help supply the food needs of the people of the Middle Atlantic States. Oysters grow well in the shallow waters along the coast.

What *have I learned?*

I

Copy these sentences on another sheet of paper. Write T before each sentence that is true, and F before each sentence that is false.

1. More than one fourth of the people of the United States live in the Middle Atlantic region.

2. Apples are our most nearly perfect food.

3. Poultry farms provide fresh vegetables.

4. Harmful germs are removed from milk by pasteurization.

5. The Atlantic Coastal Plain is a poor farming area.

6. Tobacco is grown on the Piedmont in Virginia, Maryland, and Pennsylvania.

7. Planting several kinds of crops is called "mixed farming."

8. There is less danger of frost in the valleys than on the hillsides.

9. Oysters grow best in the middle of the Atlantic Ocean.

10. Wine-making is an important industry in Western New York.

II

Copy the names in Column A. Write opposite each name the item from Column B which best fits it.

A	B
1. Oysters	Large crops from a small piece of land
2. Dairy Region	Western New York
3. Pasteurizing	Virginia
4. Soil Robber	Chesapeake Bay
5. Frost Drainage	Not a food fish
6. Wine-making	Northern Pennsylvania
7. Menhaden	Tobacco
8. Shad	Making milk safe to drink
9. "Apple Pie Ridge"	Very helpful to fruit growers
10. Intensive Farming	Delaware Bay fish

Facts *to understand*

Give a reason for each of the following facts.

1. The population of the Middle Atlantic region means great numbers of farms in the region.

2. Most of the farms on the coastal plain use intensive farming.

3. Farmers plant tobacco in different fields each year.

4. One ridge in Virginia is called "Apple Pie Ridge."

5. New York is a leading fruit-producing state.

6. Along the shores of Chesapeake Bay and other bays we find buildings called oyster houses.

7. Menhaden are used to make fertilizer, paint, printing ink, and soap.

8. The region around northern Pennsylvania and southern New York is good for dairying.

9. Great care is taken to protect milk as it makes its way from the farm to the home.

10. The fruit orchards of Delaware and southern New Jersey are in little danger from frost.

Oil Refinery. This complicated plant in Bayonne, New Jersey, receives oil by boat or pipeline and refines it into gasoline and heating oil.

6 Mineral Industries

Have you ever taken part in a guessing game called "Twenty Questions"? The first question you ask is always, "Is it animal, vegetable, or mineral?" Everything in the world can be placed into one of these three classes of things. Of course, you know what is meant by animal and vegetable, but what is mineral?

The word *mineral* takes in anything that is not animal or vegetable. Usually when we talk of mineral things we mean gold, silver, iron, copper, lead, tin, and coal. Mineral also includes salt, stone, clay, sand, oil, natural gas, and many other substances.

Some minerals can be very valuable. A man who owns a gold mine or an oil well is likely to become rich. Other minerals are not valuable. A farmer who has many rocks and stones in his fields has to spend time and money to get rid of them. Valuable minerals are not found evenly divided throughout the world. Some places are very rich in certain valuable minerals, and other places have no mineral wealth at all. You will remember that in the New England region there is very little mineral wealth.

Very few minerals can be put to use just as they are found in the earth. Something has to be done to them before they are of value. Many people make their living by getting minerals out of the ground and then changing them somehow so that they can be of use to men. We say that these people work in the *mineral industries*. In this chapter you will study the mineral industries of the Middle Atlantic region.

Mineral Industries **77**

Concrete for Highways. These men are using a huge spreader to lay concrete into forms for another new highway. It dries into a good surface.

Making Cement. All over the United States there is a huge program of building going on. New highways, homes, churches, schools, and factories are being constructed everywhere. You have probably seen many of the giant trucks called *concrete mixers* traveling along the highways. Their huge drums mix the liquid concrete on the way to the place where it is used. An important part of any concrete mixture is the cement. Let us find out how cement is made.

Cement is made from limestone and shale. These two rock materials are found together in eastern Pennsylvania near the coal fields. The Lehigh Valley is the leading cement-making region in the United States. The cities of Allentown and Easton have large plants. This region is near New York and Philadelphia, both of which need the cement to make concrete for the construction of buildings, roads, and sidewalks.

Cement is made by crushing and grinding limestone and shale into a powder. This powder is heated to a very high temperature in a long, slanting pipe which turns round and round. This pipe is called a *rotary kiln*. A very hot flame of burning oil or gas is blown into the kiln. This causes the material to form lumps called *clinkers*. The clinkers are ground up to make cement.

In order to make concrete, cement is mixed with water, sand, and gravel. Concrete is very strong and durable. It is cheap to make and is one of the best building materials. Concrete is poured into place while the mixture is wet. After a while, it dries and becomes hard as stone.

Glassmaking. It is very likely that the glass in the windows of your schoolroom or home came from the Middle Atlantic region. The familiar clear substance is made from minerals which are found in abundance throughout western Pennsylvania. More glass is made in Pittsburgh than in any other city of the United States.

Workers take pure sand and limestone and heat them together. The huge ovens are heated by electricity or by burning natural gas. When the mixture of sand and limestone melts, liquid glass results. Before it cools, this liquid is shaped on huge machines into bottles, pitchers, glasses, and other objects. Other workers pour liquid glass out onto heated steel tables. Heavy rollers pass over it. The long sheets which are formed make plate glass for windows and mirrors.

Other glass products made in Pittsburgh are shatterproof windshields for automobiles, and glass brick, which has become an important building material. All very fine glass objects are shaped and cut by hand. Skilled workers perform these delicate jobs. Glass used to make eyeglasses, microscopes, telescopes, and cameras must be carefully poured, cut, and polished.

Concrete for Buildings. Into the box-like wooden forms, wet concrete will be poured. The iron rods strengthen the concrete when it is dry.

Fine Glass Products. This highly skilled worker has used the glass blower (background) to form extremely delicate and beautiful glass items.

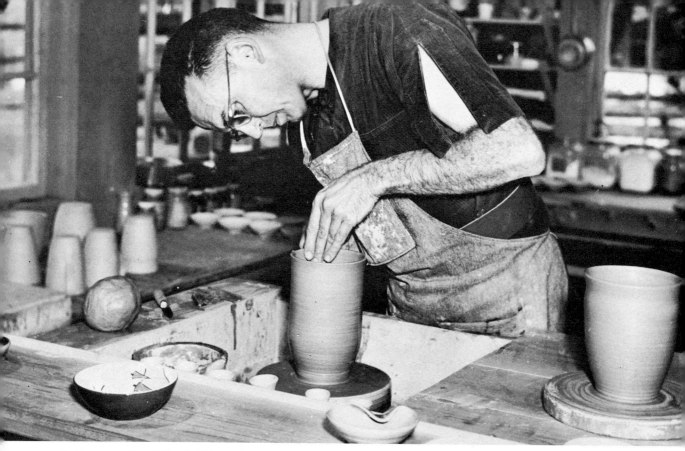

A Potter at His Wheel. This worker, another highly skilled craftsman, uses clay to create a fine vase. Pottery-making is a very ancient craft.

Stone and Clay. Rock and gravel are taken in great quantities from the highlands of the Middle Atlantic region. Together with cement, these materials find important uses in building and highway construction. A certain kind of clay found in New Jersey and New York is used for a special purpose. It is baked into bricks of all sizes and colors. These bricks are used throughout the country for construction purposes.

How Coal Was Formed. Many, many years ago parts of the earth were covered with trees and giant ferns. Huge animals called *dinosaurs* roamed in the dense forests. After these plants and animals died, they were covered by layers of mud and sand carried by streams flowing down from the mountains. This process happened over and over again, until the decayed plants and animals were buried far below the earth's surface. The weight of the layers of mud and sand produced great heat and pressure. This caused the earth's crust to fold. The buried plant and animal matter formed layers of coal under the surface of the earth. Even today miners find prints of leaves and ferns in the coal, evidence of the living things from which this mineral was formed.

The pressure and heat was not the same in all places. This unevenness caused different kinds of coal to be formed. In swampy places we find peat at or near the surface. *Peat* is the first stage in the formation of coal. In some parts of the world, in Ireland for example, peat is dried and used for fuel. In many places, soft coal called *bituminous* is mined. It is not really soft, but it is not as hard as the coal that is sometimes burned in home furnaces. Hard coal is called *anthracite* and is found in only a very few places in our country.

Mining Coal. Most of the coal mines in the Appalachian Region are deep in the earth. This is because the layers of coal, or *seams,* are buried under many layers of rock and clay. Although machinery is used more and more, it is still necessary for men to go far into the earth to get at the coal.

The miners dig out the coal, using power drills, explosives, and hand tools. They must pause from time to time to brace up the walls and roof of the tunnel they are digging through the earth. The coal is loaded on little railroad cars running through the mine. An elevator lifts it to the surface. There it is separated from the rock, washed, and sorted into different-sized chunks. It is then loaded onto railroad cars for shipment.

More coal is mined in the United States than in any other country. Our mines produce about *one half* of the world's supply. A large part of this is mined in the coal fields of the Appalachian Highlands. A coal field is a region where layers of coal lie below the surface. Pennsylvania and West Virginia have a great many coal fields. They are the leading coal-mining states.

Hard and Soft Coal. Nearly all the anthracite coal is mined in northern and eastern Pennsylvania around the cities of Scranton and Wilkes-Barre. It is a good fuel for home use because it burns slowly and does not make smoke. As it burns, it gives off a steady heat. This makes it especially valuable in certain manufacturing plants.

More than one fourth of the bituminous coal mined in the United States comes from mines in the plateau region of the Appalachian highland. The chief use for this soft coal is to make steam power for electricity. Large amounts of electricity are needed to run the mills and factories of the eastern United States. Bituminous is also used to make gas for cooking and heating.

The vast supply of bituminous coal is one of the reasons why the United States became the leading industrial country of the world. Without soft coal, the iron and steel mills, the railroads, and the factories could not have operated. The workers in these industries depend upon coal for heat and power.

Working in a Coal Mine. This coal mine worker in the Appalachian region drives a small railroad car, hauling loads of coal from the deep mine.

More than one half of the bituminous coal mined in our country is used to make *coke,* which is made from a kind of bituminous called *coking coal.* The iron and steel industry consumes large amounts of coke.

To make coke, soft coal is heated in large ovens. It is not burned in this process. When the coal is heated in a coke oven, coal gases are driven off. The light spongy material that remains is the coke. Coke is almost pure carbon. When it is burned it gives off tremendous heat, enough to melt iron ore.

One kind of coke oven is called a *beehive oven.* This type of oven allows the waste coal gas to escape. The beehive oven is not used much anymore.

Today most coke is made in *by-product ovens. By-products* are extra products that are left over after the main product has been made. For example, coke is the main product, and the coal gases are the by-products. In the by-product coke oven, the waste coal gases are not allowed to escape. They are captured and later burned to provide heat for making more coke. In addition, many chemical products, like nylon and plastics, are made from coal gases.

Changing Times. More and more today, coal is falling into disuse. This is because newer fuels, especially oil and natural gas, are taking its place in some industries. In many parts of Pennsylvania and West Virginia, towns and villages around coal mines have become deserted, and many miners have found themselves out of work. New uses for the chemicals in coal, however, are being discovered all the time. Plastics, nylon, drugs, and dyes are now made from coal. In other ways, coal may become even more important in the future.

From Ore to Iron. Iron ore is the mineral from which iron is obtained. At one time iron ore was mined in the Appalachians near Pittsburgh. Today most of it comes from mines in the Lake Superior region.

Iron is melted and separated from its ore in a blast furnace. The furnace is a large steel building lined with brick. Iron ore, coke, and limestone are poured into the top of the furnace. Then blasts of very hot air are blown through the material in the furnace.

The hot air causes the coke to burn and produce great heat. This melts the iron ore

Making Coke. When the heated coal has become coke, water is sprayed on it, making clouds of steam. It is then pushed into the waiting car.

and the limestone. The heavy, melted iron sinks to the bottom of the blast furnace. Limestone mixes with the impure parts of the iron ore. This mixture forms *slag*, which floats on top of the melted iron. Every four or five hours the melted iron and slag are allowed to run out of the bottom of the furnace. The slag is removed, leaving iron, which runs off into molds.

Men Working Together. From ore to iron is a process requiring many men of many skills, working together. Miners in the Lake Superior region go down into the earth to get the ore. Haulers then take it away by ship and rail to the blast furnaces. Quarry men supply limestone, and coal workers make coke needed for the furnaces. Still other skilled workers operate the blast furnaces. Before the mineral becomes metal, iron ore passes through many hands. Each type of worker contributes something to the final product. In making all the varied things which help us to live

Steel City. This scene along the Ohio River shows part of the reason for Pittsburgh's nickname. Note the busy railroad yards near the mills.

well, we depend upon the cooperation of many workers and suppliers.

"Tasting" the Steel. These men, their eyes protected from the brilliant glare, are taking a sample of steel from a furnace for testing.

Difficult, Dangerous Work. Men direct the movements of a huge ladle as it *charges*, or fills, an open hearth furnace with white-hot molten iron.

Making Steel. Steel is made from the pig iron in open hearth furnaces. Here more impurities are removed from melted iron.

Bessemer Converter. The pear-shaped pot in the center shoots out sparks and smoke as a blast of air passes through the hot iron, purifying it.

Other materials are added in order to make different kinds of steel. The steel can be rolled into plates or molded into any shape as it comes from the open-hearth furnace.

Some steel is made in a large furnace called the *Bessemer converter*. Steel made in this way has many uses but does not have the high quality of open-hearth steel.

The best steel is made in the electric furnace. Heat produced by electricity is used to melt the iron and make it into steel.

More steel is used today than ever before. Over 100 million tons per year are produced in this country. Steel is used in building ships, automobiles, bridges, dams, and skyscrapers. It is used also for railroad tracks, machinery, and even in tin cans.

Steel-Making Centers. Pittsburgh, Pennsylvania, and the cities around it have become one of the greatest steel-making centers in the world. You have already learned that iron ore, coke, and limestone are needed to make steel. Most of the iron ore is brought by boat from the Lake Superior region to ports on Lake Erie. A short railroad haul brings the ore from the lake ports to Pittsburgh. The best coal for making coke is mined a short distance from the city. Limestone is found nearby in the valleys of the Appalachians. These three important raw materials—iron ore, coke, and limestone—are easily brought together at Pittsburgh. Can you understand now why Pittsburgh is often called the "Steel City"?

Bethlehem, Pennsylvania, is another well-known steel center. Steel mills are also multiplying along the lower portions of the Delaware River and on Chesapeake Bay near Baltimore, Maryland.

These new mills produce huge quantities of steel to meet growing demands from all parts of the world. New nations in Asia and Africa are beginning to build their industries. Steel is one of their basic needs.

Oil. Millions of gallons of oil are used daily to supply heat for homes, power for industry, and gasoline for automobiles. Oil, or petroleum, was first discovered in the United States in the Middle Atlantic region. Colonel Edward Drake drilled an oil well in western Pennsylvania in 1859. At one time this was the leading region for petroleum. The invention of the automobile and the airplane increased the need for gasoline, which is made from petroleum. Today most of the oil comes from new fields in Texas, Oklahoma, and California, where we find deeper and more productive wells.

However, some oil is still pumped from wells in the Appalachians. Pennsylvania oil has special qualities which make it the best for lubricating and greasing automobiles and other machinery.

In the same region natural gas is found under the ground. Petroleum and natural gas are often found together. Natural gas is used to heat homes, to provide gas for cooking, and to furnish power for some industries. Natural gas is piped from the Appalachian area to nearby cities and even to cities along the coast.

Mineral Industries **85**

Building with Steel. These construction workers have a dangerous task. They assemble the steel girders to make the framework of a skyscraper.

The Uses of Energy. Of all man's needs, those for heat, light, and power are among the greatest. Long ago, wood was enough

America's First Oil Well. This shaky wooden structure was America's pioneer oil well. It ran dry in ten years, but began a huge industry.

to supply these needs. When the world population grew larger, man came upon coal as a source for heat, light, and power. Then he discovered the marvels of electricity. Still more recently, he has come to depend upon oil and natural gas. Now he has also explored the wonders of atomic energy. At some future time, man may harness the energy of the sun as his chief source of heat, light, and power.

In creating the world, God's wisdom, goodness, and care provided the means to supply all man's needs. Man, however, must seek these means. Having found them, he must use them wisely and share them with his fellow man.

Facts *to remember*

1. Valuable minerals are not evenly divided around the world. Few minerals can be put to use just as they are found in the earth. Most often, a number of different operations must be performed in order to change the minerals from raw materials into useful products or fuels.

2. Limestone and shale are used in making cement, which is one of the best building materials. The Lehigh Valley is the leading cement-making region in the United States. Allentown and Easton have large plants. Concrete is made from a mixture of cement, water, sand, and gravel. Rock and gravel found in the highlands of this region are used in highway construction.

3. The United States produces more coal than any other country. Much coal is mined in the Appalachian highlands. Pennsylvania and West Virginia are leading coal-mining states. One reason that the United States has become the leading industrial country of the world is that it has a large supply of bituminous coal. Oil and natural gas are gradually replacing coal as fuel. Plastics, nylon, drugs, and dyes are now made from coal.

4. Most of our iron ore comes from the Lake Superior region. Iron ore, coke, and limestone are used in making steel. These three important raw materials are brought together at Pittsburgh, which is often called the "Steel City." The Delaware River-Chesapeake Bay steel area is growing.

5. Oil was first discovered in the United States in the Middle Atlantic region. Only a limited amount is pumped from wells in the Appalachians today. Natural gas is piped from the Appalachian area to near-by inland cities and even to cities along the coast.

What *have I learned?*

Answer each question in a complete sentence.
1. Into what three classes of things can everything in the world be placed?
2. Why is concrete one of the best building materials?
3. What product is the result of a mixture of melted sand and limestone?
4. For what is a certain kind of clay found in New Jersey and New York used?
5. How is coal formed in the earth?
6. Define peat.
7. Tell why soft coal has helped the United States to become the leading industrial country of the world.
8. How is most of our bituminous coal used?
9. Name some new uses for coal.
10. By what method is iron melted and separated from its ore?
11. What three important raw materials are used in making steel?
12. How is natural gas used?
13. Name the rock materials which are used to make cement.
14. What is the region from which most of our anthracite comes?
15. Name one quality of coke which makes it important in the production of iron.

Facts *to understand*

In a complete sentence give a reason for each of the following statements:
1. The Middle Atlantic region no longer leads the country in producing oil.
2. Pittsburgh is often called the "Steel City."
3. Bituminous coal is very valuable to industry, but anthracite is more useful in home heating than bituminous.
4. Glass-making has become an important industry in the Pittsburgh region.
5. The gases which are produced when coke is made should not be wasted.

Beehive of Industrial Cities

Profile of a City. This view, from New Jersey across the Hudson River, shows a small part of New York City. Hundreds of cities cluster in this region.

The Middle Atlantic states have more and larger manufacturing and trading centers than any other group of states. More than half of the factories are located near the coast between New York City and Philadelphia. Another large group of busy cities lies between New York and Buffalo, in the Hudson and Mohawk Valleys of New York State.

The large population of the Middle Atlantic region requires a great amount of food, clothing, and other products that come from its factories. Food processing is a very important industry, and vast quantities of food products are prepared and packed. There are many clothing factories in this region. Those in New York State alone make more than half of all the women's clothing worn in the United States. Other important industries of the Middle Atlantic states are printing and publishing, manufacture of chemicals and electric appliances, iron and steel production, oil refining, and many others.

Let us see how the people live and work in the cities of this tremendous workshop.

New York Harbor. This is the sight which greets the millions who arrive here through the port of New York. It is always a thrilling experience.

Largest City in Our Country. New York City is the largest city, not only in the United States, but in the entire Western Hemisphere. New York City's growth to its present size was not because of any accident. Let us examine some of the reasons for the tremendous size and importance of this Atlantic coast city.

Look at the map on page 76. You will find New York City at the mouth of the Hudson River, in the southernmost part of New York State. The city occupies a group of islands which lie on the best harbor on the entire coast. Its position gives it a "front door" on the Atlantic Ocean, ideal for trading with other nations and other parts of the United States. New York City also has a "back door" on the Hudson River. This gives it a waterway route right into the heart of the country.

You remember from your study of history that the Dutch settlers bought the island of Manhattan for about $24.00 worth of beads and trinkets. The Dutch called it New Amsterdam, after a large city in Holland. From the very beginning, the location of this city made it an excellent trading center. Soon the English took over the growing city and renamed it New York. It became the most important center of trade on the Atlantic coast of North America.

Busy City. Today, New York City is so large it is divided into five sections called *boroughs*. Manhattan is an island borough, the center of trade and commerce. Richmond is an island borough. Brooklyn and Queens are located on Long Island. The Bronx is the only one of the five boroughs located on the mainland.

Because so many waterways flow around and through the city of New York, there is plenty of space along the shores for piers and docks. Many bridges and tunnels link the various parts of the city with each other and with New Jersey, across the Hudson River. In addition, old-fashioned ferryboats ply back and forth across the waters of the harbor, adding to the busy scene.

New York is also a manufacturing center. Because so many goods are shipped in and out of the harbor, there is a good opportunity for factories to be close to the source of materials and to the means of transporting finished products.

The clothing industry and the printing industry are two main businesses in this city. Many large companies have their headquarters in New York City, even though their factories are elsewhere. There are many large banks, department stores, and other commercial companies located here also.

Tourist Center. During every season of the year, thousands of visitors pour into New York City to see the "sights." They come in ships, airplanes, trains, buses, and automobiles.

Among the many attractions for tourists are the giant skyscraper buildings in the business district, especially the Empire State Building. More than 15,000 people come to work in this building every day. This is more people than live in many small cities. Electric elevator cars carry them to and from their offices high above the street.

Also of interest are the many cultural

The World's Tallest Building. The Empire State Building in New York City has 102 floors, and the tip of its TV tower rises 472 feet into the sky.

attractions of New York City. The theatres of Broadway, the opera, musical shows,

The Vast Publishing Industry. Here one of New York's seven daily newspapers is folded. In addition, many books and magazines are published.

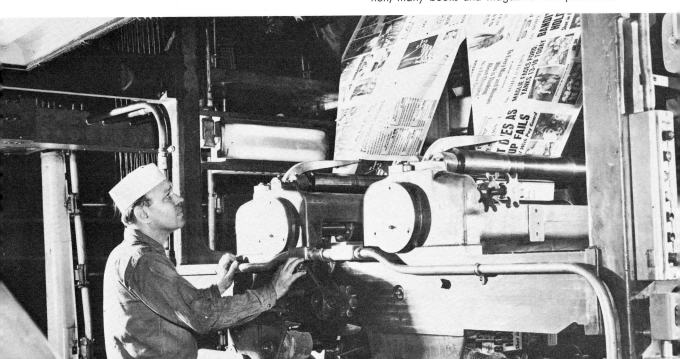

the art museums exhibits, and historic sites are all crowded. Students come to study in the many colleges and universities.

New Yorkers All. New York City has a population of nearly 8 million people. The population represents people of all nations—there are more Irish than in Dublin, more Italians than in Rome, more Jews than in Israel.

At one time, the immigrant groups which settled in New York City kept their national customs and language, and lived together in certain neighborhoods. Some of these neighborhoods still have their own national population, but gradually the differences between neighborhoods are wearing down. As in most big cities, there are areas of New York where poor housing has led to the growth of slums. Great efforts are being made, however, to tear down the slum areas and rebuild them with modern, comfortable housing.

In addition to the people who live in New York, many hundreds of thousands travel into New York City each day from their homes in nearby areas to work. A huge burden is placed on the transportation services in moving all these people to their jobs each morning and home each evening. The "rush hours" present a picture of crowded trains and buses. Millions of people are moving about quickly to keep their schedules and appointments.

The people who travel into New York City come from the *suburbs,* or towns outside the city which depend on the city to provide employment and services. In these towns, people can find more living room than in the crowded city. However, they must sometimes spend long hours commuting into the city to attend to their jobs.

Catching the 8:50. Commuters from a small town in Westchester County use this busy railroad to reach their offices in downtown New York City.

Busy Traffic Artery. The New York Thruway, a splendid 4-lane highway from New York to Buffalo, here passes Canajoharie along the Mohawk River.

The Metropolitan Area. The nearby cities and towns that usually surround a large city are called its *metropolitan area*. Let us see what the New York City metropolitan area consists of.

The state of New Jersey lies across the Hudson River from New York City. Jersey City and Newark are two of New Jersey's large manufacturing cities. Bayonne, New Jersey, is well-known for its many oil refineries. In the smaller cities and towns, there are factories making nylon and rayon products, electronics parts, and other manufactured items.

A few miles north of New York City is Yonkers, New York. It is a large manufacturing city on the Hudson River. East of New York City, in some of the towns on Long Island, are plants which manufacture airplane parts and instruments.

The New York State Barge Canal. Cities grow up where transportation is good. You should not be surprised, therefore, when the map of New York State shows a line of cities in the Hudson-Mohawk Valley. This is an old and important route in the development of our country.

Back in 1825, the Erie Canal was dug to make an all-water route from the Great Lakes to the Atlantic Ocean. These New York State cities got their start when the Erie Canal opened, and they grew rapidly in importance. Later the Erie Canal was widened, deepened, and extended. It is now known as the New York State Barge Canal.

Today railroads follow this same low-land route. So does the New York State Thruway, one of the best automobile and truck highways in the country. With all this good transportation, manufacturing developed in the line of cities from Buffalo on Lake Erie to Albany and Troy on the Hudson River.

Buffalo Harbor. The lake boat in the foreground is discharging its cargo of iron ore. In the distance are some of the city's grain elevators.

Buffalo. Buffalo on Lake Erie is the western terminal of the New York State Barge Canal. The city occupies an ideal location for trading and commerce between the eastern and western parts of the United States, and with Canada. At Buffalo, boats exchange goods with canal boats and railroads. At first, raw materials were kept in warehouses at Buffalo waiting to be transferred. Then the people of Buffalo began manufacturing items from these raw materials and selling the finished products. They made flour out of the wheat coming from the Midwest, iron and steel goods from iron ore brought by lake boats, and chemicals.

In addition to its fine location for trade, Buffalo enjoys the advantage of cheap electric power from mighty Niagara Falls nearby. This famous wonder of nature is only a few miles outside the city, and thousands of tourists come each season to see and marvel at the sight of tons of water constantly pounding down the great height of the falls. Canada and the United States share the electric plants here, and the power which is produced in these plants is used in both countries.

Rochester. Rochester began as a trading and manufacturing center for farm products. Today it is better known for its manufacture of cameras and photographic supplies. Optical instruments and electrical supplies are also made in Rochester, as well as men's clothing and shoes.

Other Cities of New York State. Along the Mohawk Valley, there are many other cities which produce a wide variety of products. Machine parts, chemicals, and typewriters come from Syracuse. Utica is famous for its textile mills. Electric light bulbs, heavy appliances, and railroad locomotives are made in Schenectady. Albany, the capital of New York State, and its sister city, Troy, stand not far from where the Mohawk River flows into the Hudson.

In scores of smaller cities along this lowland valley, all kinds of products are turned out. Among them are knitted goods, gloves, shoes, carpets and rugs, copperware, brassware, and building bricks. Because of the ease of transportation, raw materials can be shipped to this area easily, and the finished products are easily and quickly shipped all over the United States and the world. All these cities, with their busy people and their many products, help to make

Schenectady. The mighty wheels for railroad locomotives are being assembled in a huge shop. This city's factories are famous for heavy goods.

New York State known the world over as "The Empire State."

"Thunder of Waters." That is the name the Indians gave Niagara Falls. The falls on the left are in New York State, the waters to the right are in Canada.

Downtown Philadelphia. This is the Benjamin Franklin Parkway, one of the city's new traffic arteries. Much new building is going on here now.

City of Brotherly Love. Philadelphia, Pennsylvania, is the fourth largest city in the United States. It was settled by a group of Englishmen calling themselves the Friends. Sometimes they are called Quakers. William Penn, a wealthy member of this religious group, received a grant of land along the Delaware River from the king of England. The area became known as "Penn's Woods," or Pennsylvania.

Philadelphia, Pa. The statue of Captain John Barry, Father of our Navy, stands outside Independence Hall, where our great Constitution was written.

The Quakers established their colony on the Delaware River and called the city Philadelphia—the "city of brotherly love." These were peaceful people, and they invited all who were not welcome in the other English colonies to come and live with them. Among those who came were many Catholics, and to this day Philadelphia numbers many Catholics among its population, and has many Catholic churches and schools.

Philadelphia was an important center of government for the newly formed United States after the Revolutionary War. Here the Liberty Bell rang out to announce the signing of the Declaration of Independence at Independence Hall. This Hall and the cracked bell which rang out in its tower are tourist attractions in Philadelphia.

Busy Philadelphia. Although Philadelphia is one hundred miles from the Atlantic Ocean, it is a great seaport. This is because the Delaware River is deep enough for ocean vessels to sail right up to the city. Ships from all over the world bring hides, wool, sugar, wood pulp, and other raw materials into this fine harbor. Railroads and trucks also carry in coal and other

WASHINGTON, D. C.

A tract of land bordering on Maryland and Virginia is called the District of Columbia. The well-planned and beautiful city of Washington is located here. Although Washington is a large city on the fall line, it is not a manufacturing city like the others. Most of the people in Washington are occupied in some part of the huge job of governing the United States, or in serving those who govern our country and make its laws.

The Capitol Building with its large dome is the meeting place of our lawmakers, and there are many other beautiful government buildings in addition to the Capitol. Wide avenues extend out from the Capitol, as the spokes of a wheel extend from the hub. On one of these, Pennsylvania Avenue, is the White House, the home of the President of the United States.

Other important and attractive sights that tourists come to Washington to see are the Washington and Lincoln memorials, Arlington National Cemetery with the tomb of the

Where Our Laws Are Made. The Capitol Building in Washington, D. C., is the center of our government. The steel dome was erected in 1865.

Unknown Soldier, and Monticello, the beautiful home of Thomas Jefferson.

The Jefferson Memorial. This beautiful building honors the writer of the Declaration of Independence, our country's third president.

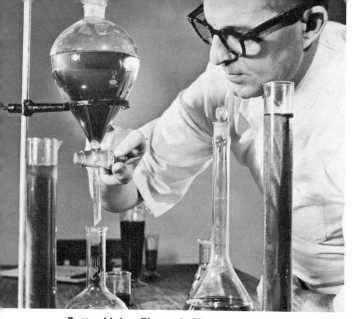

Better Living Through Chemistry. Many plants in this area are studying even newer and better ways to make helpful goods through the use of chemicals.

materials needed in Philadelphia's many busy factories. There are iron and steel

Cathedral of the Assumption. Seven Bishops of Baltimore are buried in this old church. A beautiful new cathedral has now been built in Baltimore.

mills, a great plant which builds railroad locomotives, and many shipyards where large vessels are built and repaired. Many Philadelphians work in textile mills. The mills produce large quantities of silk, cotton, woolen, rayon, and nylon goods.

Along the Delaware are many refineries, where petroleum is made into gasoline and other products.

Cities Near Philadelphia. You will recall that many cities in the Middle Atlantic region grew up along the fall line. These became centers of trade between the coastal plain and the higher lands of the interior. In addition to Philadelphia, some of the other important fall line cities are: Trenton, the capital of New Jersey, where top quality dishes and jars are made by baking clay in ovens; Camden, across the Delaware River from Philadelphia, which has large shipyards and canning factories; and Wilmington, Delaware, where there are many paint and chemical plants.

Growing Steel Industry. More and more of our nation's steel is being produced by these plants near Sparrow's Point in the area of Chesapeake Bay.

Baltimore. The city of Baltimore has an interesting Catholic history. It was named after Lord Baltimore. He founded the Maryland Colony for Catholics and others who could not practice their religion in England. It was really the only English colony in the New World where Catholics could live in peace. Today the city still has a large Catholic population.

Baltimore, Maryland, is located at the mouth of a small river about two hundred miles up Chesapeake Bay. It is a ship-building and manufacturing center. Among its many manufactured products are iron and steel goods. One of the largest steel mills in the world is located at Sparrow's Point near Baltimore. Factories also turn out electrical machinery, airplanes, and airplane parts, tobacco products, and clothing. One of its chief industries is canning fruits and vegetables. Baltimore is one of the country's ten largest cities, with a population of almost one million people.

Busy Hampton Roads. At the southern end of Chesapeake Bay, there is a large body of water called Hampton Roads. It is at the mouth of the James River.

Hampton Roads is one of the largest and deepest harbors on the Atlantic Coast. It is ice-free throughout the year. The United States has built a large *naval base* at Norfolk on this harbor. Across the harbor, at Newport News, are large shipbuilding yards. Another city, Portsmouth, has a Navy Yard where repairs to ships of our fleet are made. In addition to being a shipbuilding center, Hampton Roads is busy with merchant ships carrying exports from this region.

Tobacco from fields in Virginia and North Carolina is shipped from Norfolk and Newport News. Coal, cotton and lumber are also exported from these cities.

Facts *to remember*

1. The Middle Atlantic States have more and larger manufacturing and trading centers than any other group of states. Some important industries of this region are food processing, textile manufacture, printing and publishing, manufacture of chemicals, and making electric appliances.

2. New York City is not only the largest city in the United States but also the largest city in the Western Hemisphere. It has a population of nearly 8 million. The city is an excellent manufacturing and trading center. The borough of Manhattan is the center of trade and commerce. Broadway theatres, art museums, historic sites, the opera, and concert performances attract tourists.

3. In 1825 the Erie Canal was dug to make an all-water route from the Great Lakes to the Atlantic Ocean. It was later widened, deepened and extended, and renamed the New York State Barge Canal. A line of manufacturing cities, from Buffalo on Lake Erie to Albany and Troy on the Hudson River, arose along the canal. Railroads and the New York State Thruway have aided the growth of these cities. Buffalo occupies an ideal location for trading and commerce between eastern and Western United States and Canada. Rochester is noted for the manufacture of cameras and photographic supplies.

4. Philadelphia, "the City of Brotherly Love," is the fourth largest city in the United States. It is a great manufacturing center and seaport.

5. Baltimore, Maryland, has a Catholic history that is interesting and important in the story of religious freedom in the United States.

6. Hampton Roads is one of the largest and deepest harbors on the Atlantic Coast.

7. The Capitol Building and the White House are located in Washington, D.C., the nation's capital. Many tourists interested in history and government visit this city.

What *have I learned?*

I

Answer each question in a complete sentence.

1. Name the largest city in the entire Western Hemisphere.

2. Why are there so many factories in New York City?

3. What is a "metropolitan area?"

4. Why was the Erie Canal dug?

5. What city on Lake Erie is at the western end of the New York State Barge Canal?

6. Which city was established by the Quakers?

7. Why is Philadelphia such a great seaport?

8. Why are Catholics interested in the history of Baltimore?

9. What city is the capital of the United States?

II

Copy the names in column A. Opposite each name write one of the items in Column B that best fits it.

A	B
1. Bayonne	Bought from the Dutch for $24
2. Utica	Famous for textile mills
3. Buffalo	Capital of New York State
4. Philadelphia	Where the White House is
5. Hampton Roads	Noted for its oil refineries
	Early Catholic history
6. Newport News	Lies across the Hudson from New York City
7. Washington, D.C.	Where the Liberty Bell is
	Lies across the harbor from Norfolk
8. New York City	
9. Jersey City	Manufactures cameras and photographic supplies
10. Rochester	Obtains power from Niagara Falls
11. Albany	
12. Baltimore	One of the largest and deepest harbors on the Atlantic Coast

Facts *to understand*

Answer each of the following in a complete sentence.

1. Why has New York City grown to such tremendous size and importance?

2. Why do so many tourists visit New York City?

3. What is the importance of the New York State Barge Canal?

4. What reason may be given for saying that Buffalo occupies an ideal location?

5. Why was Philadelphia called the "City of Brotherly Love?"

6. For what is Washington, D.C., important?

Unit Two Review

Questions for Discussion and Review

1. Explain why the New England States, although small in area, are so important in the history of the United States.

2. Account for the many factories both in the New England States and in the Middle Atlantic States.

3. Why are the people of New England interested in the replanting and regrowth of their forests?

4. What part has the fishing industry played in the past and in modern times along the Atlantic Coast?

5. How did the early colonists make the soil of the New England area profitable?

6. Describe the surface, climate, and soil of the Connecticut Valley.

7. Discuss the advantages enjoyed by New England which make up for its lack of fuel and mineral resources.

8. Explain why New England's manufactured metal products are of greater value than any of its other manufactures.

9. Tell why the Middle Atlantic region has a milder climate than the New England region.

10. Compare the surface features of the New England States with those of the Middle Atlantic States.

11. Why did the early settlers locate along the Atlantic Coast?

12. What draws so many people to the Atlantic Seaboard today?

13. How is the food problem solved for the very large population of the Middle Atlantic States?

14. How are the minerals of the Middle Atlantic region used?

15. Tell how the "Beehive of Industrial Cities" of the Middle Atlantic States contributes to the glory of God.

16. List the materials needed, and describe the various steps in the production of steel.

17. What makes the Grand Banks a particularly good fishing area?

18. Why has the Hudson-Mohawk Valley of New York State always been a good transportation route?

19. Describe the fall line, and explain why the early settlers of the Middle Atlantic region were reluctant to cross it.

20. List the number of Northeastern States which were among the first thirteen states of the Union.

21. Why is the Appalachian uplands area of New York and Pennslyvania a good dairying region?

22. Describe the steps in the production of milk from the farm to the home.

23. Describe the means taken by tobacco farmers to prevent their soil becoming worn out.

24. What are some of the dangers which the New England fishermen face in their occupation?

25. Explain the fact that there is a very large Catholic population in the Northeastern States.

Using the Maps and Globe

1. Sketch the coast line of the New England States and the Middle Atlantic States.

2. On an outline map indicate all main water bodies of these two groups of states.

3. Use the wall map to point out all main cities studied in Unit Two. Try to show their historic development and their relation to the United States today.

4. Locate New York City, and tell what other cities or areas may be considered its suburbs.

5. Explain how the surface features have contributed to make the Middle Atlantic States so populous.

6. Find Washington, D.C., indicate its boundaries, and tell what types of transportation tourists use to reach it.

Using Geography Words

Here is a list of special words that have been used in Unit Two. Write a sentence using each word to show you know its meaning in geography.

peninsula	manufacturing	mouth
brush	import	current
continental shelf	source	craftsmen
quarry	bogs	suburbs
glacier	textile mills	
woodland	borough	

Getting Information from Books

Read reference books such as *Compton's Pictured Encyclopedia* to get information on the following topics. Prepare to give an oral or written report.

Puritans	Faneuil Hall
Forestry	Old North Church
Fishing Industry	Boston Harbor

New England States
Atlantic Seaboard
Liberty Bell
Independence Hall

Oyster Farming
William Penn
Revolutionary War
Lord Baltimore

Final Test

Write each sentence on your paper, choosing the correct word or words from the parenthesis.

1. An important lowland region of the Middle Atlantic States is the (Piedmont Plateau, Atlantic Coastal Plain, Connecticut Valley).

2. The process that kills harmful germs in milk is known as (sanitation, coking, pasteurization).

3. (Barley, tobacco, wheat) removes many minerals from the soil.

4. German farmers near (Lancaster, Quincy, Boston) raise more tobacco per acre than any other tobacco growers.

5. The cheapest transportation is by (airways, waterways, highways).

6. The (St. Lawrence, Mississippi, Hudson) River does not empty into the Atlantic Ocean.

7. The rivers which cross the Atlantic Coastal Plain have their sources in the (Mohawk Valley, Hampton Roads, Appalachian Highlands).

8. Cement is made from (limestone and shale, sand and limestone, clay).

9. (Anthracite coal, peat, bituminous coal) is used to make coke.

10. (Pittsburgh, Baltimore, Utica) is called the "Steel City."

11. (Jersey City, New York City, Syracuse) occupies a group of islands which lie on the best harbor on the Atlantic Coast.

12. New York City is divided into five sections called (suburbs, metropolitan areas, boroughs).

13. (Camden, Philadelphia, Norfolk) was a government center for the newly-formed United States after the Revolutionary War.

14. Today, the lawmakers of our country meet at (The Capitol Building, Independence Hall, Old South Church).

15. A lowland that is of great importance to the people of New England is (Appalachian highlands, St. Lawrence Valley, Connecticut Valley).

16. (England, United States, Germany) uses more paper than any other country in the world.

17. The northeastern United States and Canada are the only places in the world where the (spruce, oak, sugar maple) grows.

18. Fishing banks are (deep, shallow, muddy) parts of the ocean where fish come in great numbers to feed.

19. Potatoes require (sandy, mucky, firm) soil.

20. (New York, Boston, Baltimore) is the largest city in New England.

Applying Christian Principles

Select the best ending for each sentence. Then write the complete sentence on your paper.

1. God intends mineral resources to be used **a.** to build industrial nations **b.** to prepare for war **c.** for the betterment of mankind.

2. Lawmakers in large cities can contribute to the glory of God **a.** when they make laws to benefit all citizens **b.** when they obtain offices for their friends **c.** when they try to out-do other cities.

3. Farmers make wise use of natural resources **a.** when they cut down trees **b.** when they rotate their crops **c.** when they hire cheap labor.

4. Those who work to harness the waters of Niagara Falls can help their neighbors best by **a.** showing they have talent **b.** giving others electric power to turn the wheels of mills and factories **c.** showing other countries what can be done.

5. Lord Baltimore enriched the history of our country **a.** by granting freedom of religion in Maryland **b.** by bringing settlers to the New World **c.** by making Maryland a shipping center.

6. Power-operated boats, radio, radar, and other direction-finding devices can help our neighbors **a.** by letting us know the latest inventions **b.** making life more comfortable **c.** by making fishing a safer industry for those who help to feed our population.

7. The Middle Atlantic region has helped peoples of all countries by **a.** giving immigrants work and better living conditions **b.** limiting resources to white people only **c.** asking them to live in the slums until they become citizens.

8. From the variety of different occupations to be seen in the Northeastern States, we should learn **a.** that man depends upon his fellow-man for the goods of this life. **b.** that some jobs are bad because they are hard or dirty. **c.** that all men have the same skills and talents.

9. As Catholics, we should **a.** shun our non-Catholic associates. **b.** study other religions to see if they are better than ours. **c.** respect and understand those who have not yet received the great gift of Faith.

Neighbors in the Southern States

THE SOUTH

In your study of the geography of the United States, you have learned how people in the Northeastern States live, work, and play. Now you will learn about the geography and people of the region called *the South*. It takes in a group of states south and west of the New England and Middle Atlantic regions. In some ways, the South and the Northeast are alike. In many ways, however, they differ.

The South has a much warmer climate. Many tourists go there to get away from the cold, northern winters. Farmers in the South have a longer growing season.

The Southern States have more farms and fewer factories than the Northern States. Now, however, more factories are being built. The South is becoming a manufacturing region as well as a farming region.

The South has fewer large cities than the Northeast. Far fewer Catholics live in the South than in the Northeast.

How do the Southern States resemble the Northeastern States? Both regions have long coast lines. The Atlantic Coastal Plain extends through both regions. So do the Appalachian Highlands and the Piedmont Plateau.

Most important, the people of the South and of the Northeast, and, indeed, of all other regions of our country, are good, liberty-loving Americans. They are all working together to build a better United States of America.

In this Unit you will learn that:

1 The states of the southern and eastern part of our country are: North Carolina, South Carolina, Georgia, Florida, Alabama, Mississippi, Tennessee, Louisiana, Arkansas, Oklahoma, and Texas.

2 The South has generally long, hot summers and short winters, with plenty of rainfall, especially in the eastern section. Most of the surface is low and level, with some highland areas in the eastern and central sections.

3 For years, the South has been mostly a farming region, because of the ideal farming conditions—long growing season, plenty of rain, and level land. However, a change is taking place in the South today, and there is more and more manufacturing going on there.

4 Southern forests produce much wood and wood pulp. Oil, coal, and sulphur are among the important mineral products. Cities in the South are growing larger, and becoming important for mineral products, manufactured goods, and as seaports.

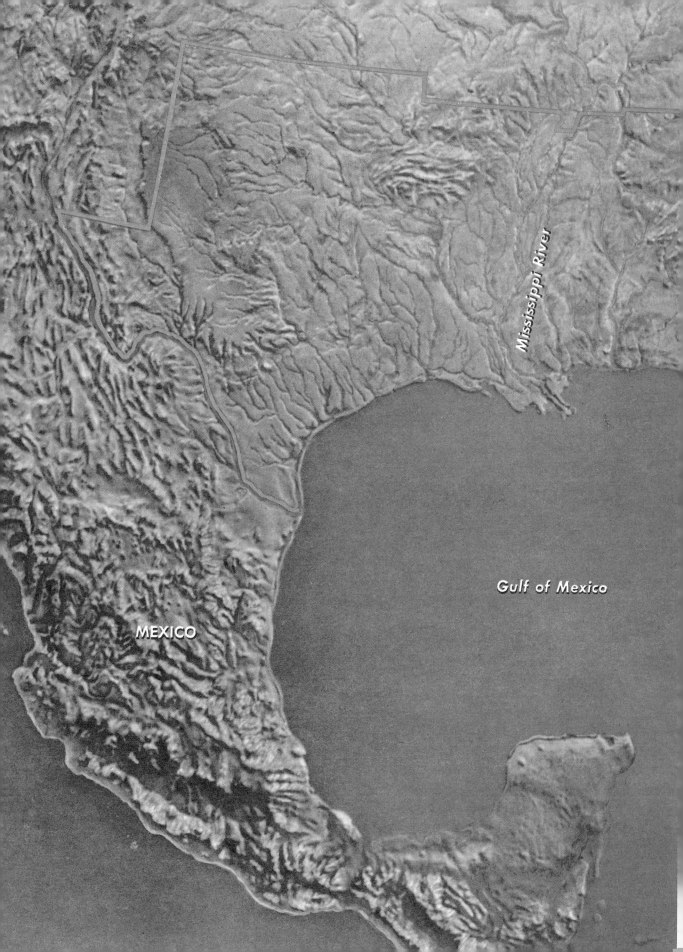

Mississippi River

Gulf of Mexico

MEXICO

THE SOUTHERN STATES

Appalachian Highlands

On this global map you can see the major surface features of the Southern States. The coast line along the Atlantic Ocean is broken by numerous capes, inlets, and river mouths. A wide coastal plain separates the Appalachian Highlands from the the east coast.

Farther west, the wide Mississippi River flows southward through the Southern States to the Gulf of Mexico. Its waters have their beginning far to the north, near Canada. West of the Mississippi, the surface is mostly a lowland plain.

Atlantic Ocean

West Indies

Caribbean Sea

The Changing South

The Old South. Greenwood, a plantation mansion in Louisiana, reflects the quiet, gracious life that was once common throughout the Southland.

The Southern States have good farmland, large forests, and a rich supply of minerals. They have mostly level land, many rivers, and a long coast line. The climate is delightful. Yet, with all these advantages, some Southern States have not prospered as well as the rest of the country. Today, many changes are taking place. It looks as if a better day is coming for the more backward areas of the South. In this chapter we shall learn about the changing South.

Location. Look at the map of the Southern States on pages 106 and 107. Here you see eleven states covering a large portion of our country. They stretch from the Atlantic Ocean in the east all the way to the foothills of the Rocky Mountains in the west. Along the Atlantic Ocean you see the states of North Carolina, South Carolina, Georgia, and Florida. Between these states and the Mississippi River you can count three more: Alabama, Mississippi, and Tennessee. West of the Mississippi River are Arkansas, Oklahoma, and Texas. Louisiana is crossed by the Mississippi.

These states have a much greater area

than the Northeastern States but are not so crowded with people. Texas, the largest state except Alaska, has only about half as many people as New York State.

Longer Summers, Shorter Winters. The Southern region has long hot summers and short winters. It has plenty of rainfall. Let us see why the Southern climate is so different from that in the North.

You know that the warmest part of the world is the equator. At the equator, the sun is directly overhead, and the weather is always hot. The closer any region is to the equator, the warmer its climate. The Southern States are closer to the equator than most of the rest of the United States. Look at the map of the United States on pages 18 and 19. You will see that California, Arizona, and New Mexico are located toward the south. This means that they are rather close to the equator. But they are not so far south as most of Texas and Florida. They are not so far south as the southern parts of Louisiana, Mississippi, Alabama, and Georgia. In all the United States, only the state of Hawaii is farther south than the Southern States. For this reason alone, we can expect the Southern region to have a warmer climate than most of the rest of the United States, and it has.

In addition, a warm current of water in the Atlantic Ocean flows north and comes rather close to the coast of the Southern States. This warm current is called the *Gulf Stream*. Warm winds from over the Gulf Stream help to keep the coastal areas warm, even in winter.

In the southern part of Florida there are many people who have never seen snow. People from the northern parts of the United States often go to southern Florida for their winter vacations. Here they can lie in the sun and bathe in the ocean even in January and February. Other parts of the Southern States are not quite so warm as Florida, but they are much warmer than the Northern States.

Along with this warm weather there is more rain than occurs in the Northeastern States. The rain falls all through the year, but there is more of it in the summer and fall months. Much of this summer rain comes in heavy, drenching showers. Thunderstorms are more frequent in the Southern States than in other parts of the country.

A region with warm weather and much rain is usually one in which crops grow very well. This is true of the South. This is the most important reason that the South has always been a farming region.

Winter in Florida. These lucky children are enjoying a December vacation at Miami Beach, Florida. The warm South attracts many visitors.

SOUTHERN UNITED STATES

Elevation	
	over 10,000
	5,000 to 10,000
	2,000 to 5,000
	500 to 2,000
	0 to 500
	Below Sea Level

ELEVATIONS IN FEET

Capital Cities ⌐ ─ ─ ─ ─ ─ ◉

International Boundaries ▬ ▪ ─ ▪ ▬

State or Provincial Boundaries ─ ▪ ─ ▪ ─

Scale of Miles

0   50   100   150   200

Studying the Map

A. The Southern States occupy the southeastern corner of the United States and are far greater in area than the Northeastern States. **1.** Name the Southern States. The second largest state of our country is in this region. Which state is it? **2.** Which of the Southern States are east of the Mississippi River? west of the Mississippi? crossed by the Mississippi? **3.** Which states border the Atlantic Ocean? the Gulf of Mexico? **4.** Which state has the longest coast line? Which states have no coast line?

B. 1. Are the Southern States mostly a lowland or a highland area? Where are the lowlands? the highlands? **2.** What highland area extends from the Northeastern States into the Southern States? Into what Southern states does it extend? **3.** Many

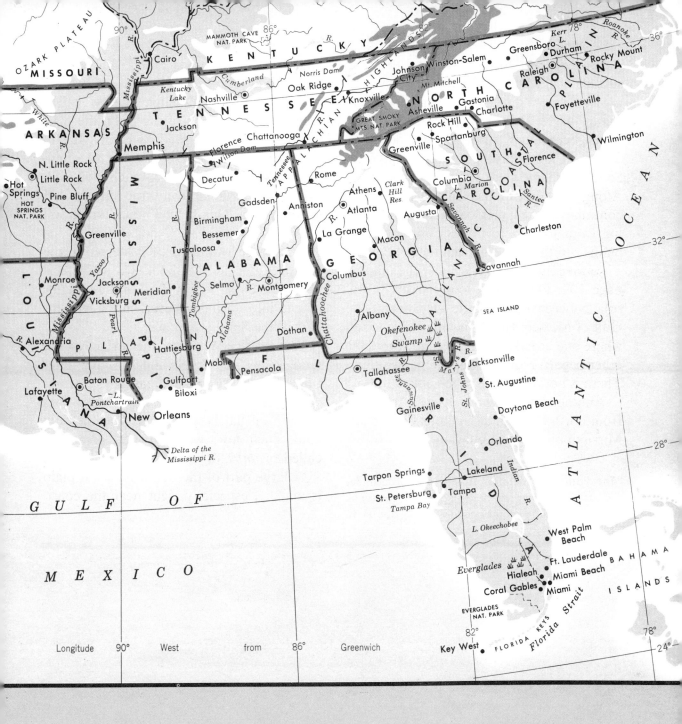

tributaries of the Mississippi are important water-ways of the Southern States. Which tributary forms the boundary between Oklahoma and Tex-as? Which flows through Tennessee, Alabama, and Kentucky? which flows through Kansas, Okla-homa, and Arkansas?

C. 1. List the Southern States and give the capital city of each state. 2. Name three cities that are seaports on the Atlantic Ocean; on the Gulf of Mexico. Why are there fewer good harbors in the Southern States than in the Northeastern States? 3. Name the three principal cities of Florida. Which is a famous winter resort? 4. Texas has more large cities than any of the other Southern States. Name three of its large inland cities. Which of these is also a seaport? Why? 5. In which Southern State is each of the following cities: Atlanta, Birmingham, Nashville, Tulsa?

The Lowland Areas. Most of the land surface of the Southern States is a low and nearly level plain. The Atlantic Coastal Plain, which you have already learned about, continues through the Southern States. It goes through North Carolina, South Carolina, Georgia, and into Florida. Along the coast of the Gulf of Mexico, it continues as the Gulf Coastal Plain, extending from Florida to Texas. These coastal plains run through eight Southern States.

As you can see by looking at the map on page 107, Florida is a long narrow peninsula between the Atlantic Ocean and the Gulf of Mexico. Here it is impossible to tell where one coastal plain ends and where the other begins. Florida is really one big plain. There is not a high hill in the entire state.

Another lowland area extends for miles from north to south along both sides of the Mississippi River. Louisiana, Mississippi, and parts of Arkansas and Tennessee are on this wide river plain.

Before men built high banks, called *levees,* on both sides of the river, the Mississippi often overflowed its banks. It still does, despite the levees, but not so often. The flood waters carried much rich soil. When they drained away, the silt was left on the plain. This helped make fertile soil for crops.

One other lowland area is located in the South. Later in this book we shall read about the Great Plains. Part of these plains extend into northern Texas, in the western part of the Southern States.

Wet Lands. Wherever the surface of the land is low and level, and the climate is rainy, there are large areas where water covers the land. This is because water does not run off flat land as quickly as off hilly land. Such low, water-covered areas are called *swamps,* or *marshes.*

A large part of the South's coastal plain is marshy, especially right near the coast.

"The Father of Waters." A level plain extends for miles on both sides of the wide Mississippi. The tugs here are paddle-wheel riverboats.

Gathering Spanish Moss. The man rowing his flatboat in the swampy canebrake searches for the soft greens used to stuff mattresses and pillows.

There are large swamps in the Carolinas, Georgia, and Florida. One of the biggest of all the swamps is the Everglades in southern Florida. There is so much water here that the land cannot be used for farms, except in the few places where it has been possible to drain the waters off. Cypress trees, saw grass, and ferns form a thick, jungle-like growth. Alligators live in the muddy waters. Bears, wildcats, and panthers roam the area. Herons, cranes, and pelicans fly about. Just about the only human beings who live deep in the Everglades are the Seminole Indians. They have learned how to live comfortably in a place where it would be very difficult for most people to survive.

Along the Gulf Coast from Texas to Florida is the bayou country. A *bayou* is a quiet, slow branch stream that scarcely seems to move. There are hundreds of bayous very close together in southern Louisiana near the mouth of the Mississippi. Much of the land between the streams is swampy. Water hyacinths grow thickly on the bayous, making it difficult to travel by boat.

Near the shores of the bayous are long, narrow strips of land. Between the narrow land strips and the shore there are narrow bodies of water called *lagoons*. With the bayous and the lagoons all around, a person is never far from water in this part of the country.

It would not be correct, however, to think that all of the coastal plain is swampy and filled with lagoons. A large part of it is well drained and makes good farm land.

Mountains of the South. Here are some of the highest mountains in the South—the Great Smokies of North Carolina. Note the thick spruce forests.

High Lands. Although much of the South consists of lowlands, there are also some highland areas. The Appalachian Highlands extend into the states of North Carolina, South Carolina, Georgia, Tennessee, and Alabama. The Great Smokies in North Carolina and Tennessee are the highest part of the Appalachian Highlands. Mt. Mitchell is in the Black Mountains of North Carolina. This is the highest peak east of the Mississippi River. It is more than a mile above sea level.

The Interior Highlands are in Arkansas, Oklahoma, and Missouri. To the north of the Arkansas River the highlands are called Ozark Mountains. To the south of the river they are called the Ouachita Mountains. Both of these highland areas are covered with forests.

In western Oklahoma and Texas, just east of the Rocky Mountains, the land is high above sea level, but is not mountainous. It is part of the Great Plains.

Early History of the South. As in New England, it was English people who established most of the settlements on the Atlantic coast of the Southern Region. Later, the French settled around the city of New Orleans, Louisiana. Before either of these groups, the Spanish explored parts of the South, especially the areas now known as Florida and Texas. St. Augustine, in Florida, is the oldest settlement in the United States. It was built by Spanish settlers in 1565, 42 years before the first English settlement at Jamestown, Virginia.

Unlike the English settlers of New England who found poor farming conditions, the English settlers of the South found ideal farming conditions. Regular rainfall, warm climate, level land, long growing season, and good soil—all these encouraged farming in the South. Remember that it was the lack of such advantages which caused New Englanders to turn to other occupations. In the South, farming became the occupation and way of life of most of the settlers. This remained true for a long time. Only recently have people in the South turned to city life and factory work in large numbers.

Three Kinds of People. After the Revolutionary War, there were really three kinds of people in the South—all three connected in some way with farming. First, there were the plantation owners. These were gentleman farmers who owned very large farms, but did very little of the actual work on them. They were mostly quite rich, lived in large, beautiful mansions, and led a life of comfort and graciousness. Second, there were the poor whites. These were less fortunate in their position than the plantation owners. They were farmers who had small pieces of land and just barely made a living. Many of them moved westward when the trails across the mountains were blazed.

Finally, there were the Negroes. They were brought into the South from Africa to work on the large plantations. These were people who were *owned* by other people. They were called *slaves*. Whole families of them would be sold at auction in the Atlantic coast ports. The plantation owner who bought slaves regarded them as cattle. In order to get his full value in work done by them, he had to feed, clothe, and house them. They were never paid, and very rarely ever became free. Naturally, the slaves were not happy with this arrangement, and many people in the Northern States, where there was no slavery, wanted to do away with it in the South. The people in the South held that our country should be half-slave and half-free. For many, many years this question was argued over and over.

EARLY DAYS IN THE SOUTH

Many well-known American songs, such as "Dixie", "Swanee River", Old Black Joe", and "Oh, Susannah" go back to the leisurely days of the South before the Civil War. Plantation owners lived in luxury and peace, banjos could often be heard from the slaves' quarters, and even the poorer farmers found satisfaction in tilling the rich soil and enjoying the warm climate.

The South has changed considerably today, but for many people the memory of a different, older way of life still lingers on.

Welcome Home. The Civil War brought many changes to the defeated South. A returning soldier often found he had to start his farm over again.

The Civil War. Tension between Northerners and Southerners grew. Then, about 100 years ago, the Civil War broke out. States in the South left the Union and set up their own union—the Confederate States of America. They fought bitterly against the United States—the Northern States—and the war dragged on for four tragic years. Finally, the South was forced to surrender. The Confederacy was broken up, and the Southern States rejoined the United States.

The South Today. Negro slaves were freed, made citizens, and given the right to vote. Their troubles were not over, however. Whites felt bitter toward the Negroes in the South and tried to hold back their progress. Even today, the Negroes in the South do not share all the privileges of citizens elsewhere in the United States. Times are changing in the South, however. One of the major changes is the gradual acceptance of the Negro as a first-class citizen in schools, jobs, and government offices.

The plantation owners are gone today. More and more people, whites and Negroes, are leaving farm work for jobs in the new industries in the cities. The city populations do not show the same international population as cities in the North. Very few immigrants settled in the South, either on farms or in cities. Most of the people of the South belong to families which have been in America for many generations.

There are few Catholics in this section of the country except for certain parts of Louisiana. Remember that almost all the original English colonies made it difficult for Catholics to settle. It was the waves of immigrants from Catholic countries during the last 100 years which swelled the numbers of Catholics in the northern cities.

They did not come in such numbers to the South because there were fewer opportunities for employment. Today, the South is a missionary area generally. Your prayers are needed to assist the priests who must travel hundreds and hundreds of miles to bring the Faith to the people of the South.

Facts *to remember*

1. The Southern States have a long coast line, mostly level land, and many rivers. There is much good farmland, large forests, and a rich supply of minerals. This section has a few large cities. Southerners are liberty-loving Americans. There are few Catholics among the population of this section of the country, except in certain parts of the state of Louisiana.
2. Southern United States has a warmer climate and a longer growing season than the Northeastern States, because it is nearer the equator. Warm winds from the Gulf Stream keep coastal areas warm, even in winter. Warm climate, plenty of rainfall, and good soil have made it a rich farming region.
3. The Atlantic Coastal Plain continues through the Southern States. The Everglades swamp is located in southern Florida. The Appalachian and the Interior Highlands, both of which are covered with forests, extend into this section.
4. Rich plantation owners, poor whites who barely subsisted on their small plots of land, and Negro slaves who were regarded as cattle lived in the South after the Revolution.
5. The Civil War freed the Negro slaves and made them citizens. Today in the South there are no large plantation owners. Some whites still begrudge human and civil rights to Negroes. Industry is growing. Catholic missionaries are needed to bring the Faith to this area.

What *have I learned?*

One item is wrong in each sentence. Write the sentence leaving out the incorrect item.
1. Some of the Southern States are Georgia, Mississippi, Maine, and Texas.
2. The Southern States differ from the Northeastern States in climate, in having been settled by English people, in number of farms, and in number of large cities.
3. The Southern States have short summers, good farmland, plenty of rainfall, and large forests.
4. Lowland areas may be found along the Gulf of Mexico, along both sides of the Mississippi, in Florida, and in the Great Smokies.
5. In the Everglades, penguins, cypress trees, wildcats, and pelicans may be seen.
6. Marshes, prairies, bayous, and lagoons are water-covered areas.
7. Negroes, industrialists, poor whites, and plantation owners lived in the South after the Revolutionary War.
8. The Civil War gave Negro slaves the good will of all whites, their freedom, made them citizens, and gave them the right to vote.
9. The Catholic Church in the South today needs more Catholics, more priests, more discipline, and more churches.
10. Regular rainfall, warm climate, good soil, and uneven land make the South a good farming area.
11. Some of the rivers which cross the Southern States are: the Mississippi, the Columbia, the Missouri, and the Ouachita.
12. The Atlantic Coastal Plain extends through Georgia, North Carolina, Louisiana, and Florida.
13. The Appalachian Highlands extends through the states of Texas, South Carolina, Tennessee, and Alabama.
14. The Southern States have good farmland, many large cities, large forests, and a rich supply of minerals.
15. The states of Arkansas, Georgia, Oklahoma and Texas are among the Southern States located west of the Mississippi River.

Facts *to understand*

Answer each of the following questions in a sentence or two.
1. In what ways do the Southern States differ from the Northeastern States?
2. Why is the Southern climate so different from that in the North?
3. How can we account for the small Catholic population of the South?
4. Why is there good farming land on both sides of the Mississippi River?
5. What brought about the tension causing the Civil war between Northerners and Southerners?

Farm Machinery. These cotton farmers in Texas, like many farmers in the South, are finding that the use of machinery can increase production.

2 Farming in the Southland

Unlike the New England colonists, the Southern colonists found level land, good soil, and a fine climate for raising crops right where they settled. The Southerners did not have to fish or make things in factories in order to earn a living. They raised two principal crops—cotton and tobacco. They sold these crops and used the money to buy the things they needed.

Since colonial days, great changes have taken place in farming. The South is still, however, a good place to raise crops. Every Southern State except Louisiana has more than one half of its land in farms. Texas and Oklahoma have more than three fourths of their land in farms or ranches.

The greatest changes in Southern farming have taken place in recent years. In the past, Southern farmers raised tobacco and cotton and very little else. Today, tobacco and cotton are still important, but the farmers also raise a variety of other crops. In addition, they keep cattle, hogs, sheep, and poultry on their farms.

In the past, almost all the farm work had to be done by hand, first by Negro slaves and later by hired hands. Today, much of the work on the large farms and plantations is done by machinery. The machinery does the work faster and better than many men working by hand. However, there are still some farmers in the South who must work their farms almost entirely by hand, without modern machinery.

The South's Oldest Crop. Christopher Columbus and his men were amazed when they saw the Indians smoking tobacco. They had never seen such a thing before. The Indians taught the colonists to use tobacco. Then it became popular in Europe.

The colonists in certain sections of the South found that the land and climate were well suited to raising tobacco. They found that money could be made on a tobacco crop. The tobacco was sold to colonists in other sections of our country and to the people of Europe. It was what the farmer called a *cash crop*. The money he made on his tobacco could be used to buy clothing and other needed articles.

Today, more than nine tenths of the tobacco used in our country is raised in the South. The state of North Carolina raises more than twice as much tobacco as any other state. South Carolina, Georgia, and Tennessee also raise much tobacco. In Florida, cigar tobacco is raised under wooden slats or cloth to protect it from the sun.

Raising Tobacco. Successful tobacco growing requires much work. The tiny tobacco seeds are planted in beds and tended carefully until they are a few inches high. In early spring, the farmer must transplant the small tobacco plants, or *seedlings*. In the fields they grow rapidly into great stalks with wide green leaves. Until harvest time the tobacco farmer must watch his plants carefully. He must spray them frequently to keep them from being damaged by insects and disease. He must cultivate often to keep the weeds from overgrowing the plants. At harvest time the leaves are picked by hand, one by one, as they become ripe. They are tied to poles and hung in a tobacco barn to dry, or be *cured*. At curing time the barn temperature must be controlled.

Soil Robber. When tobacco is planted in the same field year after year, the soil becomes worn out. Tobacco is a *soil robber*,

Personal Attention. There are many farm jobs that machines cannot do. Tending to the valuable tobacco crop requires great care and patience.

because it takes minerals from the soil. The colonists ruined much good land by allowing tobacco to weaken it year after year. Land was plentiful in those days. When the land became worn out in one section, the farmers would move farther west and start new farms until all good land was taken.

Today, the farmers use improved methods to grow tobacco. They enrich the soil by putting fertilizer in it to make up for minerals which the tobacco takes out. They do not grow tobacco in the same soil year after year. They grow tobacco in a field one year, another crop a second year, and let grass grow in the field a third year. This is called *crop rotation*. It keeps the soil from wearing out.

Selling the Crop. The tobacco crop is sold at yearly auctions. At these times, tobacco is piled in huge warehouses. Buyers from cigarette and cigar companies come to examine the tobacco and select what they need. An auctioneer sells the tobacco to the highest bidder, chanting the prices in a sing-song manner. The buyer does not use his voice to bid at this auction; he signals with his hand when he wishes to make a bid.

Large quantities of tobacco are sold in a single day. Durham, Winston-Salem, and Raleigh, all in North Carolina, lead in the manufacture of tobacco products, especially cigarettes. Many cigars are made at Tampa, Florida.

The United States, with a yearly crop of two billion pounds, leads the world in producing tobacco. Tobacco products are heavily taxed by the Government.

Future Cigarettes and Cigars. Workers in a tobacco auction warehouse unload a truckful of bright leaves. Tobacco company agents will buy them.

Cotton in Colonial Days. The colonists found that they could raise cotton in the Carolinas and Georgia. Here the summers are long and hot, and the rainfall is fairly well distributed throughout the year. These conditions are ideal for raising cotton.

Raising and harvesting cotton was very hard work in colonial days. Cotton plants required constant hoeing during the growing season. At harvest time, each boll or puff of cotton had to be picked by hand from the plant. Then the seeds had to be separated from the fibers. This, too, was done by hand.

The colonists found that they could not work such long hours under the hot Southern sun. Soon they began to bring in Negro slaves from Africa. The slaves were accustomed to the hot sun of Africa, and they could work long hours in the cotton fields.

Even with the slaves, the plantation owners were beginning to wonder whether it was worth while to raise cotton. The slaves were not paid any wages, of course, but they still had to have food, houses, and clothing. In addition, the work was very slow. A slave might work a whole month to clean one bale of cotton weighing 500 pounds. The price of the cotton scarcely paid the expenses of keeping the slaves. About the time the United States became an independent country, many plantation owners were ready to stop raising cotton. They were ready to free their slaves.

Machinery and Cotton. Eli Whitney visited the South shortly after the Revolutionary War and watched slaves picking out seeds from the cotton fiber. He invented a machine to do this work. It became known as the *cotton gin*. While a slave was cleaning four or five pounds of cotton by hand, the cotton gin would clean a thousand pounds.

Farming in the Southland 117

At the same time that Eli Whitney invented the cotton gin, other men were finding quicker ways to make cloth from cotton. Many textile mills were built in England and New England. These mills needed more and more cotton.

The plantation owners no longer wished to stop growing cotton. They raised more and more of it. They no longer wished to free their slaves. Instead, they needed more and more slaves. Plantations were even started farther west.

Plantation owners made so much money raising cotton that they seldom tried to raise much else. "Cotton is king," someone once said when speaking about the South. It is true that cotton was once the most important thing in the lives of thousands of Southern people.

Wealth of the South. A young boy displays a basketful of the fluffy raw cotton which has just been picked. Its seeds must still be removed.

Sharecroppers and Tenants. After the Civil War, the plantation owners of the South no longer could own slaves. A new system of farming grew up. A plantation owner would let out small sections of his land to families of *sharecroppers*. These sharecroppers were so poor they had nothing but their labor to invest. Father, mother, and children would work long hours to raise a crop of cotton. When the crop was sold, the family would receive a share of the money. By the time the family paid its debts, there was very little money left. They spent their lives, year after year, just barely surviving.

Sharecroppers usually had to live in bare, run-down houses and shacks. The children did not go to school. Few could afford even to have a doctor or a dentist, or to go to a hospital when it was necessary.

A *tenant farmer* was usually somewhat better off than a sharecropper. The tenant rented land and a house from the owner. He supplied his own tools and perhaps a team of horses or mules. The tenant's entire family worked to raise the cotton. Instead of paying rent, the tenant farmer paid the landlord a part of the crop he raised. When the crop was a good one, the tenant farmer would be able to save a little money for new tools or clothing or small luxuries. In a bad year, however, he might sink very deeply into debt.

The Civil War had freed the slaves, but cotton was still king in the South. Sharecroppers and tenants, Negro and white, often worked under poorer conditions than the slaves had.

In the South and elsewhere, many farm workers do not get just wages. All laborers have a God-given right to just wages. They should earn enough to support themselves and their families decently. They should be able to save for the future.

Alabama Cotton Field. This is the oldest part of the Cotton Belt. The newer sections, in the west particularly, yield greater harvests today.

Where Cotton Is Grown. The region of the South where cotton grows best is called the *Cotton Belt*. Cotton grows best where there are at least two hundred frost-free days and over twenty inches of rainfall a year. It does not grow well in areas having heavy rainfall at harvest time.

Look at the growing seasons map and the rainfall map on page 24. By comparing these two maps, you will see that the Cotton Belt extends from North Carolina to Texas. It runs through the heart of the South and includes parts of all the Southern States. Heavy autumn rains in the coastal areas along the Atlantic Ocean and the Gulf of Mexico make them unsuitable for cotton growing. Very little is grown in Florida.

The best part of the Cotton Belt by far is in east central Texas and Oklahoma. Here the black, waxy soil and long growing season are ideal for cotton. Even though the rainfall here is light, cotton does very well on the irrigated land. Texas leads all the other states in the production of cotton.

In the fertile lowlands along the lower Mississippi River, in the states of Mississippi and Arkansas, there are large cotton plantations. Some cotton is still grown where the earliest plantations were located in the Carolinas, Georgia, and Alabama. Today, however, this section of the Cotton Belt is no longer a large producer.

Problems of the Cotton Grower. A farmer who raises cotton is never certain that his crop will be a success. He must wage a constant battle against insects. The most destructive of these is the cotton *boll weevil*. This insect lays its eggs in the blossom of the cotton plant during the spring. As the cotton plant develops, the eggs hatch into worms inside the boll. The cotton is destroyed as the worm eats its way out. Unless the insects are kept under control, they can cause great damage to the cotton crop. Farmers must spray their fields with poison to kill the boll weevils.

In the western part of the Cotton Belt there is less danger. The farmer can plant his cotton earlier in the spring. This way, the blossoms fall off before the boll weevil can lay its eggs in them. This is why it pays to raise cotton in the irrigated areas of Texas and Oklahoma.

A cotton farmer also has the problem of keeping the soil fertile. Like tobacco, cotton is a *soil robber*. After a few years of growing cotton, the soil becomes poor. The cotton farmer in the Mississippi lowlands at times faces the problem of floods also. There have been times in the past when floods destroyed the entire crop. Although the United States Government spends much money trying to prevent the destructive floods in this area, they are still a danger.

The End of "King Cotton." It was the boll weevil that ended the reign of King

Cotton. Because of the boll weevil, Southern farmers began to raise many other kinds of crops. They planted fruits and vegetables. They sowed grass for pasture and raised cattle.

Scientists worked with the cotton seed to improve it. They found a cotton plant that would ripen early before the boll weevil could ruin it. But many people never went back to raising cotton. Even those who did go back to it, now raise other crops as well. In a year when cotton does not bring a good price, these farmers still get money from their other crops.

In a city of Alabama there is a monument with a large statue of a boll weevil on top. Under the statue are the words: "In Profound Appreciation of the Boll Weevil." Can you understand why the statue was erected?

Cotton is still very important to the South. Two thirds of all the cloth manufactured in the United States is made of cotton. Oil from cotton seed furnishes one third of all the vegetable oil used in salads, margarines, and cooking oils. Cotton-seed meal supplies one fifth of all the protein food given to animals. There are still many, many cotton fields in the South. Cotton is still important, but it is no longer "king."

Whirlybird Helps the Farmer. Helicopters find much work on farms today. This one dusts a chemical poison spray on crops to kill harmful insects.

A NEGRO SCIENTIST HELPS THE SOUTH

George Washington Carver, a Negro born of slave parents, became one of America's greatest scientists. As a boy, he had to work very hard. In spite of this, he managed to get an education. He was often treated unjustly, but this did not stop him.

Dr. Carver knew that growing only tobacco and cotton was bad for the South. He spent much time studying plants and finding new uses for them. He taught the Southern farmer to grow pecans, peanuts, sweet potatoes, and other crops.

Peanuts grow well in the South, and they enrich the soil. For a long time, however, few farmers raised them because they did not sell well. Dr. Carver worked many years with peanuts. He discovered 145 products that could be made from them, such as ink and axle grease. Manufacturers were soon happy to buy peanuts, and the peanut became an important crop in the South. Dr. Carver and other scientists also found new uses for sweet potatoes, wood shavings, and cornstalks.

New Machinery Helps the South. The mule and the one-man farm are fast disappearing from the South. Many of the cabins of tenant farmers and sharecroppers are now empty. There are fewer farms today than in the days of "King Cotton." Today's farms are generally larger, though, and grow a well-balanced variety of crops, using many kinds of farm machines.

In spring, tractors move over acres and acres of level land. Planting machines put in the seeds. Airplanes spray the growing plants; huge cultivators move through the rows, preventing the growth of weeds. Harvesting machines pick the crop. Today, mechanical cotton-pickers operated by four men can do the same work once done by 100 men picking by hand.

Cotton Picking Machine. Looking somewhat like a Northern snowplow, this machine is becoming a familiar sight on the more modern cotton farms.

Florida's Important Orange Crop. The juice you drank at breakfast might have come from the fruit of these trees in a grove at Windermere, Florida.

Mixed Farming. *Mixed farming* means the raising of a number of farm products, plus the raising of cattle and other livestock, on the same farm. Many Southern farmers practice mixed farming.

Corn is the second largest crop in the Cotton Belt. Corn grows tall and full when it gets plenty of rain and warm weather. Most of the Southern corn crop is fed to farm animals. The farmer, his family, and helpers also eat sweet corn, make some of it into meal, and use it in other ways.

Peanuts grow well in a sandy soil with plenty of rain and a long growing season. Most of our peanuts grow in Virginia and North Carolina. In Florida, Georgia, and Alabama, peanuts are used to fatten hogs. Peanut butter and peanut oil are made from the crops. Like potatoes, peanuts grow underground. Just before the first frost they are dug up. The vines are placed in piles to dry. The peanuts are then taken from the vines by hand or by machinery.

Early potatoes, yams, mushmelons, and watermelons are grown for the northern markets. Peach trees grow well throughout the South, especially in Georgia and South Carolina. Pecan nut trees are also common.

Fast trains and trucks rush these fresh vegetables, fruits, and nuts to markets in northern cities.

Citrus Fruits and Winter Vegetables. Grapefruit, oranges, lemons, and limes are called *citrus fruits*. The delicate trees on which they grow are easily spoiled by frosts. In Florida and along the Gulf coast, however, there are seldom any heavy frosts.

Early Spanish settlers brought the citrus trees to Florida. Today, this state leads in the production of grapefruit. Orange growing is also a major business in Florida. Central Florida is best for growing oranges and grapefruit. Limes grow farther south along the rocky keys, or islands, off the Florida peninsula. Few lemons are grown here.

Florida also excels in the raising of vegetables and small fruits. Grapes, strawberries, celery, string beans, tomatoes, cabbage, carrots, beets, white and sweet potatoes, eggplants, peppers, okra, watermelons, and cucumbers are grown in large quantities to supply winter needs of northern cities. Much fertilizer must be used in Florida to enrich the poor soil. Although rainfall is plentiful, it is necessary at times to use irrigation to produce better crops and greater yields per acre.

Sugar Cane. Every man, woman, and child in the United States consumes about one hundred pounds of sugar a year. Sugar sweetens ice cream, baked goods, beverages, and candy. Almost all vegetables and fruits have sugar in their natural juice. Some have a great deal; some have very little. Two vegetables—the sugar beet and sugar cane—are the best sources of sugar. When you study the Western States, you will learn more about the sugar beet, a major crop of that region.

We import most of our sugar cane from Cuba, Puerto Rico, Hawaii, and the Philippine Islands. Sugar cane needs fertile soil and a long growing season with plenty of rain. Along the Gulf coast in Texas and Louisiana these conditions are found. As a result, many farmers in these states, as well as in southern Florida, raise sugar cane.

Sugar cane looks something like stalks of corn when it is growing. In autumn the farmers go through the fields with long, sharp knives. They strip off the leaves and cut off the tops of the stalks. Then the stalks are cut up small and taken to the refinery. The newest way of harvesting cane is to burn away the leaves in the fields, leaving the bare stalks. The burning does not hurt the sugar if the cane is cut right away.

Harvesting Sugar Cane. This worker is stripping away the leaves from the cane, using a sharp tool called a *machete*. Note how tall the cane is.

At the sugar refinery, machines press the juice out of the cane. The juice is boiled to make sugar. Raw sugar is brown. After the impurities are removed in the refinery, it becomes white. Molasses is a by-product of the sugar industry. The pressed stalks are made into wall board, another by-product.

Sugar Refinery. A worker checks the sugar's purity. In the background, other men operate the huge machine which turns raw sugar into white sugar.

Rice. Rice is the chief grain crop grown in the Gulf Coast region. Texas, Louisiana, and Arkansas grow most of the rice of the United States. For rice growing, the land must be level and moist. The soil must be rich; the growing season long, hot, and wet.

Special care is given to the growing of rice. During the mild winters the rice field remains drained. The land is plowed in April or May. Water from a bayou is then flooded over the field to a depth of about five inches. An airplane flies low to sprinkle the seed in the water.

When the little plants are about one half inch high, the water is pumped off the field. The plants are allowed to grow to a height of 6 to 8 inches, and the field is again covered with water. This water remains until harvest time. Rice plants grow well on the flooded land, but weeds cannot. Therefore,

Louisiana Rice Harvest. After the water is drained away, machines called *combines* pick up the rice, separating the grains from the stalks, or *chaff.*

the rice farmer does not have to concern himself with cultivating his crop to control weeds, as other farmers must.

At harvest time the water is withdrawn. As soon as the ground is dry enough, combines cut and thresh the grain.

Other Southern Crops. In northern Texas and Oklahoma much wheat is grown. It is stored in high bins, called *elevators,* built on the level plains. Some of the crop is sent to nearby cities to be made into flour. Oklahoma is one of the five largest wheat-producing states. Wheat grows in a drier climate than most other crops.

Soybeans are grown throughout the Southern States. They grow well in the climate of the South. The oil pressed from soybean seeds has hundreds of uses in manufacturing.

Texas excels in the growing of sorghum. Sorghum is a stalk plant somewhat like corn. It yields a grain which is used chiefly as a feed for livestock.

Livestock and Dairying. Still another example of the changing South is the gradual switch from crop production to livestock production. Hogs are now a major livestock item throughout the Atlantic and Gulf Coastal Plain areas. Dairy cattle are being raised more and more, especially near the large cities, where large amounts of fresh milk are sold. Beef cattle production has become very important. In fact, in the last ten years, the South has gone ahead of the Western States in beef production. In Texas, on the Edwards Plateau, sheep-raising has become very important.

The increase in livestock raising is partly due to the discovery that much of the land of the South once used for farming is better suited to pasture. Many of the old plantations where cotton and tobacco were once raised are now cattle and sheep ranches. Regular rainfall and mild winters keep the pastures green almost all year round. This means that the livestock farmer need not

Scene on a Cattle Ranch. The brand burned onto a young calf hurts only for a moment. It helps the rancher identify his cattle on the range.

spend so much for winter feed. His animals can graze outdoors most of the year.

Texas was always noted for its large herds of beef cattle. Today, Texas is the leading state in the country, not only for cattle, but for sheep, horses, and goats as well. Over one half of the land in this enormous state—over 100,000 square miles—is set aside as pastureland. Although Texas leads the nation in cotton production, it also leads in production of wool from sheep. Throughout the Red River Valley, in eastern Texas, there are over one million head of beef cattle grazing on the rich pastureland.

Florida has become an important beef-producing state. In fact, Florida now has more beef cattle than the state of Wyoming. In Alabama, there is a region known as the Black Soil Belt. This region was famous

Pork on the Hoof. Shortly before they are sent to market, these hogs are made fat and plump by being fed on a rich mixture of corn and peas.

once as a cotton-growing area. Today, it is almost one continuous cattle pasture. In Georgia and Alabama, great numbers of hogs are raised.

Facts *to remember*

1. Cotton and tobacco were once the principal crops of the Southern colonists. Great changes have taken place in Southern farming in recent years. Mixed farming, modern machinery, livestock raising, and dairying have been introduced.
2. Tobacco is the South's oldest crop. Today, nine tenths of our tobacco crop is still raised in this section.
3. Long, hot summers and sufficient rainfall throughout the year in the Southern States make ideal conditions for raising big crops of cotton. The invention of the cotton gin by Eli Whitney made the saying, "Cotton is king," a reality.
4. Scientists have perfected improved cotton seeds that ripen early; machines have replaced the hand labor necessary in cotton raising; cotton is no longer "king," though much is still raised.

5. Southern farmers now practice mixed farming by raising many crops as well as a variety of livestock on the same farm. Citrus fruits are raised in Florida and along the Gulf coast.
6. Recently the South has switched from crop production to livestock production. Much of the land once used for tobacco and cotton is now used as cattle and sheep ranches. Texas leads in raising cattle, sheep, horses, and goats.

What *have I learned?*

Rewrite each sentence, using only the correct word or phrase in italics.
1. Today, much of the work on the large farms and plantations is done *by hand* or *by machinery*.
2. Tobacco is called a "soil robber" because it *enriches* or *takes minerals from* the soil.
3. A farmer uses crop rotation when he *fertilizes the soil,* or *grows different crops in the field.*
4. Slave labor insured the plantation owner of *little* or *much* profit.
5. *A tenant farmer* or *a sharecropper* was sometimes able to save a little money.
6. The greatest problem of the cotton grower was *a short growing season* or *the boll weevil.*
7. *George Washington Carver* or *Eli Whitney* found many uses for the peanut.
8. Mixed farming means growing *cotton and tobacco* or *different crops plus livestock.*
9. Florida leads in the production of *peaches* or *citrus fruits.*
10. *Rice* or *wheat* is the chief grain crop grown in the Gulf Coast region.

Facts *to understand*

In a complete sentence give a reason for each of the following statements.
1. The early colonist called tobacco a *cash crop.*
2. Even with the slaves, the plantation owners were beginning to wonder whether it was worth while to raise cotton.
3. "In Profound Appreciation of the Boll Weevil" are the words under the statue of a boll weevil.
4. Many of the cabins of tenant farmers and sharecroppers are now empty.
5. Many of the old plantations where cotton and tobacco were once raised are now cattle and sheep ranches.

3 Forests, Furs and Fisheries

Valuable Animals. A Louisiana trapper's family helps dry muskrat pelts. Furs to help keep out Northern winters often come from the warm South.

You have learned that the South is a great farmland. In addition to farming, what other occupations are there which cause people to work outdoors?

Working in the forests is certainly an important outdoor occupation. In New England men work in the forests to produce paper pulp and maple sugar. In the South, the forests also provide very important products. Many Southerners are busily employed obtaining these products from the forests.

Fishermen also spend most of their time outdoors. They can be said to make their living in the world of nature. Along the coasts of the Atlantic Ocean and the Gulf of Mexico there are many areas where food

fish are plentiful. These are not the same fish caught in northern waters, as you will see. The Southern fishermen face the same hardships and dangers, and do much the same kind of work as the fishermen on the Grand Banks or in Chesapeake Bay.

In addition to the men who make their living in the forests and on the seas, there is a group of Southern workers who make their living outdoors in the bayou country. This area of the South, with its countless streams, flooded land, and marshes, abounds with fur-bearing animals like muskrats, opossums, and minks. Men trap these animals for their valuable furs.

In the last chapter you learned about the farmers of the South and how they live and work. In the following pages you will study the three different outdoor workers of the South—the lumberman, the fisherman, and the fur-trapper.

Logs Into Boards. This huge, powerful saw cuts into a log on its first step toward becoming useful lumber. Next, it must be *cured*, or dried.

Southern Forests. The forests of the South produce more than one third of all the wood used in the United States. Only the Pacific Northwest has a bigger output of lumber. There are two general kinds of wood produced in the forests of the South—hardwoods and softwoods. These come from two different forest belts extending from the Northeast into the South.

The Softwood Belt is the more important. It extends from the Atlantic Coast westward through the Gulf Coast States to Texas. The chief softwood tree is called the yellow pine, or southern pine. The wood of this tree is yellowish, and it grows well in the sandy soils of the softwood belt. It grows much more quickly than the hardwoods of the northern forests.

You will remember reading how the lumber of New England is dragged over snow-covered ground and down swift streams to the sawmill or the pulp mill. An entirely different method of lumbering is used in the South. The land is level here, and the trees may be cut down at any time of the year. Those chosen to be cut are first marked with paint. After being *felled*, or cut down, with power-driven saws, the trees are dragged away. A *donkey engine*, usually run by steam, pulls a long cable to which the cut logs are attached. The logs may be dragged to a sawmill right in the woods, or to a railroad or truck loading point. From there they are shipped to more distant sawmills. At the sawmills, the logs are cut and trimmed into planks, or ground into wood pulp for paper-making.

Most yellow pine lumber is used for building purposes. It makes a cheap, strong wood. Recently, more and more yellow pine has been used in making wood pulp for paper. At first it was used only for making Kraft paper—the strong, brown paper you see in grocery bags and cartons. Now men have found ways to bleach this wood pulp in order to make finer grades of paper. Thus, the Southern softwood forests are providing a much-needed supply of wood pulp for our huge paper needs. As you already know, the forests of New England alone cannot fill these needs.

Naval Stores. An unusual use is made of some yellow pines. While the tree is growing, a big V-shaped scar is cut into its bark. A collecting cup is put at the bottom of the scar. During the spring and summer a thick gummy liquid collects in this cup. Every day this sticky liquid is gathered and brought to a building in the forest. Here the liquid is boiled to produce turpentine, resin, and wood tar. These products, called *naval stores,* are an important product of our Southern forests.

Wood tar was once used for filling cracks in the wooden ships of the Navy. That is how the name "naval stores" came to be used. Turpentine is used for making varnishes and paints. Resin is used in making soap, oilcloth, linoleum, and other products.

Hardwood Lumber. The Hardwood Belt extends from New England west and south, along the Appalachian Highlands. These hardwood forests once grew so thick that a pioneer hunter on horseback could not thread his way through the trees. Later, these valuable hardwoods were cut down or burned to make room for farms. The only hardwood trees that now remain are growing high on the slopes of the Appalachian and Ozark Mountains, where the land is too steep for farming. Hardwoods are used mostly for making furniture. The leading furniture manufacturing center of the South is located at High Point, North Carolina, near the Hardwood Belt.

Another Forest Product. Even while they are still growing, Southern trees are producing half the world's supply of turpentine, resin, and tar.

A Truckload of Future Homes. Huge trucks loaded with logs on their way to the sawmills are a familiar sight on the roads of the softwood belt.

Magic with Wood. Man is always finding new uses for wood. Rayon that is woven into cloth for suits and dresses is made

Forest Observatory. Forest rangers are stationed at lookout posts to watch for the outbreak of a fire begun by dry weather or careless campers.

from wood pulp. Rayon is also used in making the linings of automobile and airplane tires. Wood pulp is used in making plastics such as cellophane. *Plywood* is made by gluing thin layers of wood together. It is much stronger than ordinary boards of the same thickness. Plywood panels make beautiful walls for homes and offices. They are easy to work with and need little care.

As more uses for wood are discovered, more trees must be cut to supply the demand. This means that we must be careful of our future supply of trees. Otherwise we shall run out of them.

Trees for Tomorrow. When minerals are removed from the ground, they cannot be replaced by nature. When trees are cut down, they can be replaced. It is well to remember that God created trees for the use of man. In the past man did not replant trees in place of those he cut down. As a result, trees became more and more scarce.

It is man's duty to see that there is enough lumber for the future. He can do this by replanting trees in place of those he

Deep-Sea Fishing Fleet. These boats at a pier in Florida are hired each day by sportsmen who enjoy the thrill of catching a large ocean fish.

cuts down. This is called *reforestation*. Only trees marked by experts should be cut. They must be cut with skill and care so that other trees are not damaged by their fall. Branches and other parts of trees should not be wasted. Stumps, bark, and limbs can be used to make chemicals and other products. By careful planning it is possible to have a supply of lumber always available.

In addition, reforestation has other advantages. Wherever trees cover hillsides, water soaks into the ground and is held. This prevents floods, which carry away valuable soil where they are allowed to run down unchecked from higher land. Forested areas control the amount of water flowing into streams and rivers. This constant flow insures a steady water supply for home use and farm irrigation. In addition, forests provide excellent recreation areas for the larger numbers of people who live in our growing cities. Even before trees are cut, they are serving man. For these reasons we must plan to use carefully the great gift of the forests which God has provided for us, just as we must use carefully all His great resources.

Coastal Fisheries. Fishing in the Southern States has never been as important as in the Northeastern States. There are several reasons for this. First, in the early days the settlers of the South did not need to turn to the sea for food. They had excellent farm land on which to raise their food. Secondly, food fish is found more abundantly in the cool waters farther north. The warm waters along the southern coasts do not provide the huge catches of herring, mackerel, cod, and others which are found on the Grand Banks. In addition there are fewer good harbors in the South. Even so, there are many fisherman and many fishing fleets harvesting the sea crops of Southern waters.

Most of the commercial fishing of the South is *inshore* fishing. This means that the fishermen work very close to the shore. Among the Southern States, Louisiana, Florida, and North Carolina lead in the value of fish caught. Sport fishermen come to Florida's waters to match their skill with giant sailfish, tarpon, swordfish, and tuna.

Sponge Fisherman. The heavy gear and special suit worn by this Tarpon Springs man help him to descend to great depths when gathering sponges.

Shellfish Waters. Shrimp, oysters, and crabs are the chief kinds of shellfish taken in the bays along the shore of the Gulf of Mexico. Shrimp are caught in bag-shaped nets dragged through the water. They are sold fresh, frozen, or canned. Oysters are raked from the floor of the sea, and taken to packing houses where the shells are removed. The oysters are packed in ice for shipment to all parts of the country. The crab sheds its shell once a year. While it is growing a new shell, it is called a *soft shelled* crab. In this form it is regarded as a delicacy. Both hard-shell and soft-shell crabs are taken in Gulf waters.

Gathering Sponges. Sponges are gathered in the Gulf of Mexico off Tarpon Springs, Florida. The sponge is a sea creature which builds for itself a skeleton full of tiny holes. This skeleton is left behind when the sponge dies. Where the waters are deep, men wearing diving suits cut the sponges from the bottom. Where the waters are shallow, men stand in rowboats and cut the sponges from the bottom. They use long hook-like knives fastened to the ends of long poles.

The sponge fishermen are mostly of Greek descent. In Greece many sponges grow offshore as they do in Florida. When sponge fishermen came to our country, many of them settled in Tarpon Springs to work in a business with which they were familiar.

Although natural sponges are still gathered, artificial sponges of rubber or plastic are being used more and more.

Fur Trapping. In the bayou country of Louisiana, trapping muskrats for their furs is an important occupation for many people. In this "half land and half water country," as it has been called, trappers really operate "fur farms." In the marshes, swamps, and stream banks, the food supply of muskrats is protected, the natural living conditions of the animals are safeguarded, and the trapping is strictly controlled by state law. In this way, an abundance of furs is assured from season to season.

At one time, trapping was a risky and lonely occupation. Fur trappers roamed the deep woods, especially around the Great Lakes and Pacific Northwest, and in Canada. They traded guns and trinkets to the Indians for furs, and kept their own line of traps. Each year their furs were sold at auction. Some years they were lucky, and some years they were not. They had to brave freezing weather, hostile Indians, and loneliness.

The trapping done in Louisiana today is a much steadier kind of business. It is like livestock farming. The trappers supervise the feeding and housing of the animals which will later provide the furs. Louisiana supplies most of the country's muskrat furs —far more than any other state. In addition, the trappers in the bayou country obtain furs from opossums, raccoons, minks, otters, and nutria.

These trappers are mostly of French descent. Their ancestors were French people exiled from the island known as Acadia many years ago. New Orleans, Louisiana, as you will learn, now resembles a French city, because of the large numbers of French people who settled in this region.

Facts *to remember*

1. Southern forests produce more than one third of all the wood used in the United States. The Softwood Forest Belt is the most important. Strong, cheap wood, which today can be bleached to make finer grades of paper, is obtained from the yellow pine. This tree provides a much-needed supply of wood pulp for our huge paper needs.
2. An important product of the Southern forests is naval stores. Hardwoods are used mostly in the making of furniture. Rayon, plastics, and plywood are products of the softwood trees.
3. God created trees for man's use; therefore, man has an obligation to replant trees in place of those he cuts down.
4. Reforestation will provide us with lumber, prevent soil erosion, insure water supply for irrigation, allow for recreation areas, and produce stumps, bark, and limbs that can be used to make chemicals and other products.
5. Because in the early days the South did not need to turn to the sea for food, because food fish is not so abundant as farther north, and because there are fewer good harbors, Southern Coastal fisheries are not as important as the fisheries of the New England States.
6. Shrimp, oysters, and crabs are the chief kinds of shellfish caught in the bays along the shore of the Gulf of Mexico. Sponges are gathered in the Gulf of Mexico off Tarpon Springs, Florida.
7. Trappers operate "fur farms" in the bayou country of Louisiana. Here muskrat trapping is an important occupation.

What *have I learned?*

Complete each of the following sentences, choosing the correct word or words in parentheses.
1. (Factory workers, lumbermen, chemists) work outdoors in the South.
2. The yellow pine belongs to (the rare wood, the hardwood, the softwood) tree.
3. In Southern forests logs are (floated downstream, hauled on a sled, dragged to a sawmill).
4. Hardwood trees are used in (making furniture, rayon, plastics).
5. Trees became more and more scarce in our country because of (poor soil, cool climate, man failed to replace those he cut).
6. Most of the commercial fishing of the South is (inshore, deep-water, surf fishing).
7. (Tuna, oysters, sponges) are known as shellfish.
8. (Raising cranberries, gathering sponges, muskrat trapping) is an important occupation in the bayou country of Louisiana.
9. Sponge fishermen are mostly of (French, Greek, Spanish) descent.
10. (Resin, wood pulp, rayon) is a naval store.
11. Kraft paper is used in (newspapers, paper bags, books).
12. (Scottish, Greek, French) people from the island of Acadia settled in Louisiana.
13. (Oysters, shrimp, crabs) are raked up from the bottom of the sea.
14. (Sealskin, mink, sable) is a fur produced in Louisiana.
15. Reforestation guarantees our water supply by (providing wood to build dams, controlling the flow of water into streams and rivers, storing water in tree leaves.)

Facts *to understand*

Give a reason for each statement.
1. The Southern yellow pine is a valuable forest resource.
2. Fishing never became as important in the South as it did in New England.
3. A group of Southern workers make their living outdoors in the bayou country.
4. The trapping done in Louisiana today is like livestock farming.
5. It is man's duty to see that there is enough lumber for the future.

4

Mineral Wealth

Offshore Drilling Operations. Oil companies are now pumping oil from deposits under the bottom of the sea off the coasts of Texas and Louisiana.

In the early days of the South, as you already know, most people made their living by farming. Because they found they could make money by raising tobacco and cotton, they did not try anything else. More recently, however, the people of the South have been discovering that they have a great wealth of minerals. Today, more and more people are making a living in the mineral industries.

As you know, minerals have little value in their raw state. Generally, man must do three things in order to profit by mineral riches. First, of course, he must find the minerals. Second, he must get them out of the ground. Third, he must discover the best way to use the minerals.

In this chapter we shall see what the mineral resources of the Southern States are and what they have done for the South. We shall learn how men in the South are using the minerals which God has provided.

Petroleum Is Important. We usually think of minerals as being hard, like iron ore and coal. Petroleum, unlike most other minerals, is a liquid. The name *petroleum* comes from two Latin words: *petra* and *oleum*. *Petra* means rock, and *oleum* means oil. Petroleum means "rock oil." Most often, we use the word "oil" when we speak of petroleum. It is found deep in the earth, tightly sealed in rock formations.

From petroleum we get gasoline, kerosene, lubricating oil, fuel oil, and many other products. Today, it would be hard to imagine a world without petroleum. Gasoline runs our automobiles and airplanes. Fuel oils run our locomotives and ships, and heat our homes. Every kind of machinery needs lubricating oil in order to keep it running.

Like other minerals, petroleum cannot be replaced once it has been taken from the ground. We must make wise use of it and never waste it.

Drilling for Oil. Most of our oil comes from beneath the ground. Men who study rocks tell the oil producers where they think oil can be found. Then the work of drilling an oil well begins. The oil men build a tall steel tower over the place they wish to drill. The tower is called a *derrick*. A cutting tool, or *bit*, is put on the lower end of a piece of pipe and lowered from the derrick. This tool is like a dentist's drill, but it is much larger. This drill is turned by a motor. As it turns, it grinds and chews its way through the ground and the rock. More lengths of pipe are fastened as the bit goes down into the earth.

When the drill bores into a rock pocket containing oil and natural gas, the gas pushes the oil up the pipe. It gushes out, and the oil men say they have a *gusher*. They cap the pipe as soon as they can and use a pump to get the oil out of the ground. The dark brown liquid is called *crude oil*. The oilmen are happy when they succeed in finding a well. Sometimes they dig almost a mile into the earth before they find the precious oil. Sometimes they do not find any at all. Even the good wells do not last forever. They run dry, and oilmen must then drill others. Various methods are used in locating new oil deposits. They are usually found in layers of porous sandstone. Layers of shale

Portable Drilling Rig. Petroleum engineers calculate where oil deposits may lie. Then crews like this bring their drills to probe for the oil.

imprison the oil in the sandstone until it is tapped by the new well.

"Cracking" Plant. At Baton Rouge, Louisiana, there are hundreds of plants like this. *Cracking* the oil means breaking it into its various products.

Transporting Oil. Most crude oil reaches the refineries by pipe lines. These are laid a few feet below the ground. Every few miles pumps force the oil along on its way to the refinery. One of these pipelines runs all the way from oil fields in Texas and Oklahoma to refineries in Bayonne, New Jersey. In the refinery many oil products are obtained.

Crude oil is also transported overland in railroad tank cars and tank trucks. Tugboats push fleets of oil barges up the Mississippi and other rivers and bays. Long ships called *tankers* carry oil to ports along the coast and across the ocean. One tanker can hold enough oil to heat 10,000 homes for a whole winter.

Oil Fields. Four Southern States west of the Mississippi River—Texas, Oklahoma, Arkansas, and all but a small part of Louisiana—produce millions of barrels of oil each year. This area is called the mid-continent field. Texas is by far the greatest producer of oil in the United States. Only one country in the world—Venezuela—produces more oil than the State of Texas.

Men are now hunting for oil under the sea and finding it, too. Oil companies are spending a million or more dollars a day drilling in the Gulf of Mexico, near the coasts of Louisiana and Texas. Drilling in deep water is expensive, but when the companies find oil, it pays off. Pipelines have already been built to carry oil to the mainland from offshore fields. One underwater pipeline is 48 miles long.

Southern Refineries. Until recently, almost all the crude oil went to the refineries along the Middle Atlantic coast on New York Bay, Delaware Bay, and Chesapeake Bay. Now more and more of it is being refined in Southern cities. One of the biggest refineries in the world is at Baton Rouge on the Mississippi River. Baton Rouge is the capital of Louisiana and one of the chief ports of the United States. Nearby are about a dozen chemical plants which use the various oil products produced in the Baton Rouge refineries.

More refineries are located near the Gulf Coast in the states of Louisiana and Texas than are found in any other section of the United States. The largest centers are at New Orleans, Baton Rouge, and Lake Charles in Louisiana, and Beaumont-Port Arthur, Houston-Baytown, Texas City, and Corpus Christi in Texas. These centers are near the cheapest form of transportation—water. They are also near the supply of crude oil and near the supply of natural gas, which they use for fuel.

Small refineries are in the interior. El Paso in western Texas, Tulsa in Oklahoma, and Little Rock in Arkansas have important refineries. They have connections with the transcontinental pipe lines to the Great Lakes and the Northeastern States.

Gulf of Mexico Oil Shipping. Through the pipes and valves of this dock at Houston, Texas, thousands of barrels of oil flow into a tanker.

Natural Gas. Natural gas is usually found near the oil pockets in the ground. Formerly, it was allowed to escape into the air, or it was burned on the oil field. Today, much of it is piped to cities and towns all over the United States. It has many uses in homes and factories. Its principal use is as a fuel. Texas and Louisiana supply the United States with one half of its supply of natural gas.

Coal and Iron of Southern Appalachians. The third fuel mineral of the South is neither a liquid nor a gas. It is a solid—coal. It is found in large quantities in the Appalachian Highlands where they extend into northern Alabama near the city of Birmingham. It is soft coal, and much of it is turned into coke. Besides having soft coal nearby, Birmingham has iron ore and limestone. These three are burned together in blast furnaces to produce iron and steel.

Laying Gas Lines. These men are putting down gas pipelines to carry Oklahoma's natural gas to stoves and heaters as far away as Milwaukee.

Birmingham is sometimes called the "Pittsburgh of the South."

The city of Birmingham supplies many of the manufacturing cities with the iron and steel they need for machinery. Much iron and steel for derricks and pipes is necessary for the oil and gas industries.

Aluminum. You have seen many things made of aluminum. It is a light, strong metal which does not tarnish. Your mother's cooking utensils may be made of aluminum. It is used in the manufacture of airplanes and automobiles. You can see more and more of it being used as a building material on modern skyscrapers. Aluminum windows and panels are used extensively in home building. Where does this metal come from?

Mineral Wealth **137**

A Yellow Mineral. This freighter at the gulf port of Galveston, Texas, loads up with a cargo of sulphur from the mines of Texas and Louisiana.

Bauxite is an ore mined chiefly in Arkansas. From this mineral ore, aluminum is removed by electricity. Aluminum factories require great amounts of electric power. Many of them are located near water power which can be used to generate electricity. In the South, however, the largest producers are now using natural gas to produce power. Their plants are located on the lower Mississippi River near the source of the bauxite ore. This saves the cost of transporting the ore over great distances.

Sulphur. The best sources of sulphur in the world are along the Gulf of Mexico in the states of Texas and Louisiana. These two states produce most of the sulphur used in the United States.

Sulphur is a very important mineral, but is seldom used alone. It is blended with other minerals, in nearly all kinds of chemical industries. It is useful in the bleaching, tanning, and dyeing industries. Farmers use it in their fertilizers, and in their powders and sprays to kill insects.

Sulphur is not difficult to mine. A well is bored into the sulphur beds. Pipes of different sizes are placed down in the well, deep enough to reach the sulphur. Very hot water, or steam, is forced down one of the pipes. This causes the sulphur to melt. Then air is blown down another pipe. It forces the melted sulphur, in liquid form, up to the surface through a third pipe. The liquid sulphur is piped to large yards where it cools and becomes hard as rock. It is broken into lumps, and big steamshovels scoop it up into railroad cars. The cars carry it to the industrial plants where it will be used to make sulphuric acid and other chemical products.

The chemical plants need much fresh water. Is it any wonder that many of these plants are located on the lower Mississippi? The flow of the huge Mississippi River water in this area is twice the amount of water used daily in the United States. All the new plants have large intake pumps along the river. They also have large return pipes. After the water is used, it is made clean again and returned to the river.

Salt. Salt is found in thick beds in the states of Louisiana, Texas, and Oklahoma. In its raw form, it is hard and resembles rock. Much of it is quarried on Jefferson Island in Louisiana. Besides its use as a seasoner for foods, salt is used in factories, on farms, and in manufacturing. It is used to preserve and flavor meats and fish. Large blocks of salt, called *salt licks,* are placed in fields for cattle. Salt is used in many chemicals and as a cleanser.

Phosphate and Nitrate. *Phosphate* rock is mined in Florida. It was originally formed from the bones of sea animals that became imbedded in sediments. The sediments turned to rock under the pressure of the sea waters that once covered much of Florida.

Mined phosphate rock is crushed to make fertilizers and chemicals.

Nitrate is a mineral found in the ground in certain parts of the world. Today, nitrogen can be taken from the air and made into nitrates. Nitrate plants use hydroelectric power. In the South they are located in northern Alabama and in Tennessee. Nitrate is used in many kinds of fertilizer.

Magnesium. *Magnesium* is a metal which is even lighter than aluminum. It is not mined from the ground. At Freeport, Texas, it is extracted from sea water. Huge pumps force water from the Gulf of Mexico into the magnesium plant. There, chemicals are used to separate the magnesium from the salt water. This metal, often mixed with steel, is used to make airplane parts. It is known for its strength and lightness.

Phosphate Mine in Florida. A huge machine, called a *dragline,* scoops up phosphate from the surface. Next the rocks will be crushed into a powder.

Magnesium for Fine Steel. White-hot molten magnesium is being poured into molds to harden. It will then be sent to a mill to be mixed with steel.

Facts *to remember*

1. Many people in the South are turning from the raising of cotton and tobacco to the mineral industries. God provides the minerals in their raw state; man must alter them to make them useable.
2. Petroleum is found deep in the earth in rock formations. From it we obtain gasoline, kerosene, lubricating oil, and fuel oil. Texas is the greatest oil producer in our country. Oil is now being discovered and produced from under the sea, in the Gulf of Mexico particularly. The Southern States refine their own crude oil, mostly in the Gulf coast cities of Texas and Louisiana.
3. Natural gas, which is found in the South, was formerly allowed to escape or was burned on the oil fields. Today, it is pumped through pipelines all over the country and used as a fuel.
4. Besides having soft coal nearby, Birmingham has iron ore and limestone, which are used to produce iron and steel. This city is sometimes called the "Pittsburgh of the South," because of the great amounts of iron and steel produced there.
5. Sulphur, which is used in bleaching, tanning, and dyeing, and as a fertilizer and insect spray, is mined along the Gulf of Mexico. Bauxite is mined chiefly in Arkansas. Aluminum is removed from this ore by electricity.

6. Deposits of salt, phosphate, and nitrate are found in the Southern States. Magnesium is extracted from sea water from the Gulf of Mexico at Freeport, Texas.

What *have I learned?*

Name the mineral.
1. I am the ore from which aluminum is removed.
2. Men drill for me with a huge bit lowered from a derrick.
3. Formerly I was allowed to escape into the air, or I was burned on the oil field. Now I am used as a fuel.
4. I am lighter than aluminum and used to make airplane parts.
5. In my raw form I resemble rock. I am used mostly as a seasoner for food.
6. Gasoline, kerosene, lubricating oil, and fuel oil are my products.
7. I am used in making coke.
8. I am extracted from sea water.
9. Bleaching, tanning, dyeing, and fertilizing industries consider me important.
10. I am used together with coal and limestone to produce steel.
11. I am usually transported to refineries by long pipelines.
12. I can be taken from the air. I am used in many different kinds of fertilizers.
13. After I am melted, I am forced up a pipe into a yard, where I cool and become hard.
14. I am used to lubricate machinery to keep it running smooth.
15. I was originally formed from the bones of sea animals that became imbedded in sediments.

Facts *to understand*

Answer each of the following in one sentence.
1. Why do minerals have little value in their raw state?
2. Why are the sulphur chemical plants located on the lower Mississippi?
3. Why has Birmingham become such a great steel-producing city?
4. Why is it profitable to have oil refineries located in the South?
5. How is oil taken from the ground?

Air View of Galveston, Texas. After being destroyed by a tropical storm in 1900, Galveston was rebuilt. Today it is a major port of the South.

5
Manufacturing and Cities

We have read about many changes that have taken place in the South. Eli Whitney caused a big change when he invented the cotton gin. The Civil War brought about great changes. The little insect called the boll weevil caused a great change when the farmers of the South had to plant other crops besides cotton. Another change came about when the owners of large farms began to use farm machinery. One machine could do the work of many men; so the owners of large farms no longer needed many men to work in the fields. The sharecroppers and tenant farmers had not been making enough money. Now with larger farms competing against them, many of these people could make no money at all at farming.

Southern leaders gave much thought to this problem. "What we need are factories," they said. "Then the people who cannot make a living on the farms could work in the manufacturing cities." The South had never had many factories. The Southern people went to work to get Northern businessmen to build factories in the South.

Advantages for Manufacturing. The South has many advantages for manufacturing. The climate is warm, and factories do not have to be heated as they do in the North. There is a ready supply of workers who can no longer be kept busy on the farms. Factories need raw materials. The South has an abundance of cotton, timber, pulpwood, natural gas, oil, coal, iron, phosphate, and bauxite. The products of Southern mills and factories are made chiefly from these raw materials.

Factories need power. Oil, natural gas, and soft coal are near at hand in Southern states. Water power is available on the fall line in the Southern Piedmont.

Transportation is excellent over the level land. So is water transportation, which is the cheapest kind for bulky goods. Excellent ports on the rivers and coasts receive and send cargoes to the North Central states and even into Canada by river and lake routes. Cargoes are sent on the ocean to all the continents of the world, especially South America.

Southern Mills and Factories. One third of all factory workers in the South work in the textile mills. The Southern Piedmont section is now the leading cotton-goods

manufacturing region of the country. The machines in the mills spin cotton fiber into thread and weave the thread into cloth. Every state in the South has cotton mills, but North Carolina leads in this industry. Raleigh, North Carolina, Columbia, South Carolina, Atlanta, Georgia, in the Piedmont region, and Birmingham, Alabama, and New Orleans, Louisiana, are important textile-producing centers.

More than half of all the new chemical plants in the United States are being built in the South. The Texas Gulf coast has become the greatest chemical manufacturing area in the world, and it is still growing. Chemical plants must spread over large areas. High steel towers, enormous tanks shaped like globes, and miles and miles of complicated, colored pipe lines cover the Texas Gulf coast.

These plants consume large quantities of oil, natural gas, water, wood pulp, coal, and air. They produce plastics, nylons, artificial rubber, fertilizers, dyes, medicines, and many other products. Scientists are doing research work all the time to find new ways

Textile Mill in South Carolina. Here, women are examining large bolts of cloth to check its quality. This is one of many modern Southern mills.

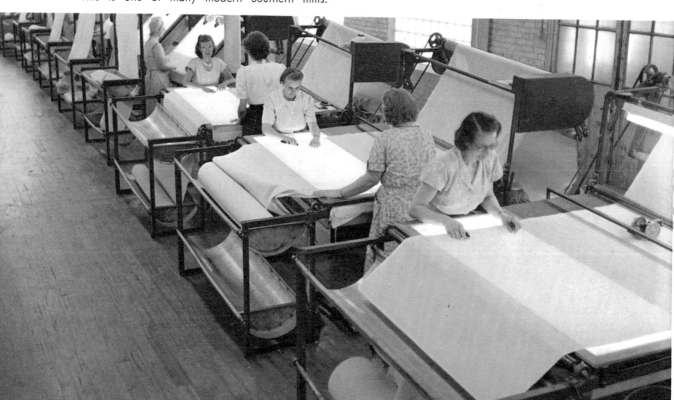

Making Petroleum Products. The round tanks store oil under pressure. In the background is special equipment used to make rubber from petroleum.

of combining raw materials chemically to produce new substances. Their discoveries help satisfy life's needs and comforts.

In our second largest state, Texas, airplane plants grew up during and after World War II. Much of the work in aircraft production in Texas can be done outdoors all the year round because of the warm climate and wide level spaces.

Iron and steel mills in Birmingham and other Southern cities supply the iron and steel for the machines needed in factories and on large farms. Larger farms with fewer hand laborers need tractors and harvesting machinery. Food-processing factories, refineries, and mills also require heavy machinery.

Factories Bring Changes. Factories are helping the South in many ways. First of all, they give work to many people. The factory workers now have more money to spend on farm goods; so the farmers are

also helped by the factories. Owners of factories must pay higher taxes than owners of farm land. With the extra tax-money the Southern States have been able to build better schools and better roads. They have been able to do many other things for their people.

The South is changing from a strictly farming district to a district that has both farming and manufacturing. This may turn out to be one of the most important changes that has ever taken place in the South—a change for the better.

The boom in manufactured products has brought prosperity to many Southern cities. There is still no city of the South with more than a million people, but some have grown rapidly in the last few years. Let us look at some of them.

Atlantic Coast Ports. Charleston, South Carolina, and Savannah, Georgia, have been important Atlantic seaports since early days. Tourists are attracted today to historic Charleston and nearby Fort Sumter, where the first shot of the Civil War was fired. Savannah is noted especially for paper-making. Both ports export turpentine, resin, cotton, and peanuts.

Cities in the Highlands. Manufacturing and trading cities are located in the foothills of the Appalachians. In these cities goods are stored in warehouses, elevators, and tanks. Business men from smaller cities and towns come to buy raw materials and finished products from this kind of sales center. Atlanta, Georgia, is a good example of such a city. It began as a railroad

town. Today, it is a state capital and a large manufacturing center as well. Thousands of products, from pins to automobiles, are made in the city and surrounding areas.

Raleigh, North Carolina, and Columbia, South Carolina, are state capitals. Both cities manufacture textiles, furniture, fertilizers, and cottonseed oil.

Greenville, South Carolina, has one of the largest cotton textile mills in the world. Within 100 miles of this city are over 500 more textile mills.

Winston-Salem, North Carolina, is one of the oldest tobacco cities in the country. Charlotte, North Carolina, manufactures cotton and rayon cloth. Asheville, North Carolina, is a growing city at the entrance to Great Smoky National Park.

St. Augustine, Florida. Here is the oldest mission in the oldest city of the United States. It was built 400 years ago by Spanish missioners.

Florida's Coastal Cities. On Florida's northeastern coast is our oldest city, St. Augustine. It was founded in 1565 by missionary priests from Spain. Originally, St. Augustine was a fort and trading center. By the time the Puritans were about settled in Massachusetts, the Franciscan Fathers in Florida had over forty missions with 30,000 Catholic Indians. Later, Florida became an English colony.

Florida's coastal cities attract thousands of tourists each year. Many visitors like living in this state, and they settle down here to stay. Jacksonville is a vacation resort and manufacturing city. Miami, West Palm Beach, and Miami Beach are the most important vacation centers. Fishing, bathing, and sunning on the beach are the great attractions in these cities. Miami is noted for its large international airport.

Key West is the most southern city of the forty-eight states. A line of small islands, called the *Florida Keys,* stretches out into the Caribbean from the tip of Florida. Key West is at the end of this chain. On Florida's west coast are Tampa and St. Petersburg, both on Tampa Bay. A bridge connects these two resort cities. Tampa is especially noted for the manufacture of cigars and the shipping of phosphates. Farther north is Pensacola with its excellent harbor and airport. It is a training base for the United States Navy.

New Orleans. New Orleans is the oldest major port of the South. Over one half million people live in this busy and colorful city. New Orleans has an interesting history. Years ago French explorers from Canada discovered a low, flat plain of deep, rich soil at the mouth of the Mississippi River. The silt carried down by the river formed this rich plain called a river *delta.* Soon a French settlement was established and called New Orleans after the city of Orleans in France. The territory around

New Orleans was called Louisiana after King Louis of France.

The King of France made a present of the city to his cousin, the King of Spain. Spanish people came to settle there also. The city and its people to this day still show traces of French and Spanish influence in their speech, their buildings, and their way of life. Sometimes these people are called *Creoles*.

New Orleans, together with a large area of land in the central part of the continent, became part of the United States by being purchased from its European owners. New Orleans rapidly became an important port for the American settlers along the Mississippi. They sent their goods down the river and out to the ocean through this city.

Some Irish immigrants later came to New Orleans. They found they could live peacefully here as Catholics. The French and the Spanish had already made New Orleans a city with a Catholic tradition and Catholic way of life. New Orleans today is one of the few places in the South where Catholics are very numerous.

Over the years, the Mississippi delta has continued to grow. As more and more silt is deposited by the river, the delta extends farther out into the Gulf of Mexico. Today, ships must travel a hundred miles up the Mississippi River to reach the city of New Orleans. Ocean steamers from coastal ports of the United States, from the West Indies, Central America, and South America come to New Orleans with raw materials, and take away finished products for many countries of the world. In addition, river boats ascend the river to Minneapolis, to Pittsburgh, to the Great Lakes ports, and on to the Canadian ports.

New Orleans is a manufacturing city as well as a major port. Factories make boxes, burlap bags, cigars, cigarettes, canned food, clothes, cotton goods, furniture, and ships. Sugar refineries, grain elevators, and cotton warehouses are located in and around the city. Furs, sugar, and oil are the leading exports.

French Quarter, New Orleans. A typical scene in this colorful city, showing court and terrace, reminds us that France helped settle our country.

Gulf Ports. On such a long coast as that of the Gulf of Mexico, you would expect many seaports. Mobile, Alabama, has an excellent port with fine docks for loading and unloading cargo. Lumber, cotton, coal, aluminum products, canned fruits, and seafood are shipped from the city. Biloxi and Gulfport are important seaports along the Gulf coast of the state of Mississippi.

Texas has several major Gulf ports. Beaumont and Port Arthur are noted for their large oil refineries. Texas City and Galveston are large cotton, grain, and petroleum markets. In both cities, oil refineries, chemical plants, and flour mills cover a large area.

In southern Texas, Corpus Christi and Brownsville ship products from the inland sections to other coastal cities of the United States and to ports of many foreign countries. In Corpus Christi the aluminum industry receives its bauxite from the island of Jamaica in the West Indies.

Busy New Orleans Pier. Freighters line up at this long New Orleans pier to take aboard a varied cargo of oil, sugar, and furs for world trade.

Products from the Rio Grande valley have increased because of the Falcon Dam recently built on the river by the United States and Mexico. Farmers in the valley are better off because of the increased electric power and the irrigation projects. Their farm products pass through Brownsville, near the Mexican border.

Texas ports have the space necessary for storing products—warehouses for cotton, elevators for grain, and tanks for oil. These Gulf ports can be expected to continue growing rapidly.

Other Texas Cities. Texas has several large inland cities. Fort Worth is the center of the Texas cattle industry. Cattle, sheep, and goats are brought here from the surrounding ranches. Fort Worth is also a cotton and meat-packing center. Dallas buys and sells much cotton from the huge Texas cotton farms. It has become famous as a center for women's clothing.

The oldest city in Texas is San Antonio, founded as a Spanish mission in 1744. Here is the famous *Alamo*, a fort where brave Texans died fighting rather than give up their independence. San Antonio deals in wool, hides and skins, and citrus fruits. Many tourists visit its old Mexican section.

Austin, Texas, is 75 miles northeast of San Antonio. It is the state capital and an important distributing center for cattle. It manufactures furniture, brick, building stones, and food products. El Paso is a gateway city on the western boundary of Texas. Like all the other cities of Texas, it is rapidly increasing in trade and manufacturing industries.

Largest City of the South. Houston, Texas, is now the largest city among the Southern States. It began as a railroad and cattle center. Later, cotton and pine lumber were shipped from Houston. Much of the country's supply of petroleum lies within a few

hundred miles of Houston, so today oil and gas are its leading products. However, cattle, cotton, lumber, and rice continue to be important. Houston is an inland city, but a ship canal connects it with the Gulf of Mexico. This makes it possible for Houston to become one of our major ports. Houston has more than one half million people who work in shipyards, iron and steel mills, and factories turning out chemicals, airplanes, machinery, processed foods, and textiles. Houston exports wheat from Kansas and Oklahoma, and salt and sulphur from the coastal region.

"Remember the Alamo!" That was the cry which inspired the Texans in their fight for freedom from Mexico. Davy Crockett and Jim Bowie died here.

Some State Capitals. Florida's capital city is Tallahassee. Montgomery, Alabama, and Jackson, Mississippi, are state capitals and noted as cotton and cattle centers. Nashville is the capital of Tennessee.

Arkansas' capital, Little Rock, is almost in the exact center of the state. Important bauxite mines are nearby. Little Rock is also a lumber center.

Oil wells are pumping right in front of the capitol building in Oklahoma City, Oklahoma. This capital city is also a center for stockyards, flour milling, and meat packing. Tulsa in Oklahoma is also a kind of capital. It is called the "Oil Capital of the World." Main offices of most oil companies are located in Tulsa.

Facts *to remember*

1. When Southerners failed to make a living from the soil, they turned to factories for a living.
2. Warm climate, ready supply of workers, abundance of raw materials, available power, and good transportation give the South manufacturing advantages.
3. Every state in the South has cotton mills. The Southern Piedmont section is now the leading cotton-goods manufacturing region of the country.
4. The Texas Gulf Coast has become the greatest chemical manufacturing area in the world. Here plastics, nylons, artificial rubber, fertilizers, dyes, medicines, and other products are produced.
5. People are attracted to the historic Atlantic Coast port of Charleston. Businessmen from smaller cities and towns come to the manufacturing and trading cities in the foothills of the Appalachians to buy raw materials and finished products.
6. St. Augustine, our oldest city, founded in 1565 by missionary priests from Spain, is on Florida's northeastern coast. Key West, Florida, is the most southern city of the forty-eight states. New Orleans is the South's oldest major port.
7. A low, flat plain of deep rich soil at the mouth of the Mississippi was formed by silt carried down by the river. On the long coast of the Gulf of Mexico there are many seaports. Mobile, Alabama, has fine docks for loading and unloading

cargo. Texas has several large inland cities. Houston, its major city, is now the largest city of the South.

What *have I learned?*

I

Answer each question in a complete sentence.
1. What effect did machinery have on the South?
2. What effect did factories have on the South?
3. What advantages does the South have for manufacturing?
4. Why did the Gulf Coast become a great chemical manufacturing area?
5. Why does New Orleans have a favorable location for trade?

II

Copy the names in Column A. Write opposite each one the item in column B that best fits it.

A	B
1. New Orleans	oil wells in front of the capitol
2. Port Arthur	founded as a Spanish mission in 1744
3. Austin	important vacation center
4. San Antonio	largest city of the Southern States
5. Houston	has a large Catholic population
6. Oklahoma City	a state capital noted as a cattle center
7. Birmingham	capital of Tennessee
8. Greenville	supplies iron and steel for factory machinery
9. Miami	Gulf port with large oil refineries
10. Nashville	largest cotton textile mills in the world

Facts *to understand*

Give a reason for each statement.
1. Manufacturing is becoming more and more important in the Southern states.
2. A large supply of workers is available to the owners of factories in the South.
3. Many textile mills moved from New England to the Southern states.
4. The increase in the number of factories is helping the South in many ways.
5. Houston, Texas, is a port even though it is an inland city.

Unit Three Review

Questions for Discussion and Review

1. What change has the development of mineral resources brought about in the South? 2. Discuss how the surface features of the South have benefited the region. 3. How have the occupations of the Southerner kept him in close contact with God's world of nature? 4. Give the advantages of the South in regard to manufacture. 5. Why has farming always been a major occupation of the Southerner? 6. Give reasons for the rise of cotton as an important crop in the South. 7. Give reasons for the decline of cotton as the most important crop of the South. 8. Why are so many oil refineries located along the Gulf Coast? 9. Why does the South, with a larger area than the Northeastern States, have a smaller population? 10. What are some of the reasons for the popularity of Florida as a winter vacation area? 11. Discuss the ways in which the Southern tobacco farmer prevents his soil from wearing out. 12. Why do Southern farmers feel a kind of gratitude toward the destructive boll weevil? 13. In what ways did George Washington Carver help the farmers of the South? 14. Give reasons why Florida is especially suited to raising citrus fruits. 15. Why did livestock raising replace farming in certain areas of the South? 16. Discuss the advantages to everybody in a careful program of reforestation. 17. What are some of the reasons for the importance of Birmingham, Alabama, as a steel-producing city? 18. Discuss the many uses of sulphur in manufacturing and farming. 19. Why have the Southern States become much more important than New England in the production of cotton textiles? 20. Why has Houston, Texas, become one of the busiest ports in the United States? 21. How have the Southern mineral industries made use of natural resources found off the coast line? 22. Discuss the effect of the Gulf Stream on the climate of the Southern States. 23. Why are there fewer Catholics in the Southern States than in the Northeastern States? 24. Why is there less danger from the cotton boll weevil in the western part of the Cotton Belt? 25. What are the advantages in the Gulf Coast region which make it ideal for growing rice?

Using the Maps and Globe

1. On an outline map of the United States, label all manufacturing cities of the South.
2. Compare the latitude of the Southern States with that of the Northeastern States.
3. List all the principal water bodies bordering or within the Southern States and state one use for each.
4. Make an outline map of the Southern States, and indicate by color the surface features of the region.
5. Use a globe to point out 2 advantages the South may have in regard to world trade.

Using Geography Words

Here is a list of special words that have been used in Unit Three. Write a sentence using each word to prove you know its meaning in geography.

seedlings	*derrick*	*naval stores*
reforestation	*sharecropper*	*Gulf Stream*
soil robber		*gusher*
boll weevil		*plywood*

Getting Information from Books

Read reference books, such as *Compton's Pictured Encyclopedia,* for information on the following topics. Prepare to give an oral or written report.

Cotton Gin	George Washington Carver
Steel	Petroleum
Wood Pulp	

Final Test

Write each sentence on your paper, choosing the correct word or words in parentheses.
1. When the farmers of the South could not make a living from the soil, they turned to (fishing, manufacturing, mining) for a living.
2. (The Florida Keys, The Southern Piedmont, The Gulf Coast) is now the leading cotton-goods manufacturing region of the country.
3. The Texas Gulf Coast has become a great chemical manufacturing area because (good farms, suitable climate and rainfall, raw materials) needed by chemists are near at hand.
4. In the Southern States there are fewer (farms, cities, boll weevils) than in the Northeastern States.

Southern United States 151

5. (Many farmers, Seminole Indians, The Spanish) are the only human beings who live deep in the Everglades.

6. Immigrants did not come to the South in such large numbers because (it was hard to find a landing place, nobody told them about it, there were fewer employment opportunities).

7. (The South, New England, Pacific Northwest) has the largest output of lumber.

8. (Fishermen, chemists, office workers) can be said to make their living in the world of nature.

9. In the bayou country of Louisiana, furs are assured from season to season (by government control, by the presence of much water, by inexperienced trappers).

10. In the early days of the South most people made their living by (mining, farming, fishing).

11. Most crude oil reaches the refineries by (pipe lines, truck, railroad).

12. A mineral that is not mined from the ground is (iron ore, sulphur, magnesium).

13. One reason that cotton is raised in the South is that (there is a long growing season, it enriches the soil, slaves could be obtained more easily).

14. The greatest enemy to cotton growing was (frost, few factories, the boll weevil).

15. Over half of the land of Texas is used (as pastureland, by miners, by fur trappers).

16. Protective banks along the Mississippi River are called (levees, dikes, sea walls).

17. The (Great Smokies, Blue Ridge, Catskills) are mountains of the South.

18. The largest Catholic population of the South is in and around the city of (Miami, Florida; Houston, Texas; New Orleans, Louisiana).

19. (Corn, tobacco, cotton) is the oldest crop of the South.

20. A (tenant farmer, slave, sharecropper) rented land and a house from the plantation owner.

21. (Peanuts, cotton stalks, sweet corn) are often used as feed for hogs.

22. The newest way to harvest (cotton, sugar cane, soybeans) is to burn away the leaves in the fields.

23. The leading state in the United States for the production of beef cattle is (Florida, Wyoming, Texas).

24. (Maple syrup, sawdust, turpentine) is one of the forest products called naval stores.

25. Fur trapping is carried on mostly in (Alabama, Louisiana, Tennessee).

Applying Christian Principles

1. Northern people are worthy of praise in helping Southern people build factories because **a.** they aided the Southerner to make a better living **b.** showed how skilled they were **c.** received pay for their help.

2. When we drain swamps, we benefit our neighbor by **a.** driving out the wild animals **b.** keeping away the Indians **c.** giving him more land on which to raise crops.

3. Whites are most unjust to the Negro **a.** when they hire him to do hard work **b.** when they refuse to give him a fair share of the profits they receive **c.** deny him a share in the rights and the privileges of citizens elsewhere in the United States.

4. Fishermen can best thank God for allowing them to make their living in His world of nature by **a.** trying to become wealthy **b.** sharing the resources with the needy **c.** using scientific methods.

5. Although God could have made minerals valuable in their raw state, He did not do so in order that man **a.** would not use them for war purposes **b.** might perfect them and praise God for their value **c.** would be able to take all the credit himself.

6. Changes in farming in the South have been good because they **a.** now encourage the Southern farmer to make the best use of his land. **b.** increased the price of cotton **c.** make the farmers work easier.

7. The increase in manufacturing in the South will be a good thing for Southerners because it **a.** will help them to compete with other regions of the country **b.** increase the size of their cities. **c.** provide employment for people who could not make a living at farming.

8. Reforestation is important because **a.** wood is no longer important **b.** it insures that there will be lumber, topsoil, and water for future Americans. **c.** it covers up land that is no longer useful for farming.

9. People in every part of the world cooperate best with God's plan when they **a.** fight hard to obtain good land and resources **b.** don't look for ways to change their condition **c.** make the best use they can of the blessings which God has bestowed upon them.

Neighbors in the North Central States

In this Unit you will learn that:

1 The thirteen North Central States are often called the Middle West, or simply the Midwest.

2 The surface of the Midwest is mostly level—part of the great Central Plain of North America. Summers are often quite hot, and winters cold. Except along the Great Lakes, there are no large bodies of water nearby to moderate the climate.

3 Level land, fertile soil, and a long growing season make the Midwest a great farming region. Corn, wheat, dairy products, beef, and pork are produced.

4 The Midwest is a tremendous workshop. Mineral industries are especially important. Transportation assists manufacturing. In this region there is cheap water transportation and many miles of railroads and good highways.

5 Some of the largest cities of the United States are in the Midwest. Their huge populations engage in different industries, turning out a variety of manufactured items.

THE MIDWEST

The section of the United States we are going to learn about next is known by several names. It is often called the North Central region. This is because it is in the center of the country and to the north. This section is also called the Midwest, or the Middle West.

The North Central region might be called "the food basket of the nation," because food crops like corn and wheat are grown in large quantities. Vegetables, many dairy products, and much of our meat also come from the North Central States.

But the North Central region is more than a "food basket." Valuable mineral deposits are located here, and a great deal of manufacturing is carried on. For example, almost all the automobiles manufactured in the United States come from this region.

When the thirteen original states won their independence, only the Indians and a few French settlers lived in the Middle West. In time, people from the Eastern Seaboard and newcomers from Europe moved across the Appalachian Mountains. In less than a hundred years the wilderness changed into a great food-producing and manufacturing region.

CANADA

Appalachian Highlands

River

THE
NORTH
CENTRAL
STATES

The five Great Lakes, lying between
the United States and Canada, form
the most outstanding feature of this
region. Connecting waterways link
the many cities along their shores.

From the Appalachian Highlands
in the east, all the way to the west,
extend the vast fertile farmlands of
the Central Plain. Three mighty rivers
flow southward through this plain.

Rich Harvest. Tons of golden wheat grains pour from a combine on a Midwestern field. The fruitful Midwest is truly "food basket of the nation."

1

The Middle West

The North Central States, or Middle West, is a group of thirteen states lying together in the center of the United States. Look at the map on pages 158 and 159. Six of the North Central States border on the Great Lakes. They are: Minnesota, Wisconsin, Michigan, Illinois, Indiana, and Ohio. The other seven states in the region are North Dakota, South Dakota, Nebraska, Kansas, Iowa, Missouri, and Kentucky.

The Mississippi River, together with its two most important branches, the Missouri and the Ohio, flows through the North Central region. These three rivers touch twelve of the thirteen North Central States. Michigan is the only state in the Midwest which is not on one of these rivers, and Michigan touches three of the Great Lakes.

Fifty-four million Americans live in these thirteen states. They supply the United States and many other countries of the world with food and manufactured goods.

A Wide Open Corridor. Turn back to the map of North America on pages 6-7. Notice that one continuous plain extends from the Arctic Ocean south to the Gulf of Mexico. This low-lying area is bordered on the east by the Appalachian Highlands, and on the west by the Rocky Mountains. It forms a wide open corridor down through the central part of North America.

During the winter, cold, dry air moves into this corridor from the north, and during the summer warm, moist air moves in from the south. The part of the corridor which lies in the United States is one of the great farmlands in the world. It forms an important part of the North Central region we are now going to study.

Mostly a Low-Lying Plain. The surface of the Middle West is mostly a low-lying plain, part of the great North American lowland you just read about. Most of this Great Central Plain is less than 1000 feet above sea level. Throughout the North Central States, the surface of the land is gently rolling to nearly level. There are some hilly or highland areas, as you will see. The Black Hills in South Dakota and the Ozark Mountains in Southern Missouri are examples of these.

The western part of this plain slopes gradually upward until it reaches a height of 5000 feet, near the Rocky Mountains. For the most part, however, the surface of the North Central region is a gently rolling, nearly level land.

Once Beneath the Sea. Many thousands of years ago, a vast inland sea covered the central part of our continent. The present states of Indiana, Iowa, Missouri, and Illinois were at the bottom of this sea. In fact, only the highlands of the Ozark Mountains stood up above the level of this tremendous inland sea.

Many rivers and streams poured into this sea from all sides. They carried with them fine silt, or mud. Deep blankets of this material spread over the bottom of the sea. Dead plant and animal life dropped to the bottom and formed more layers on the sea floor. The weight of each additional layer pressed down on the others. All this helped form the fertile soil which now covers the North Central States.

Then came a time when the land was gradually uplifted, and the vast area that had once been the sea floor became dry land. The great Mississippi River and its branches formed. They helped to drain this level lowland.

Rolling Farmlands. Fertile soil, plenty of sunshine, and enough rainfall favor the grains and mixed crops on the farms in the hills of Wisconsin.

Studying the Map

A. 1. Make a list of the North Central States. **2.** Which of the states touch the Canadian border? **3.** Which of the North Central States border the Great Lakes? **4.** Name the Great Lakes that are crossed by the boundary between the North Central States and Canada. **5.** Which of the Great Lakes lies entirely in the United States? which is largest? which lies farthest east? **6.** Name those North Central States which touch the Southern States. **7.** Use the scale of miles on the map to find the distance across the North Central States from the eastern boundary of Ohio to the western boundary of Nebraska.

B. 1. What does the map tell you about the surface of most of the North Central States? **2.** Where in this region are the highest elevations above sea level? How are they shown on this map? **3.** Which great river crosses the region from north to south? Where is its source? Name the North Central States east of this river. west of this river. **4.** The two most important tributaries of the Mississippi River cross the region. Name these tributaries and trace their courses on the map. **5.** Small ships and barges can travel between Lake Michigan and the Mississippi River. What waterways would they use? **6.** Through which lakes and connecting waterways would an iron ore boat have to travel in going from Duluth, Minnesota, to Buffalo, New York?

C. Most of the largest cities of the North Central States are located on the Great Lakes or on the important rivers of the region. **1.** The largest city of the North Central States is at the southern end of Lake Michigan. Name this city. **2.** Which large city is located on a river between Lake Huron and Lake Erie? in Wisconsin on the western shore of Lake Michigan? in Ohio on the southern shore of Lake Erie? **3.** Which large river city is located near the junction of the Missouri and the Mississippi rivers? on the Ohio, midway between Pittsburgh and the Mississippi? on the Missouri River where it forms the boundary between Kansas and Missouri? **4.** Name the "twin cities" on the Mississippi River in Minnesota. Name the city of Minnesota which is located at the extreme western edge of Lake Superior.

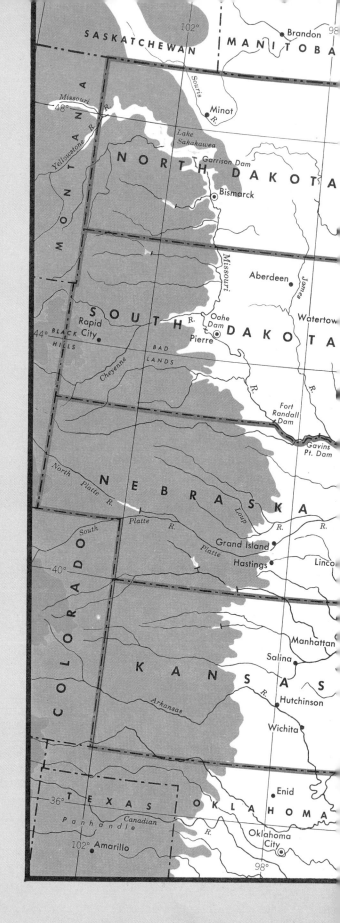

over 10,000
5,000 to 10,000
2,000 to 5,000
500 to 2,000
0 to 500
Below Sea Level

ELEVATIONS IN FEET

Capital Cities ⊙
International Boundaries
State or Provincial Boundaries

Scale of Miles

0   50   100   150   200

Winnipeg

Lake of
the Woods

O N T A R I O

Port Arthur

ISLE ROYALE
NATIONAL PARK

L A K E   S U P E R I O R

St. Marys R.

Sault Ste. Marie

Grand Forks

Hibbing

MESABI RANGE

MINERAL RANGE

Marquette

M

Str. of
Mackinac

L.Itasca
Source of
Mississippi R.

Duluth

Superior

Georgian
Bay

Fargo

Mississippi R.

St. Croix R.

St. Cloud

Menominee R.

Green Bay

C

H

I

L A K E   H U R O N

82°

St. Paul

Falls of St. Anthony

St. Louis Pk.

Minneapolis

Minnesota R.

Wausau

Eau Claire

Appleton

Green
Bay

Oshkosh

Saginaw Bay

G

A

Bay City

Saginaw

Flint

Port
Huron

Toronto

L.
ONTARIO

44°

Rochester

Winona

La Crosse

Sheboygan

Muskegon

Lansing

Pontiac

St. Clair Lake
St. Clair

Austin

Mason
City

Wisconsin R.

Milwaukee

Madison

Racine

Kenosha

Grand
Rapids

Jackson

Detroit

Hamtramck

Royal Oak

Sioux Falls

Waterloo

Dubuque

Beloit

Battle Creek

Ann Arbor

Dearborn

Windsor

L A K E

Erie

Sioux
City

Ft. Dodge

Des

Cedar
Rapids

Rockford

Waukegan

Evanston

Kalamazoo

Wyandotte

Detroit R.

Cleveland

PENNA.

I O W A

Iowa City

Daven-
port

Clinton

Elgin

Cicero

Chicago

E. Chicago

South Bend

Ft. Wayne

Lima

Toledo

Lorain

Youngs-
town

E R I E

Des Moines

Council Bluffs

Omaha

Moines R.

Ottumwa

Rock Island

Aurora

Joliet

Gary

Hammond

Maumee R.

Mansfield

Akron

Canton

Z

O H I O

Pittsburgh

Burlington

Peoria

Bloomington

Danville

Anderson

Kokomo

Muncie

Springfield

Marion

Columbus

Zanesville

Wheeling

Keokuk

I L L I N O I S

Champaign

Decatur

Indianapolis

Richmond

Dayton

Fairmont

Quincy

Springfield

Terre Haute

Hamilton

Cincinnati

Parkersburg

Clarksburg

Leavenworth

Topeka

Kansas City
Missouri

Independence

Kansas City

Columbia

University City

St. Louis

Alton

East St. Louis

Covington

Newport

Portsmouth

Ohio R.

W E S T

Lawrence

Jefferson City

Illinois R.

I N D I A N A

Frankfort

Louisville

Lexington

Huntington

V I R G I N I A

Charleston

Pittsburg

Osage R.

Lake of
the Ozarks

M I S S O U R I

Springfield

Mississippi R.

Wabash R.

Evansville

Owensboro

Ohio R.

K E N T U C K Y

Wolf
Cr. Dam

APPALACHIAN MTS.

VIRGINIA

Johnson City

N O R T H

82°

Lake O' the
Cherokees

Joplin

O Z A R K   P L A T E A U

Kentucky
Dam

MAMMOTH CAVE
NATIONAL PARK

Dale Hollow
Dam

Cumberland R.

Kentucky
Lake

Paducah

CUMBERLAND MTS.

Oak
Ridge

Asheville

Charlotte

C A R O L I N A

Tulsa

Muskogee

A R K A N S A S

T E N N E S S E E

Jackson

Nashville

Knoxville

94°

90°

86°

The Work of the Glacier. You remember learning about the work of the glacier in shaping the surface of New England. The North Central States were also strongly affected by the ice sheet that moved into the region from Canada. It came as far south as the Ohio and Missouri Rivers.

As the glacier moved southward, its enormous mass bore down with grinding force on the surface of the Middle West region. Here, as it reached the end of its journey, it started to melt. As it melted, tons of the rock material it had picked up and carried frozen in its ice were deposited. Wrinkles and folds in the old sea floor were filled in, and a deep covering of glacial soil was left over much of the surface. Glacial soils are usually fertile because they are well mixed and contain the mineral matter growing plants need.

In Minnesota, Michigan, and Wisconsin, the rocks and soil left by the melting glacier kept some of the water from running off

Corn, Wheat, and Dairy Belts. Notice the states located in each belt. Compare this map with the rainfall and growing seasons maps on page 24.

the surface. As a result, thousands of small lakes were formed. This region is sometimes called the "Land of Lakes."

Deep, Rich Prairie Soil. The inland sea and the glacier helped to form deep level layers of soil. The rainfall and warm, sunny days encouraged the growth of forests and grasslands. Again, century after century, layers and layers of dead leaves, roots, sticks, and remains of animals piled up. When living plants and animals die and decay, a rich dark substance forms. This is called *humus*. Under the heavy growth of forests and prairie grass, a rich store of humus piled up. The soil grew deeper and deeper, and its fertility increased.

The Climate Favors Farming. In addition to the advantage of good soil, farmers in the Middle West enjoy a climate which favors the production of various crops. There are four areas, or *belts*, in which certain crops grow well. Each belt is named after the particular crop which grows best in it. They are the Corn Belt, the Hay and Dairying Belt, the Winter Wheat Belt, and the Spring Wheat Belt. There are no

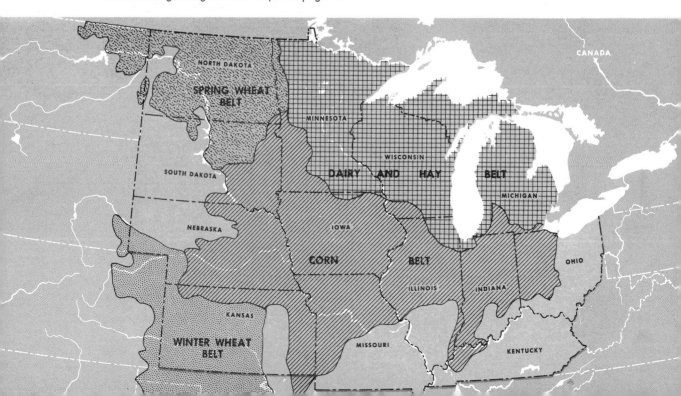

Plowing the Rich Midwest Soil. A four-bladed plow turns over the fertile soil in spring to prepare it for the corn crop, soon to be planted.

sharp dividing lines separating these belts —one changes very gradually to another.

The Corn Belt extends westward from Ohio, through Indiana, Illinois, Iowa, Missouri, and Kansas, to Nebraska. Here the summers are hot, with frequent showers, and the winters are cold and moist.

North of the Corn Belt, in the upper Great Lakes states, the growing season becomes shorter. Corn will not ripen in a short growing season like this. Here the climate with its shorter, cooler summer favors pasture land particularly. This section is called the Hay and Dairying Belt.

In the drier western parts of the North Central region, there are two wheat belts. One is centered in Kansas and in part of Nebraska. It is called the *Winter Wheat Belt*. Here wheat seeds are planted in the fall. The wheat crop begins to grow and resembles grass by the time winter sets in. During the winter, the wheat remains in the field, without further growth. In spring, it

begins to grow again and is harvested in midsummer. As you have already learned, parts of this Winter Wheat Belt extend into the states of Texas and Oklahoma.

The Spring Wheat Belt includes North and South Dakota, and reaches right up into Canada. If wheat were in the fields during the long cold winters here, it would freeze. For this reason, it must be planted in the spring and then harvested in late summer.

Of course, in each of these belts, other crops, fruits, and vegetables are also grown wherever the soil, the climate, and the growing season are favorable.

To say that the North Central States have warm, moist summers and cold, dry winters is to present an incomplete picture. It is really a region of changeable weather. Often on the plains the wind will change

A Refreshing "Break." Harvesting the wheat crop during the Midwestern summer can be hot work. A cool drink from the water jug is very welcome.

suddenly, and temperatures may go way up or way down in a very short time. Someone once said jokingly of the weather in Kansas: "If you don't like this weather, just wait an hour; it will be different." That was an exaggeration, of course, but the weather can change very suddenly in this part of the United States.

This changeable weather can be frightening and damaging. In winter, storms called *blizzards* sweep across the plains from the northwest. Snow piles high. Traffic stops, and stray travelers and animals may freeze to death.

In summer, sometimes the hot air grows very still, and thunderstorms develop and bring welcome showers. Another kind of storm that sometimes occurs is called a *tornado*. A tornado does a great deal of damage because of the high winds that come with it. After it passes, people and

livestock lie killed or injured, and hundreds of homes and crops may lie in ruins. Fortunately, tornadoes do not occur often and cover only a small area.

Even though the overall weather is changeable, the growing season is long enough for cereals and other food crops.

Farming with Machinery. The North Central States had a big advantage over New England for farming, because machinery could be used on the level surface.

In 1832 Cyrus Hall McCormick invented a machine which cut wheat. It was called a *reaper*. The machine saved the farmer a great amount of time and work. In 1847 McCormick went to Chicago to build machinery for the wheat farmers of the Middle West. As the years passed, the company he formed made many improvements in the reaper and invented some new machines for the farmer.

Before this time the size of a man's farm depended upon how much work he and his family could do on it. With the aid of the reaper and other farm machinery, a farmer was able to take care of a much larger farm. The machines helped him to work ten times as much land as he could by hand. Today, the machines that wheat farmers use do fifty times as much work.

Farm machinery has played an important part in making the North Central States such a great food producing region.

Railroads and the Farmer. The level surface of the plains was also excellent for the building of railroads. As soon as railroads reached the North Central States, more settlers came to this region, and the farmers began to increase the size of their farms. They produced larger and larger crops and sent them by railroad to the East where they were needed. The railroads brought machinery and other manufactured goods to the farmers from the factories of the East.

People in different parts of our country learned to depend upon one another for things they needed. Each section of our country was able to engage in the industries for which it was best suited. The railroads helped in the exchange of products.

Cleared Land. At one time, most of the North Central region east of the Mississippi River was heavily forested. Remember that this section receives more rainfall than the section of the North Central region west of the Mississippi. When the first settlers came over the Appalachians, they found the good soil they were looking for. Only they had to clear the trees away first.

Lumber from the felled trees was used to build houses, fence posts, and barns. Even so, there was too much lumber. Some was burned, and some was used later to build railroad ties. Much of this great natural resource was not used wisely as God intended.

The heavy forest never returned to the eastern part of this region. The rich black soil, the long growing season, and the plentiful rainfall encouraged the people to keep the land in use as cropland. Gradually, however, small stands of new trees are now being developed in the North Central States by people who think that forests should be encouraged. There is very little lumbering done; the greatest use of these new forests is for recreation and sport—hunting, fishing, and camping.

Farther west, where the rainfall is considerably less, there were no trees. Early farmers found tough, high grass covering the rich land. The trees and the grass are mostly gone, but the land they enriched is being used to feed people all over the United States today.

The First Midwesterners. This man is a Sioux Indian of South Dakota. He is dressed in the outfit worn by the Plains Indians many centuries ago.

Indian Country. Centuries before the settlers came to this region and carved thirteen states out of it, the Indians found it a good place to live. There were two kinds of Indian living in the region. To the east

Father Marquette Converting the Indians. The French priest started a mission on Lake Superior and explored the length of the Mississippi River.

of the Mississippi, in the great forest, were the Algonquins and other tribes. These people lived in the forest. They did not farm, but hunted wild animals for their food. To the west, in the grasslands, tribes like the Dakotas roamed about. These wandering people hunted the huge herds of wild buffalo. In this way they obtained meat, clothing, and shelter—all provided by buffalo.

None of the Indians ever seemed to be aware of the riches that lay about them—the fertile soil, the wooded forests, the herds of useful animals. They lived simply and used just what they needed. When the white settlers came, many Indians either moved west, or died fighting the newcomers, or took up life in the white man's way. We are aware of their heritage when we see names like Mississippi, Minnesota, Michigan, and Kansas—all Indian words.

The Frenchmen Come. The French explorers were first to arrive. They discovered with awe and pleasure the vast Mississippi —which the Indians called "Father of Waters." Among the French explorers were brave missionary priests like Father Marquette who risked their lives to convert and teach the native Indians.

Most of the Indians they met were friendly. Father Marquette told them the good news of salvation. They listened and were eager to hear more about the Savior and His Church. Father Marquette, whom the Indians called "Black Robe," promised to return and found a mission among them.

The French explorers did not settle in great numbers. They set up trading centers where fur-trappers and hunters could exchange their catch for money or food. Others were busy searching in vain for a "Northwest Passage"—a waterway to the Pacific. Very few realized the true wealth of the region, even though it lay all about them.

The Midwest Grows. It was not long before greater and greater numbers of settlers came across the Appalachians. Some of these people were farmers who wanted to settle on good ground, and they recognized it when they found it. Some came all the way from New England, where the soil would not permit much farming. The little trading posts grew up to be cities. Men discovered the forests and cut them down to make room for farms or for lumber to build the railroads.

The Government of the United States encouraged more and more people to come into the North Central region. As each part of this region became settled and populated, it was admitted as a state into the United States. Immigrants, many of them Catholics, arrived from Europe. They, too, came to this region to avail themselves of the good farmland.

Today, all these people of the Midwest live in a prosperous and favorable land— the heartland of the United States. Many live in big cities and many live on farms. Many came in the last fifty years from Germany, Ireland, Poland, or some other land; others have ancestors who came to this sec-

Wisconsin Camping Ground. A young Indian boy of the Winnebago Tribe enjoys the annual gathering. Many tourists now attend these gatherings, too.

tion more than 150 years ago. In the following chapters you will learn more about the different ways all these people live and work and play.

The Vanishing Herd. This mighty animal is one of the 600 remaining buffaloes protected on a wildlife refuge. Millions once roamed the plains.

Working Together on a Farm. A farmer and his son are operating a tractor. This valuable machine is used in performing many jobs on the farms.

Facts *to remember*

1. The North Central or Midwest region may be called "the food basket of the nation." It has valuable minerals and is a great manufacturing region.

2. The Mississippi River, together with the Missouri and the Ohio Rivers, flows through the Midwest. Minnesota, Wisconsin, Michigan, Illinois, Indiana, and Ohio border on the Great Lakes. This region was once covered by a vast, inland sea. Deposits of silt from this sea enriched the soil. Glacial soil also added to the fertility of the land.

3. This broad, level plain, enriched by deposits from the inland sea and the glacier, has a favorable climate for most crops and has ideal surface features for using farm machinery and for building railroads. Although once heavily forested, the land is now mostly cleared.

4. Today, the people of the Midwest live, in cities and on farms, in a prosperous, favorable land.

What *have I learned?*

The word in italics makes each sentence right or wrong. If wrong, rewrite the sentence, putting in the correct word.

1. The surface of the Midwest is mostly *hilly*.

2. Glacial soils are usually *fertile*.

3. *Few* of the automobiles manufactured in the United States come from the Midwest.

4. The area near the Great Lakes is a great *manufacturing* district.

5. The Ohio, the Missouri, and the Mississippi rivers touch all the states in the Middle West except *Illinois*.

6. When living plants and animals die, they *destroy* the soil.

7. The Spring Wheat Belt extends farther *north* than the Winter Wheat Belt.

8. In the Corn Belt, the growing season is *short*.

9. Cyrus McCormick invented the reaper to cut *corn*.

10. The *railroads* brought machinery from the East to the Midwest.

11. East of the Mississippi was heavily forested because it received *more* rainfall.

12. *Much* lumbering is done in the Midwest.

13. The Algonquins lived by *farming*.

14. The "Father of Waters" was discovered by a *German* explorer.

15. The Government of the United States *discouraged* people from coming to the North Central region.

Facts *to understand*

Give a reason for each statement.

1. The Midwest may be called the "heartland of the United States."

2. As soon as railroads reached the North Central States, more settlers came to this region.

3. Farm machinery helped to make the Midwest a great food-producing region.

4. The North Central States is a region of changeable weather.

5. The North Central region is more than a "food basket."

6. Farmers of the North Central States are taking advantage of events which occurred millions of years ago.

7. Spring wheat is grown in the more northern areas of the Midwest.

8. The coming of the railroads was a great help to the farmers of the Midwest.

9. The first Europeans to come to the Midwest did not leave many permanent settlements.

10. The herds of buffalo which once roamed our country were very important to the Indians.

2
Corn and Wheat Farms

Corn and wheat are the principal cereal crops raised in our country. The North Central States lead in their production. You are probably familiar with corn as a tasty vegetable eaten on or off the cob. Corn for our tables, or *sweet corn,* is not the major crop of the Corn Belt. Here the farmers grow a rough, darker kind of corn. It is used mostly as feed for livestock.

Wheat is our most important food crop. It furnishes about one fifth of all the food we eat. Bread, cake, pies, crackers, breakfast cereals, spaghetti, and many other foods are made from wheat. It is also fed to hogs and cattle.

The Corn Belt. Nearly every state in the country has farms which raise some corn. In the Corn Belt of the North Central region, however, corn is by far the most important crop on more than three fourths of all the farms. The states of the Corn Belt, in the order of greatest corn production, are Iowa, Illinois, Indiana, Nebraska, Minnesota, Ohio, Missouri, and Wisconsin. Together, these eight states raise more than one half of the total corn crop of the United States.

During the summer in the Corn Belt, a traveler might go for hundreds of miles and see field after field of green rustling corn. Near the corn fields, there are also fields sown in other crops. But the corn fields occupy the greatest amount of space. They stretch out for miles and miles.

Mechanical Seeding. The machine which this tractor pulls across a field automatically drops seeds into four rows at a time and adds fertilizer.

How Corn Is Grown.

Corn is a warm-weather plant. In the Corn Belt the summer days are hot with plenty of sunshine, and even the nights are warm. Corn needs plenty of rain during its growing season. In this region the rain comes in frequent thundershowers. Many of these occur at night, and those that come during the day do not last long. This makes it possible for corn to get enough sun and enough rain. Throughout most of the Corn Belt the growing season is at least six months long. This is long enough for the corn to grow well and to ripen before frosts come in the fall.

Corn Belt farmers have to work very hard during the spring. Their first job is plowing. This begins as soon as the frost is out of the ground. To turn the soil over, the farmers use large plows pulled by a tractor or two teams of horses. After plowing is finished, the harrow is used. This machine breaks up the soil and makes the surface smooth. The soil is now ready for the mechanical seeder. It drops the corn seed and covers it with soil and fertilizer.

Main Product of the Corn Belt. Here you see a close-up view of corn in a crib. This corn is cattle feed, much coarser than the sweet corn you eat.

After a few weeks the corn begins to sprout. It must be cultivated to keep the soil broken up and free from weeds. On most Corn Belt farms, the farmers have a corn cultivating machine that takes care of several rows at a time.

In one month the stalks grow from the height of one foot to about six or seven feet. In another month the plant makes big ears of corn. During the entire growing season, Corn Belt farmers must guard against insects that kill the corn plants. They spray their fields regularly with a chemical which is poisonous to the insects.

The Corn Harvest. Harvesting time is the most interesting part of the summer for the Corn Belt farmer. There are different ways in which a farmer harvests his corn. Some of it is cut while the stalks are still green. These stalks and the ears are chopped up by a machine. This cut corn is stored in *silos*—tall, round buildings built of wood, brick, or concrete. Corn *silage,* as the cut corn is called, is used to feed hogs, cattle, and other animals kept by Corn Belt farmers.

Most of the corn crop is allowed to ripen

Storing Corn Feed. The farmer stands on a ladder to attach the lid on one of the large wire cribs where the dry ears of corn fodder are stored.

in the fields. After the stalks turn brown, harvesting machines cut them down. The farmers pile these stalks into large bundles called *shocks.* Later the ears are picked and the outer cover, called the *husk,* is removed.

Corn Makes Good Pork. Ears of corn, together with the green cornstalks, are chopped up and fed to these hogs. The rich mixture makes them fat.

Life on a Corn Belt Farm. This boy and girl, children of a Corn Belt farmer, spend happy summer days roaming around barns and haystacks.

Often the cornstalks are allowed to stand in the field until the ears dry out in the sun. A horse-drawn wagon moves along between the rows of stalks. The corn pickers walk alongside the wagon and throw in the ears as they are picked. The ears are hauled off and stored in a bin called the *corn crib*. Contests are held each year to select the champion corn-picker.

On some of the farms a corn-picking machine is used. This machine is pulled along a row of corn stalks. It removes the ear of corn from the stalk, husks it, and tosses it into the wagon.

Even the corn plants that remain in the field are not wasted. Livestock owned by the farmer is turned into the fields. They eat the stalks, husks, and ears that are left.

Corn and Animals. Throughout the Corn Belt, farmers keep many kinds of livestock, especially hogs. Iowa and Illinois, the top two corn-producing states, are also the nation's top pork-producing states. Pork is the meat we get from hogs. Herds of beef and dairy cattle also graze in pastures throughout the Corn Belt. Chickens and turkeys occupy large poultry ranges, houses, and sheds. All these animals are fed on the corn raised right in the region.

Some farmers feed all or most of the corn they raise to their own livestock. Others, with more corn than they can use, sell it as feed grain. It will be bought by livestock farmers who cannot raise enough corn to feed their meat animals. Very little corn is exported as feed grain out of the Corn Belt to other parts of the United States.

Because so many meat animals are raised on corn, it can be said that we eat our corn "on the hoof." People of the United States eat more meat than people anywhere else in the world. It is partly because of the plentiful corn crop of the Middle West that Americans receive so much meat for their tables.

Other Uses for Corn. Even though more than nine tenths of our corn crop is used to fatten livestock, it does have some other uses as well. Some is ground up to make corn meal. Some is used to make cornstarch

Watching the Cattle. Like many other farmers of the Midwest, the twins' father raises fine cattle. This breed of cattle is called *Hereford*.

and corn syrup for bakers and candy manufacturers. Some is used to make a favorite breakfast cereal, corn flakes. However, "corn on the cob"—sweet corn raised as a vegetable for man's use—is raised on smaller farms throughout the other states of the country. It is canned, frozen, or delivered fresh to vegetable markets.

Each year, farmers in the Corn Belt harvest more corn than they can use right away. Some of the surplus is kept in cribs right on the farms. It will be used to feed livestock in a year when the harvest is not so great.

Some Corn Belt farmers also raise *hybrid* corn. This is corn grown especially as seed. They sell this seed throughout the region to farmers who will be planting their fields the following year.

Other Corn Belt Crops. Farmers in the Corn Belt have found that it is not good practice to plant corn in the same field year after year. The reason is that corn would take the same minerals from the soil each season. Soon the soil would become weak, and the crops would suffer.

Instead, Corn Belt farmers *rotate* the crops in their fields. This means that they plant a different crop in a field each year. In this way, the richness of the soil does not become exhausted. Some crops even put back into the soil minerals which corn needs. Sometimes a field is rested for an entire season by not being planted at all. This is called lying *fallow*.

Crops which are rotated with corn include wheat, oats, barley, rye, and sorghum. We call these *grain* crops. Barley is used to make malt, one of the chief ingredients in brewing beer. Wheat and rye go to make flour for baking. Oats and sorghum are cut up for livestock feed.

In addition, Corn Belt farmers grow hay and clover for dairy cattle, keep orchards for producing fruit, and raise some vegetables for their own use.

As you can see, many other crops are grown in the Corn Belt in addition to corn. Some are grown to provide cattle feed, some as food crops for the city markets, and some to provide rotation of corn fields.

Disc Harrow at Work. This wide machine breaks up the soil before wheat planting. Tractors are used to pull various machines in the Wheat Belts.

Two Wheat Belts. There are two wheat belts in the North Central region. The difference between them lies in the times of the year in which wheat is planted. One is the Spring Wheat Belt; the other is the Winter Wheat Belt.

Spring wheat is planted in the early part of the year, around April and May. It grows all summer, and the tall crop is cut and harvested in September or October. Spring wheat is planted by farmers in parts of North Dakota, South Dakota, Minnesota, Montana, and across the border in Canada. This region is called the Spring Wheat Belt. A large part of this belt lies in the North Central States.

Winter wheat seed is planted in the fall of the year. It begins to sprout, develop roots, and take on a grassy appearance. As winter comes on, the ground is usually covered with a blanket of snow. Underneath, the grassy-looking wheat "goes to sleep." It stops growing but does not die. In spring it starts to grow again and is ready to harvest in early summer.

Winter wheat plants would freeze during the colder winters of the more northern states like the Dakotas, Minnesota, Montana, or in Canada. However, farther south, the winters are not so severe. Wheat does not freeze in the ground, and winter wheat farming can be carried on. The states in the Winter Wheat Belt are Kansas, in the region we are studying, and parts of Oklahoma and Texas in the Southern States.

Kansas leads in the production of winter wheat; North Dakota leads in spring wheat production. Four fifths of all the wheat grown in the United States is winter wheat.

Planting Wheat. The wheat farmer does not have to hire a large force of workers, even though his crop may cover many square miles. Machines do most of his work. Before the planting season, either in the spring or the fall, the wheat farmer must prepare the soil by plowing. He uses a tractor to pull his wide plow. Then a machine called a *harrow* is attached to a tractor. As it passes over the plowed ground, it breaks the soil up into fine pieces.

Next, a planting machine scatters the seeds on the earth and covers them over automatically. Wheat is not set out in rows like corn. It grows widespread like grass. Therefore, it does not have to be cultivated as corn does from time to time.

Wheat is unlike corn in one other important way. It does not require so much rain. Remember, corn grows best in the eastern section of the Middle West. This is the rainier section, where the thick forests once stood. Wheat grows best in the drier west. Since it is a grain, or grassy crop, it succeeds as well as the prairie grass once did in this drier climate.

Harvesting Wheat. During the dry, sunny days of summer and fall, the wheat ripens and is ready for harvesting. This work is done by large, complicated machines which are called *combines*. These amazing machines cut the wheat and thresh it in one operation. *Threshing* means separating the kernels of wheat from the stalks. The kernels are poured like sand into waiting trucks. Then they are taken to grain storage tanks, called *elevators*. The elevators may be near the field or farther away at a shipping port.

The stalks which are discarded are called *straw*. Sometimes straw is burned; most often it is left on the field and later plowed under the soil. It is a good fertilizer.

Miles and Miles of Wheat. Harvester combines reap a huge harvest. Can you tell why farms in this region are sometimes called "factory farms"?

Where the Wheat Is Stored. These huge, round buildings in Kansas City, Kansas, are called *elevators.* Next step from here is the flour mill.

Milling Wheat. Special agencies and companies agree to buy the farmer's wheat from his fields or his wheat bins. Then they send it to a mill, where it will be processed

Fresh-Baked Bread. Flour from Midwestern mills keeps ovens busy all over the country, baking the many foods necessary to form strong bodies.

to make flour. The kernels of wheat are carefully cleaned. Then they pass through sets of rollers which grind them into flour. The white flour is packed in bags and sent to bakeries throughout the United States and to many foreign countries.

The material left after the white flour has been milled is called *bran.* It is rich in vitamins. Bran has a high food value, and much of it is made into cereals and baked goods. Some bran is also used to make feed for livestock.

Many cities throughout the Midwest have flour mills. Buffalo, New York, however, is now the leading flour-milling city in the United States. The grain is sent there in large boats which carry it over the Great Lakes. Kansas City, Missouri, and Minneapolis, Minnesota, are the next two flour milling cities in importance. Both are located within the wheat belts. Kansas produces more flour than any other state in the country.

174 North Central United States

Other Crops in the Wheat Belt. Like the corn farmers, wheat farmers have learned that it is best not to grow one crop in the same field year after year. In the wheat belts, when a field is not planted with wheat, it is planted with corn, oats, rye, barley, flax, or potatoes. Some fields are kept as pasture land for beef cattle. The cattle supply animal manure which the farmer plows into the soil to keep it fertile.

Sometimes a crop like clover will be planted in a field. Instead of harvesting it, however, the farmer will plow it under the soil when fully grown. This returns many of the minerals to the soil and enriches it for the next season's crop.

Facts *to remember*

1. The North Central States lead in the production of corn and wheat, the principal cereal crops raised in our country. Iowa, Illinois, Indiana, Nebraska, Minnesota, Ohio, Missouri, and Wisconsin raise more than half the total corn crop of the United States. Corn requires much rain and a long growing season.

2. People in the United States eat more meat than people anywhere else in the world. Nine tenths of our corn crop is used to fatten livestock. Iowa and Illinois, the top two corn-producing states, are the nation's top pork-producing states. Little corn is shipped as feed grain to other parts of the United States from the Corn Belt.

3. Corn Belt farmers must rotate their corn crops with other crops to replace the minerals taken out of the soil by corn. When clover is plowed under, it returns many minerals to the soil and enriches it. Hay and clover are grown for dairy cattle. Farmers keep orchards and raise vegetables for their own use.

4. Winter wheat is raised in the southern section of the Midwest, and spring wheat in the north. Machines do most of the work for the wheat farmer. Most of the wheat is used to make flour. Buffalo, New York, is the leading wheat-milling city in the United States.

What *have I learned?*

Write each sentence by completing it with the correct word or phrase in the parenthesis.

1. (Wheat, corn, rye) is the most important crop of the Corn Belt.

2. Corn needs (a short growing season, plenty of rain, little rain).

3. A crop of (wheat, clover, corn) gives the farmer the most work in cultivating.

4. Dried ears of corn are stored in (corn cribs, silos, seeders).

5. Most of the corn crop is (exported, eaten by humans, used to fatten livestock).

6. When a field is rested for a season, we say it is (lying fallow, rotating, fermenting).

7. Winter wheat is planted in the (fall, winter, spring).

8. A (reaper, harrow, combine) is used to break plowed ground into fine pieces.

9. (Bran, hybrid wheat, sorghum) is the vitamin material left after the white flour is milled.

10. (New York, Missouri, Kansas) produces more flour than any other state in the country.

11. Sweet corn is raised mostly as (cattle feed, a vegetable crop, a fertilizer).

12. (Cotton, tobacco, other grain crops) are most often rotated with corn.

13. Wheat requires (more rain, less rain, the same amount of rain) as corn.

14. Storage tanks for grain are called (elevators, refineries, cribs).

15. North Dakota, South Dakota, Minnesota) leads in the production of Spring wheat.

Facts *to understand*

Answer each of the following questions in a sentence or two.

1. What food crop furnishes about one fifth of all the food we eat?

2. How does the growing of wheat differ from the growing of corn?

3. Why are many livestock raised in the Corn Belt?

4. What is one reason that the people of the United States eat so much meat?

5. What is the difference in the two wheat belts?

3
Other Midwest Farms

Making Hay in Wisconsin. This important dairy state produces great amounts of hay for dairy cattle feed. Here the new-mown hay is stacked to dry.

As you have learned, corn and wheat are the most important crops of the North Central region. But there are farmers in this region who do not raise corn or wheat as their principal crop.

Remember that corn and wheat are crops which grow best under certain conditions of climate and soil. Corn requires a climate with plenty of summer sunshine and rain in showers. Wheat requires a drier climate, with moderate winters. Both corn and wheat grow best in the dark, rich *prairie soil*. Both crops do best on level land.

There are sections of the North Central region where we do not find such conditions. In these sections, other kinds of farming are carried on. In this chapter we shall learn how these other farmers live and work together.

Hay and Dairy Belt. In the section of the Midwest north of the Corn Belt, dairying is the most important kind of farming. Wisconsin, Minnesota, and Michigan are important dairy states. The land is somewhat hilly and makes ideal pasture land for herds of dairy cows. There are many lakes, streams, and wells, which furnish plenty of clear water, a necessity for dairy cows. Dairy cattle raised for milk require more water and richer pasture than cattle raised for beef.

The soil in the Hay and Dairy Belt is thinner and lighter than that of the Corn Belt or the Wheat Belt. In addition, the growing season is shorter in the Hay and Dairy Belt. There are crops which are well suited to these conditions. Most often they are animal feed crops, raised on the same farms which have large herds of dairy cows. In this way, dairy farmers grow most of the feed their cows need. By doing so, they save both time and money.

"Making Hay." First of all, there is hay. Certain kinds of grass make good hay. It is cut and dried in the sun, and then used as feed for livestock. The grass which is sown to make hay may be any one of a number of different varieties. Among the most common grasses are timothy, clover, and alfalfa. Soybeans, oats, rye, and wheat are also cut and used as animal fodder. In the northern part of the North Central States, alfalfa is the chief hay crop.

Hay is best when the farmer cuts, or *mows,* it while it is in flower. If it grows too long before mowing, it becomes dry and useless.

When the hay is at the correct stage of growth, the farmer mows it down. Usually the stalks are left right in the field, where the curing process begins. Most of the water in the hay is given off, and it turns light brown or yellow. From time to time, it is turned over to help the curing and prevent rotting. After four or five days, it is gathered. Sometimes a farmer will store the loose hay in his barn. Most often, a special machine squeezes it into square blocks, called *bales.* These bales, tied with wire, can be stored and used when needed as winter food for animals. Sometimes hay is chopped up fine, mixed with corn, and stored in a silo.

Sometimes two crops of hay can be cut from the same field in one season. Sometimes also, after hay is cut, the field is re-seeded. Then cattle are brought in to graze on the second crop when it begins to grow. Often a farmer will find it wise to plow a field of hay right back into the soil. This helps to enrich the soil for next year's crop.

Hay is the fourth crop in importance in the United States, after wheat, corn, and cotton. Wisconsin is the chief hay-producing state in the country. After Wisconsin come New York, Minnesota, California, Iowa, and Nebraska.

Another Useful Farm Machine. These men are operating a hay baler. Cut hay, which has been dried in the field, is pressed and tied into bales.

Dairy Farms and Products. One of the richest dairy regions in the United States is in southeastern Wisconsin. Farmers here ship their fluid milk to dairies and bottling plants in the nearby large cities of Chicago and Milwaukee. Other farmers of the Dairy Belt, farther from the city markets, must make other products from the fresh milk which cannot be shipped long distances. They make butter and various kinds of cheese.

The region which includes large parts of Wisconsin, Minnesota, and Michigan has more dairy farms than any other part of the country. Most of these farms are smaller than the farms in the Corn and Wheat Belts. On them, strips of pasture land for summer grazing lie side by side with strips of land where hay and corn for silage are grown. This practice, called *strip farming,* helps to prevent soil erosion.

The North Central States contribute

Dairy Cattle. Sleek, well-fed cows can be seen on farms throughout the Hay and Dairy Belt. They make this region famous for its milk products.

about three fourths of all the milk products used throughout the United States. In addition to butter and cheese, these include ice cream, canned evaporated milk, dried milk solids, and products for candy-making and baking. Milk and milk products help to keep Americans everywhere healthy and strong.

Cool Climate Cereal Crops. In the upper Great Lakes region, where the climate is cool and moist, small grains such as oats, rye, and barley grow well.

Oats do not require so rich a soil as corn or wheat. This grain is planted either in the spring or fall. Most of the oats are used as livestock feed in the form of hay, or as grain. A small part of the oat crop is used for making oatmeal.

Barley is a feed grain for cattle. In some places, barley is used in making beer and some food products.

Rye is used in several ways. It can be cut for making hay. It is plowed back into fields to enrich the soil. It is ground into flour for making certain kinds of bread.

Soybeans. In recent years, the soybean has become a major crop in the United States. It is grown extensively throughout the Northeastern States. Originally soybean plants were imported from China. They were intended to be used to enrich the soil and as animal feed. Chemists have since found that soybeans are rich in food values for human beings. Their oil is used in margarines and salad oil. It is also widely used in manufacturing of plastics. Chemists are discovering more uses for this crop. The demand for soybeans becomes greater and greater each year. As a result, Midwestern farmers are planting larger crops of soybeans. Illinois leads in this production.

Flax for Seed. There are two kinds of flax. One kind is grown for the fiber, and the other for seed. Minnesota raises flax chiefly for its seed. In the mills of Minneapolis, flaxseeds are crushed to obtain a pale yellow oil called *linseed oil.* This oil is used to make paint, varnish, printer's ink, linoleum, and soap.

Linseed cake is the material left when the oil is squeezed from the seed. It makes excellent feed for animals. Flax straw is used in making heavy paper and as packing. In some countries, where there is much hand labor available, flax produces the fiber which is used for making linen.

Fruit and Vegetable Regions. Fruits grow well along the eastern shore of Lake Michigan and the southern shore of Lake Erie. In spring, the cool winds blowing from the lakes keep the trees from blooming until the danger of a frost is passed. In summer, cool lake breezes keep the weather from getting too hot; in the fall, warm winds delay the frost and help ripen the fruit.

Grapes grow well in Ohio and Indiana, along the southern shore of Lake Erie, as well as on the Door Peninsula in Wisconsin. Cranberries grow in the sandy marshes

Ripe Peaches. Fruit like this does well along the lake shores, due to the moderate climate and long period between spring and autumn frosts.

of central Wisconsin. Apples, peaches, cherries, grapes, strawberries, raspberries, and other fruits grow well also in the hilly sections just south of the Corn Belt.

Large quantities of vegetables are grown on the plains that border the Great Lakes. Michigan has great canneries where tomatoes, string beans, peas, and many other vegetables are canned. Some vegetables and fruits are quick-frozen; some are sold fresh in local markets. Potatoes are an important crop in Michigan, Wisconsin, Minnesota, and North Dakota.

Farmers and Forests. Michigan and Wisconsin were once leading lumbering states. Much of the forest in this region was cut down to make room for farms. Some of it was destroyed by fire. The white pine forest supplied excellent building lumber to the farmers in these states for many years. Only a few forest areas remain in the extreme northern parts of Michigan and Wisconsin. Here lumbering is still important.

Many of the farmers here do part-time work in these forests. During the winter they haul logs on sleds to the frozen lakes and rivers. By spring, when the farmers are back in their fields doing the plowing, the ice melts, and the logs float down to the saw mills.

In some areas, where the trees were cut down long ago, new trees have grown. They are called *second growth* trees. Such trees do not make good lumber but can be used to make wood pulp. Wisconsin, Minnesota, and Michigan produce a large amount of pulp for paper mills.

In Ohio, Indiana, and Illinois, a small amount of lumber is still uncut. These states are in the Central Hardwood Forest, but very little of this once-great forest remains standing. Some of the farmers in these states have kept small wood lots. The wood lots supply the farmer with lumber for building and for fuel.

Winter Lumbering. While his snow-covered fields are idle, this farmer keeps busy hauling out logs which will be floated to the mills in spring.

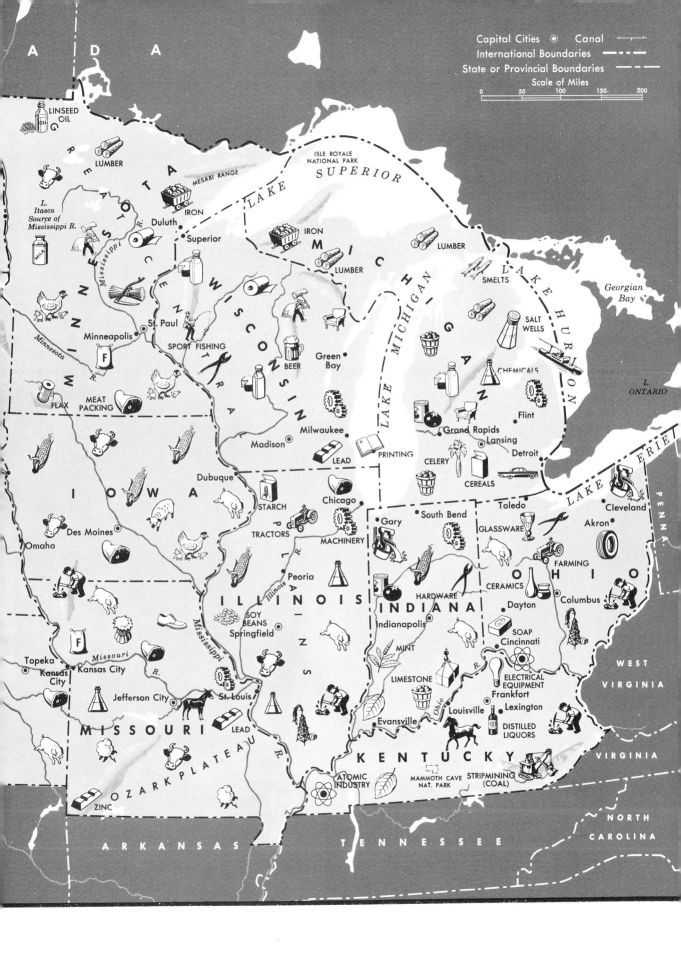

A   D   A

LINSEED OIL

LUMBER

MESABI RANGE

IRON

Duluth

LAKE SUPERIOR

ISLE ROYALE NATIONAL PARK

L. Itasca Source of Mississippi R.

Superior

IRON

M

LUMBER

MILK

Mississippi R.

LUMBER

SMELTS

LAKE HURON

Georgian Bay

Minneapolis

St. Paul

SPORT FISHING

BEER

Green Bay

SALT WELLS

L. ONTARIO

CHEMICALS

FLAX

MEAT PACKING

Milwaukee

Madison

LEAD

PRINTING

CELERY

Grand Rapids

Lansing

Flint

Detroit

CEREALS

IOWA

Dubuque

STARCH

Chicago

Toledo

Cleveland

Akron

PENNA.

Des Moines

TRACTORS

MACHINERY

Gary

South Bend

GLASSWARE

FARMING

Omaha

Peoria

ILLINOIS

HARDWARE

INDIANA

Indianapolis

CERAMICS

Dayton

Columbus

OHIO

SOY BEANS

Springfield

MINT

SOAP

Cincinnati

ELECTRICAL EQUIPMENT

WEST VIRGINIA

Topeka

Kansas City

Missouri R.

Kansas City

LIMESTONE

Frankfort

Louisville

Lexington

Jefferson City

St. Louis

LEAD

Evansville

Ohio R.

DISTILLED LIQUORS

MISSOURI

KENTUCKY

VIRGINIA

OZARK PLATEAU

ATOMIC INDUSTRY

MAMMOTH CAVE NAT. PARK

STRIPMINING (COAL)

ZINC

ARKANSAS

TENNESSEE

NORTH CAROLINA

MINNESOTA

CENTRAL

WISCONSIN

LOWLAND

Minnesota R.

Illinois R.

Mississippi R.

Missouri R.

LAKE MICHIGAN

MICHIGAN

LAKE ERIE

GREAT

THE 4-H CLUBS

Over two million boys and girls in this country belong to the 4-H Clubs. There are almost 90,000 4-H Clubs in our 50 states and Puerto Rico. The 4-H motto is "To Make the Best Better." Most members live in farm communities and are between the ages of 10 and 20. By following the 4-H program, boys and girls learn to be better farmers, home-makers, and citizens.

The 4-H's stand for Head, Heart, Hands, and Health. The emblem of the 4-H club is a four-leaf clover, with an H on each leaf. At their meetings farm boys and girls recite this pledge:

I pledge—
    My Head to clearer thinking,
    My Heart to greater loyalty,
    My Hands to larger service, and
    My Health to better living, for
    My Club, my Community, and my
      Country.

Catholic boys and girls may add another H—for Heaven. They will do all their work with the idea of pleasing God. A boy can raise good food as a corporal work of mercy —"to feed the hungry." A girl can learn to become a good Christian mother and house-keeper.

The 4-H clubs are important to our country. The United States Department of Agriculture in Washington, D.C., directs them. A local leader organizes a group of from 5 to 50 members. The county leader, or county agent, gives him advice and help.

County agents are experts in farming. They are the farmer's friend. Often they visit farms to show the farmer better ways to save his soil. They know where to plant crops in order to get the highest return. They advise the farmer on many other things— how to care for his animals and poultry, how to drain his land, and how to make a pond and stock it with fish.

Here are a few things the 4-H'ers in America did in a single year:

1. raised over 1,000,000 head of livestock.
2. produced over 1,000,000 acres of crops.
3. raised over 9,000,000 chickens, turkeys, and other poultry.
4. preserved over 3,000,000 quarts of food.
5. painted or redecorated 900,000 homes.
6. made 2,000,000 articles of clothing.

Best of all, they learned to live together and work together for a better America. They helped save the soil for future generations. They camped together and learned to understand each other.

Making the Dry Soil Bloom. Rows of vegetables receive life-giving moisture from the irrigation ditches. Without irrigation, they could not grow.

Farms in the Bluegrass Region. In northern Kentucky there is a section called the Bluegrass region. It gets its name from the bluish-green grass which grows there. The rock in this region is mostly soft limestone, which breaks up easily and makes rich soil.

The region has long been famous for the fine horses raised there. The lime in the soil is taken up into the grass and drinking water. It helps the horses who graze on the grass to grow big, strong bones and fine teeth.

Tobacco is an important crop of the Bluegrass region. The city of Louisville is noted as a tobacco market.

Land Use in the Great Plains Region. The western sections of North Dakota, South Dakota, Nebraska, and Kansas lie in the Great Plains region of our country. The Great Plains extend into Oklahoma and Texas in the South, and westward to the foot of the Rocky Mountains. They are dry, grassy plains that gradually rise to higher elevations in the west.

The eastern boundary of the Great Plains is marked by the 20-inch rainfall line. Find this line on the map of rainfall on page 24. West of that line the annual rainfall is 20 inches, or less. The Great Plains are so far from large bodies of water that the winds carry little moisture. The moist winds from the Pacific Ocean have long since lost their moisture on the western slopes of the mountains.

There is good soil and plenty of sunshine on the Great Plains. Crops will grow well wherever they can get enough water. Some farmers of the Great Plains are able to *irrigate* their farms. They do this by digging ditches which conduct water to the farms. Water is obtained either by digging deep wells or by damming up a river.

Among the crops grown on the irrigated lands in the Great Plains region are grasses like alfalfa, clover, and timothy. Wheat, potatoes, melons, and sugar beets are also grown in this region under irrigation.

Facts *to remember*

1. In parts of the Midwest where the soil is thin and the growing season short, the land is used for dairying, cool-climate cereal crops, and forests.
2. Hay is the fourth crop in importance in the United States, after wheat, corn, and cotton. Timothy, clover, and alfalfa grass are sown to make hay. Oats, rye, and barley grow well in the upper Great Lakes regions, where the climate is cool and moist.
3. The region which includes large parts of Wisconsin, Minnesota, and Michigan is the chief dairy area of the United States. The Bluegrass region of Kentucky is famous for its horses.
4. Soybeans are rich in food value and are used to enrich the soil and as food for livestock. Linseed oil is obtained from flaxseed and is used in making paint, varnish, printers' ink, linoleum, and soap.
5. Lumbering is still important in northern Michigan and Wisconsin. These two states, together with Minnesota, produce a large amount of pulp for paper mills.
6. Crops do well under irrigation in the dry, grassy Great Plains, which extend into Oklahoma and Texas in the South, and westward to the foot of the Rocky Mountains.
7. In 4-H Clubs children learn to live and work together for a better America.

What *have I learned?*

Rewrite each statement, using only the item in the parenthesis which correctly completes it.
1. North of the Corn Belt (dairying or cotton-raising) is the most important kind of farming.
2. The growing season is (longer or shorter) in the Hay and Dairy Belt than in the Corn Belt.
3. Hay is best when it is mowed (while it is dry or while it is in flower).
4. The (northern or southern) region of the Midwest has more dairy farms than any other part of our country.
5. Most of the oat crop is used (to feed livestock or to make oatmeal).
6. Chemists have found that soybeans are (poor or rich) in food values for human beings.
7. Winds that blow over the Great Lakes (hasten or delay) frost in the fall.
8. (Few or Many) forest areas remain in the northern parts of Michigan and Wisconsin.
9. Second growth trees are used (for lumber or for wood pulp).
10. The Bluegrass region is in (Kentucky or Indiana).
11. The Great Plains are (close to or far from) large water bodies.
12. "To Make the Best Better" is the motto of (the 4-H Clubs or the Boy Scouts).
13. The North Central States contribute about (three fourths or one third) of the milk products of the United States.
14. Rye is (a vegetable or a grain).
15. Tobacco is an important crop (in the Great Plains region or in the Bluegrass region).

Facts *to understand*

In a complete sentence give a reason for each of these statements.
1. In certain sections of the North Central States, corn and wheat are not grown.
2. Southeastern Wisconsin is a rich dairy region.
3. Only a few forest areas remain in Michigan and Wisconsin.
4. There is little moisture on the Great Plains.
5. The Hay Belt is a good place for dairy cows.
6. Some Dairy Belt farmers ship milk products rather than fresh milk.
7. Fruit grows well along Lakes Michigan and Erie.
8. The Bluegrass Region of Kentucky is famous for the fine horses raised there.
9. Soybeans are becoming a very valuable crop.
10. The 4-H Clubs help to make good Americans and good Catholics.

4
Minerals, Transportation, Manufacturing

The North Central region is not only the "food basket of the nation" but a great "workshop" as well. A large part of the nation's manufactured goods is made in this region. From the very beginning of its settlement, factories sprang up throughout the Midwest.

Why were business men so successful when they started factories in the North Central region? First, the rich natural resources supplied them with raw materials which they needed. Coal, petroleum, and natural gas were available for fuel to turn the wheels in the factories. Iron, copper, and other minerals were plentiful. From them, machinery and other manufactured products could be made. Second, land transportation was good because the land was level. This made it easy to build railroads and highways. In addition, the Great Lakes provided fine water transportation, and so did the Mississippi and some of its more important tributaries. Fine transportation made it possible to bring the fuel and raw materials to the factories at low cost and to carry the manufactured products to markets where they could be sold.

In this chapter you will learn more about the mineral resources of the Midwest.

Fuel Resources. There are large beds of coal and many fields of petroleum and natural gas in the North Central region. Coal is mined in parts of Illinois, Indiana, Kentucky, Ohio, Missouri, and Kansas. It is bituminous, or soft coal. Most of the soft coal lies deep in the earth between layers of rock. It is brought out by miners who must work far below the surface of the earth. In eastern Ohio, however, some soft coal lies close to the surface. It is mined by steam shovels that uncover the layers and scoop up the coal. This is called *strip mining*.

The soft coal is used to make coke for the iron and steel mills around Chicago and Cleveland. It is also used to produce steam for generating plants that supply electricity to Midwestern factories and homes.

Still another fuel, petroleum, is found in Kansas, Illinois, Indiana, and Ohio. You remember reading about oil wells and the uses of oil when you studied the Southern States. While the North Central States do not have nearly so much oil as the South, there is enough in the region to satisfy at least part of the people's needs. Some natural gas is also found with the oil. However, in addition to the region's own supply of oil and gas, some has to be piped in from the South.

Iron Ore. West and south of Lake Superior, in northern Minnesota, there is a world-famous iron-mining district. It is called the Mesabi range and is famous for its *open-pit* iron mines.

No shafts or tunnels have to be dug into the earth to obtain the iron ore. An open-pit iron mine is a wide hole in the ground. In this respect it is like the strip-coal mines of Ohio. But the iron mines in Minnesota are much bigger and deeper than the coal

The World's Largest Iron Mine. Trucks and equipment seem dwarfed in this view of a vast open-pit mine in Minnesota. Note the different levels.

mines in Ohio. Within an open-pit mine, huge shovels pick up tons of iron ore at one time and load it into railroad cars. One of these shovels can do the work of several hundred men.

The Mesabi district once contained the largest iron ore deposit ever discovered. However, by now the richest and most easily mined iron ore from the Mesabi Range has already been used in the blast furnaces of the iron and steel mills. There is still a large amount of ore to be taken out of the ground at Mesabi. This remaining ore, called *taconite,* is not so rich nor easy to mine. However, scientists have found new and profitable ways of taking the iron out of the taconite ore, and the Mesabi region is busy once again.

Copper. In northern Michigan, along the shores of Lake Superior, copper ore is found deep in the earth. It is not easy to mine this copper ore. Unlike the Mesabi iron ore, copper ore has to be removed

Michigan Copper Mine. The ore is conveyed on belts to the top of this hopper. A chute is opened, filling up each car as it passes underneath.

from the earth by digging deep shafts. Some copper mines are more than a mile deep. Copper ore can be obtained much more easily in some of our western states. For this reason, it is not so important in the Midwest as certain other minerals.

Copper is a metal which has many uses. Copper wire is used everywhere to carry electricity. Mixed with other metals, copper is valuable in many industries. Copper mixed with zinc makes brass. Copper and tin make bronze. These mixtures of minerals are called *alloys.* Scientists are making many new alloys for different purposes.

Lead and Zinc. Lead and zinc are found in the Ozark Plateau region of Missouri. Lead is a soft and heavy metal. It is combined with certain chemicals to make *solder,* a soft, easily-melted substance. Solder is used to join other metal pieces together. Lead also has some use in making water pipes. However, its greatest use is in making the lead plates for automobile storage batteries. Sometimes lead is combined with other metals to form alloys which are not so soft as lead but have its qualities of weight and strength.

Zinc is much harder than lead. Buckets, pipes, fences, and other steel objects are covered with zinc to keep them from rusting. The zinc coating is called *galvanizing.* Zinc is used also in many other ways. It can be mixed with copper to form an alloy called brass. Zinc is also used in paint, in certain medicines, and in rubber products.

Joplin, Missouri, became a center of lead and zinc production in the North Central states because it is near the mines. The supply at these mines is almost gone now, but lead and zinc is still shipped into Joplin from mines in other parts of Missouri, and from Kansas and Oklahoma. From Joplin, these metals are then sent to manufacturing areas all over the country.

Tons of Salt. Here you see huge piles of the familiar white substance found on every table. The worker wears a mask to protect himself from dust.

Salt. Salt mines are found in Michigan, Ohio, and Kansas. Scientists tell us the sea once covered these areas and left deposits of salt behind. As time went by, the salt deposits became covered by layers of earth. Now they are far below the surface.

Today, two methods are used to get salt from the mines. One way is to dig a shaft down to the salt beds. Then the salt can be mined like any other mineral. The other method is to bore a hole and sink pipes down to the salt beds. This is called a *salt well*. Water is forced down the pipes, and some of the salt is dissolved. The salty water is then pumped to the surface. Here the water is allowed to evaporate, or pass into the air. The salt remains behind in the flat pans.

Salt from the North Central region, like salt from other areas, has many uses. It is packaged for table and cooking use, it is used in certain chemical industries, and it is sold to livestock producers for their cattle.

Transportation and the Midwest. When the pioneers crossed the Appalachian Mountains into the North Central region, they found a vast area stretching all the way to the Rocky Mountains.

Fortunately, the pioneers found three great rivers in the North Central Region. They are the Missouri, the Ohio, and the Mississippi. The new settlers floated their farm goods down these rivers to New Orleans, on the Gulf of Mexico. Then the goods were put on ocean ships and taken to the eastern part of our country or to other parts of the world.

It was quite simple for farmers and boatmen to get their goods down the river on rafts. But is was almost impossible to get the rafts back up the river against the powerful current. Usually the rafts were broken up at New Orleans and sold for lumber.

Minerals, Transportation, Manufacturing **189**

Partners in Industry. The close ties between transportation and manufacturing can be seen here. Trains and boats carry this factory's products.

In time, better means of transportation came to the Midwest. Roads were built, and horses began to pull wagons and carriages over the roads. Then the steam engine was invented, and steam railroads were built.

Steam engines were also used to push the boats that traveled the rivers and the Great Lakes. With a steam engine, a boat could travel up a river almost as easily as it could travel down. In New York State, the Erie Canal was dug. This connected Lake Erie with the Hudson River. As a result, Midwest farmers could send their products through the Great Lakes, the Erie Canal, and the Hudson River all the way to New York City.

Next came gasoline engines. When these engines were put on carriages, the carriages ran without being pulled by horses. The "horseless carriage" became the first model of our present automobile. Over the years, millions of automobiles and trucks have been carrying people and products over the North Central states.

Transportation and Manufacturing. Mineral resources alone did not make the North Central states a manufacturing region. Good transportation also helped. It did this in three ways.

First, transportation was necessary to bring fuel and raw materials to the factories. It was necessary to take the manufactured goods from the factories to the places where they would be sold.

Second, good transportation enabled many people to come to the Midwest. These people needed many manufactured goods. This meant that more and bigger factories had to be built to supply them.

Third, the means of transportation themselves—railroad trains, trucks, automobiles, and airplanes—had to be manufactured. Almost all the automobiles manufactured in the United States, for example, now come from the Midwest. The huge auto industry is one of the most important in the entire country. It gives work to many thousands of people. Factories in the Midwest also manufacture steel railroad parts and tracks, tractors, airplanes, and large amounts of rubber tires.

Farmers and Manufacturing. The first people to come into the North Central states were farmers, and farming is still very important today. There is a very close connection between farming and manufacturing.

Farmers raise food for the factory workers in the cities. The factory workers must eat in order to live, and almost all their food comes from the farms. Farmers also supply some of the raw materials for mills and factories. Wheat is ground into flour. Corn is made into dry cereals and many other food products. Fruits are made into jams and jellies.

Most important, farmers buy many of the things made in the factories. Factories would have to close down if there were no customers to buy their products. Farmers are good customers for factory products. They buy many of the same things that city people do—automobiles, television sets, refrigerators, and washing machines. They also buy all kinds of farm machinery which city people do not buy.

Just as farmers help manufacturing, so manufacturing helps farmers. With the farm machinery, Midwest farmers are able to raise larger crops. This means more money for the farmers.

Working Together. In this chapter on minerals, transportation, and manufacturing in the North Central states, we have seen that people need each other. Factory workers and other city people could not live if they did not have the food raised by the farmers. Factory workers make farm machinery and other products that are a big help to the farmer. People who work in the mineral industries have an important part to play also. Factories could not engage in manufacturing if they did not have fuel and raw materials.

It takes thousands of miners, oil workers, and others to bring the fuels and other minerals out of the ground. The minerals must

Shipping Tractors by Rail. The great farm districts throughout the Midwest depend on the railroads to transport necessary machines and equipment.

be taken to the factories. So must other raw materials. This is the job of the railroad men, truck drivers, and other transportation workers. The transportation workers must also carry the manufactured products to the people who wish to buy them.

In the Midwest, as in every other section of our country, the different kinds of workers need each other. We can learn an important lesson from this. No matter where we are or what we do, we depend upon a great many other people.

THE McCORMICK REAPER

The *reaper* is one example of the way Midwest farmers help manufacturing. At one time, farmers had to cut their crops with hand tools. It was hard, slow work. Then a man named Cyrus McCormick invented a machine called a *reaper* which would be pulled by horses. It harvested more grain than could be harvested by many men working with hand tools, such as scythes and sickles.

The reaper would not work well on the hilly, stony farms of New England, but it worked fine on the wide, level fields of the Midwest. Cyrus McCormick built a large factory near Chicago. Before long, he was selling many reapers to the farmers of the Midwest. He had to make his factory larger.

In time, many improvements were made in the reaper. When the gasoline engine was invented, the reaper no longer had to be pulled by horses. It could work even better when pulled by the faster and more dependable tractor.

Facts *to remember*

1. Early in the history of the United States, manufacturing became an important industry in the North Central region. It is an ideal area for factories because it has raw materials and good land and water transportation.

2. The Midwest has large beds of bituminous coal, which is used to make coke and to generate electricity. It has many fields of petroleum and natural gas. Some gas and oil must be piped in from the South.

3. Large deposits of iron ore from the Mesabi range in northern Minnesota have been used, but scientists have found ways of using the taconite ore now mined there. There are also deposits of copper, lead, zinc, and salt.

4. Pioneers used the Missouri, the Ohio, and the Mississippi rivers to transport goods to New Orleans or to the Gulf of Mexico. Road construction, the steam engine, and the horseless carriage solved the east-west transportation problem.

5. Good transportation helped make the North Central States a manufacturing region because it brought fuel and raw materials to the factories, brought many people to the Midwest, and caused conveyances to be manufactured.

6. People engaged in mining, transportation, and manufacturing find that they need one another.

What *have I learned?*

I

On a separate piece of paper, write each statement, using only the word or words in the parenthesis that make it correct.

1. Factories in the North Central States were successful because of (good transportation, good soil, government).

2. Bituminous coal is used for (making paper, coke, home heating).

3. The (Midwestern, Southern, New England) States have the most oil.

4. The Mesabi range is famous for (iron ore, salt, copper).

5. Copper is used in (galvanizing, synthetics, electrical wiring).

6. Taconite is an ore which yields (copper, lead, iron).

7. (The Ohio, The Penobscot, The Hudson) is a great river in the Midwest.

8. An invention that aided transportation in the Midwest was (the cotton gin, the reaper, the steam engine).

9. The Midwest became a manufacturing region because good transportation brought (raw materials, food products, irrigation).

10. (Negroes, factory workers, manufacturers, farmers) were the first to come to the North Central States.

II

Copy each item in Column A. Opposite each, write the item from Column B which best matches it.

Column A	Column B
1. Alloy	good, cheap water transportation
2. Taconite	
3. Lead	Mesabi Range
	Ohio
4. Iron ore	Copper mixed with zinc
5. Reaper	metal coated with zinc
	automobiles
6. Great Lakes	produced mostly in
7. Solder	Joplin, Missouri
8. Galvanized	inferior iron ore
	cement for joining metals
9. Horseless carriages	mineral used for flavoring
	important piece of farm equipment
10. Strip-coal mines	
11. Copper	brought into the Midwest from the South
12. Salt	transportation to Gulf of Mexico ports
13. Brass	
14. Natural gas	a mixture of different minerals
15. Rivers of the Midwest	found in northern Michigan

Facts *to understand*

Give a reason for each statement.

1. The surface of the North Central region helped to make it a manufacturing area.

2. The reaper helped industry and the farmer.

3. The presence of raw materials allowed the Midwest to have many factories.

4. Transportation aided the manufacturing in the Midwest.

5. Different kinds of workers need one another.

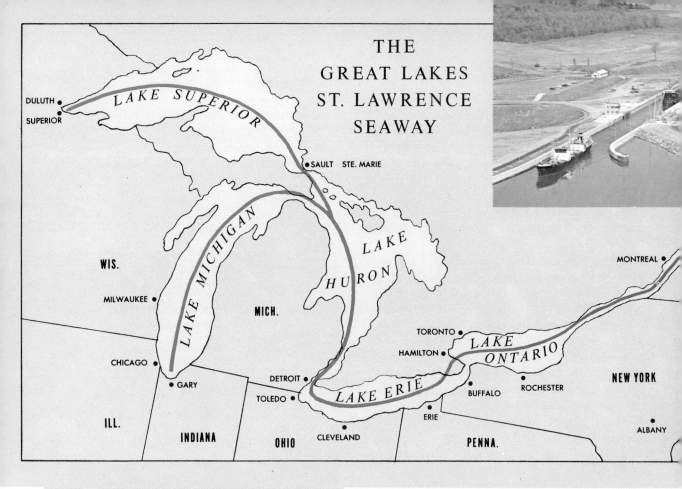

THE
GREAT LAKES
ST. LAWRENCE
SEAWAY

DULUTH
SUPERIOR
LAKE SUPERIOR
SAULT STE. MARIE
LAKE MICHIGAN
LAKE HURON
MONTREAL
WIS.
MILWAUKEE
MICH.
TORONTO
HAMILTON
LAKE ONTARIO
NEW YORK
CHICAGO
ROCHESTER
GARY
DETROIT
BUFFALO
TOLEDO
LAKE ERIE
ERIE
ALBANY
ILL.
INDIANA
OHIO
CLEVELAND
PENNA.

5

Cities of the North Central States

Cities grow for various reasons, but the chief reason is manufacturing. In the Northeast, where there is much manufacturing, we find many large cities. In the South, where there is less manufacturing, we find fewer large cities. However, the cities of the South will continue to grow as manufacturing grows.

In the last chapter we read how mineral

From Inland to the Sea. Freighters pass through the Eisenhower Lock (inset above) and the Welland Canal (right), important links in this waterway.

resources and good transportation helped the growth of manufacturing in the North Central states. This means we should expect to find many large cities in this region. It contains four of the ten largest cities in the United States. They are Chicago, Detroit, Cleveland, and St. Louis. Look at the map on pages 158 and 159, and find these four cities. Each has good water transportation.

Ports on the Great Lakes. Look at the map of the North Central region on pages 158 and 159. Find the Great Lakes and the major cities along their shores. The cities on the Great Lakes are far from the ocean; yet many of them are really ocean ports today, thanks to the St. Lawrence Seaway.

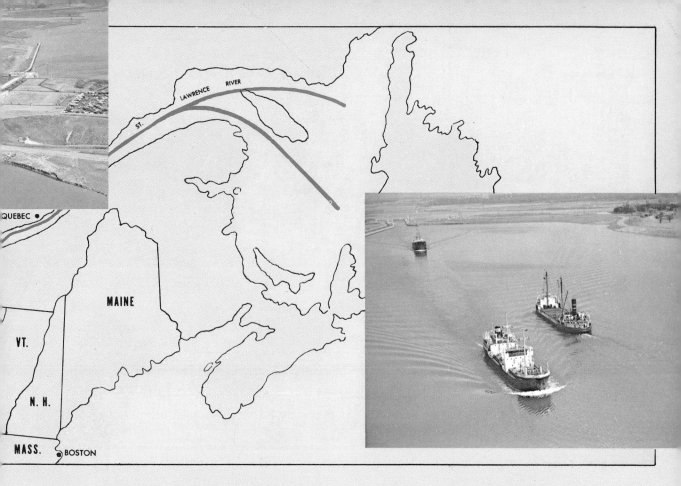

QUEBEC

MAINE

VT.

N. H.

MASS.   BOSTON

The governments of Canada and the United States worked together for years to build the St. Lawrence Seaway, and it was completed in 1959. As a result, all but the very largest ocean vessels can now sail up the St. Lawrence River from the Atlantic Ocean to the Great Lakes.

Of course, the ports on the Great Lakes were busy long before the Seaway was built. The lakes were an ideal water route between the cities which lie along their edges. Today, however, these cities carry on trade with the rest of the world as well. Study the diagram of the St. Lawrence Seaway above and below to see how it operates.

Men deepened the channel of the St. Lawrence River, dug canals, and built dams so that big ships could come into the Great Lakes. But they cannot keep the waterway open all year round. Why?

From November to March the lakes are frozen. Some years, ice blocks the harbors until late in April. This means that the boats must do all their work in six or seven months of the year. During the summer months, boats and ships race against time to carry minerals, grains, and manufactured goods to their destinations. During the coldest winter months, other means of transportation have to be used.

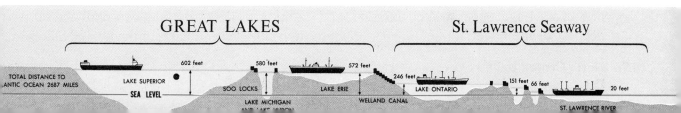

GREAT LAKES   St. Lawrence Seaway

TOTAL DISTANCE TO ATLANTIC OCEAN 2687 MILES   602 feet   580 feet   572 feet   246 feet   151 feet   66 feet   20 feet

LAKE SUPERIOR   SEA LEVEL   SOO LOCKS   LAKE MICHIGAN AND LAKE HURON   LAKE ERIE   WELLAND CANAL   LAKE ONTARIO   ST. LAWRENCE RIVER

Lake Freighter. This enormous ship is taking on iron ore at Duluth, a major Lake Superior port. It loads 35,000 tons of ore in only three hours.

Duluth and Superior. Let's take a trip on the Great Lakes. We shall begin our trip on a freighter in the port of Duluth, Minnesota. This city is at the western tip of Lake Superior. Nearby is the city of Superior, Wisconsin. Large amounts of iron ore from the Mesabi district are shipped from both cities. Wheat from the Spring Wheat Belt is also shipped from these cities, and so is lumber from the forests of Wisconsin and Minnesota. Boats returning to these cities bring coal from Pennsylvania and West Virginia. Some coal is used to make coke for the iron and steel mills in Duluth.

Our ship is loaded at Duluth with a cargo of spring wheat. It will go to the flour mills in Buffalo on Lake Erie. We first cross Lake Superior, the largest and deepest of the Great Lakes.

The "Soo Canal". Our ship enters the St. Mary River, which flows from Lake Superior into Lake Huron. At the city of Sault Sainte Marie, the level of the river falls 20 feet. The fall makes rapids in the river which are unsafe for ships and boats. A canal with locks has to take the boats up and down by "water steps." This canal is called "Soo" for short. The Soo is the busiest canal in the world.

Once our ship passes through the Soo Canal, we are sailing on Lake Huron. Sailing southward, we pass through the St. Clair River, then the St. Clair Lake, and finally enter the Detroit River. We pass the city of Detroit and enter Lake Erie.

Eastward to Buffalo. On Lake Erie, we can sail as far as Buffalo, New York. For a short time we leave the North Central region and enter the Middle Atlantic region. Some cities, like Buffalo, can really be said to be in several regions of the United States.

In the port of Buffalo there are large *grain elevators*. These are huge warehouses waiting for the spring wheat our ship carries. We watch the men unload our cargo and store it in the grain elevator. It will remain there until the mills are ready to use it.

The Welland Canal. Joining Lake Erie with Lake Ontario is the Niagara River. It is 33 miles long. Near Lake Ontario, the waters of the river drop suddenly. This is the famous Niagara Falls. Below the falls, water is churned into foam along a turning, twisting gorge seven miles long.

Our ship could go around the falls by using the Welland Canal, but we do not wish to go farther. Canada built the Welland Canal. Using it, ships can go out through Lake Ontario into the St. Lawrence River, and then to the Atlantic Ocean. From Duluth to the Atlantic Ocean is a journey of 2350 miles.

After a few days, we leave Buffalo on a Great Lakes passenger ship heading west again toward Chicago. Our ship will make stops at the most important Great Lakes ports. These port cities are also great manufacturing centers.

Cleveland. Cleveland, with a population of more than one million people, is the largest city on Lake Erie and the largest city in the state of Ohio. Factories in the Cleveland area make heavy steel products such as lake freighters, diesel and electric locomotives, motor trucks, auto bodies, aircraft, and all kinds of valuable machine tools. Oil refineries are numerous in Cleveland, and clay industries continue here from early days.

Cleveland has great iron and steel mills. It receives iron ore from both directions on Lake Erie. Iron ore from Labrador comes through the St. Lawrence River into Lake Erie. Iron ore from the Mesabi region

The Soo Canal. An ore freighter is steaming through the world's busiest canal. The locks operate like elevators, raising and lowering the ship.

comes by way of Lake Superior and Lake Huron. Ships unload their iron ore and return loaded with coal from the Appalachian coal fields.

At Cleveland we also see trucks piled high with auto tires. They come from the city of Akron, Ohio, just to the south of Cleveland. Akron produces more rubber tires than any other city in the world. Each year, the rubber companies of Akron make millions of tires of all sizes for automobiles, airliners, tractors, bicycles, and baby carriages. They also produce huge quantities of rubber footwear and raincoats. The giant balloons used in airships are made in Akron. Fire hose and bathing caps are among the many other products of Akron, the "Rubber Capital" of America.

Airplane Tires. These huge tires have been especially made for use on a giant airliner. They are being shipped from Akron to Cleveland by truck.

Exchanging Cargoes. Here at Toledo, a lake freighter unloads iron ore and takes on a cargo of coal. These ships seldom make a trip with empty holds.

Toledo. Leaving Cleveland, we sail west on Lake Erie to Toledo. We find that it is located on a small river flowing into Lake Erie. It, too, has advantages for trade and manufacturing. Iron ore is received by boat, and coal is brought in by rail. Pipe lines

bring petroleum to Toledo's many refineries. Large ships called *tankers* carry gasoline and oil from Toledo to the other lake cities.

With cheap fuel at hand, and much good sand nearby, Toledo has also become a great glass manufacturing center. Glass is made mostly to supply the need for automobile windows and windshields, as well as for other industries which require glass and fiberglass. The factories of Toledo also supply the automobile industry with small parts such as spark plugs.

Detroit, the Automobile City. From Toledo, our ship sails north on Lake Erie into the Detroit River. We dock at Detroit, one of the largest and busiest cities in the United States. At the piers on the Detroit River and the Rouge River, we see vessels from many parts of the world. They are bringing tons of raw materials for the factories of this city. They will take away autos, machine tools, chemicals, paper, and farm implements.

Automobile Factory. At Detroit, workers are busy putting locks on car doors. Hoods to cover the engines are not yet in place — do you know why?

Mackinac Bridge. Here you see one end of the world's largest suspension bridge. In the foreground, a family takes snapshots along the lake shore.

Detroit is the center of the automobile industry. Large ships can easily carry raw material and finished products to and from the cities on the St. Lawrence Seaway. Even more important is the fact that many of the raw materials needed by the automobile industry are nearby. Coal and iron ore are available for making the iron and steel. Auto workers need food, of course. Fresh vegetables, fruits, milk, meat, and other foods are produced on nearby farms.

Detroit is in a section of the United States where there is a ready market for automobiles. People on the farms and in cities want to buy automobiles. The automobile industry got an early start in Detroit. Companies in the Detroit area once built wagons and carriages. When the automobile was invented, the skilled wagon builders began making automobile bodies. They made them first with lumber and then later with metal. As the demand for cars increased, more factories opened in and near Detroit.

Detroit ranks second only to Chicago as the largest manufacturing city in the Midwest. The automobile industry caused other industries to grow up in the Detroit area— among them are steel mills, glass works, oil refineries, rubber factories, and chemical plants. Do you wonder that it is a crowded, busy city?

After our tour of Detroit we again board the lake steamer. It sails north, crossing Lake Huron. Finally, we sail through the Straits of Mackinac under the great Mackinac Bridge which connects the upper and lower peninsulas of the state of Michigan. It is the world's largest suspension bridge.

Milwaukee. Sailing south on Lake Michigan, we reach Milwaukee, Wisconsin, on the western shore of the lake. Milwaukee's harbor on Lake Michigan is excellent. Freighters bring coal from the Appalachians for the city's industries. Wheat, iron, copper, and lumber are brought to the city from the surrounding areas.

There are meat-packing, textile, glass-making, and farm-implement factories in Milwaukee. The city is also famous for the fine beer made in its breweries.

The nearby cities of Racine and Kenosha, also in Wisconsin, manufacture electrical machinery and automobiles.

Busy Chicago. This view looks east across the Chicago River. Notice the many bridges, the modern highway, and the tall office buildings downtown.

Our Second Largest City. Chicago, near the southern tip of Lake Michigan, is the largest city in the North Central states and second largest in the country. Only New York City is larger. Over three and one half million people live and work in the city of Chicago. Many more people live in Chicago's many suburbs.

Chicago has always been an important trading city. Grain comes in from western cities. It is stored and later shipped from Chicago. Oil comes by pipe line, river barge, and rail from the Gulf Coast states. Coal and iron ore come by Lake freighters.

Coal also arrives by way of rail and barge from the southern Illinois coal fields. Livestock from the northern plains and from the Corn Belt arrive by rail. Sulphur, fiber, sugar, and chemicals arrive from the South by way of the Mississippi and Illinois Rivers.

The railroad was introduced in Chicago about one hundred years ago. Today, Chicago is the greatest railroad center in the world. Many railroad lines cross Chicago, or link up at Chicago with other lines going north, south, east, and west.

Chicago is a great meat-packing center. Many farmers and stock-men ship their cattle, hogs, and sheep to Chicago. The livestock is kept in stockyards. The animals are brought from the stockyards to the meat-packing plants where they are slaughtered. The skin or hide is removed. Next the animals are *dressed*. This means removing those parts which cannot be used for meat. Then the meat is cut, inspected, and graded according to its quality.

Some of the meat is hung in great ice-boxes until ready for shipping. Some is quick-frozen and stored in freezer plants. Refrigerator cars and trucks carry the meat to all sections of the country. Some of the meat is processed before it leaves the packing plant by cooking, smoking, salting, or baking.

Chicago is also an educational center. Many fine universities and colleges are located in and around the city. One of the finest and largest systems of Catholic schools in the United States has grown up in the Archdiocese of Chicago. The Catholic population in this city is very large.

Chicago is sometimes called the "Windy

The Chicago Stockyards. Steers and hogs fattened in the Corn Belt are shipped by rail to Chicago. They are then kept in pens until the slaughter.

City." It is windy because a large body of water—Lake Michigan—lies northeast of

Crossroads of Transportation. A view south over the world's busiest railroad center shows miles and miles of track near the Chicago River shore.

The Growth of Chicago. This skyline view shows the many new parks, offices, and residence buildings that are being built in modern Chicago.

it. The winds which arise over large bodies of water are usually quite strong. Also, the

Recreation Center. This is Lincoln Park in Chicago. Many visitors are attracted daily to its famous gardens, art museums, and conservatories.

wide level plains to the west and south leave Chicago open to winds blowing from the west and the south.

With our stop at Chicago, we bring to an end our trip on the Great Lakes.

River Cities. We have just seen the large number of Midwest cities which lie along the shores of the Great Lakes. Other important North Central cities are on or near the Mississippi River and two of its tributaries, the Ohio and Missouri rivers.

The Twin Cities. The cities of St. Paul and Minneapolis in Minnesota are on opposite sides of the Mississippi River and are called "the Twin Cities." Minneapolis, the larger city, began as a sawmill town, using the waterpower of the Mississippi at the Falls of St. Anthony. The falls also made power for grinding wheat into flour. Minneapolis remains an important flour-milling city today. St. Paul, the other "twin," is the capital of Minnesota. St. Paul is as far up the river as steamboats can go. Like Minneapolis, it is a trading center for the surrounding farm area. It has large meat-packing plants. Canadian skins and furs are bought and sold in St. Paul.

There are hundreds of lakes within a short distance of the Twin Cities. Many people go there for recreation. Fishing and camping are popular outdoor sports in this region.

St. Louis on the Mississippi. The city of St. Louis, Missouri, is on the Mississippi River just below the spot where it is joined by the Missouri. St. Louis is an important river port and a great railroad center.

From the early days of our country, St. Louis has been a trading post for furs. It is still a center for the fur industry, receiving furs from Louisiana especially.

St. Louis today is a manufacturing center. Raw materials for its factories come from all directions. Fuel for its factories

St. Paul, Minnesota. A bridge crosses the Mississippi at Robert Street, St. Paul. This "twin" is famous as a meat-packing and fur-trading center.

comes from the coal fields of south Illinois and also from the oil fields of Oklahoma and Texas. Some important manufactured products of St. Louis are aluminum, oil, chemicals, meat, airplanes, farm tools,

Minneapolis. Using the water power of the Mississippi River, the many mills of this Minnesota "twin" have always turned out great amounts of flour.

Ohio River Scene. The "Delta Queen", last of the old stern-wheel river boats, passes the city of Louisville on its way southward to New Orleans.

leather and shoes, and a variety of other different machines and goods.

Since early days, many Catholics have made their home in St. Louis. There are many beautiful Catholic churches and schools in this city. St. Louis University is a famous Jesuit school.

Famous River Port. Looking across the Ohio River, you can see downtown Cincinnati, Ohio. Many items are shipped from this city's factories.

East St. Louis, in Illinois, is a large city across the Mississippi River from the city of St. Louis. Bridges join the two cities.

Cincinnati. Since the days of the steamboats, Cincinnati, Ohio, has been an important river port on the Ohio River. This city is located on a beautiful spot not far from the place where the Ohio River bends northward. Find it on the map on page 159. Spring floods on the Ohio have damaged the lower parts of the city from time to time.

Huge plants line both sides of the Ohio River at Cincinnati. Some of the older plants turn out machine tools, clothing and shoes, paper, and heating equipment. Now newer plants are working on atomic energy and chemicals. River barges and railroad cars bring in coal from the Appalachian coal fields. Iron and steel are obtained from the Pittsburgh district.

Louisville. Louisville, Kentucky, is famous as a tobacco market for the tobacco farms of the Bluegrass region of Kentucky. Because of its location, Louisville has always been a trading center. At one time,

ONE NATION UNDER GOD

You have been studying about the United States for some time now. You have learned that our country is one blessed with the material things of this world. Farms and forests, fisheries and prairies, mountains and valleys, rivers and lakes—all are part of the great wealth which our country enjoys.

Huge factories are found throughout our land, giving worthwhile employment to millions of people and producing the many good things of life which we use daily. We Americans have good food, and more of it than most people in the world. We have tremendous amounts of cheap electricity, we have cars, trains, and airplanes to make travel a pleasure, and we have many parks and playgrounds for our recreation.

Wonderful as these things are, they alone do not make a strong nation. It is the people who make this country strong, and the people draw their strength from God. The families of America, working together, praying together, and cherishing one another,

The Church at Work. The National Shrine has just been built in Washington. The NCWC sends food all over the world. A missioner preaches from his trailer-chapel.

The Church at Prayer. In your daily prayers, never forget to pray for our country, that we may enjoy the blessing of peace.

dren in other lands. The National Catholic Welfare Conference sends food, medicine, and other necessary items overseas from Catholics who have gladly donated them.

"More things are wrought by prayer than this world dreams of." Americans should find it easy to pray. God has been good to this land. America was founded by religious people, religious freedom is part of our nation's law, and we daily pledge our allegiance to "one nation, under God."

Hour by hour, day by day, year in and year out, the prayers of the Church ascend to God. Bishops and priests, during their daily Masses, pray that this land may enjoy the blessing of peace and thank God for His magnificent gifts. The little child who kneels to say her night prayers, the laborer who pauses to say grace before his lunch, the busy mother who makes a visit to the Blessed Sacrament, and the Sister who offers her daily Rosary—all add to the huge chorus of praise to God. The prayer of the Church is that this nation, under God, may continue to serve Him and give thanks for His many blessings.

provide America's most important natural resource.

Schools and churches fill our cities and towns, and splendid cathedrals and shrines glorify God and our nation. These schools and churches form the young men and women of today who will be the leaders and parents of the future. The great strength of America is in its people, and the schools and churches which make young Americans devoted to God and proud of their land.

The National Shrine to the Immaculate Conception in Washington, D.C., draws millions of Catholics yearly to honor our Blessed Mother. Yet there are many more millions, even in our own land, who have not been granted the great gift of Faith. These millions are yearning to hear the Word of God, and many Catholic missioners are bringing to them the good news of salvation.

Catholics show their thanks to God for His many blessings on America by sharing their blessings with His less fortunate chil-

The Leadership of the Church. Our bishops, our priests, and our teachers show us how to be good Catholics and Americans.

Kansas City, Missouri. In the background is Kansas City, Kansas. The elevated highway joining the two cities is called the Interstate Viaduct.

the falls in the Ohio River forced boats to stop and unload at this point. A town grew up to care for the trade. Today, a canal enables ships to go around the falls.

Other Midwest Cities. Where the Missouri River forms the boundary between Kansas and Missouri, there are two cities with the same name. They are both called Kansas City. To the visitor they would seem to be one city, but they have different governments because they are in different states. Kansas City, Missouri, is larger than Kansas City, Kansas, and has about three times as many people. Both cities are grain and livestock markets.

Kansas City, Missouri, is also a center for the aircraft industry. Omaha, Nebraska, is a railroad center, livestock market, and flour-milling city. In the center of Indiana is the state's capital—Indianapolis. It is an important railroad and trading center.

Columbus is an industrial city and the capital of Ohio. It is in the center of the state. In the center of Illinois is its capital city, Springfield. The tomb and monument of Abraham Lincoln is in a beautiful park in Springfield, Illinois. Lincoln lived in Springfield as a young man and practiced law there.

There are only a few large cities west of the Mississippi River. Fargo, North Dakota, and Sioux Falls, South Dakota, are the largest cities in the Spring Wheat Belt.

Topeka, Kansas, is a railroad center with large railroad repair shops. Wichita, Kansas, is noted for its airplane works. Lincoln, Nebraska, distributes farm products. The capital and leading city of Iowa is Des Moines. It has many meat-packing houses.

Cities of the North Central States 207

A FARM BOY USES HIS HEAD

On a Michigan farm a boy named Henry Ford used to tinker with machinery whenever he could. He left his father's farm to work for an engine company. Henry was an industrious young man. In the evenings he repaired clocks and watches. Soon, he got a better job as chief engineer for the electric light company in Detroit, Michigan. He kept thinking about the new automobiles that only a few people could afford to buy. He thought, "If watches can be made for everyone, why cannot automobiles be made for everyone?"

One day, Henry Ford borrowed some money, rented a factory, and set up the Ford Motor Company. He hired workers and paid them good wages. He put the best materials into the cars he made in his plant. Ford soon worked out a new system by which each worker does only one job in the manufacture of a car.

Ford's workers did not walk from car to car. The cars, placed on a moving belt came to the men. This was soon called the *assembly line*. It was Ford's own invention and has become the way in which most manufacturing is done today.

This new way of making autos turned out finished products faster and cheaper than the old way. *Mass production* methods started to appear in many different kinds of factories throughout our country and Europe.

Other manufacturers copied Ford's methods. Good small cars soon were selling at a price almost anyone could pay. Many people bought them. In a few years our highways became jammed with cars and trucks and buses. Today, the automobile has become a familiar part of every American's life.

The use of so many cars increased the need for other services. New highways had to be built. Asphalt and concrete pavement made the roads smooth and even. The need grew for service stations, motels, and eating places all along America's miles of major highways. Millions of people are now affected daily by the automobile, made possible by the ideas of a Midwest farm boy.

Facts *to remember*

1. The chief reason for the growth of cities is manufacturing, together with the presence of good water transportation. Chicago, Detroit, Cleveland, and St. Louis—four of the ten largest cities in the United States—are in the North Central region.
2. The St. Lawrence Seaway makes many cities, far from the ocean, really ocean ports which carry on trade with the whole world. The Seaway is frozen from November to March, and other means of transportation must then be used.
3. The Soo is the busiest canal in the world. It connects Lake Superior with Lake Huron. The Welland Canal permits ships to go out through Lake Ontario from Lake Erie into the St. Lawrence River, and then to the Atlantic Ocean.
4. Cleveland, with a population of more than one million people, is the largest city on Lake Erie and the largest city in Ohio. The Cleveland area is noted for heavy steel products, valuable machine tools, oil refineries, and clay industries.
5. Detroit is one of the largest and busiest cities in the United States. Its location gives it a ready market for automobiles.
6. Chicago, near the southern tip of Lake Michigan, is the second largest city in the United States, next to New York City. In it over three and one half million people live and work. Chicago is an important trading and meat-packing center, and is the greatest railroad center in the world.
7. From early days of our country, St. Louis has been a trading center for the fur industry. Today, it is a manufacturing center, receiving raw materials for its factories from all regions of the country.
8. Cincinnati has been an important port on the Ohio River since the days of the steamboat.
9. Millions of people are now affected daily by the automobile, made possible by the ideas and ambition of a Midwest farm boy, Henry Ford. He also invented the assembly line, which gave us the mass-production method.

What *have I learned?*

I

On a separate piece of paper, identify the following cities and canals:

1. I am located near iron and coal deposits. I am

the center of the automobile industry.

2. I am the largest city on Lake Erie. Factories in my area make heavy steel products.

3. Although I am located on a small river, I have become a great glass-manufacturing city.

4. I was built by the governments of the United States and Canada, and I allow ocean vessels to go from the Atlantic Ocean to the Great Lakes.

5. I am on the western shore of Lake Michigan and am famous for fine beer.

6. I am the greatest railroad center in the world.

7. I am the busiest canal in the world.

8. I am a manufacturing center, as well as a center for the fur industry.

9. I am located on the Ohio River. I have plants that are now working on atomic energy and chemicals.

10. I am a center for the aircraft industry. I am larger than another city of my name.

11. I am located near the tip of Lake Michigan, and I am a great meat-packing center.

12. I am an important flour-milling city. I am a twin.

13. I am the capital of Indiana, as well as an important railroad and trading center in the heart of a rich farm area.

14. Ships can use me to go around Niagara Falls.

15. I am proud of one of my farm boys who, by inventing the assembly line, made the automobile possible for nearly everyone.

II

The word in italics makes each sentence right or wrong. If wrong, rewrite the sentence, using the correct word.

1. During the *winter* months, parts of the Great Lakes waterway cannot be used.

2. The city of Duluth, Minnesota, is at the *eastern* tip of Lake Superior.

3. The *Welland Canal* is the busiest canal in the world.

4. *Cincinnati,* Ohio, is the largest city on the shores of Lake Erie.

5. Akron, Ohio is famous for the many different *rubber* products made there.

6. The city of *Racine,* Wisconsin, is famous for its fine beer.

7. Detroit, Michigan, is the center of the *automobile industry.*

8. The city of *Chicago,* Illinois, is a great meat-packing center.

9. St. Paul, Minnesota, and Minneapolis, Minnesota are on opposite sides of the *Missouri River.*

10. *St. Louis,* Missouri, is a center of the fur industry.

Facts *to understand*

Answer the following questions in a sentence or two.

1. Why are there large cities in important manufacturing areas?

2. What reason may be given for most large cities being on good water-transportation routes?

3. Of what value is the St. Lawrence Seaway?

4. Why are so many large cities situated on the Great Lakes or on the Mississippi?

5. How has the automobile industry helped other manufacturers?

6. How do the lake freighters manage to have full cargoes sailing west as well as east?

7. What is the transportation importance of the Welland Canal?

8. What are the advantages which Detroit enjoys, and which make it the center of the automobile industry?

9. Why is Chicago sometimes called "the windy city?"

10. In what ways do Kansas City, Missouri, and Kansas City, Kansas, differ from each other?

Unit Four Review

Questions for Discussion and Review

1. Why may we call the North Central States "the food basket of the nation"? **2.** How has the surface of the Midwest helped it become a great farming and manufacturing area? **3.** Account for the importance of the corn crop in the Midwest. **4.** Explain the fact that other countries do not eat so much meat as we do. **5.** Why are there so many large cities in the North Central region? **6.** Describe the work of the glacier in forming the rich soils of the Midwest. **7.** Why do we say that the North Central States is a region of changeable weather? **8.** What has the use of machinery done to help crop production in the Midwest? **9.** Why is this region particularly suitable to the use of farm machinery? **10.** Describe the importance of the railroads to the growth of Midwestern farms and manufacturing. **11.** How did the Indians live and work in the North Central region before the coming of the white settlers? **12.** Describe the importance of the buffalo to the early Indians. **13.** List the crops which Corn Belt farmers grow to rotate their corn fields. **14.** Describe the planting, growing, and harvesting of winter wheat. **15.** How can you account for the fact that Buffalo, New York, is the leading flour-producing city, even though it is far from the wheat belts? **16.** What are some of the uses to which soybeans are now being put? **17.** In which parts of the Midwest is lumbering still an important industry? **18.** What are the advantages to an individual boy or girl in belonging to a 4-H Club? **19.** Describe some of the uses for copper, lead, and zinc. **20.** How have the cities along the Great Lakes become ocean ports in addition to being lake ports?

Using the Maps and Globe

1. Measure the width and the length of the North Central region. Use the scale of miles to estimate how long and how wide an area you studied about in Unit Four.
2. Trace the bodies of water you would sail on if you made a trip from the Atlantic Ocean to Detroit.
3. Locate Chicago, Detroit, Cleveland, and St. Louis, and indicate the methods of transportation each uses for trade.
4. Use the wall map to explain why Detroit is ideally located as a ready market for automobiles.
5. Use the physical-political map to describe the surface of the Midwest.

Using Geography Words

Here is a list of special words that have been used in Unit Four. Write a sentence using each word to prove that you know its meaning in geography.

humus	*belts*	*harvester combine*
tornado	*reaper*	*strip farming*
elevator	*bales*	*open-pit mining*
	irrigate	

Getting Information from Books

Read reference books such as *Compton's Pictured Encyclopedia* for information on the following topics. Prepare to give an oral or written report.

Henry Ford	St. Lawrence Seaway
reaper	Great Plains
silo	buffalo
Father Marquette	Chicago fire
railroads	Mesabi Iron Range

Final Test

Write each sentence on your paper, choosing the correct word or words from the parenthesis.
1. (Wheat, Corn, Oats) is a cool-climate cereal crop.
2. The (Welland, Soo, Suez) Canal joins Lake Erie with Lake Ontario.
3. Many (chickens, buffalo, fish) are raised in the Corn Belt.
4. (Timothy, Clover, Alfalfa) is the chief hay crop in the northern part of the Midwest.
5. (Bran, Straw, Hay) is high in food value and is made into cereals.
6. (Cyrus McCormick, Henry Ford, Thomas Edison) made mass production possible.
7. (Iron, Zinc, Petroleum) is a fuel.
8. An important product of flaxseed is (linen, linseed oil, nylon).
9. The most important food crop in the United States is (corn, wheat, cotton).
10. The North Central region is mostly (mountainous, plain, desert).
11. The word that best describes the weather of the Midwest is (mild, hot, changeable).
12. (Milwaukee, Detroit, Chicago) is the second largest city in the United States.
13. (Sweet, Hybrid, Field) corn is used as a vegetable.
14. (Corn, Rye, Tobacco) is a leading crop of the Midwest.
15. (Open-pit mining, Strip farming, Baling) prevents soil erosion.
16. Louisville, Kentucky, is famous as a trading center for (furs, tobacco, corn).
17. The "Twin Cities" are Minneapolis and (Kansas City, St. Louis, St. Paul).
18. (Toledo, Cleveland, Detroit) is famous as a Midwestern glass-producing city.
19. The (Soo, Welland, St. Clair) is the busiest canal in the world.
20. (Cleveland, Chicago, Detroit) is the largest city on the shores of Lake Erie.
21. Wheat is stored in tall buildings called (silos, barns, elevators).

22. Brass is an alloy of (copper and lead, zinc and lead, copper and zinc).

23. The Bluegrass region of Kentucky is famous for (dairy cows, horses, mules).

24. Minnesota, Michigan, and Wisconsin are sometimes called (the Corn Belt, the Great Plains, the Land of Lakes).

25. Corn is sometimes used to make (plastics, syrup, nylon and rayon).

Copy Column A. Opposite each product in Column A, write the name of the state from Column B which leads in its production.

Column A	Column B
1. corn	Kansas
2. spring wheat	Wisconsin
3. winter wheat	Iowa
4. milk products	Missouri
5. horses	Minnesota
6. iron ore	North Dakota
7. lead	Kentucky

Copy Column A. Opposite each item in Column A, write the name of the city in Column B which best fits it.

Column A	Column B
1. automobiles	Chicago
2. stockyards	Milwaukee
3. tires	
4. beer	Cincinnati
5. flour	Cleveland
6. Ohio River port	Detroit
7. steel center on Lake Erie	Akron
8. port on Lake Superior	Duluth
	Minneapolis

Applying Christian Principles

1. We show that we depend upon other people when **a.** we pull the weeds in the garden **b.** we wash dishes **c.** we trade farm goods for manufactured goods.

2. God's gifts of fertile soil, wooded forests, and herds of useful animals found in the Midwest were best appreciated by the **a.** Indians **b.** white settlers **c.** French explorers.

3. A girl can be most pleasing to God when she **a.** becomes popular **b.** learns how to become a good Christian mother **c.** learns how to invest her money.

4. People living in the "heartland" of the United States practice the corporal works of mercy best when they **a.** share their prosperity with other nations **b.** live in large cities **c.** farm large areas.

5. Immigrants bestowed the greatest benefits on our United States when they **a.** helped us in industry **b.** built schools **c.** brought the Catholic faith.

6. The farmer and the factory worker have the correct attitude towards each other when they **a.** try to compete with each other for this world's goods **b.** recognize each other's needs and problems **c.** try to become free and independent of each other.

7. Henry Ford's greatest contribution to the good of mankind was **a.** making automobiles cheaper **b.** giving an example of how a poor boy can become rich **c.** showing how the increased production of factories can benefit everybody by making more products available.

8. The Catholic Church is important to the United States because **a.** by the prayers and good works of its members blessings can be brought to the American people **b.** Catholics pay high taxes **c.** Catholics buy many manufactured products and help manufacturers.

9. The worst danger of city life is **a.** the danger of being run over by automobiles **b.** the ignorance and disease which may be caused by crowded conditions **c.** falling from windows in tall buildings.

10. The St. Lawrence Seaway is a good example of **a.** making the best of a bad situation **b.** naming new canals and locks after famous people **c.** the cooperation which should exist between governments of different countries.

The Western States

THE WEST   ALASKA   HAWAII

The group of thirteen Western States you are now going to study is the youngest of all the groups of states in our country. The first of these states to enter the Union was California, in 1850. Most of the others entered the Union only fifty to seventy-five years ago, and the last two became states only in the last few years.

Youngsters grow rapidly, are quick to learn new ways of doing things, and look toward the future more than toward the past. This is true of our Western States. New minerals, vital to the atomic age, are being mined throughout the West. Land that was once considered useless is now being watered by irrigation from huge dams and flowering with many crops.

Alaska, the largest of the United States, contains many mineral deposits that have not yet been tapped. Its people are pioneers; they are working to make a good life in a new and often dangerous land. Hawaii is a melting pot of many races and nationalities, showing us the way to live in peace with neighbors who are different.

Throughout the West, new industries are springing up—airplane and rocket factories, atomic power plants, and electronics manufacturers. Most important, however, the people of the Western States are ambitious and energetic, eager to make America a better place to live.

In this Unit you will learn that:

1 There are thirteen Western States. Eleven of them lie within the borders of the forty-eight states, and are called the West. The twelfth is Alaska, far to the north; the thirteenth is Hawaii, far out in the Pacific Ocean.

2 Four natural regions make up the West. They are: the Great Plains, the Rockies and Great Basin, California, or the Pacific Southwest, and the Pacific Northwest.

3 Farming and livestock-raising are done in the Great Plains. Mining is the chief occupation in the Rockies and Great Basin. Large cities in California turn out many kinds of manufactured products, and its farms produce over 200 kinds of crops. Lumbering, farming, and fishing are important in the Pacific Northwest.

4 Alaska is a storehouse of mineral wealth, not yet fully developed. Its population is still very small.

5 Hawaii, a group of volcanic islands, is a tiny state with a population larger than that of Alaska. Its rich farmlands produce sugar cane and pineapples.

HAWAII

Pacific Ocean

Sierra Nevada

Coastal Ranges

Cascade Mountains

Columbia

River

Great Basin

Colorado River

Rocky

Mountains

MEXICO

CANADA

Great Plain

THE WESTERN STATES

Our new state of Alaska is far to the north, a huge peninsula extending outward from the coast of North America. Hawaii, our most recent state, occupies a tiny group of islands far out in the Pacific Ocean.

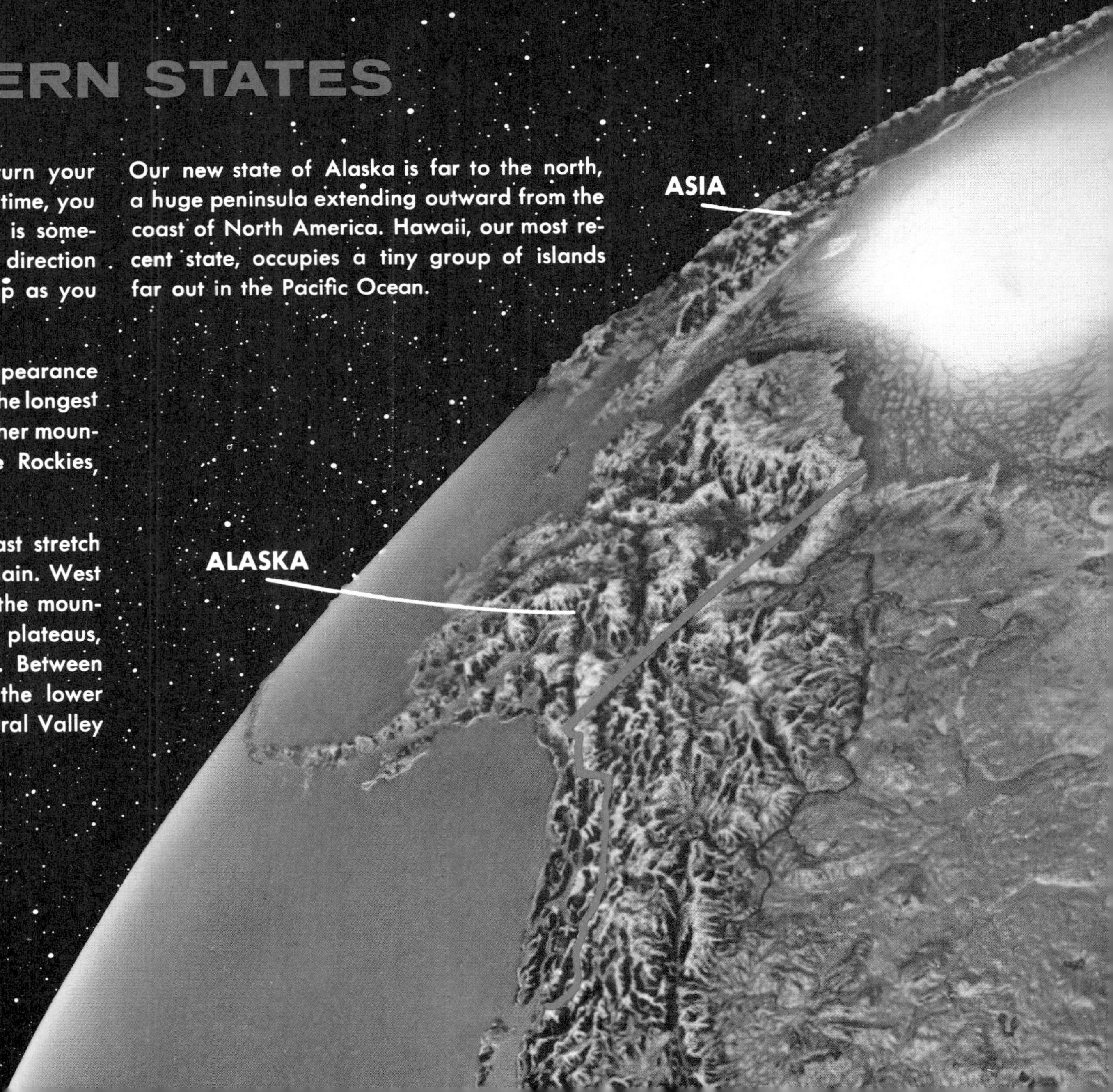

In order to read this, you had to turn your book part way around. At the same time, you also turned your map around. This is sometimes called orienting a map. The direction north is now at the top of your map as you look at it.

Notice first the extremely rugged appearance of the surface throughout the West. The longest chain of mountains is the Rockies. Other mountain groups, some higher than the Rockies, stand near the Pacific coast.

To the east of the Rockies is the vast stretch of dry lowland called the Great Plain. West of the Rockies, between them and the mountains of the coast, is an area of hills, plateaus, and deserts called the Great Basin. Between the towering Sierra Nevada and the lower Coastal Ranges lies the green Central Valley of California.

ALASKA

ASIA

Region of Great Contrasts

How the Land Looks. In this picture you can see some of the widely contrasting features of the Western landscape — mountains, prairie, and brush.

Westward from the Mississippi Valley, the Great Plains rise gradually, stretching out wide and lonely toward the sunset. Suddenly, dark, tree-covered mountains loom up from the silent plains. Over their summits more peaks, higher still, can be seen, snow-capped among the clouds. These are the Rocky Mountains, the "backbone" of North America. They extend north and south for thousands of miles, from Alaska, across Canada and the United States. Their highest peaks rise almost three miles above sea level.

Still farther west, near the Pacific Coast, there are more mountain ranges, some with peaks even higher than those of the Rockies. In the north are the Cascades, and in the south the Sierra Nevada. Extending almost the entire length of the Pacific Coast are the Coastal Ranges. Between these mountain ranges on the coast and the Rockies farther inland lies a wide area of lower mountains, great plateaus, and lowland deserts. This land between the mountains is known as the Great Basin.

The Western States display a great variety of surface features. In addition, there are wide differences in climate, population, agriculture, and way of living. It is truly a region of many contrasts.

Location and Extent. Look at the map on pages 218-219. You see that the Western States of our country lie between Canada to the north and Mexico to the south. To the east are two groups of states —the North Central and the Southern. To the west is the wide Pacific Ocean.

This great extent of land takes in more

than one third of the total land area of the United States. It is made up of eleven states. They are: Montana, Wyoming, Colorado, New Mexico, Idaho, Utah, Arizona, Nevada, Washington, Oregon, and California.

Some of these states have very small populations. Only in the states bordering the Pacific do we find large centers of population. These states—Washington, Oregon, and California—have the most people and are very rich in natural resources. They are well located for trade with world markets. California has more people than any state in the Union except New York State.

Let us see how this vast Western region came to be settled and why the people came.

The First Westerners. For many years, only the American Indians lived in the Western mountains and plains. Food, clothing, and shelter were easy to get. Indian families "camped out" as though on a lifelong vacation trip. The mountains were rich with wild game—deer, elk, moose, antelope, bear, rabbit, and grouse. Streams were full of trout. Blueberries, raspberries, strawberries, and blackberries spread like a carpet across the green mountain valleys. Over the dry plains roamed thousands of buffalo. Clean, cold water ran in mountain streams.

Some Indian tribes built up villages on the mountainsides that looked like apartment houses. Some raised corn and other crops. In those early days Indians knew how to irrigate their fields with water brought from streams by canals and ditches. This is the same thing that white men now do in the drier parts of the West, turning deserts into productive farms and orchards.

Deep below the surface lay oil, coal, iron, silver, gold, copper, and lead. This natural wealth meant very little to the

Indian Reservation Village. This young girl sitting outside her apartment-like dwelling is one of the Pueblo Indians of the Taos Reservation.

Indians, who did not need it. However, it was later to bring many settlers to the Western United States in search of fortune.

"Mercy Running Rabbit." This young man has been named in the old Indian fashion. He is pictured in Glacier National Park in the state of Montana.

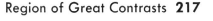

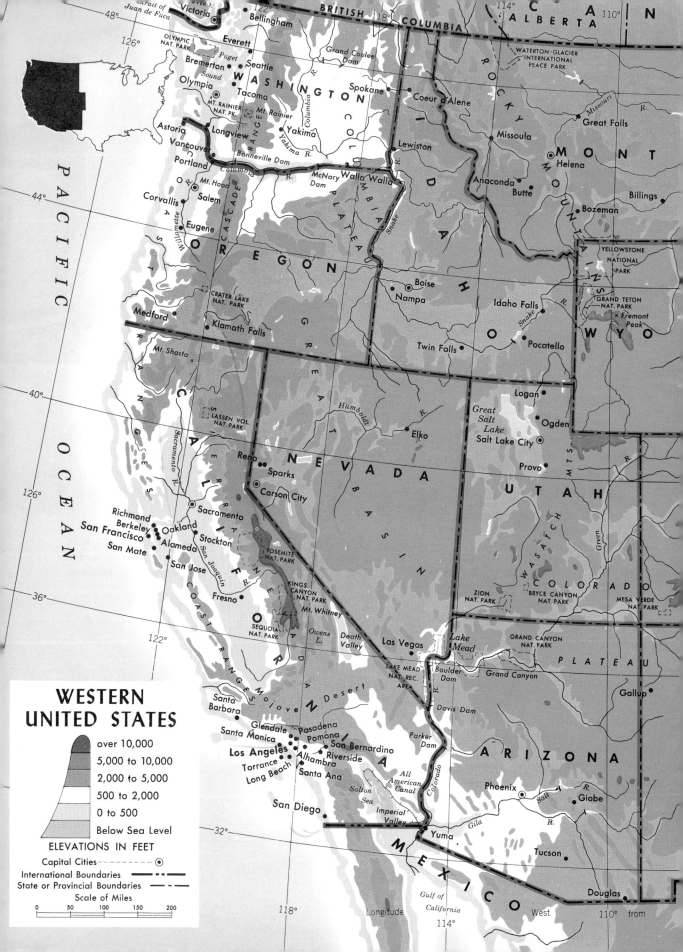

Studying the Map

A. The Western States are a group of eleven large states extending from the North Central and Southern States westward to the Pacific Ocean and from Canada southward to Mexico. They form about one third of the total land area of the United States. **1.** Name the eleven Western States. **2.** Which states border Canada? Mexico? the Pacific coast? **3.** There are many large national parks in the West. See how many you can find on the map. In what state is each located? **4.** Locate Carson City in Nevada and Los Angeles in California. Which city is farther west? How can you tell? **5.** Find the latitude and longitude of San Francisco and of Los Angeles. Which city is farther north? farther west?

B. With the exception of Alaska, the highest elevations in the United States are in the Western States. **1.** What color is used on the map to show the highest elevations? **2.** Find the Rocky Mountains on the map. Through what states do they extend? **3.** Find the Sierra Nevada in California. In what part of the state is this range located? **4.** The highest mountain peak in the Western States and the lowest point in the United States are near Sequoia National Park in California. What is the name of the peak? the name of the lowest point? **5.** What mountain range is located in central Washington and Oregon? Name a high mountain peak in each of these states. **6.** What is the name of the large plateau region of the Pacific Northwest? Into what states does it extend? **7.** Find the Central Valley in California. Between which mountain ranges is it located?

C. The rivers of the Western States are of great importance for irrigation and power. **1.** Find the Colorado River on the map. Where is its source? Into what body of water does it empty? In what state is the Grand Canyon of the Colorado River? **2.** What river forms the boundary between Washington and Oregon? Where is its source? Into what body of water does it empty? **3.** What river forms the boundary between Idaho and Oregon? Of what river it is a tributary? **4.** Name the river that flows down a wide low valley in western Oregon. What city is located where this river joins the Columbia? **5.** Name the two rivers that drain the Central Valley of California. **6.** In what state is the Great Salt Lake located?

Region of Great Contrasts 219

Pueblo Village and Church. The early Mission Church and the Indian dwelling in New Mexico are reminders of the two earliest people of the West.

The Spanish Come. The Spanish were the first Europeans to settle in the West. They had started settlements in New Mexico be-

Mission of Santa Barbara. In California, Franciscan missionaries erected many chapels like this. Some are kept as historic sites to this day.

fore the English came to New England and Virginia; before the Dutch came to New York; before the Catholics came to Maryland; and before the Quakers came to Philadelphia.

About one hundred years after the voyage of Columbus, Spanish colonists began to move northward from Mexico across the Rio Grande. *Rio Grande* means "Big River". Four hundred men, women, and children from Mexico settled in the region of New Mexico. They named their town Santa Fe, meaning *Holy Faith*.

In 1769, Franciscan missionaries opened their first mission on the west coast at San Diego. They built a string of Indian missions stretching six hundred miles up the coast of California as far as San Francisco. Father Junipero Serra was the famous leader of these missionary priests. Today, most of these missions have been restored, and thousands of visitors come to see them.

Exploring the West. When our country was very young, President Jefferson sent two men, Lewis and Clark, to explore the region of the Rocky Mountains and the lands lying between them and the Pacific Ocean. They spent two years and four months traveling from St. Louis, Missouri, to the Pacific coast and then back again. They traveled chiefly by means of rivers— the Missouri, the Snake, and the Columbia. Their exploration helped to make Oregon first a territory, then a state.

Soon more trails were opened to the West. The Oregon Trail crossed the mountains and plateaus northwest to Oregon and Washington. The Sante Fe Trail led to the Southwest. Men, women, and children traveled in covered wagons, drawn by slow oxen. They pushed their way across the continent to build new homes in the West for themselves and the descendants.

Later, cattlemen pastured their herds on the Great Plains, and the day of the cowboy and the "Wild West" began. Sheepmen also started to run huge flocks over the open range. Fierce fights sprang up between the cattlemen and sheepmen over the rights of each to pasture their animals. This rough frontier region, with harsh contests and bitter fights, is the old West we often hear about in stories.

The "Forty-niners." In 1848, somebody found nuggets and grains of shining gold in the sands of California streams. Men thirsty for riches rushed to the Pacific Coast from all parts of the United States. They came to be known as "Forty-niners", because 1849 was the year the "gold rush" started. Some made the long, hard journey around Cape Horn in little sailing ships. Others sailed to Panama, traveled overland across the isthmus, and took another ship on the Pacific side north to California. Many more crossed the Great Plains in oxcarts and struggled painfully to travel over the Rocky Mountains.

Before long, gold and silver were also found in the Rockies, in the states of Montana, Colorado, Idaho, Nevada, Arizona, and Utah. Mining towns sprang up almost overnight. Other towns grew up as trading and supply centers. Prospectors and miners swarmed over hills and up streams, washing the sands in "gold pans," looking anxiously to see if heavier grains of gold had settled to the bottom. Many found no gold at all, and the towns they established so quickly became deserted. Some of these "ghost towns" can still be seen today.

Historic Meeting. In order to signify the importance of the completed railroad, the last spike was made of gold, and the work gangs celebrated.

Settlers and Railroads. Many of the gold-seekers who were disappointed found good valley land with water nearby for irrigation. There they settled down and began to farm. The Union Pacific Railroad was built, running from Omaha to San Francisco on the Pacific coast. Great numbers of Irishmen worked to build the eastern part of this road. Thousands of Chinese workmen were brought over from China for the western part, which was started from San Francisco and built eastward. The two ends of the railroad met near Ogden, Utah, and the road was finished. Trains ran from the Atlantic Coast to the Pacific Coast.

The railroad company offered cheap rates of travel from the East, and the government gave free land to *homesteaders*. A man and his family could hire a whole box car, load into it his household furniture, farm implements, horses, cows, pigs,

and chickens, together with food for the trip.

With his own bed in one corner of the "immigrant car," the farmer traveled and took care of his stock until the car was set off on a side track near his future home. Then everything was unloaded. Each man lived on his acres, built a house, and started farming. The land became his own. Range lands, where cattle had pastured, were cut up, fenced in, and planted to crops. Stagecoaches and freight wagons ran from railway stations to villages and farm lands in faraway valleys.

The Trickle Becomes a Stream. People from everywhere came pouring into the West. Mountaineers from Virginia, Tennessee, and Arkansas, and "Yankees" from New England became cowboys, propectors, and miners. Irishmen drifted west from New York, Philadelphia, and Boston to work in the mines, on the railroad, or as teamsters and freighters. A few Italians and Jews began as peddlers and set up grocery and dry goods stores in mining camps and railroad towns. Chinese started restaurants and laundries. Mexicans worked as sheep herders, farm hands, and railroad laborers. Here and there a Catholic priest built a little church in some railroad town and spent his time trying to gather in the people who had forgotten what it means to be a Catholic.

Hard-working, patient people from crowded Japan came to California, cultivated truck gardens, and operated fishing boats off the coast. The Western States today have a mixed population from many nations and races. All have become "just plain Americans."

The Changing West. The first farmers in this region settled only in fertile valleys where water for irrigation was close at hand. Then the people began urging their government to build dams to hold the water in reservoirs. Two big dams were built. They are the Grand Coulee Dam on the Columbia River in Washington, and Hoover Dam on the Colorado River between Nevada and Arizona. They now produce electric power and also irrigate millions of acres of land. Shasta Dam in the Sacramento River in California is another big project.

Factories, canneries, smelters, and machine shops made their appearance as towns grew into cities. Farmers plowed up more land as soon as irrigation water was made possible. Great sections on the eastern side of the mountains were still too dry and too far away from any water supply for farming. Here the soil was still unbroken, and cowboys herded cattle across the range. Some of the range was plowed up for wheat farms, but during unusually dry years, the topsoil blew away leaving almost a desert. As you know, this was a waste of a valuable resource.

Man-made Lake. The Grand Coulee Dam is the world's largest concrete structure. This dam provides water and electricity for surrounding areas.

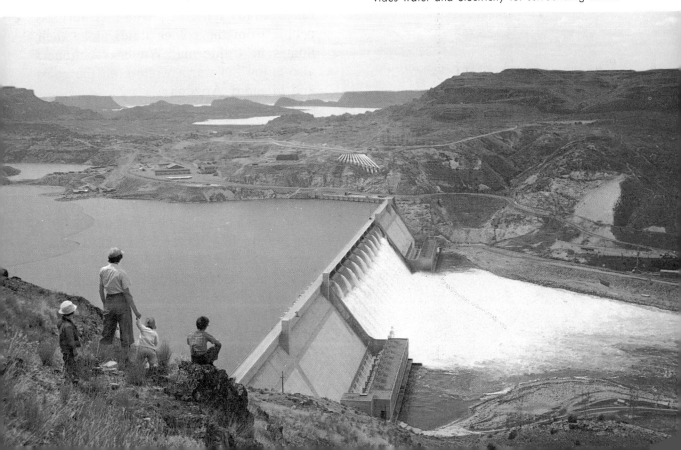

The West Today. The flow of automobiles added more changes to the West. White ribbons of highways now wind across sagebrush plateaus and zigzag up steep peaks and down breath-taking canyons. Cars with New York or Massachusetts license plates pass cars from California and Oregon at service stations in Utah and Colorado. Tourists with camp equipment hurry along through the glare of the wide deserts of Nevada and Arizona. Tourists camp in forests or in cabins along the highways. Houses on wheels, called *trailers,* rumble along the roads.

Today, the jet airplane roars over the Rockies, crossing the United States in less than six hours. Planes fly over the Grand Canyon and the Painted Desert where travelers used to die of thirst. Streamlined trains thunder across the continent in three days or less.

Gold is still mined in the West, no longer by the single miner rocking his little pan, but by powerful machinery owned by great corporations. Coal is needed for railroads and industries, and miners dig in dark tunnels here and there along the foot of the great mountain ranges.

Along the Pacific coast, as well as in the mountain states, orchards, arranged neatly in squares, dot the irrigated valleys. Railroads and trucks furnish quick transportation for the fruit, which spoils easily. Melons grow big and juicy under the sunny desert skies. In late summer the farmers and their families are busy from dawn till dusk, picking, packing, and trucking melons to the towns for shipment.

Cowboys still herd cattle up the mountains in summer and out on the dry range in winter. They often ship their steers east to be fattened on Iowa corn.

Tourists and vacationers lean dizzily over the rim of the Grand Canyon. They shoo away bears from their camps in Yellowstone Park. Dude ranches give city people a chance to ride a horse and hear imitation cowboys sing songs of the old range. Many retired farmers and business people from the colder states make their homes in California. Winter vacationers also enjoy the warm winters on the coast and in sunny Arizona.

The West is not only an attractive place for tourists and vacationers. Every year, more and more people leave their homes in the East, the South, or the Midwest, and travel to the West. There they hope to find a new way of life, a new job, better opportunities for a career. Sometimes they are disappointed; often, however, they find that the West is the "land of their dreams."

The populations of cities on the Pacific Coast continue to grow larger year after year. This is true especially in California. In other places, like Arizona, the favorable climate attracts many people suffering from certain ailments.

224 Western United States

Dividing the West. In order to study the Western States we shall divide their vast area into four regions: (1) the Great Plains (2) the Rocky Mountains and the Great Basin (3) the Pacific Southwest (4) the Pacific Northwest. The boundaries of these regions are shown on the map on page 224.

In each region we shall see what man has been able to do with the resources he has found. Man always has some choice as you will see. In some places, where he plowed up the grasslands, winds blew the topsoil away until crops could no longer be raised. Now he is re-seeding the grasslands, hoping to restore them so that they can again be used for grazing. In other places, where the soil was fertile but without enough rainfall, huge dams were built on mountain streams to store water for irrigation.

From age to age, man makes decisions on how land and other natural resources shall be used. Resources are God's gift to man and God intends man to use them intelligently. Let us think about man's use of the natural resources of the Western United States as we study each region.

Facts *to remember*

1. The Western States are bounded by Canada on the north, Mexico on the south, the North Central and the Southern states on the east, and the Pacific Ocean on the west. The Rocky Mountains, the Cascades, and the Sierra Nevada Mountains are located in this region. The West has a variety of surface features and wide differences in climate, population, agriculture, and way of living.
2. American Indians were the first people to make their homes on the Western mountains and plains. They were not interested in the great stores of mineral wealth buried there. The Spanish were the first Europeans to settle in the West. Franciscan missionaries built missions along the California coast. Father Junipero Serra was the leader of these missionary priests.

3. Gold-seekers, cattlemen, and sheepmen settled down in the fertile valleys of the West where water could be obtained. The Union Pacific Railroad brought many others. The Grand Coulee Dam, the Hoover Dam, and the Shasta Dam were constructed by the Government at the request of the people. Today, these dams generate electricity and are used to irrigate the land.

What *have I learned?*

Write each sentence by completing it with the correct word in the parenthesis.
1. The (Sierra Nevada, Rockies, Cascades) are called the "backbone" of North America.
2. The Western States take in more than (one-third, one-half, four-fifths) of the total land area of the United States.
3. (Colorado, California, Utah) has more people than any other state in the Union, with the exception of New York.
4. (Mining, Plowing, Irrigation) brought water to the dry West.
5. Gold was first discovered in (Idaho, Arizona, California).
6. The government gave free land to (homesteaders, business men, missionaries).
7. The Union Pacific Railroad extended across the Western States from Omaha to (Denver, Boise, San Francisco).
8. The Grand Coulee Dam and the Hoover Dam produce (minerals, electric power, ships).
9. Many people travel to parts of the West in winter to (lumber, vacation, build).
10. In the West the (eastern, northern, western) sides of the mountains are dry.

Facts *to understand*

Give a reason for each statement.
1. The West has changed since the time when the American Indians roamed the Plains.
2. The work of the Spanish had a great influence on the development of the West.
3. The Oregon Trail and the Sante Fe trail aided in increasing the population of the West.
4. The Western States today have a mixed population from many nations and races.
5. The Union Pacific Railroad brought farmers from the East to settle land in the West.

2
The Great Plains

Great Plains Cattleman. "The cowboy" is a familiar figure in all stories about the West. Today, herding cattle is still a hard, lonely job.

A traveler journeying westward from one of the North Central States would cross the Central Plains. You read about this wide, level area when you studied the North Central States. Gradually, as he went west, the traveler would find himself in a different region. The land rises slightly, and fewer and fewer trees are seen, except along the rivers. Rainfall becomes much less; this can be seen from the tough, wiry grass which is the new region's chief vegetation. He is now in a natural region of our country called the Great Plains.

Location. It is not possible to say exactly where the Central Plains end and the Great Plains begin. Where they merge, the two areas are really quite similar. To the east, however, the Central Plains enjoy moderate rainfall, deep rich soil, and numerous sources of water. To the west, the Great Plains have little rain, soil that is suited only for grassland, and scattered water supply. Their general boundary line is just about at the 20-inch rainfall line. Find this line on the rainfall map on page 24.

You will see that the Great Plains extend into three different sections of the United States. They cover the western parts of North Dakota, South Dakota, Nebraska, and Kansas. These are among the North Central States. They also include the western parts of Oklahoma and Texas, in the Southern States. Finally, the Great Plains cover the eastern parts of Montana, Wyoming, Colorado and New Mexico. These are among the Western States which you are now studying.

Settlement of the Great Plains. Plains Indians once roamed this vast area. They hunted buffalo—the huge animals which traveled in herds and supplied the Indians with food, clothing, and shelter. As settlers from the East and the Midwest crossed the Plains, or settled there, the vast herds of buffalo began to disappear. Work crews building the railroads, cattlemen, and many others slaughtered large numbers of buffalo needlessly and wastefully.

The roaming tribes of Indians were soon without their major source of food and raw material. In addition, the Indians were displaced by whites who wanted the land wherever it was fertile or profitable to use.

After being driven from place to place and after fierce battles with the white men, most of the Indians were located on areas of government land called *reservations*. Here most of them live today—a much different kind of life from that which their ancestors enjoyed.

The Great Plains region is still very sparsely settled, however. Cattle and sheep graze on the open range, and a few scattered farms appear wherever there is enough rainfall or a close supply of water for irrigation. Many hundreds of acres are owned by the United States government. They can still be obtained by homesteaders who are willing to live there, endure the loneliness, and work against difficult conditions to farm the land. Let us see what the conditions are which make farming so difficult and so costly on the Great Plains of the West.

Water for the Dry Grasslands. Where rainfall is so slight, a wind-operated pump must be used to bring up the water from deep beneath the soil.

A Wasted Land. The horrible effects of careless farming can be seen clearly here. Topsoil, with nothing to hold it, has completely blown away.

Little Rain on the Great Plains. Along the eastern boundary of the Great Plains there is an average of 20 inches of rain a year. This is not very much. Most crops need more than 20 inches of rain a year. But the climate becomes even drier to the west. The part of the Great Plains that is in the Western States receives an average of only ten inches of rain a year. This ten inches of rain is an *average*. In some years there may be more than ten inches. In some years there is much less.

The Prairie Grass. You have just learned that before the white men came, the Great Plains were the home of Indians and buffalo. The buffalo fed upon the grass but did not harm the roots. More grass would grow up again from the roots. The roots kept the rich topsoil in place. Since the Plains Indians did not try to plant crops, the grass roots and the soil were never disturbed.

When the white men came to the Great Plains, they plowed the soil and planted corn, wheat, and other grains. This worked fine in the years when there was enough rain. But it did not work at all in the years when there was little rain.

At the time of the first World War, in 1916, our country needed much food to send to its soldiers. Large amounts of food were also needed to send to the countries who were fighting on our side. More land on the Great Plains was cultivated. Thick prairie grass that had been growing for hundreds of years was plowed up. Wheat and corn were planted in place of the grass. For a number of years following World War I, the Great Plains had more rain than usual. Large amounts of wheat and corn were harvested. The Great Plains farmers were happy with their big crops— but not for long.

A Dust Bowl. In the 1930's, for year after year, there was hardly any rain at all. The hot sun beat down on the dry fields. In the old days, the thick prairie grass had protected the soil from sun and wind, but now the grass was gone. The sun made the soil so dry that it became like powder. Then the winds blew the powdery dry soil away. This caused "dust storms." At times, the air was so filled with dust that people could scarcely see the sun, even in the middle of the day. The dust storms blew from the Great Plains across the Central Plains and as far east as Pennsylvania. The Great Plains seemed to be nothing but a region of dust, and people called part of the region the "Dust Bowl."

The dust that was blowing away was really rich topsoil. It had taken hundreds of years for this topsoil to form, and now it was blowing away—tons and tons of it. Farmers watched their cattle die for lack of feed. They watched the corn and wheat wither away, unable to grow without fertile topsoil. They watched their fields blow away in great clouds of dust. They could do nothing to stop all this. Many farmers had to leave their farms on the Great Plains, never to return.

Best Suited for Ranching. From the dust storms of the 1930's the people of the Great Plains learned a valuable lesson. Never again would they plow up so much of the land. They would still raise some crops, but they would be sure that the crops received enough water even in a dry year. In many places this water is now pumped from deep wells.

Since grass grows better than other crops on the Great Plains, the people decided to raise grass on most of the land. In rainy years, water soaks through the grass and goes deep into the soil. In dry years, the grass prevents the sun from drying out the soil, and there is still enough moisture deep in the ground to keep the grass alive. The soil does not blow away because the grass roots help hold it in place. As long as the land is covered with grass, there is little danger of great dust storms.

Can the owner of grass-covered land make money from his land? He can, by letting beef cattle graze on it. The cattle eat the grass and grow. Then they are sold to Corn Belt farmers who fatten them for market. Cattlemen must be careful, however, not to have too many cattle on their land. A large herd grazing on a small range might eat the grass right down to the roots. If there are not too many cattle, the grass grows up again from the roots, just as it did when the buffalo grazed on it.

A man who raises beef cattle is called a *rancher,* and his land is called a *ranch.* Most ranches on the Great Plains are very large in area and keep thousands of head of cattle. The people of the Great Plains have found that their land is better suited for ranching than it is for farming.

Riding the Range. The modern rancher still travels best on a horse. The cattle in this picture are the famous "longhorns" — strong and tough.

Great Plains Sheep Herds. On the higher pastures of Wyoming, vast herds of sheep are raised. Wyoming ranks very high as a wool-producing state.

Sheepherding. Sheep as well as cattle are raised today on the Great Plains. They can feed where the grass is too poor for cattle. Their sharp hoofs enable them to graze on hillsides and in rough areas where cattle cannot climb. In addition, sheep can stand a colder climate because of their coat of wool.

The sheepherder of the Great Plains often leads a lonely life. In the summer he drives his flock into the cool mountain meadows to graze on the green grass. He may live alone with them with only a faithful sheep dog as his companion. The dog is trained to round up the sheep and protect them from wild animals. In the fall the sheep are driven down from the mountains to the plains again. The fat lambs are separated from the flock and shipped to market to be butchered. The rest of the flock grazes on the more sheltered ranges. In the spring their wool is cut off by shearing machines and sent to market.

Dry Farming. As we have seen, farming is still done on some parts of the Great Plains, but the farmers have learned to be very careful about the way they use their land. They use the method known as *dry farming,* or else they use irrigation.

When a farmer practices dry farming, he makes use of what little rain there is. He chooses crops that can grow with a small amount of moisture, such as wheat and alfalfa. He plants his crops in narrow fields, leaving some fields fallow. The word "fallow" means *idle.* Sometimes, he cultivates this field so the weeds do not grow

Dry Farming in Utah. Notice the way in which the fields have been plowed according to the contours of the land. This helps hold the water.

230 Western United States

and so that it will catch the rainfall. Sometimes he covers his fallow fields with a *mulch*—straw or dried roots—so the soil will not blow away. If it is covered with mulch, the water in the ground does not pass away into the air. Thus the water from the rain is stored for the next year.

The Great Plains farmer also rotates his crops from one field to another to make use of the stored water, as well as any rain that falls during the growing season. There are many millions of acres of dry-farming lands in the western states.

Irrigation. Carrying water to fields by means of canals, ditches, or overhead sprinkler pipes is called *irrigation*. This is very expensive. A farmer cannot afford to do it unless he feels that he will get a big return on his crop, both in yield per acre and selling price.

On the map on this page you will see that the irrigation regions in the Great Plains are near rivers that flow east from the Rocky Mountains. Look along the branches of the Missouri River, especially the Platte River. Here great dams hold back the river water in artificial lakes, or *reservoirs*. Canals and gates regulate the flow of water from the reservoirs to the farms.

In other parts of the Great Plains farmers need water for irrigation so badly they have tunneled through mountains to get it. One such tunnel is 13 miles long and carries water from the more rainy western slopes to the dry lands of the Great Plains east of the mountains.

Irrigation. Precious water flows through the pipes and down the muddy ditches of this irrigated farm. Very rich crops can be raised this way.

Crops of the Great Plains. In the last unit, on the North Central States, you learned about the Spring and Winter Wheat Belts. These belts extend into the eastern part of the Great Plains. Here the climate is not so dry as in the western part nearer the Rockies. Where the Great Plains extend into Oklahoma and Texas, a kind of cotton that needs less rain is grown. Corn is raised on the Great Plains where they extend into the states of Nebraska and South Dakota.

On the drier parts of the Great Plains the most productive farms are in eastern Colorado. Here the soils are good and hold irrigation water fairly well. In the valley of the Arkansas River, in southeast Colorado, irrigated farms produce melons, peaches, pears, small grains, and vegetables. The most important center for raising sugar beets in the United States is in the irrigated valley of the South Platte River in northeastern Colorado.

Sugar beets give the farmer a high return per acre. Machines do nine tenths of the harvesting of this crop. Sugar refineries are located near the sugar beet fields because the beets are bulky and heavy and would be expensive to transport. Beet tops and beet pulp are not thrown away. These parts are used to feed hogs and other livestock.

Mining on the Great Plains. In the northern part of the Great Plains are the Black Hills of South Dakota and Wyoming. Some of the famous Western adventurers and outlaws, such as "Wild Bill" Hickok and "Deadwood Dick," once worked in the rich gold mines of this region. A few of the gold mines are still being worked in the Black Hills. During the World War II, however, many of the gold miners left these mines to work in the copper mines of the Rocky Mountains. Although not a precious metal like gold, copper is of great value today.

All along the Great Plains at the foot of the Rocky Mountains, stretching from Canada to Mexico, are many productive oil wells. Casper, Wyoming, is at the western end of a pipe line from these oil fields. It runs eastward all the way to the Atlantic Coast.

Wyoming, Colorado, and New Mexico each produce large quantities of uranium ore. This important mineral is necessary to the production of atomic energy. The deposits of uranium in the Great Plains states, therefore, are of great value.

Much soft coal lies in the Great Plains. It is of poor quality, however, and is mined only where it is needed for refineries and factories. Colorado and Wyoming lead the Western States in amount of coal mined.

In New Mexico, near Carlsbad, there are extensive beds of *potash*. Potash is a chemical used in many kinds of artificial fertilizers and plant foods.

Where the People Live. Settlements on the Great Plains are few and far apart. In this region of large farms and ranches the population is small and scattered over a very wide area.

Sugar Beet Harvest. The complicated machine in this picture picks and loads the crop. With irrigation, these fields produce 17 tons per acre.

At the Foot of the Mountains. Denver, Colorado, is located on the Great Plains near the Rockies. The high mountains can be seen from downtown.

Small towns grew up at cross-roads to serve the needs of the farmers over a large area. The towns usually consist of a street or two of houses, a few stores, a post office, a couple of gasoline stations, a high water tower, and sometimes a row of grain elevators near the railroad track. The few large cities are located at the high western edge of the Great Plains.

The "Mile High" City. Denver, Colorado is the only large city of this region. The discovery of gold brought settlers to Denver in 1858. Not much gold was found there, but the city became a trading place for miners. Denver has a fine location on the Great Plains, at the foot of the Rocky Mountains. It is over 5000 feet above sea level.

Miners from the mining camps in the mountains come to Denver for mining equipment and other supplies. Many mining companies have offices in Denver.

Farmers bring their products to Denver. Here the sugar from sugar beets is refined, wheat is milled, cattle and sheep are butchered, and meat products packed. Farmers and ranchers buy their farm machinery and other manufactured products which they need in Denver.

Denver is a center of commerce and transportation. Railroads, airlines and highways connect Denver with the rest of the country. Warehouses in Denver store supplies for the people of smaller settlements scattered in isolated sections of the plain.

Denver is an attractive stopping place for tourists on their way to other resorts. From Denver, a tourist can easily reach Pikes' Peak, the Garden of the Gods, the famous Royal Gorge of the Arkansas River, and other natural wonders.

Other Cities of the Great Plains. Pueblo, Colorado, is called the "Pittsburgh of the West," because so much steel is produced there. Steel mills in Pueblo get their iron ore from the Rocky Mountains and their coal from Trinidad, Colorado. Farm machinery, mining machinery, and steel rails are manufactured in Pueblo.

Great Falls, Montana, is on the Missouri River. It is noted for the many plants which refine Montana's copper. It is also a stop on an important transportation route by air and land to Alaska.

Cheyenne, Wyoming, is the capital city and a transportation center. It is the Northern terminus of an old cattle trail from the south. Livestock and agricultural products are shipped from Cheyenne.

Facts *to remember*

1. The Central Plains merge with the Great Plains. The Great Plains extend into the North Central States, the Southern States, and cover a section of the Western States. This section has few trees and little rainfall. Tough, wiry grass is the chief vegetation.

2. After being driven from place to place, the Plains Indians who once roamed the West were finally located on Government land called reservations.

3. Before the white men came, buffalo fed on the grass that grew on the dry prairie land. During World War I, the Great Plains were cultivated, and so the prairie grass was destroyed. Dust storms blew away the rich topsoil. Many farmers had to leave their farms.

4. Ranchers raise large herds of beef cattle which now graze on the replanted grassland. Sheep feed where the grass is poor. Crops are raised by using dry-farming. Great dams hold back river water in reservoirs. Canals, ditches, and overhead sprinkler pipes provide water for irrigation.

5. Some gold is still mined in the Black Hills. Copper, oil, and a poor grade of coal are also mined on the Great Plains. Large beds of potash are found in New Mexico. Potash is used mostly to make various kinds of chemical fertilizers.

6. In this region of large farms and larger ranches, the population is small and scattered. There are few large cities. Denver, Colorado, the most important one, is a center of commerce and transportation. Its warehouses store supplies for the smaller settlements on the plain.

7. The most important area for raising sugar beets in the United States is in Colorado. Sugar refineries are located near the beet fields. They convert the vegetable into valuable refined sugar.

What *have I learned?*

Copy these sentences on another sheet of paper. Write T before each sentence that is true, and O before each sentence that is false. If a sentence is false, write it a second time correctly.

1. The Great Plains have little rain.
2. The Plains Indians who roamed the West hunted buffalo.
3. By plowing up the prairie grass, topsoil was saved.
4. After the dust storms of 1930, farmers plowed up more land.
5. Beef cattle can graze where the grass is short and sparse.
6. When a farmer practices dry farming, he chooses crops that need much water.
7. Irrigation regions in the Great Plains are near rivers that flow east from the Rocky Mountains.
8. Sugar beets give the farmer a high return per acre.
9. This region produces more copper than gold.
10. Denver is the only large city of this region.
11. Sugar beets require much hand labor.
12. Steel is produced in Pueblo, Colorado.
13. There are no oil wells in the Great Plains.
14. Carrying water to fields is called irrigation.
15. Sheep and cattle are raised on the Great Plains.

Facts *to understand*

Answer each of the following questions in a sentence or two.

1. Why were the Indians happy when they alone lived on the Great Plains?
2. Why did many farmers have to leave their farms in the West after 1930?
3. How is the land of the Great Plains used today?
4. Why are there few large cities in this area?
5. Why are sheep able to get along on poorer pastureage than cattle?

3
The Rockies and Great Basin

Colorado National Monument. This area in western Colorado has been set aside by the Government to preserve its dramatic and breathtaking scenery.

The two regions of the Western States which you will next study are very different from the Great Plains region. These two regions have an appearance which contrasts sharply with the wide, level plains area. In general, they have even a smaller population than the Great Plains, they have even less land suitable for farming, and hardly any industries or cities at all.

At the western edge of the Great Plains, in the states of Montana, Wyoming, Colorado, and New Mexico, the surface of the level plain changes abruptly. The Rocky Mountains rise up to their great heights. Trees cover the slopes, replacing the miles and miles of level prairie grass. Sparkling streams in the lower valleys provide water for the irrigation canals which lead to many farms. Great areas of woodland are set aside as National Parks.

Farther west still, but not so far west as the Pacific coast mountain ranges, there is an area between the mountains called the Great Basin. This is a region of lower mountains, plateaus, and lowland deserts. It is a hot, dry land, as different from the Rockies as the Rockies are different from the Great Plains.

The Rocky Mountains. The Rocky Mountains extend north and south almost the whole length of our continent. Trace them on the map of North America on pages 6-7. Begin in the northern part of Canada, then south across the United States, and into Mexico. In Mexico the mountains are called by another name, but they are really part of the same chain. You will learn more about the mountains in Canada and Mexico when you read about those countries in another part of this book.

In this chapter you will learn about the part of the Rocky Mountains in the United States. They extend from the northeast corner of the state of Washington, across Idaho, Montana, Wyoming, Utah, Colorado, and into New Mexico. You can see how wide this chain of mountains is by finding the city of Denver, Colorado, on your map (page 219). Then find Salt Lake City, Utah. Denver is on the Great Plains at the foot of the eastern slope of the Rockies. Salt Lake City is on the other side of the mountains at the foot of the western slope. The cities are more than 400 miles apart. Between the two cities are some of the highest peaks in the Rockies.

The Rocky Mountains are very high and very rugged. They are much higher than the Appalachian Mountains in the East. Some of the peaks are almost three miles above sea level. The highest peaks in the Rockies have snow on them even in the middle of summer.

The Rockies were a great barrier to pioneers trying to reach the Pacific coast. Today they are no longer a barrier, but are crossed by railroads, by automobile highways, and, of course, by airplanes.

Not very many people live in the Rocky Mountains because there are very few ways to make a living on the steep slopes. There are no large cities in the mountains. The people of the mountains make their living chiefly by mining, lumbering, farming, raising livestock, and caring for tourists.

"Backbone of America." The Rocky Mountains stand out in majesty against the sky. These are the rugged peaks the Western pioneers had to cross.

Gold-mining in the Rockies. In a stream near Black-hawk, Colorado, a dredge sifts the gravel to find any grains of gold that may be present.

Mining the Precious Metals. On the map of the Western States on pages 218-219, you will notice a Colorado city named Leadville. Like other Western cities, it was named for the mineral found nearby. At one time there was so much gold mined in Colorado that they covered the entire dome of the Capitol Building in Denver with this precious metal.

The Rocky Mountains were a troublesome barrier to the "Forty-niners" who were on their way west to mine gold in California. They followed trails that led them over these high mountains, bypassing the precious metals which lay, unknown, all about them. It was not until ten years later that gold was discovered in the Rockies. Then a second gold rush started, this time to the state of Colorado.

There are still mining centers in the Rockies, but in many places the supply of gold has run out. The mines are deserted, although the buildings were left standing. These abandoned towns are called *ghost towns*.

Where gold mining is still carried on, more modern methods are now used. Huge dredges separate particles of gold from loose gravel found in the beds of streams.

These places where gold and gravel are found together are called *placer deposits*.

Another mining method uses powerful streams of water to wash gravel with gold deposits out of a mountain into a long, washboard trough. The heavy gold catches in the grooves of the trough, and the loose gravel runs off.

Where the gold is buried deep in a mountain, the miners dig a shaft down to it. The ore is then removed just like coal. Cable cars carry the ore down to the nearest refinery. Cripple Creek and Leadville, Colorado, are the most important gold mining centers in the Rockies today.

Silver is often found mixed with gold. In Nevada, the first miners were so anxious to discover gold that at first they threw away huge chunks of rich silver ore. They did not realize how valuable it was. Later, when the value of silver was discovered, one of the gold mines became the richest silver mine in the world. It was called the Comstock Lode. Some silver is still mined in the West, but our country is no longer a large producer of silver.

Open Pit Copper Mine. Here in Utah, and in Oregon, great open pit mines are producing vast amounts of valuable copper. Notice how wide this pit is.

Copper Mining. Much more copper is mined in the Rocky Mountains than silver and gold. The United States leads the world in producing this reddish metal. It is important in the electrical industry for making wire and parts for radios, stoves, irons, and electric refrigerators. It is often mixed with other metals to make alloys such as brass, bronze, and duralumin.

Some copper mines first started as gold or silver mines. At Butte, Montana, the copper is mixed with gold and silver. A shaft more than a mile deep has been driven into "the richest hill in the world." In all, there are 2700 miles of shafts and tunnels under the city of Butte. The copper ore is shipped to nearby Anaconda, where water and coal are available for refining it. At the refinery, the copper is separated from rock and other metals.

At one time, poisonous gases from the copper refining furnaces were allowed to escape into the air. This killed all the trees and shrubbery for miles around. Now the gases are collected and made into useful products. In this way plant life is saved, and useful products are not wasted.

Much copper is also mined in Oregon and Utah. In fact, these two states are now leading copper producers. Here the ore is of lower grade, but located near the surface. It is not necessary to build expensive mine shafts. The ore is mined from open pits similar to those of the Mesabi Range where iron ore is mined. At one place, called "The Pit," nothing remains now of the mine but a huge hole from which all the ore has been removed. It is a reminder that we must be careful of our remaining supply of minerals. If they are wasted, we shall soon have nothing but "Big Pits" like the one in Arizona. The resources of the earth must be used wisely.

Other Minerals of the Rockies. In the Coeur d' Alene district of Northern Idaho, great amounts of lead and zinc are mined and refined. The Rocky mountain area is also the source of a number of minerals which find special uses in strengthening certain kinds of steel. One of these is *manganese,* found mixed with copper in the mines near Butte, Montana. *Tungsten,* also used for making the filaments in electric light bulbs, helps make good steel. It is mined in Idaho. *Chromium,* used in making stainless steel, comes from mines in Montana. Also used in the manufacture of steel are *molybdenum* and *vanadium,* but mined farther south in Colorado. This region is the world's chief source of these two rare and valuable metals.

Uranium ore, highly valued because of its part in the production of atomic energy, is also found in large amounts throughout the Rockies.

Tourists Visit the National Parks. The Rocky Mountains are so beautiful and so awe-inspiring that many tourists come to visit them each summer. The United States Government owns most of the land in the mountains. This means that the land belongs to all of the people of the United States. Some parts are so beautiful that the Government has set them aside as national parks.

In the northwest corner of the state of Wyoming, and extending partly into Montana, is Yellowstone National Park. Good roads and hotels are maintained in the park area. No hunting is allowed, in order to protect the birds and animals.

Yellowstone National Park is filled with natural wonders. Hundreds of hot springs boil up and over the ground. In some places

Nature's Great Spectacle. A large crowd of tourists at Yellowstone National Park enjoys watching "Old Faithful" as it spouts high into the air.

OLD FAITHFUL

Snake River in Wyoming. This is Grand Teton National Park, where the Teton Mountains rise 7000 feet straight up from the level floor of the valley.

there are *geysers,* springs out of which water is blown high into the air by escaping steam from under the earth. One big and beautiful geyser is called "Old Faithful", because it spouts regularly about once an hour. It throws a beautiful stream of water straight up into the air like a firehose.

Other national parks are Glacier National Park in Montana and Rocky Mountain National Park in Colorado. Thousands of Americans enjoy visiting these parks every summer.

Land Between the Mountains. Between the Rocky Mountains and the mountains near the Pacific Coast, there is an extensive area of lower mountains, plateaus, and basins. Different parts of this varied area have one thing in common: everywhere it is dry. Because the elevation here is lower than the mountain areas, the temperatures are higher. Moisture-bearing winds from the ocean have dropped their moisture on the Pacific, or western, side of the mountains long before they descend into the Great Basin. Instead of giving up moisture then, these winds absorb moisture as they are heated. The southern part of this region is so dry that most of it is considered desert or near-desert.

The Great Salt Lake. You can see on the map on page 219 that most of the state of Utah is in the Great Basin. In the northeastern part of the state you will see a large lake. It is not at all like the Great Lakes. In the Great Lakes there is fresh water. The water in this western lake however, is very salty.

How did the water of the lake get so salty? Salt is a mineral contained in some rocks. Some of it is dissolved by rain water as it runs off the surface of the rock. Rivers carry some of this salt into the ocean. They carry only a little bit at a time. The water in the ocean evaporates; that is, it passes into the air as moisture. The salt, which is a solid material, is left behind. It has no way of getting out.

This is exactly what happens in Great Salt Lake. Rivers flow into the lake, but no rivers flow out. The salt in these waters is deposited in the lake. As the lake water evaporates, salt is left behind. The Great Salt Lake is getting saltier and saltier all the time. It is already six times as salty as the ocean. You can stand in the water, sit in the water, or lie down in the water, but you cannot sink into it. You just bob around like a cork on the sea. Visitors always enjoy a swim in this strange lake.

West of the lake there is an extensive salt desert. The salt here looks like snow on the ground.

Salt Lake City. Salt Lake City is the capital of Utah. This beautiful city lies at the foot of the Wasatch mountains, near the shores of the lake from which it got its name.

The city was founded by the Mormons, a religious group, one hundred years ago. Brigham Young, their leader, led them to the West when they could not get along with their neighbors in the East. The Mormons took a year making their way across the country to the western side of the Rockies. There they found a great, flat land between the mountains, bordering the large, silvery lake. They started a community which they called Salt Lake City.

It was not long before they started plowing, planting, and building. They used water from the mountain streams, bringing it into their fields by irrigation ditches. Where only desert plants had been before, there soon were green fields of vegetables and hay.

The region around Salt Lake City is still a garden spot and the city itself has a population of over 200,000. Today Salt Lake City is an important crossroads for railroads, highways, and airlines running east, west, north, and south to the other parts

No Waterwings Needed. Tourists demonstrate the odd fact that it is almost impossible to sink in the Great Salt Lake. Note how easily they float.

of our great country. It is a trading and manufacturing center for the people who live nearby on the farms and ranches, or who work in the mines. Salt, which is obtained by evaporating water from the Great Salt Lake, is refined in the city and shipped to other parts of the country. Oil, meat, and metals are other products.

Salt Lake City. Lying on the shores of the lake, the beautiful capital of Utah is surrounded by fertile farmland and shadowed by high mountains.

THE NATIONAL PARKS OF AMERICA

In some countries of the world, the most beautiful areas of woodland, mountains, and hills are reserved as the private estates of rich men and aristocrats. These fortunate few keep their parks for their own private use, and the public seldom has the opportunity to enjoy these stretches of natural scenery.

This is not so in America. Throughout our land, the choicest areas of natural beauty are kept by the Government for the use of all the people. These are called the National Parks. Every citizen shares in the ownership of towering mountain ranges, hot springs, vast forest areas, canyons, glaciers, and waterfalls.

Each year, millions of Americans visit their national parks. They find wonderlands

Natural Wonders of the West. (Right) Two views of the Grand Canyon. (Below) The Royal Gorge. (Below, right) Painted Desert.

of nature, unspoiled by the work of man. There are park rangers who see to it that the laws are obeyed, and that the natural features of the region are not changed or altered in any way. There are also scientists who give lectures and tours of each area, pointing out the varieties of wild life and explaining some of the spectacles of nature. Tourists often rent tents for camping overnight.

Perhaps the best known of the national parks is Grand Canyon National Park in Arizona. Here the magnificent sight of the deep gorge cut by the Colorado River thrills many visitors each year. It is possible to take a donkey ride along the rim of this vast canyon, and look deep within its shadows to see the tiny ribbon of the Colorado River far below. A few of the other famous national parks and monuments in the West are Yellowstone, Petrified Forest, and Yosemite. Perhaps you will have the opportunity some day to visit one of these exciting places.

Canyon Road. U. S. Highways 6 and 24 enter Glenwood Canyon at this point. Throughout Colorado and most of the West there are excellent roads.

The Grand Canyon. One of the greatest wonders of the region is the Grand Canyon in Arizona. This canyon is really a very big ditch, cut by the Colorado River

Driving Through the West. This excellent highway crosses the Inyo Mountains of California. Death Valley lies beyond the peaks in the background.

as it crosses the Colorado Plateau. It is a mile deep! From the top of the canyon the river looks like a slender little thread of water running at the bottom. Yet the river has cut this huge canyon all by itself. The walls of the canyon show the different layers of sandstone and limestone, colored yellow, red, green and purple. Each layer of rock has been colored by the minerals it contains. Copper turns rock green, iron turns rock red, and other minerals each have their own colorings.

There are other canyons cut by branches of the Colorado river, but the Grand Canyon is the biggest of them all. Long, long, ago people called "Cliff Dwellers" built their homes high up on the walls of these canyons. They built caves in the rock to be safe from their enemies.

Fast-growing City. Phoenix, Arizona, has tripled its population in recent times. It is now the largest city between the Rockies and the mountains near the Pacific. Around the city is an irrigated farm area. Water for irrigation is supplied by dams that have been built on the Salt River. The city itself depends on this river for its water supply and hydroelectric power.

The sunny, dry climate has brought many vacationers, as well as year-round residents, to Phoenix. While midday temperatures are high in summer, nights and mornings are comfortable. Homes, buildings, and factories are usually air-conditioned. Most vacationers come from colder climates to enjoy the mild Arizona winters.

Facts *to remember*

1. The Rocky mountains are on the western edge of the Great Plains. They are much higher than the Appalachian Mountains. Trees cover the slopes. Streams in the lower valleys provide water for irrigation. The Rockies acted as barriers to the pioneers who traveled west. Today, there are many kinds of transportation crossing the Rockies. In the mountains, however, there are few people and no large cities.
2. Between the Rockies and the Pacific lies the Great Basin. It is a region of lower mountains, plateaus, and lowland deserts. The climate is hot and dry.
3. Many minerals are found in the Rockies. The richest copper mine in the world is located in Butte, Montana.
4. Tourists visit Yellowstone National Park to see its many natural wonders. "Old Faithful," located in this Park, is a big geyser. There are other national parks in the Western States. The Grand Canyon in Arizona is one of the greatest wonders of this region. It was cut by the Colorado River.
5. Since no rivers flow out of Great Salt Lake, it is getting saltier and saltier. Salt Lake City was founded by the Mormons. They made a garden spot out of a desert in Utah.

What *have I learned?*

I

Answer each of the following questions in a sentence or two.

1. How far do the Rocky Mountains extend on the continent of North America?
2. What methods are used to mine gold in the Rockies?
3. How is the copper mining in Utah different from the copper mining in Michigan?
4. Describe the climate of the Great Basin.
5. Why has the area around Phoenix, Arizona, become a favorite spot for vacationers?
6. How do the Rocky Mountains compare with the Appalachian Highlands in height and extent?
7. What are some of the noticeable contrasts to be found in this region?
8. Why is the Great Salt Lake becoming more and more salty each year?
9. Why are there no large cities and few people in the Rocky Mountains area?
10. What are some of the natural wonders which tourists come to see in this region?

II

Copy the items in column A. Write opposite each one the item from column B that best fits it.

Column A	Column B
1. A barrier to the "Forty-niners"	Salt Lake City
2. Abandoned mining towns	Butte
3. Location of the world's richest copper mine	Yellowstone National Park
4. Used for making filaments for electric light bulbs	Rocky Mountains
5. Areas where gold and gravel are mixed	"Ghost Towns"
6. Cut by the Colorado River	Tungsten
7. City founded by the Mormons	Uranium Ore
8. A dry area between the Rockies and the Pacific	Grand Canyon
9. Used in the production of atomic energy	Great Basin
10. Place of natural wonders	Placer Deposits

Facts *to understand*

Give a reason for each statement.

1. The Rocky Mountain Region differs from the Great Plains Region.
2. Different methods are used to mine gold.
3. Many tourists come to the Rocky Mountain region.
4. The Great Basin has little moisture.
5. Salt Lake City and Phoenix are important cities in this area.

4

Sunny California

The Golden Gate. The famous bay and the long bridge across it at San Francisco have been the West Coast gateway for millions of travelers.

California, one of the Pacific Coast states, is quite different from those parts of the West which you have already studied. The Great Plains, with its large farms and ranches, does not have a large population, nor does the rugged Rocky mountain area or the dry Great Basin. There are few large cities in these regions because there is little manufacturing. In contrast, along the California coast we find such large cities as San Francisco, Los Angeles, and San Diego. All are busy ports and important manufacturing centers.

California is our third largest state. Only the new state of Alaska and Texas are larger in area. The population of California has grown so rapidly in recent years that today only the state of New York has more people. Many expect that the growing population of California may soon surpass even that of New York. California is a good place to live and work.

The California Coast. The map on page 218 shows you that California has a long coast line on the Pacific Ocean. The coast curves rather sharply. Los Angeles and San Francisco are both on the Pacific, but the curve of the coast puts Los Angeles far to the east of San Francisco. Los Angeles is even east of the inland city of Reno, Nevada, and Reno is over 200 miles from the ocean.

There are not so many good harbors along California's coast as there are along the Atlantic coast. However, San Francisco Bay is an excellent harbor because it is almost surrounded by land. Two peninsulas protect it from the storms which build up at sea. Monterey Bay, south of San Francisco, has a wide opening and faces the open sea. For this reason, it is not a very good harbor. Los Angeles has a good man-made harbor. While San Diego's harbor is smaller than San Francisco Bay, it is quite useful, and the city serves as our chief naval base on the Pacific Coast.

California's Mountains. Now let's look at California's mountains. There are low mountains near the coast which run from the Oregon border all the way south to Los Angeles. These mountains are called the Coast Ranges. Unlike the Middle Atlantic States, California has no wide coastal plain. In some places, the mountains of California come almost to the ocean shore.

To the east of the Coast Ranges is a chain of jagged, high mountains called the Sierra Nevada. The name is made up of two Spanish words which mean *sharp-toothed* and *snowy*. The Sierra Nevada is much higher than the Coastal Ranges. Moisture-bearing winds from the Pacific Ocean are cooled as they rise up the western slopes of the Sierra Nevada. As a result, large amounts of rain fall on the western slopes. When the winds go down the other side of the Sierra Nevada, they are

Sierra Nevada Mountains of California. Here the jagged peaks overlook the Owens River Valley on the eastern, drier side of the mountain range.

Mount Whitney. This famous peak is the highest point in the forty-eight states. It is located in eastern California, part of Sequoia National Park.

causes the Great Basin to be so dry. By the time these winds have crossed the high mountains, they have released all their moisture on the Pacific, or *windward* side.

Land of Contrasts. From what you have read so far, you can see that California is a land of great contrasts. The deserts get almost no rain at all, while other sections of the state get large amounts of rain. There are few plants of any kind on the deserts in the southern and western parts of California. In the northern section we find the huge redwood and sequoia trees. Some of these trees are said to be three or four thousand years old. There are places in the southern part of the state where snow never falls, while the peaks of the Sierra Nevada, not far away, have snow all year.

warmed and release very little moisture. That is why the land is so dry in the Great Basin to the east of the Sierras.

In the southern part of California are the San Bernardino Mountains. They are really a continuation of the Sierra Nevada, but they are not so high.

There is also a large expanse of desert land in California. It is mostly in the southern part of the state, west of the Sierra Nevada. The dryness of this area is due to the same action of the Pacific winds which

There are other contrasts, too. There are large areas in the deserts and mountains that are scarcely ever visited by human beings. On the other hand, millions of people live in Los Angeles and its surrounding metropolitan area.

In the Sierra Nevada is a peak called Mount Whitney. It is 14,495 feet above sea level, and is the highest peak in this part of North America. Only 80 miles away from Mount Whitney, however, is Death Valley, 280 feet below sea level. This is the lowest place in all the Western Hemisphere.

Death Valley. Badwater, in California's Death Valley, is at the lowest point in the United States — 280 feet below sea level. Mt. Whitney is nearby.

Variety of Climates. California has every kind of climate—from very dry to very wet, from very cold to very hot. The lowlands from San Francisco south to the Mexican border have a *Mediterranean climate*. This means that the weather is warm both in the summer months and in the winter months, although it is a little warmer in summer. All during the long summer there is scarcely a drop of rain. The sun shines brightly day after day. The rain comes in the winter months.

This is a very pleasant climate to live in. Many people from other parts of the country have moved to California because they enjoy the climate. Many others come to enjoy the climate in California during their vacations.

High in the mountains, the weather is much cooler. Summer days are cool, and winter days are very cold. It is impossible to drive through parts of the mountains in winter, because the roads are covered by many feet of snow. Mountain blizzards are often very severe.

On the deserts the days are very hot all year round, although the evenings are cool. The temperature often reaches 120 degrees in desert areas like Death Valley. There is seldom any rain in the deserts.

Water is a problem everywhere in the southern part of the state. The rain that falls during the winter months is not enough to take care of the needs of the people all year round. Los Angeles has to bring in its water from the mountains many miles away.

In the northern part of the state and on the western slopes of the Sierras, there is plenty of rain brought by the westerly winds blowing in from the warm Pacific Ocean. The giant redwood and sequoia trees grow here. These huge trees, the biggest living things in the world, could not have grown so big without great amounts of rain.

Hillside Farming. Here on the slopes of California's Great Central Valley a farmer plows his field. The excellent climate and soil produce rich crops.

Fertile Valleys. Between the coast ranges and the Sierra Nevada is a flat valley running from north to south. It is about 50 miles wide and 400 miles long. This is the Great Central Valley of California. It consists of two river basins, or areas drained by rivers—the Sacramento and the San Joaquin. The Sacramento River flows south, and the San Joaquin flows north. They meet and flow together into San Francisco Bay. These two rivers are fed by water from the mountains. In turn, they supply water for the fields in the valley. The best farm land in California is found in this valley.

Another good farming section is the Imperial Valley in the south of the state. This was once a desert, but now water is brought to it by irrigation. It has become one of the richest farming lands in the world.

Remember these things and you will

have a good picture of the surface of California: a long curved coast line with two natural ports; mountains near the coast and higher mountains about fifty miles to the east; the rich Central Valley between the mountain ranges.

A Giant Industry. Today, farming in California is a giant industry. No state raises more crops than California. New methods in farming, plus the use of irrigation where there is not enough rainfall, have made this tremendous growth in agriculture possible.

Farming began in California with the old Spanish missions. Mediterranean crops were brought from Spain and transplanted in American soil. You can see on the maps in your Atlas that Spain borders on the Mediterranean Sea. There the climate is mild and rainy in winter, dry and hot in summer. When the Spanish found that southern California had a similar climate, they planted the same kind of crops they had grown in Spain. Some of these were lemons, oranges, olives, and grapes. The early Spanish settlers also herded livestock, chiefly sheep

Fruit from the Vine. The Cella Vineyards of Reedly, California, produced these juicy grapes. The warm climate favors grape-growing especially.

and cattle. Wheat, fruits, and vegetables were raised for the gold-seekers who came in 1849.

Fast transportation and refrigerator cars make it possible to ship fruits and vegetables to the eastern cities during the winter season. Special crops that bring high returns are grown with the use of expensive irrigation systems. They are canned or quick-frozen for markets at home and abroad. Today, these same crops, as well as many new ones, are raised in the Central Valley and other farm areas in California.

Over 200 Kinds of Crops. Today, California farmers send to market over 200 different farm products. Truck farmers produce a great variety of vegetables and fruits, including asparagus, carrots, celery, lettuce, spinach, sugar beets, tomatoes, and cantaloupes, grapes, peaches, pears, and prunes. Other farmers grow potatoes, barley, wheat, rice, and cotton, or raise dairy and beef cattle. Poultry farmers raise chickens and turkeys, and market eggs.

The rich soil, the long growing season, and the abundance of water for irrigation favor the growth of fruits and vegetables. In the irrigated areas, melting snows from the mountains feed the reservoirs where the water is stored.

The long, dry, sunny days of the Southern California summer are ideal for drying fruits. Fresno is the center of the raisin industry. Raisins are made by drying grapes. Other dried fruits from California are apricots and prunes. Prunes are made by drying plums. Much of California's fruit is also dried by artificial light and heat.

Large quantities of wine grapes are raised in the Central Valley. California is our leading wine-producing state. The first grapes for making wine were introduced by the Franciscan Fathers who came as missionaries to the west coast of America.

Oranges. Everyone associates the growing of oranges with California, especially the popular seedless oranges. Let us see how this big industry grew up.

Much planning is necessary for an orange grove. The trees are set out in rows. In California there are usually from 80 to 130 trees to an acre. When the trees are about six years old, they begin to bear fruit. A large tree may bear 500 or more oranges at a time.

Orange trees can be easily damaged by insects and disease. They must be carefully watched for any sign of sickness, or of the insects that feed on their leaves. Several times a year the trees are carefully *pruned,* or trimmed. They must also be irrigated.

There is another danger which orange trees are subject to—they cannot take extremes of cold. In order to avoid the danger of frost, orange growers usually set the trees out on the hillsides instead of in the valleys. Cold air is heavier than warm air and, therefore, settles into the lower areas. By placing their trees on the slopes, the growers often avoid the lower temperatures which occur in the valleys.

Orange Groves. Oranges are only part of California's fruit crop. This state produces more than one third of the fruit grown in the United States.

Orange growers, however, must constantly watch the thermometer for frosty weather. When the weather gets cold enough to damage the trees, the farmers place oil heaters in the rows between the trees. It is costly to heat an orchard, but the farmer must save his crop from killing frost.

Great care must also be taken in picking and packing oranges. The picker must place the orange in a bag at his side without bruising it. The filled bag is emptied gently into a box or trunk. In the packing house oranges are sorted, washed, dried, and separated according to size. Some are wrapped in paper and boxed for shipping. Others are used in canning factories to make juice, most of which is quick-frozen. Orange oil, marmalade and candied orange peel are some of the by-products.

In recent years, some California orange orchards have been cut down to make room for housing developments to take care of the growing population. California even imports some oranges now from Florida.

APPLES
LUMBER
MACHINERY

SALMON

COFFEE
TEA
SPICES

CANNED
SEAFOOD

FOOD
PROCESSING

CRANBERRIES

PETROLEUM PRODUCTS
MANUFACTURED GOODS
FISH DRIED FRUIT

RUBBER HEMP SILK
COPRA BANANAS
PINEAPPLES QUININE

COMMERCIAL
FISHING

PETROLEUM PRODUCTS
CANNED FRUIT
RAW COTTON

SILK
RUBBER
COFFEE
COTTON

C A N A

CANADA

OLYMPIC
NAT. PK.

ALUMINUM

Seattle

Olympia   Tacoma

WASHINGTON

Spokane

WATERTON-GLACIER
INTERNATIONAL
PEACE PARK

ROCKY

M O N T

Helena

MT. RAINIER
NAT. PARK   Mt. Rainier

PLUTONIUM

Lewiston

Butte
COPPER

Billings

Portland

FOOD
PROCESSING   Salem

O R E G O N

CRATER LAKE
NAT. PARK

COPPER

I D A H O

Boise

ZINC

LEAD

YELLOWSTONE
NATIONAL
PARK

GRAND
TETON
NAT. PARK

W Y O

LASSEN VOL.
NAT. PARK

N E V A D A

Carson City

Sacramento

San Francisco

Oakland

YOSEMITE
NAT. PARK

KINGS
CANYON
NAT. PARK
Mt. Whitney

SEQUOIA
NAT. PARK

Death
Valley

MOVIES

Los Angeles

Long Beach

SANTA CATALINA
ISLAND

San Diego

COPPER

Great
Salt
Lake

Ogden

Salt Lake City

COPPER

U T A H

LEAD

ZINC

URANIUM

ZION
NAT. PARK

BRYCE CANYON
NAT. PARK

MESA VERDE
NAT. PARK

C O L O R A D O

URANIUM

PLATEAU

GRAND CANYON
NAT. PARK

Las
Vegas

Lake
Mead

NATURAL
GAS

Mojave Desert

Salton
Sea

A R I Z O N A

Phoenix

Gila

Tucson

MEXICO

P A C I F I C

O C E A N

CASCADE RANGE

COLUMBIA PLATEAU

GREAT BASIN

SIERRA NEVADA

COAST RANGE

C A L I F O R N I A

Snake R.

Colorado R.

Sacramento R.

Capital Cities - - - - - - - ◉
International Boundaries ———
State or Provincial Boundaries —·—·—
Scale of Miles

TUNA

0   100   200   300   400

Farmers Without Land. In California, as well as in some other parts of our country, there are huge farms of thousands of acres where only one crop is grown. It may be wheat, or lettuce, or sugar beets, or some orchard crop. The owners may be a farm family, or some large grocery company or canning industry. A few men are hired to plant and cultivate these *factory farms* by machinery.

At certain seasons, however, they need many more hired helpers—usually at harvest time. For a few weeks great numbers of people are hired to cut lettuce or asparagus, to pick peaches or pears, and to thin sugar beets. Thousands of workers with their families come in trucks or in their own broken-down cars to work for day wages during these busy times. They are welcomed for a short season; then they are no longer needed. They must move on to look for more work. Many of these roving workers were once farmers who left their own small plots of land because they could not make a living.

Workers who are always on the move have little chance to go to church or receive the sacraments. Fathers, mothers, and children must work in order to make a living. They have no real homes, their children have little chance to go to school, and many of them are very poor. Much of the fruit and vegetables eaten by city people come from these huge *factory farms,* harvested by these poor workers. Our government and a few of the farm owners furnish good camp cottages, but in some places the workers are forced to sleep in old shacks. The life of a traveling worker is not good. It is better for families to have their own small farms and work on their own land.

Mining in California. Minerals have had much to do with the prosperity of California. Remember it was the discovery of gold that brought people in large numbers to settle this state. At present it is not gold but oil that is bringing mineral wealth to California. One of the largest oil fields is in the Long Beach area near Los Angeles.

California is also one of the leading states in the production of natural gas. Oil and natural gas are especially important to the people of California, since it is not a coal-producing state. Most of California's power is produced by these two fuels.

Some gold, silver, lead, zinc, and copper are mined in the mountains. One steel plant near Los Angeles uses iron ore mined in California.

Los Angeles. The largest city in the Western States is Los Angeles, California. This modern city was named by the Franciscan missionaries in honor of Our Lady, Queen of the Angels. They came upon the site of the city the day after the feast of Our Lady of the Angels.

It remained a small town until oil was discovered nearby. Then the city grew very rapidly, and in less than 25 years it has become one of the busiest and biggest cities of the United States. Its population now exceeds two million people, with another two million living in surrounding smaller cities and towns. This makes a total of four million for the metropolitan area of Los Angeles.

In area, Los Angeles is one of the largest cities in the world. The main part of the city is about twenty miles inland. At one time Los Angeles had only a very poor port called San Pedro. The people dredged out its harbor, built a breakwater two miles long, and bought a narrow strip of land leading to it, called the "shoestring." Now the port of Los Angeles handles more business than any other port on the west coast.

Los Angeles is also a city of many industries. Some of the products sent out from

here are packed meats, clothing, food products, machinery, metal products, rubber tires, petroleum products, automobiles, and aircraft. The Los Angeles area assembles more automobiles than any other place except Detroit; is a leading producer of airplanes; makes more rubber tires than any other city except Akron; ranks third in the preparation of food, and fourth in the making of clothing among the other states.

Two Big Problems. A big problem for Los Angeles is the water supply. Factories and city dwellers need large quantities of water. An *aqueduct,* a big wide steel tube, brings water 240 miles from Owens Lake, high in the Sierra Nevada mountains. It runs across mountains and deserts on its

A Busy Road. This is the famous Los Angeles Freeway. Millions of vehicles pour in and out of the city each day along this modern, high-speed road.

way. It soon became clear, however, that the aqueduct could not supply all the water needed by a fast-growing population. A second aqueduct was built to Hoover Dam on the Colorado River, 242 miles away. By means of this aqueduct, water comes all the way from the Rocky Mountains by way of the Colorado River. As the Los Angeles area continues to grow in population, the need for water will become more urgent. Plans will have to be made to get more water from the rivers to the north.

Hemmed in by the sea on the west and a wall of mountains on the east, Los Angeles rests in a basin. This location creates another problem. Warm air from the interior deserts comes over the mountains and keeps the cool lower air from rising. It is trapped there for days and days. This air becomes polluted by fumes from auto exhaust pipes and smoke from industrial plants. The bright California sunshine has a chemical effect on the fumes. The polluted air at times burns people's eyes and chokes them.

The smoky air is called *smog*. Los Angeles has already made some progress in lessening the smog conditions by forbidding the burning of wastes in the city. Other large cities of our country have similar air pollution problems, but none are as serious as that of Los Angeles.

Hollywood. The motion picture industry brought fame to this Los Angeles suburb. Most of the movies shown in the United States are produced here.

Movie and TV Land

It is hard to believe that there was no such thing as moving pictures sixty years ago and that home TV was unknown twenty-five years ago. Four out of every five motion pictures made in our country today are produced in Hollywood, a suburb of Los Angeles. So are many of the television films.

The industry started in Hollywood be-

Disneyland. The delightful Land of Tomorrow is one of the many attractions at Walt Disney's famous amusement center located in Anaheim, Calif.

cause strong sunlight was needed in taking the pictures. This meant the actors had to work out-of-doors practically all year round. The dry, sunny climate of Los Angeles area was ideal for making movies. In addition, all kinds of scenery can be found near Hollywood—deserts, mountains, ocean.

Nowadays much of the scenery is artificial and is made right in the studio. Electric lighting is now so good that bright sunlight is no longer needed. The studios are now used as much for TV films as for movies. Actors, carpenters, electricians, stage hands, and directors are needed to make a picture. Thousands of people in the Los Angeles area work in the movie and TV industry.

San Francisco

The city of San Francisco was founded by the Franciscan missionaries in 1775. It was the last of the twenty-one California missions. When gold was discovered in California in 1849, many people flocked to the city. Since then it has grown very rapidly.

San Francisco is built on steep hills overlooking one of the best natural harbors in the world. Ships that enter the large harbor pass under the beautiful Golden Gate Bridge. Canned goods, petroleum products, grain, dried fruits, flour, and leather are among the many products which are shipped from San Francisco. Coffee, silk, sugar, tea, coconuts, and tin are some of the imports. San Francisco is the business center of the California Valley. The city handles about one fourth of the Pacific Coast trade.

Many large business firms and banks have offices in San Francisco. It is the financial center of the west coast, just as Chicago is for the Middle West and New York City is for the Eastern United States.

If you visited San Francisco, you would want to see its famous Chinatown. It looks like a real Chinese city.

Sights of San Francisco. (left) An old-fashioned cable car toils up one of the steep hills. (right) San Francisco's Chinatown is now world-famous.

Panorama of the City. This picture of San Francisco was taken from Nob Hill, high over the city. It looks out toward the bay in the background.

Other California Cities. Two other important cities on San Francisco Bay are Oakland and Berkeley. The eight-mile Oakland Bridge, longest in the world, joins these cities with San Francisco.

California's capital city is Sacramento. The city was born with the discovery of gold in 1848. It is located near the center of the fertile Central Valley. Just south of Sacramento is Stockton. Both cities are marketing centers for the farm products of the Central Valley.

The oldest city in California is San Diego. Father Serra, the Franciscan, built his first mission here. Since then, many of the offices and dwellings in the city have been built along the same Spanish style. A huge naval base has been constructed here by our government. The excellent natural harbor and delightful climate permit open-air training of men all year round. The city also has an important airplane industry.

Part of California's fishing fleet works out of San Diego's fine harbor. They bring in large catches of tuna and sardines.

Facts *to remember*

1. California, our third largest state, has a long, curved coast line with two natural ports. There are mountains near the coast and higher mountains about 50 miles to the east. The rich Central Valley lies between the mountain ranges. Many people live in this state.
2. There are not so many good harbors along the California coast as along the Atlantic coast.
3. California is a land of contrasts because it has great differences in rainfall, climate, vegetation, number of large cities, and land level. Water is a problem in southern California. It is brought to the cities by means of a long aqueduct.
4. The rich soil, the long growing season, and the abundance of water for irrigation favor the growth of fruits and vegetables in California. Farmers send to market more than 200 different farm products. The long, dry summers are ideal for drying fruits. Orange-growing is a big industry.

5. Hired workers help with the work at harvest time. They have few opportunities for education, proper religious training, or good home life.
6. In area, Los Angeles is one of the largest cities in the world, and one of the biggest and busiest cities in the United States. Water must be piped long distances to this city. The air is easily polluted. In Hollywood, a suburb of Los Angeles, many movies and television programs are produced.

What *have I learned?*

In each of the following sentences, the word in capitals makes the sentence right or wrong. Write all the sentences correctly on a piece of paper. Change the wrong words to correct words.
1. California has a LONG curved coast line with two natural ports.
2. The Coast Ranges are HIGH mountains.
3. The Great Basin is WEST of the Sierras.
4. Winds going down on the eastern side of the Sierra Nevada are WARMED and release little moisture.
5. Mount Whitney is the highest peak in the state of COLORADO.
6. The huge redwood and sequoia trees live for THOUSANDS of years.
7. Summer days are COOL in lands having a Mediterranean climate.
8. ANIMALS are the biggest living things in the world.
9. Death Valley has a RAINY climate.
10. The Great Central Valley is drained by the MISSISSIPPI and the San Joaquin Rivers.
11. No state raises more crops than OREGON.
12. Large quantities of WINE grapes are raised in the Central Valley.
13. To avoid danger of frost, orange trees are set out in the VALLEYS.

Facts *to understand*

Answer each of the following questions in a sentence or two.
1. How does California differ from the Great Plains?
2. To what natural dangers are orange trees exposed?
3. What contrasts are found in California?
4. Why are so many crops raised in California?
5. What problems must Los Angeles solve?

5 The Pacific Northwest

A Mountain Trail. Happy vacationers on horseback are riding across Edith Creek. In the background is Washington State's beautiful Mount Rainier.

The Pacific Northwest region, in the northwest corner of the United States, consists of the states of Washington, Oregon, and part of northern California. Look at the map on page 218. You will see that all three of these states have a Pacific coast line. The region is one of high mountains, fertile river valleys, and interior plateaus.

This was the part of our country first explored by Lewis and Clark when Thomas Jefferson was President of the United States. They took their canoes down the Snake River and into the Columbia River,

finally arriving at the Pacific Coast. It took over two years to make their journey over the rugged mountains from St. Louis to the Pacific Coast and back. Today, this once-distant corner of the United States is closely bound to the rest of the country.

Surface. A very narrow, almost barren, coastal plain lies between the Coastal Ranges and the Pacific Ocean. The coast line is very regular and there are few good harbors. The mouth of the Columbia River affords transportation to Portland, Oregon. Puget Sound, an arm of the Pacific Ocean, enables large ships to reach Seattle and Tacoma in Washington.

Between the low Coastal Ranges and the high Cascades, farther inland, lies the

Mount Hood. The magnificent peak of this mountain in Oregon soars 11,245 feet into the sky and is covered with snow throughout the entire year.

fertile Puget Sound—Willamette lowland. The location of this valley between mountain ranges is similar to that of the Central Valley of California.

The western slopes of the Cascade Mountains are a vast, forested wilderness. High in the Cascades, Mt. Rainier in Washington, Mt. Hood in Oregon, and Mt. Shasta in northern California raise their snow-covered peaks over 10,000 feet into the clouds. In southern Oregon, deep blue Crater Lake lies in the crater of an extinct Cascade volcano. Many tourists find delight in the beautiful scenery of this part of the Pacific Northwest.

To the east of the Cascades, in Washington, Oregon, and extending into Idaho, lies the Columbia Plateau. Many centuries ago in this region there were volcanoes from which great quantities of lava flowed. *Lava* is melted rock from below the earth's surface. It cools and hardens after it comes to the surface. The Columbia Plateau was built from layers of this lava. As years passed, the surface layers of lava decayed and formed fertile soil.

Climate. Cool summers and mild, wet winters describe the climate of the Pacific Northwest, on the Pacific, or windward, side of the Cascades. When winds blow in from over the Pacific Ocean, they are forced upward over the low coast ranges and climb the western slopes of the high Cascades. The warm, moist air from the ocean cools as it rises. As a result, the Pacific slopes of these mountains have the heaviest rainfall in the United States. Some of the mountain slopes receive as much as 150 inches of rainfall in a year, with the average between 80 and 100 inches.

During the winter, the winds blow over the land from the ocean, which is warmer. There is seldom any frost in the Puget Sound —Willamette Valley. However, there is some danger of floods in the late winter and spring. That is when the rivers carry off the heavy rains and the water from the melting snows of the Cascades.

In summer, the ocean is cooler than the land, and the winds blowing in from over the sea give the areas west of the Cascades a delightfully mild summer climate. The average winter temperature usually differs less than 20 degrees from the average summer temperature. Roses bloom in the month of December in Portland, Oregon.

On the east side of the Cascades, on the Columbia Plateau, the rainfall is light, averaging less than 20 inches a year. Temperatures on the plateau are not so mild as they are west of the mountains. Summers are much warmer, and winters colder.

The Puget Sound—Willamette Lowland. Some of the best farm land in the Pacific Northwest lies in the valley of the Willamette River and in the lowland bordering Puget Sound. The fertile soil and the long growing season provided by the warm summers and mild winters are good for farming. More than half of the farms in Oregon are in the Willamette Valley, and many of Washington's farms are near Puget Sound.

Fruit farms produce prunes, cherries, pears, strawberries, and apples. Truck farmers raise onions, celery, peas, beans, and tomatoes. Northwest lowland farmers also raise wheat, oats, and other grains, and keep sheep, dairy cattle, and poultry.

Many of the products of the farms in the Willamette—Puget Sound lowland are sent to markets in the larger cities of Seattle, Tacoma, and Portland, to supply local needs. However, the farmers of this region also send their crops to canneries and frozen food plants. The farms could supply even greater amounts of foodstuffs, and probably will in the future as the population of the region increases. One reason why more crops are not produced here at this time is the shortage of labor for harvesting. There is no point in growing more than can be picked.

The Columbia Basin. Another important farm area of the Pacific Northwest is located in eastern Washington and northeastern Oregon. This region, part of the Columbia Plateau, is called the Columbia Basin because it lies between the Cascades and the Rockies. The region is drained by the Columbia River and some of its tributaries. The Columbia rises in the Rockies, flows south, west, south again across the state of Washington, and finally west again to the Pacific. During the last part of its journey to the Pacific, it forms the boundary between Washington and Oregon.

The Columbia Basin has fertile lava soil. Although the rainfall is light, the Columbia River supplies plenty of water for irrigation. In many places dry farming is carried on. You will remember from your study of the Midwest that wheat is a crop which does not require much rainfall. Some of the largest spring and winter wheat farms in the coun-

try are in this region. The wheat is harvested by combines as in the Midwest. Three important wheat markets in the Pacific Northwest are Spokane and Seattle in Washington, and Portland in Oregon.

The Hood River in Oregon, and the Yakima and the Wenatchee Rivers in Washington, flow down the eastern slopes of the Cascades into the Columbia. In their irrigated valleys are extensive apple orchards. Washington is usually the leading apple-producing state in our country each year.

In Washington the waters of the Columbia River are held back by the huge Grand Coulee Dam. The water is used to irrigate thousands upon thousands of acres of fields in the Columbia Basin where sugar beets, vegetables, fruits, potatoes, and alfalfa are grown.

Farming in Oregon. A farmer pauses to accept a drink of water brought by his daughter on horseback. This is at Klamath Falls, near California.

California Redwood Tree. People standing at the base of this Pacific Northwest tree seem tiny by comparison. It is one of the oldest living things.

Land of Giant Trees. The greatest forest area of the United States is in the Pacific Northwest. Dense forests of huge evergreen trees cover the rainswept western slopes of the Coast Ranges and Cascades. In Washington and Oregon the chief trees are red cedar, Douglas fir, western pine, hemlock, and spruce. In northern California, on the Pacific slopes of the Coast Ranges, grow the famous redwood trees. They are among the tallest and largest trees in the world. It is said that one of these redwood trees could supply enough lumber to build twenty-two average-sized homes. The western pine is another giant. It grows tall and straight, sometimes reaching a height of 200 feet or more, with a trunk 7 to 8 feet around.

The Pacific Northwest now produces almost half the timber cut in the United States. Oregon is the leading state, followed by California and Washington. Most of this timber is used for construction lumber. Some more is used to make plywood. Plywood consists of a number of long, very thin sheets of wood glued together under great pressure. It is very strong and makes an excellent building material for walls, floors, doors, and siding. Some wood, especially bark and scraps that cannot be used for lumber, is made into wood pulp for rayon and paper mills.

Timber! Let us imagine that we are visiting a lumber camp in the Pacific Northwest. After a long slow journey by train, we arrive at a small mountain station on the western slopes of the Cascades in Oregon. A truck belonging to the lumber company is at the station to meet us. We drive along a road through a forest of tall evergreen trees to the lumber camp, deep in the woods.

The boss of the camp shows us through the camp buildings. We visit the bunk houses where the lumbermen sleep, the cook house, the storerooms, and the tool house. Some of the buildings are on railroad flatcars. This makes it easier to move them when the timber in an area is cut and the camp must be moved to a new location. We are introduced to some "lumberjacks," and they ask us to have supper with them. Like the boss of the camp, they are big, friendly men with amazing appetites.

The next morning we watch the men work in the forests. They are experts at their jobs. We see a lumberjack, called a "high climber," cutting off the top of a tree. He has reached the top with the help of a safety belt and sharp spikes strapped to his shoes. Other lumberjacks called "fallers," are cutting the trees using power saws. When a tree is about to fall they shout a warning cry of "Timber!"

A cutting team saws the fallen tree into giant logs. They are usually dragged by tractor and cable to a loading point. A man called a "donkey engineer" runs a derrick that loads huge logs onto flatcars. Sometimes the trees are sent down the mountain to the sawmill in a long chute called a *flume*.

Because of the great size of the logs, the sawmill has to be a very large building. An expert can tell at a glance what a log will be used for when it enters the sawmill. He signals an operator who controls the machines that saw each log into beams, planks, or sash. The machines change what was once

Outward Bound Logs. Thick cables lift the huge logs onto flatcars. Almost half the lumber cut in the U. S. is produced in the Pacific Northwest.

a tall tree into a pile of lumber, chips, and sawdust. In this way, men work together in teams to produce the lumber that is needed for so many purposes.

A Giant Is Cut Down. With a mighty roar, another of the forest "giants" falls to earth. Care has been taken that it does not strike another tree.

Saving Our Forests. Natural resources have been put on this earth not only for our use but for future generations as well. Our lumber resources were shamefully wasted in many parts of our country. Those that are left will not last forever at the present rate of use unless more is done to conserve our forests.

Some steps have been taken in the Pacific Northwest to use these forests wisely. Lumber companies have started to replant trees where they had been cut down before. Others use *selective lumbering*. By this method, they cut down only tall trees and allow the smaller ones to remain. These smaller trees then have a chance to grow. This helps to keep a steady supply of lumber always on hand. It is much more sensible than cutting down every tree in sight and then waiting for years and years for a new crop of trees to grow.

Conservation. Trees cut down must be replaced. Seedlings like these are planted by hand, or grow from cones dropped by flying helicopters.

The government is also doing its part to conserve the forests of the Pacific Northwest. Large areas have been set aside as parks and forest reserves. There lumbering is not permitted, and trees are specially cared for. Forest rangers are ever on the watch to protect against the greatest enemy of forests—fire.

Fisheries of the Pacific Northwest. Along the Pacific Coast, from San Francisco north to Alaska, thousands of people are employed catching and canning salmon. The industry is not so important in the Pacific Northwest today as it was some years ago. Once the Columbia River was the most productive salmon fishing area in the world.

The breeding habits of the salmon make it an easy fish to catch. The salmon hatch from eggs in the quiet upstream waters of rivers and swim downstream to the ocean. After two or three years in salt water, they are full-grown. The salmon try to swim back to lay their eggs in the same waters they came from. When they come back, they are

A Large Haul of Salmon. These fishermen return to port at Blaine, Washington, with their day's catch. Nearby canneries will buy and pack these fish.

large and fat, and in such great numbers that it is easy to catch them offshore or in the rivers.

The building of the Bonneville and Grand Coulee Dams on the river, however, has produced changes. Large numbers of salmon no longer swim up the Columbia and its tributaries to lay their eggs. At Bonneville, *fish ladders* were built alongside the dam. By using the ladders, salmon could leap up a series of water steps and then continue upstream. The fish ladders were not too successful, however. Large numbers of salmon could not get to their usual egg-laying grounds. Fish ladders were not tried at the Grand Coulee Dam because of its great height. Instead, a fish *hatchery* was built below the dams. As the salmon come upstream, they are caught and their eggs are taken. When the baby salmon hatch out they are put back into the Columbia river. From there they swim downstream to the ocean.

Salmon is still a major catch in the Columbia and other rivers, in Puget Sound, and in the other coastal waters of the Pacific Northwest. Most of this catch is sent to the salmon canneries located along the shores of Puget Sound.

Other fish caught in the waters of the Pacific Northwest are halibut, sole, trout, shad, oysters, and pilchard. Pilchard are not food fish, but are used to make oil and fertilizer. Seattle is a great fishing port and is called the halibut capital of the world. It has more fishing boats than any other North Pacific port.

Fish provide food for man, feed for livestock, and fertilizer for the soil. We also use fish to make medicines and vitamins. We use it to make oil, paint, soap, and ink. Fishing, one of our country's oldest industries, supplies many needs and wants.

Producing Shiny Aluminum. Inexpensive electric power makes the production of this metal profitable. This machine rolls aluminum into sheets.

Manufacturing. Manufacturing is increasing in the Pacific Northwest. Aluminum, aircraft, heating equipment, iron,

Pacific Port of Seattle. Lumber is one of the most important items shipped from this busy Washington port. A great amount now goes to Alaska.

wool textiles, and leather are manufactured.

Furniture is manufactured in Portland and Tacoma. Packing cases for canned goods are made in the sawmills. Power for manufacturing comes from the big dams built on the Columbia River. This river furnishes more power for industry than any other river in the United States.

The cheap electricity supplied by hydro-electric power stations at the Bonneville and Grand Coulee Dams is very important. It led to the building of large aluminum-manufacturing plants in this region. The bauxite ore, from which aluminum is extracted, must be shipped long distances from Arkansas and South America. The cheap power available in the Pacific Northwest, however, makes aluminum manufacturing profitable.

Cities on Puget Sound. Some of the best harbors along the Pacific coast are on Puget Sound in the state of Washington. Seattle and Tacoma are the two chief ports on Puget Sound. Much of the lumber cut in the forests of the Pacific Northwest is shipped from these ports. Seattle has become an important trading center for the surrounding region. It is the chief port of the Pacific Northwest. The city was founded in 1852. At first, it grew slowly. Then gold-seekers, on their way to Alaska in the north, aided its growth and increased its importance as a trading center.

Lumber, machinery, cotton cloth, canned goods, and grain are exported. Silk, burlap, copra, tea, copper, rubber, and vegetable oils are some of the imported products. Most of them are brought from countries on the other side of the Pacific. Much of the trade with the new state of Alaska passes through the port of Seattle.

Port Angeles, Bellingham, and Everett in Washington are other busy trading ports on Puget Sound.

River Port. Portland, the largest city in Oregon, is one hundred miles up the Columbia River near the point where the Willamette flows into it. Although ocean ships sail up the river to Portland, few foreign vessels visit this port. Most of its commerce is with other ports along the Pacific Coast. From the interior, Portland receives much wheat and wool. Portland's factories manufacture clothing, wool textiles, chemicals, and machinery. It exports more lumber and other wood products than any other city of the Pacific Northwest.

Other Cities. Spokane, in eastern Washington, is the largest interior city of the Pacific Northwest. It is the gateway city for people traveling over the Rockies to the irrigated lands of the Columbia Basin. The city is an important wheat market.

Olympia, on the Puget Sound lowland, is the capital city of Washington. Salem, located on the Willamette River, is the capital city of Oregon.

Facts *to remember*

1. The Pacific Northwest is a region of high mountains, fertile river valleys, and interior plateaus. It has a regular coast line with few good harbors; however, some of the best harbors along the Pacific Coast are on Puget Sound in the State of Washington. Lewis and Clark first explored the Pacific Northwest.
2. East of the Cascades is the Columbia Plateau, which built up over the years from layers of lava which cooled and hardened.
3. Winds blowing from the Pacific and climbing the western slopes of the high Cascades give this area the heaviest rainfall in the United States. Winds from the ocean also prevent frost in the Puget Sound—Willamette Valley. Fertile soil and a long growing season make this a good farming area.
4. The Columbia River supplies water for irrigation to the Columbia Basin. Much spring and winter wheat is raised in this region. Washington is a great apple-producing state.

5. The greatest forest area of the United States is in the Pacific Northwest. Oregon is our leading timber state. We must save our natural resources for future generations.
6. Along the Pacific Coast, from San Francisco to Alaska, salmon is still a major catch.
7. Manufacturing is increasing in the Pacific Northwest. The Columbia River furnishes more power for industry than any other river in the United States. Cheap power makes aluminum manufacturing profitable, even where the bauxite ore has to be brought great distances.

What *have I learned?*

Rewrite each sentence, using only the correct one of the two words or phrases in italics.
1. *The Columbia Plateau* or *Puget Sound* is an arm of the Pacific Ocean.
2. The *eastern* or *western* slopes of the Cascade Mountains are a vast forested wilderness, receiving heavy rainfall.
3. The Columbia River rises in *Northwestern United States* or *Southwestern Canada*.
4. It took Lewis and Clark *two years* or *six months* to travel from St. Louis to the Pacific Coast and back.
5. Rainfall is light *west* or *east* of the Cascades.
6. More than half the farms in Oregon are in the *Willamette Valley* or *near Puget Sound*.
7. Wheat requires *much* or *little* rainfall.
8. The most important lumber state of the Pacific Northwest is *California* or *Oregon*.
9. *Spokane* or *Portland* is the largest interior city of the Northwest.
10. *Pilchard* or *Salmon* caught in the waters of the Pacific Northwest are used for food.

Facts *to understand*

Answer each of the following questions in a sentence or two.
1. What gives the Pacific slopes of the Cascades the heaviest rainfall in the United States?
2. Why is the Columbia Basin so important to the Northwest?
3. For which different purposes is the timber of the Northwest used?
4. Why are salmon easily caught?
5. What steps have been taken in the Northwest to preserve our forests?

The Pacific Northwest 267

6

Alaska

The Aleutian Islands. This chain stretches for 1500 miles into the North Pacific Ocean. The narrow inlets of the sea between high banks are *fiords.*

In your study of the United States so far, you have now learned about forty-eight states. In this chapter, you will study our forty-ninth state, Alaska. To learn about it, you will have to leave the borders of the forty-eight states and travel far to the northern part of our continent.

The state of Alaska is a large peninsula extending outward from northwestern North America. Strings of islands, which are part of the state, extend westward far into the Pacific and southward along the coast line of Canada. In area, Alaska is our largest state, more than twice the size of Texas, our second largest. There are still very few people in this new member of the United States, however. In the following pages you will read about them, and how they live and work.

A Great Bargain. A little more than 200 years ago, people from Russia crossed the Bering Strait to explore Alaska. On the map on pages 6-7, see how close Alaska is to Asia. The commander of the Russians was named Vitus Bering, and the sea and the strait there were named for him. The Russians did not have far to travel from Asia because the Bering Strait is only about 50 miles wide. They did little to settle the country during the years they owned it. They seemed interested only in furs and in trading with the native Eskimos.

In 1867, just after our Civil War ended, the United States bought Alaska for $7,250,000. Many people in the United States said we made a mistake when we bought Alaska. Because they thought the land contained nothing but ice and snow, they called it "Uncle Sam's Icebox."

Alaska was neither an "icebox" nor worthless. Before many years had passed, these people discovered they were very wrong. The fish, gold, and furs obtained in Alaska in a single year were worth many times the amount of money paid for it. Since its purchase, Alaska has become more and more valuable each year. Today, it is the largest of the fifty United States, an untapped storehouse of valuable resources, and an important base for our country's defenses.

Natural Wonders of Alaska. Tourists coming to Alaska by car, plane, or ship see some of the most beautiful scenery in the world. Flower-carpeted valleys lie at the foot of snow-capped mountains. Hundreds of blue lakes, winding inlets from the sea called *fiords,* glittering glaciers, and smoking volcanoes make fascinating sights throughout this state.

Along the southern coast of Alaska, just north of Kodiak Island, is the "Valley of Ten Thousand Smokes." Smoke appears everywhere in the valley, coming up through cracks in the surface. The area is set aside by our government as a national monument. Here, in 1912, the volcano, Mt. Katmai erupted. The explosion threw thousands of tons of earth, dust, and ashes into the air. It left a hole in the earth, called a *crater,* 2½ miles wide from which lava flowed, covering the surrounding land. Underground fires still smolder in the crater of Mt. Katmai. Tourists enjoy watching the dramatic show of underground power.

Valley of Ten Thousand Smokes. In this natural wonder of southern Alaska, a constant cloud of smoke is sent up from cracks in the surface.

Mt. McKinley in central Alaska is the highest peak in North America. It is in the Alaska Range, and towers to 20,320 feet above sea level. In Alaska there are at least eight other peaks higher than Mt. Whitney in California. The area around Mt. McKinley is called Mt. McKinley National Park.

Slowly-moving masses of snow and ice, called *glaciers,* can be seen on the mountain slopes. They are smaller versions of the huge sheet of ice which once covered most of North America. Where the mountains are close to the coast, the glaciers slide slowly toward the sea. Huge chunks of ice break off them and fall into the sea. These become floating icebergs.

If you are in Alaska at the right time of year, you will see the *Aurora Borealis,* or "Northern Lights." At night the whole northern sky is lit with beautiful colors which seem to shoot up from the horizon far into the heavens. It as an amazing sight.

These and many other strange and wonderful things make the new state of Alaska an exciting and fascinating place to visit.

Meet the People. Alaska has fewer people than any other state, but its population is growing at a rapid rate. Eskimos and Indians make up nearly one third of the population. The remaining two thirds are white Alaskans, many of whom came north from the United States while Alaska was still a territory.

The Eskimos live along the coast of the Arctic Ocean and Bering Sea. For many years, these people have made their living by hunting and fishing, moving their homes from place to place. Today, however, many of them are studying in good schools and working at modern trades. They are no longer a wandering, uncivilized people.

Indians live mostly in the interior, generally along the streams where they can

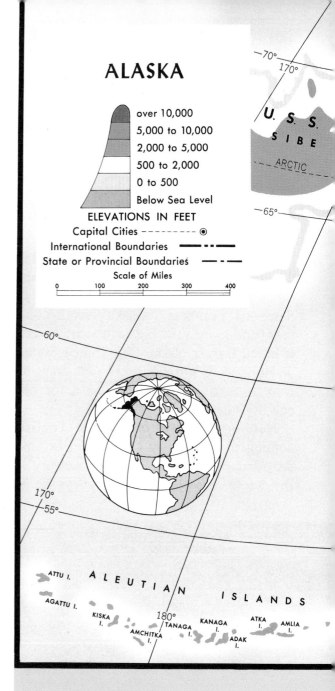

Studying the Map

Alaska, the forty-ninth state, is the largest in area of all the states but has the smallest population of any.

1. In what part of North America is Alaska located? On which country does it border?
2. Alaska is a peninsula and has water boundaries on three sides. What large bodies of water wash the coasts of Alaska? **3.** On the map find Pt. Barrow, farthest north in

Alaska. What is its latitude? **4.** Find the "Panhandle" that extends southward along the western boundary of Canada. What does the map tell you about the coast of this part of Alaska? **5.** Locate the Arctic Circle on the map. What part of Alaska does it cross? What kind of climate would you expect to find there? **6.** The Bering Strait separates Alaska from Siberia on the continent of Asia. Use the scale of miles on the map to measure the distance across the Bering Strait. **7.** What island group extends from the Alaska Peninsula far into the Pacific Ocean? **8.** The highest mountain peaks in North America are in Alaska. Which is the highest peak on the continent? Name another high peak in Alaska. **9.** The Yukon River is an important means of transportation in Alaska. Find this river on your map. Where is its source? Into what body of water does it empty? **10.** Find the Alaska Highway. At which city in Alaska does it end? Into what country does it extend? **11.** Which city now serves as capital of Alaska? In what part of the state is it located?

Eskimo Children. Two young boys enjoy playing with their puppy—an Alaskan "Husky." What can you tell of the climate from the clothes they wear?

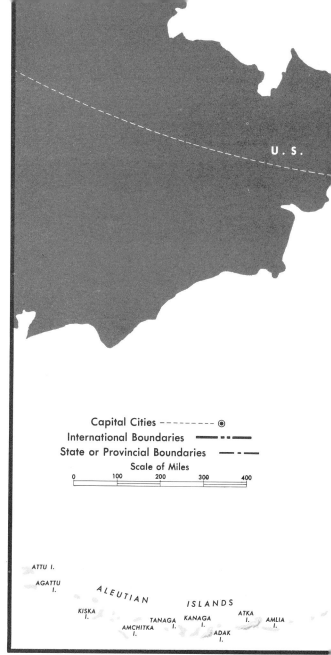

U. S.

Capital Cities - - - - - - - - ◎
International Boundaries —— ■ ■ ——
State or Provincial Boundaries — ■ — ■ —

Scale of Miles

0   100   200   300   400

ATTU I.

AGATTU I.

ALEUTIAN ISLANDS

KISKA I.

TANAGA   KANAGA   ATKA I.   AMLIA I.

AMCHITKA I.   I.   I.   ADAK I.

make a living by hunting and trapping. They live together in small villages. In the center of each village they put up a tall pole carved and painted in the forms of birds and animals with big, ugly faces. In a way, these poles, called *Totems,* are the Indian's "family tree." Each tribe or family has some bird or animal—such as a bear or an eagle —for its mascot. Reading from the top to the bottom, you can tell by the carved figures the success or failure of family matters. Some totem poles are only a few feet high; others are 80 feet high. The totem pole has become Alaska's trade mark.

White settlers first came to Alaska attracted by exciting tales of the gold discovered there in 1897. Over the years they came in larger numbers to labor in the mines, to fish for salmon or work in the fish canneries, to cut lumber in the forest, and to farm in the warmer valleys. Others came to start a business, or practice as doctors, dentists, and lawyers.

You see that Alaskans work in many of the same industries as the people of the Pacific Northwest. They live in towns and villages similar to those in the less populated parts of the United States. In the larger towns and cities there are stores, hotels, banks, and theaters. Some houses date back to log cabin days, and some are as modern as any in our cities. Every large town and city has its airport, because air travel is the most important means of transportation to the interior of Alaska.

The Panhandle. Over one third of Alaska's people live in the *Panhandle,* a region which extends south along the coast like a handle from the main part of Alaska. The Panhandle stretches for 400 miles along the western border of Canada. It is a land of many islands which lie along the coast against a background of snow-covered mountains and forests.

Alaska's capital, Juneau, is a port city located about halfway between the north and south borders of the Panhandle. In the mountains back of Juneau there is an abandoned gold mine. It was this mine that brought people to the city in the early days of Alaska's settlement. Other important cities located here are Sitka, the old Russian capital, and the port city of Ketchikan, the biggest salmon canning center in the world.

The climate of the Panhandle is rainy, and much milder than you would expect from its northern location. It is affected by the warm, moist winds which blow in from over the Pacific. In addition, the warm Japanese Current flows along this coast, somewhat like the Gulf Stream which flows along our Atlantic coast. The thermometer seldom falls below zero. In summer it rises to 80 degrees on some days. Flowers and vegetables grow rapidly during the long summer days. The winters are never so cold here as they are in New England or in the North Central States, even though the Panhandle is farther north.

The Panhandle has a treasure of natural resources. It is covered with a dense growth of forests that thrive in the mild, moist climate. The future of the lumber and paper pulp industries looks bright in this region. All kinds of minerals lie in the islands of the Panhandle. Prince of Wales Island is a storehouse of iron, copper, and coal. All these resources are waiting to be developed. Now that Alaska has become the forty-ninth state, more money, machinery, labor, and transportation facilities will become available, and the lumbering and mining industries will become more productive.

Southern Alaska. Anchorage, Alaska's largest city, is on Cook Inlet in southern Alaska. Mountains that lie back of the city shut off the cold winds from the north. However, the coast of Southern Alaska is colder and drier than the Panhandle. Anchorage is an important center for world air travelers. Planes going from various parts of the United States to cities in Asia stop at Anchorage to refuel. It is Alaska's most modern city.

Seward, across the Kenai Peninsula from Anchorage, is an important port for southern Alaska. The Alaska Railroad connects Seward with Anchorage and the interior city of Fairbanks. Seward handles Southern Alaska's trade with Seattle and other west coast cities.

The Alaska Peninsula stretches more than 500 miles west of southern Alaska. It is a cold, wet, unfriendly land. Its rocky surface is dotted with many active volcanoes. Little vegetation grows there.

Beyond the Peninsula are the Aleutian Islands. These islands are really tops of mountains rising from the sea. They, too, have volcanoes which pour out steam, ashes, and melted rock. Fog, rain, and strong winds make life difficult for the *Aleuts,* the people who live here. On some of the islands, the people raise blue foxes, very valuable for their furs.

The Fur Industry. The fur industry has been important in Alaska for many years. Millions of dollars' worth of furs have been shipped from Alaska since it has belonged to the United States. Trapping is an important occupation among the Indians. Muskrat, mink, beaver, marten, weasel, and otter are caught, and their skins are sold.

There are a few farms where fur-bearing animals are raised. Fox and mink are the

Anchorage Airport. A Pan American Boeing "707" jet airliner makes a stop at this busy airport. Today, most flights to Asia refuel at Anchorage.

chief animals raised by the fur farmers. The blue fox is also important. There are many blue-fox farms along the coast and on some of the islands. Furs grow fine, thick, and long on the animals of the rocky, moist wind-swept islands.

The best known fur-bearing animals in Alaska are the seals. The seals swim over to the rocky Pribilof Islands in the Bering Sea every summer. Some years ago, so many seals were killed that there was danger that they would disappear altogether. Laws were then passed to protect the seals. Now only a certain number of young male seals are permitted to be killed each year. Today, the seals are again increasing in numbers on the Pribilofs.

Seal and fox skins are shipped from Alaska to St. Louis, Missouri, where they are prepared for use as articles of clothing.

The government has established *wildlife refuges,* or game preserves, for certain animals so that they will not die out. Some of these are on Kodiak Island, for the brown bear; on the Aleutian Islands, for the sea otter; on the Kenai Peninsula, for the moose; and on Nunivak, for the musk ox.

The Yukon Uplands. The interior of Alaska is a plateau region lying between high mountain ranges. The Yukon, longest river in this part of the world, cuts through this region and finally flows into the Bering Sea. This river is deep enough and wide enough for large boats to use. They can travel across Alaska and into Canada on the Yukon during the summer months. However, it is frozen over from October to June.

Interior Alaska has long, cold winters and short, warm summers. The land is nearly level in some places, but it is mostly hilly and mountainous. There are some warmer valleys which could be used for farming. However, poor roads, or no roads at all, make it difficult to use this land.

Fairbanks is the chief city of the Yukon uplands. It is on a branch of the Yukon River. A railroad connects Fairbanks with the Pacific Ocean by way of Anchorage and Seward.

Fairbanks looks like other towns in the United States. It has many of the comforts

and conveniences of a modern community. Fairbanks is the center for the gold-mining industry in the interior of Alaska. The University of Alaska is located here, and so is a United States Agricultural Experimental Station. The Alaska Highway joins Whitehorse in Canada with Fairbanks. Actually this highway runs all the way from Great Falls, Montana, through western Canada into Alaska. It was built during World War II and is kept open all year round.

Within the Arctic Circle. About one third of Alaska lies north of the Arctic Circle. This land is sometimes called "The Land of the Midnight Sun." During the short summer, the sun does not set for several weeks. During the long, cold winter, the sun does not rise for several weeks.

There is little rain or snow in this region. In summer, coarse grasses and flowers grow. Mosses and lichens cover the frozen soil. Reindeers imported from Siberia feed on the mosses that grow on the *tundra* or treeless Arctic plains. The reindeer are used

to supply food and skins for the small Eskimo population of northern Alaska.

Point Barrow on the Arctic Ocean is our northernmost city.

Matanuska Valley. Very little land in Alaska is farmed—less than one hundredth of the state. This tiny farmed area is mostly in Matanuska Valley. It is in south central Alaska, not far from Anchorage.

A visit to this valley would present some surprises. Mountains to the north shut out the very coldest winds and make a frost-free period possible between the months of May and September.

During the summer season, southern Alaska has a very long day and a short night. The number of hours of sunshine on a summer day may total as much as 16 or 17. Plants grow rapidly with all this sunshine, and do not require as long a growing season as they do in those climates where the days are shorter.

Some years ago, while Alaska was still a territory, our government carried out a plan to settle a group of farmers in the valley. Large log houses of six to eight rooms, plus a good-sized barn, were built for each family that came to farm. Berries, potatoes, cabbages, oats, peas, hay, poultry, and dairy products are now produced in the Matanuska Valley. Crops that are not needed by the farm families are sent to markets in the towns along the railroad.

Farmers receive high prices for their farm produce. The produce is marketed by a cooperative association run by the farmers. This cooperative has established a vegetable canning plant, a cold storage plant, and even a creamery. The Matanuska Valley has schools, a trading post, warehouses, a power plant, and a hospital to take care of its community needs.

Despite Matanuska and other farming areas, however, Alaskans must still import nearly all their food. Most of it comes by boat from Seattle to ports in the Panhandle and southern Alaska. Alaskans hope that this dependence on other states for food will soon change. Thousands of acres are available to homesteaders in the northern State. Families willing to face pioneer conditions are moving there. They find satisfaction in meeting the challenge of the cold, unfriendly land. It is likely that Alaska will become settled just as our other "pioneer" States were settled—by strong people willing to face hardships.

Fishing in Alaskan Waters. Alaskan waters provide some of the best fisheries in the world. The warm Japanese current which flows south along the coast contains a wealth of vegetation and tiny animals

Treasure of Alaska's Waters. These fishermen use a purse seine, just as in New England, to bring in a rich catch of salmon off the Alaska coast.

upon which millions of fish can feed.

Alaska leads the world in catching, canning, and exporting salmon. The fish are caught during the summer months and canned during this season. The city of Ketchikan is the center for this industry.

Cod, halibut, herring, shrimp, and clams are also caught in Alaskan waters. The value of the fish caught here is now several times the value of the fish caught off the Atlantic coast.

Game fishing attracts many sportsmen to Alaska. They fish in the coastal waters and in the many lakes and streams.

Facts *to remember*

1. Alaska, our largest state, is a big peninsula extending outward from northwestern North America. Few people live here. Eskimos and Indians make up one third of the population; the rest are mostly white Alaskans. Alaskans work in many of the same industries as the people of the Northwest. Every large town and city has an airport.

2. Alaska was explored by the Russians, but was bought by the United States just after the Civil War. It is an untapped storehouse of valuable resources, and it is an important base for our country's defenses. About one third of this state lies north of the Arctic Circle.

3. Tourists coming to Alaska by car, plane, or ship see some of the most beautiful scenery in the world. Mt. McKinley is the highest peak in North America. Fires from volcanoes still smolder. Glaciers can be seen on the mountain slopes. In the fall of the year the *Aurora Borealis* lights up the northern sky.

4. Over one third of Alaska's people live in the Panhandle. The climate is rainy here, and milder than would be expected from its northern location. It has a dense growth of forests and many minerals. Now that it has become a state, Alaska's lumbering and mining industries will become more productive.

5. The coast of southern Alaska is colder and drier than the Panhandle. The Aleutian Islands are tops of mountains rising from the sea. The tiny farmed area is mostly in the south central area. Here plants grow rapidly in the summer, when days are very long and nights very short. Crops are marketed by a cooperative association run by the farmers. Food is imported.

6. Alaska leads the world in catching, canning, and exporting salmon. Trapping is an important industry.

What *have I learned?*

One item in each group is wrong. Write the sentences, copying only the items which make them correct.

1. Alaska has many lakes, fiords, crowded cities, glaciers, and volcanoes.

2. Pineapples, fish, gold, and furs make Alaska a valuable land.

3. Aurora Borealis, Mt. McKinley, Crater Lake, and the "Valley of Ten Thousand Smokes" are of interest to tourists in Alaska.

4. Alaskan Indians use totem poles, have their homes along the Pacific Coast, and live together in small villages.

5. Alaskan cities have airports, modern homes, theaters, and torrid jungles.

6. The Panhandle has a Mediterranean climate, salmon, canneries, and fishing boats.

7. Dense forests, rice fields, many minerals, fish, and fur-bearing animals are some of Alaska's resources.

8. Juneau, Anchorage, Seward, and the Aleutian Islands are in southern Alaska.

9. Matanuska Valley has a farming area, long summer days, a power plant, schools, and many hotels.

10. An important river, Fairbanks, penguins, a university, and an Agricultural Experimental Station will be found in the Yukon Uplands.

Facts *to understand*

Give a reason for each statement.

1. The climate of much of Alaska is not as cold as one would expect it to be.

2. Tourists come to Alaska to see its natural wonders.

3. Over one third of the Alaskans live in the Panhandle.

4. The fur industry has been important in Alaska.

5. Alaska may become settled just as our "pioneer" states were settled.

7

Hawaii

Sun, Sand, and Surf. Beautiful Waikiki Beach in Honolulu is a famous Hawaiian vacation spot. In the background is the hill called Diamond Head.

The English explorer, Captain James Cook, is famous for his voyages of discovery throughout the Pacific Ocean. In the course of his voyages, Cook visited many of the Pacific island groups. One of the island groups he discovered he named the Sandwich Islands. The name was given to honor an English admiral, the Earl of Sandwich. Later, however, this group became known as the Hawaiian Islands—the name which the native people used.

At first, the Hawaiian Islands were visited only rarely, and the native people continued their peaceful existence. As time went by, New England whaling ships began to use the Hawaiian Islands as a base. These ships came from New England, thousands of miles away, in search of whales. They found the islands convenient for resting and obtaining food on their long voyages.

Gradually, as ocean traffic in the Pacific grew heavier, more and more ships made use of the Hawaiian Islands as a stopping-off place. Their location, about in the middle of the ocean, made them an ideal place for ships to stop off on their trips between America and Asia or Australia. When airplanes started to cross the Pacific, they too found the Hawaiian Islands convenient for refueling.

In 1898, the native people of the islands asked to be annexed to the United States as a territory, in the same way that Alaska was, and that many parts of our country had been before statehood. The United States Navy built a base for the Pacific fleet at Pearl Harbor in the Hawaiian Islands. It was the Japanese sneak attack on this base that brought our country into World War II.

Because of the close ties which always existed between our country and Hawaii, the islands were granted statehood in 1959. Hawaii is our fiftieth state, and a very valuable one, as you will see when you read further about these islands and their people and their way of living.

The State of Hawaii. How very different is Hawaii from the state of Alaska we have just been studying! The islands are strung out over 400 miles in the blue Pacific. They form our most southern state, only one thousand miles from the equator. Alaska is our most northern state. When the area of all the islands is added together, it is a little more than the combined areas of Connecticut and Rhode Island. By contrast, the huge state of Alaska has ninety times this area. Yet the population of Hawaii—about 500,000 people—is more than twice the population of Alaska.

Unlike Alaska, Hawaii is not a "frontier" state. There are no vast open spaces waiting for settlers to come and develop the land and its resources. Hawaii has a well-developed farming industry, and large cities visited by thousands of tourists every year. Transportation facilities in the islands are modern in every sense. By jet, the island state is only a few hours from our west coast. Hawaii, two thousand miles out in the Pacific, is closer to San Francisco than New York City is.

Formation of the Islands. It is said that the Hawaiian Islands are really mountain tops pushed above the sea by the action of volcanoes. Hawaii, the largest island, is really the highest mountain on earth. If you measure its height from the bottom of the Pacific Ocean, it is higher than Mt. Everest measured from sea level. One of Hawaii's two volcanoes is still active.

The Hawaiian Islands were formed ages ago. Hot melted rock, called *lava,* was pushed up through cracks in the ocean floor. The lava hardened into rock. As layer was deposited upon layer, the islands poked up above the ocean and grew to different sizes. Hawaii, the largest island, is also the newest. Its size is still increasing as hot lava hardens into new rock. Visitors to Hawaii National Park watch this volcano in action. It has exploded violently several times, but most often it just oozes lava down its slopes.

Extinct Volcano on Oahu. This dead crater is called the Punchbowl. It is a military cemetery, where many of the dead of World War II are buried.

The Islands Today. Although Hawaii, as you have just seen, is the largest island, it is not the most important. Find the island of Qahu on the map on page 282. Three fourths of the Hawaiian people live on Oahu. Honolulu, the capital and chief city, is located here. So is Pearl Harbor.

Other islands are: Nihau, the northernmost island, where many of the original Hawaiian people live; Kauai, oldest of the islands; Molokai; Lanai, a privately-owned island; Maui; Kahoolawe, used as a target by Navy and Air Force bombers, and uninhabited; and Hawaii.

In addition, a string of tiny islands and reefs continues to run northwestward for one thousand miles from Nihau. Most of these are too small to support life, but traces of past civilizations can be found on some of them. Like a string of beads thrown down in the water, these reefs and tiny islands extend the length of our new state of Hawaii to more than 1500 miles.

The Hawaiian People. There are not many native Hawaiians left. Most of the people are of foreign stock. Immigrant Japanese and their children, crowded out of their own small islands, came to the Hawaiian Islands seeking new homes. Today, people of Japanese descent make up about half the population. There are also large numbers of Chinese, Filipinos, and Portuguese who came as plantation workers. There are also many Americans and Europeans who came after the annexation as government officials and business men. They make up about one fourth of the population.

The true, native-born Hawaiians are called *Kanakas*. They have beautiful brown skin and dark hair. Once they were pagans, but today many of them are Catholics.

In olden times the Hawaiians lived in grass huts. Many flowers grew wild on the

"Aloha" means Welcome. The Hawaiian Islands are famous for hospitality toward guests. Music and flowers are part of the entertainment.

islands, and the natives used to string them in wreaths around their shoulders. The girls wore flowers in their hair and pretty grass skirts over short tunics. Today, the Kanakas live in wooden houses, some of them very fine. They wear the traditional costume only to parties and on holidays.

The natives often hold great banquets called *luau*. They serve chicken cooked in coconut milk, pig roasted whole with crabs,

Famous Outdoor Feast. A festive meal like this is called a *luau*. A whole roast pig is cooked with clams and fruit in an *imu*, or rock-heated pit.

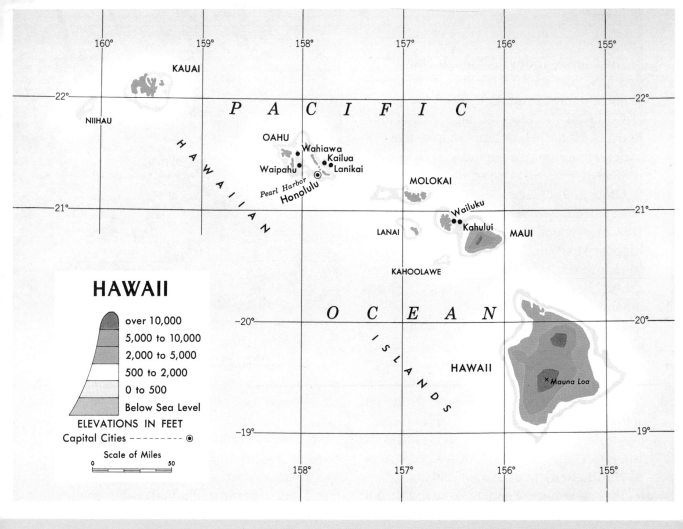

Studying the Map

Hawaii, our newest State, is very small in area when compared to Alaska. The population of the islands, however, is more than double that of Alaska.

1. In what ocean are the Hawaiian Islands located? Between what continents do they lie? 2. Of the eight larger islands shown on the map, which is the largest? 3. Which of the islands lies farthest east? farthest west? farthest north? farthest south? 4. In what latitude are the Hawaiian Islands? in which climatic zone? 5. From their location in the Pacific Ocean, what kind of climate could you expect to find in these islands? 6. What does the map tell you about the surface of the Hawaiian Islands? 7. On which of the islands do we find the highest elevations above sea level? 8. Mauna Loa is a volcanic peak on the island of Hawaii. About how high is it above sea level? 9. On which island would you expect to find the largest population? How can you tell this from the map? 10. Which city is the capital of our newest state? On which island is it located?

and yams and bananas cooked in a sandpit over hot stones. After the feasting, they play ukuleles and guitars, and tell stories in song and dancing.

The native Hawaiians are a smiling, handsome, and easy-going people who love music and swimming. They work and live together, proud of their new state.

A Tourist Paradise. The Hawaiian Islands are very beautiful. Because they lie just within the Tropics, they are the only state in the Union where the sun can be seen shining directly overhead. The climate in the islands is always mild, never too hot nor too cold. The trade winds blow steadily and carry moisture picked up over the ocean. In some parts of the islands, the rainfall is very heavy; in other places, there is not enough rain for crops. It all depends upon which side of the mountains you are located on. Slopes which face into the wind are rainy, and those away from the wind are generally dry.

On these lovely islands great snow-covered mountains rise to nearly 14,000 feet. Sharp cliffs drop thousands of feet into the sea. There are hundreds of waterfalls, and streams have cut canyons deep into the earth. One can find cool forests not far from the sunny beaches. Hawaii is a state of contrast and variety.

Visitors to our newest state are met with the greeting *Aloha*, meaning "welcome." They are given a necklace of fresh flowers, called a *lei*, as a token of friendship. The people of Hawaii are very friendly and have learned how to live in peace with one another without regard for race or nationality. For these and other reasons Hawaii is visited by thousands of vacationers and tourists every year.

Sugar Cane and Pineapples. When you think of our state of Hawaii, think of sugar

A Sun-drenched Field. The Hawaiian soil and climate are ideally suited to growing pineapples. This is one of the chief industries in the islands.

Hawaii **283**

Hawaiian Dairy Farm. Under the calm tropical sky, it is somewhat odd to see a pasture and dairy cattle resembling those in northern United States.

cane and pineapples. These crops bring the most money to the people. Sugar cane is called the "king crop." Most of it is shipped to the states on the continent.

The Hawaiian climate is ideal for sugar cane. The islands are near enough to the equator so the weather in the lowlands is warm all year. The northeastern side is the rainy side on the islands. Winds from the

Hawaiian Orchid. Exquisite flowers like this one cover the islands. Three different types of orchid from Hawaii are very much in demand over here.

ocean bring heavy rainfall. Sugar cane grows well in the moist fertile soil. If sugar is to be grown on the dry side of the islands, irrigation must be used. In some places tunnels have been dug through the mountains to carry water to the fields on the dry side.

Many pineapples are raised on the higher and drier lands where sugar cane will not grow. A pineapple plantation may cover 15,000 acres. About three fourths of all the world's canned pineapples come from Hawaii.

Pineapple is a fruit which requires careful attention. Over the years growers in Hawaii have developed the best methods of raising large and juicy pineapples. The island of Lanai belongs to a pineapple company, and many people of the islands work in the huge pineapple industry.

Other Products. Rice is grown on some of the lowlands. The warm climate and the wet, fertile soil favor its growth. Rice is the chief food of many of the Hawaiian people. Coffee, corn, vegetables, bananas, nuts, and tobacco are also grown in Hawaii.

Even though farming is the most important industry in Hawaii, only about one tenth of the land can be used for crops. As a result, the people must import more than two thirds of all their food. They are able to pay for this with money earned by working on sugar and pineapple plantations or in the tourist industry.

The cattle business is growing in Hawaii. One of the largest beef cattle ranches in the world is on the island of Hawaii. On this ranch they raise pure-bred Herefords, noted for the fine quality of their beef. The Hawaiian cowboy is called a *paniola*.

Magnificent orchids are grown outdoors in Hawaii. They are collected in aluminum baskets and poured on loading trays. Over 50 million orchids are sent by air freight to the states on the continent every year.

Honolulu. Honolulu, on the island of Oahu, is the capital and largest city of the state of Hawaii. It has many stores, modern hotels, and beautiful homes. In its fine harbor are ships from all over the world. Many products are imported and exported at Honolulu. The chief exports are sugar and pineapples. The chief imports are food, machinery, clothing, and oil.

Pearl Harbor, near Honolulu, is still a great naval base for our Pacific fleet. Great air bases have been built both there and in Honolulu.

Island Possessions in the Pacific. The United States has several island possessions in the Pacific Ocean. Midway Island is northwest of the state of Hawaii. It is called Midway because it lies halfway between the United States and Asia. Wake Island is southwest of Midway. West of Wake Island is Guam. Guam is used as a naval base.

A smaller group in the South Pacific are known as American Samoa. The United States Government holds a trusteeship over the island groups of the Marianas, the Marshalls, and the Carolines for the United

Reminder of a Tragedy. Navy men visit the sunken *USS Arizona*, tomb of many Americans who died during the Japanese attack on Pearl Harbor.

Nations (UN). This means our country watches over their affairs and helps them.

The islands of the Pacific are especially important to the United States in this age of airplanes and rockets. They provide air and naval bases in the Pacific Ocean.

Hawaiian Street Scene. Kalakaua Avenue is a modern thoroughfare at Waikiki. The cities of Hawaii seem quite similar to those on the mainland.

FATHER DAMIEN OF MOLOKAI

When the white men came to the Pacific Islands, they brought white men's diseases with them. Many of the natives caught these diseases and died. One of the worst diseases was leprosy. Those afflicted with this disease had to be separated from others.

On the northern coast of the island of Molokai, a section was given over to a leper colony. Here Father Damien, a Belgian priest, came to bring spiritual comfort to the unfortunate lepers. He himself caught the disease and died of it. Later, Franciscan Sisters came to the island to care for the afflicted women and girls.

Today, modern methods of treatment have reduced the numbers of people suffering from this disease. A modern leprosy hospital is now located where Father Damien worked among his people.

Facts *to remember*

1. Since the Hawaiian Islands lie in the middle of the Pacific Ocean, they are an ideal place for ships to stop on their way between America and Asia or Australia. Because the Japanese attacked these islands at Pearl Harbor, we were brought into World War II.
2. In 1898, the people of Hawaii asked to be annexed to the United States as a territory. Hawaii was granted statehood in 1959. The islands are strung out for 400 miles in the Pacific. They are only 1000 miles from the equator. Although the state of Hawaii is much smaller than Alaska, its population is twice that of Alaska.
3. Hawaii has a well developed farming industry and large cities. Transportation facilities are modern. It has one of the world's chief cattle ranches. Sugar cane and pineapples are the chief money crops. Much of the food is imported.
4. Most of the people of Hawaii are of foreign origin and descent. They are friendly and live in peace. Many tourists visit this beautiful land. It has many stores, modern hotels, and beautiful homes. Ships from all over the world are seen in its fine harbor.
5. The United States has several island possessions in the Pacific Ocean. Among them are Midway Island and Wake Island. Our country also holds a trusteeship over other island groups. The islands of the Pacific serve as air and naval bases.

What *have I learned?*

Copy the following. Add the word or words which will complete the sentence.
1. Our fiftieth state is
2. The Hawaiian Islands are mountain tops formed by the action of
3. Three fourths of the Hawaiian people live on the island of
4. True native Hawaiians are called
5. The "king crop" is
6. From Hawaii comes three fourths of all the world's canned

7. The chief food of the Hawaiian people is
8. The name of a Belgian priest who brought spiritual comfort to the lepers is
9. The capital and largest city of the state of Hawaii is
10. The people of Hawaii must import more than two thirds of all their

Facts *to understand*

Give a reason for each statement.
1. Many tourists visit the Hawaiian Islands.
2. Some of the Hawaiian Islands have very small populations.
3. Hawaii is populated by many national groups.
4. Sugar cane and pineapples are Hawaii's money crops.
5. Even though farming is an important industry in Hawaii, food must be imported.
6. Statehood was desirable to the people of Hawaii.
7. The area of Hawaii is still increasing.
8. Many ships and airplanes stop at the Hawaiian Islands.
9. Hawaii has a very pleasant climate, seldom very hot or very cold.
10. Father Damien's memory is revered by the Hawaiian people.

Unit Five Review

Questions for Discussion and Review

1. What great contrasts are to be found in our Western States? 2. What can our two newest states contribute to our country? 3. Explain how the West today differs from the West at the time of Lewis and Clark. 4. Tell how the four sections into which the Western States are divided differ from one another. 5. What are the chief occupations of the people of the West? 6. How was the West settled? 7. Why is the West regarded as a "young" section of our country? 8. In which region of the West do we find the greatest centers of population? 9. Who were the first Europeans to settle in the West? 10. Why were the gold-seekers called the "forty-niners"? 11. What is the general boundary line between the Central Plains and the Great Plains? 12. Why is the Great Salt Lake be-

coming saltier each year? 13. What are some of the conditions which make farming difficult on the Great Plains? 14. What is dry farming? 15. Where are the irrigated sections of the Great Plains mostly located? 16. What are some of the most important minerals of the Rockies? 17. In what way are the National Parks of value to all Americans? 18. What is a Mediterranean climate? 19. Why are orange trees safer on the hillsides than in the valleys? 20. What are some of the riches of Alaska not yet fully developed?

Using the Maps and Globe

1. On an outline map of the Pacific Ocean, locate the Hawaiian Islands and other island groups. Indicate by arrows the routes used by different continents in their trade with one another.
2. On an outline map of North America, show routes taken by Americans to reach Alaska.
3. Sketch a map of the Western States. Shade it to show the rainfall lines.
4. Make a product map of the Western States.
5. Use the globe to show how the Western States are well located for trade with other lands.

Using Geography Words

Here is a list of special words that have been used in this unit. Write a sentence using each word, to prove you know its meaning in geography.

reservations	*trailers*	*dry farming*
placer deposits	*aqueduct*	*windward side*
mulch	*fiords*	*selective lumbering*
irrigation		

Getting Information from Books

Read reference books such as *Compton's Pictured Encyclopedia* for information on the following topics. Prepare to give an oral or written report on each topic.

Alaska	Klondike Gold Rush
Lewis and Clark Expedition	Pineapple Growing
Rocky Mountains	Ghost Towns of the West
Hawaii	How Movies are Made
Sante Fe Trail	California Missions

Final Test

Write each sentence on your paper, choosing the correct word or words from the parenthesis.

1. The Western States take in more than (one half, three fourths, one third) of the total land area of the United States.

2. The (Spanish, French, English) were the first Europeans to settle in the West.

3. The Great Plains are best suited for (farming, industry, ranching).

4. An artificial lake is called a (dam, reservoir, ditch).

5. The (Rocky, Cascade, Appalachian) Mountains are called the "backbone" of North America.

6. The metal mined in the largest quantity in the Rocky Mountains is (silver, copper, gold).

7. (Tungsten, Chromium, Vanadium) is used in making stainless steel.

8. Farming was begun in California by the (Dutch, Spanish, French).

9. A popular fruit of California is the (pineapple, apple, orange).

10. Great quantities of (lava, fertile soil, sand) flow from volcanoes.

11. A fertile farming area in the Pacific Northwest is near (Puget Sound, the Dust Bowl, the Coast Ranges).

12. Along the Pacific Coast many people make a living by (raising sugar cane, fishing, diving for pearls).

13. The state closest to Russia is (California, Montana, Alaska).

14. For its size (Alaska, Hawaii, California) has a very small population.

15. The state that is used as a stopping-place in the Pacific is (Oregon, Hawaii, Utah).

16. Lewis and Clark explored the region of (the Rocky Mountains, California, Alaska).

17. The Grand Coulee Dam is on the (Colorado, Mackenzie, Columbia) River.

18. Plowing up the prairie grass led to (floods, eruptions, dust storms).

19. (Los Angeles, Salt Lake City, Denver) is known as the "mile high" city.

20. Places where gold and gravel are found mixed together are called (open pits, placer deposits, ghost towns).

21. (Salt Lake City, Phoenix, Denver) was founded by the Mormons.

22. (San Francisco, Los Angeles, San Diego) serves as our chief naval base on the Pacific Coast.

23. The only state in the United States where the sun can be seen shining directly overhead is (New Mexico, Alaska, Hawaii).

24. A tall pole painted in the forms of birds and animals is a (kayak, tundra, totem).

25. A feast of meat and fruits roasted in a sandpit is called a (lei, luau, aloha).

Applying Christian Principles.

1. The people of the United States can best show their appreciation of Alaska by **a.** mining her minerals **b.** assisting her to progress **c.** enjoying her natural beauty.

2. Father Damien should be remembered most because **a.** he helped the unfortunates **b.** made Molokai more modern **c.** made the Pacific Islands better known.

3. Lumber companies can help the people of the United States by **a.** cutting down many trees **b.** using selective lumbering **c.** ridding our country of forest ranges.

4. Los Angeles helps her people conserve their health by **a.** modern industries **b.** giving men mining jobs **c.** lessening the smog conditions.

5. Our government can best assist migrant workers by **a.** letting them alone **b.** providing better living conditions. **c.** urging people to hire them.

6. The National Parks help Americans to **a.** find a good spot for a picnic **b.** preserve the natural beauty of much of our country **c.** enjoy a greater variety of sports.

7. Men were wrong to plow up the prairie grass because **a.** the topsoil soon blew away **b.** the soil underneath was too poor for agriculture anyway **c.** the grass roots damaged the plows.

8. Collecting poisonous gases from copper refineries **a.** is impossible **b.** is foolish, because they are of no use **c.** is a good means to help make the best use of our resources.

9. The people of Hawaii show a very important example to us of **a.** how to raise pineapples **b.** how to live in peace with different races and nationalities **c.** the value of swimming.

Neighbors in Canada

In this Unit
you will learn that:

1 In some ways, the people, the surface, and the history of Canada are similar to those of the United States. Both nations enjoy friendly relations.
2 Canada has generally a cool climate. Most of the people live in the southern part, away from the extremes of cold found in the north. The climate on the west coast is rainy and mild.
3 Eastern Canada is made up of the Atlantic Provinces and the St. Lawrence Provinces. Fishing, farming, lumbering, and mining are carried on, and most of Canada's large cities and major industries are located in the East.
4 Western Canada includes the Prairie Provinces, with a surface like that of our Great Plains, and British Columbia, in the Canadian Rockies. Wheat farming, lumbering, fishing, and mineral industries are important in Canada's West.
5 Northern Canada is divided into two territories. It is a varied area of mountains, plateaus, and frozen plains. Very few people live in this cold region.

I n most parts of the world, the borders between countries are heavily guarded. In order to pass from one country to another in Europe, Asia, and in other places, it is necessary to show special papers and passes, submit to a search of baggage, and sometimes wait through long delays.

Between the United States and Canada there is a border which extends for more than 3000 miles. What makes this border different from those in most parts of the world is the ease in crossing. Americans going into Canada or Canadians coming in to the United States have very little difficulty at all because of the friendly relations which exist between these two North American nations.

As you study the geography and the people of Canada, you will find that they are similar to those of the United States in many ways. Of course, Canada is a country which extends farther north than the United States; as a consequence, we can expect its climate to be a good deal colder than ours.

The St. Lawrence Seaway which you learned about when you studied the North Central States is the best symbol of the friendship and cooperation which exists between the two nations. Both the United States and Canada built the seaway; both the United States and Canada share in its benefits.

CANADA

The northern part of North America is occupied almost entirely by Canada. Only Alaska and Greenland do not belong to this vast country, the second largest in the world.

Notice that in the southern part of Canada many of the surface features are continuations of surface features which cross the United States as well. Farther north is the wide Laurentian Upland. The extreme north is a cold and barren waste land.

The coast line of Canada, which touches three oceans, is broken everywhere by islands, bays, and river mouths.

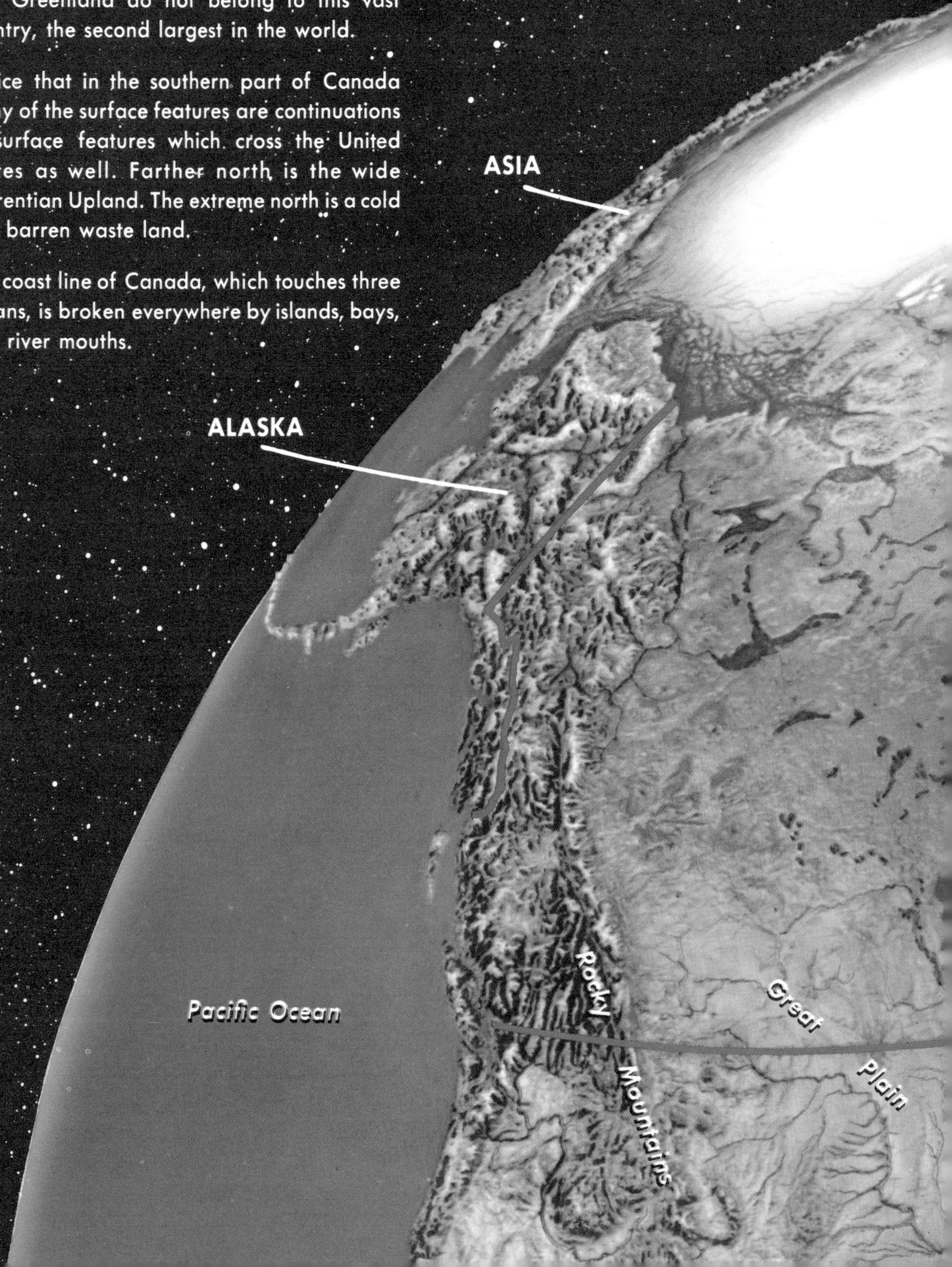

ASIA

ALASKA

Pacific Ocean

Rocky Mountains

Great Plain

Arctic Ocean

EUROPE

GREENLAND

Atlantic Ocean

Hudson Bay

Laurentian Uplands

Appalachian Highlands

Let's Learn About Canada

There are many ways in which the United States and Canada are similar. The United States once was a colony of England, and so was Canada. In fact, Canada is today a member of the British Commonwealth of Nations and has close ties with Great Britain. English is the principal language of the United States, and it is also the principal language throughout most of Canada. The ancestors of most Americans came from the continent of Europe, and so did the ancestors of most Canadians.

In Canada and the United States, the principles of government and religion are very much the same. Our school systems are similar. Many American businessmen have invested money in Canada, and many Canadian businessmen have invested money in the United States. One Canadian-owned railroad actually cuts across our state of Maine, instead of taking a longer route to the north. The line ends at St. John in New Brunswick. As you know, the United States and Canada worked together to build the St. Lawrence Seaway, making it possible for large ocean-going ships to enter the Great Lakes and reach the lake ports of both countries.

The United States and Canada are partners and neighbors working together to make North America a better continent.

Location and Size. Canada spreads across the northern portion of the continent of North America. In area, it is the largest country in the Western Hemisphere and the second largest country in the world. Only the Soviet Union in Eurasia is larger. Canada faces three oceans: the Atlantic on the east, the Arctic on the north, and the Pacific on the west. To the south lies the greater part of the United States, and on the northwest boundary of Canada is our new state of Alaska.

Provinces and Territories. Canada consists of provinces and territories, just as our country consists of states. On the map of Canada on pages 294 and 295 find the names of the ten provinces and two territories.

The provinces of Canada are: the Pacific province of British Columbia; the Prairie provinces of Alberta, Saskatchewan, and Manitoba; the St. Lawrence provinces of Ontario and Quebec; and the Atlantic provinces of Newfoundland, New Brunswick, Prince Edward Island, and Nova Scotia.

Farther north, crossed by the Arctic circle and bordering on the Arctic Ocean, are two territories: the Yukon Territory and the Northwest Territories of Mackenzie, Keewatin, and Franklin. We shall learn about each of these divisions in the following pages.

The Surface of Canada. You have studied the surface features of the United States, from the regions of the east coast to those of the west. In Canada you will find mostly an extension of the same surface features.

The Appalachian Highlands, which stretch into New England, continue north through the Atlantic Provinces of Canada. These provinces are sometimes called the *Maritime Provinces,* because they are close to the sea. The coast line here is rugged, and the land is a succession of mountain ridges, uplands, and wide valleys.

One part of Canada is entirely different from any part of our country. That is the Laurentian Upland. This northern region is shaped like a large horseshoe around the Hudson Bay and extends south to the Great Lakes. In some places there are miles of barren rocks; in other places there are pine forests, lakes, and rivers.

The Laurentian Upland takes in about one half the entire area of Canada. Until rich stores of minerals were discovered in the rocks, the people did not bother much about this area. It now seems probable that this huge, barren section of Canada will become more and more populated and productive.

The most thickly settled part of Canada is the rolling farmland that makes up the St. Lawrence Valley. This small but valuable area extends along both sides of the St. Lawrence river and takes in the Ontario Peninsula between Lake Huron and Lakes Erie and Ontario as well as other parts of the region bordering the Great Lakes.

Canada's Eastern Coast. A scene on the Nova Scotia peninsula, one of Canada's Atlantic Provinces. The old name for Nova Scotia was Acadia.

Studying the Map

Canada, our neighboring country to the north, has an area slightly greater than the United States but has only about 1/10 as many people.

A. 1. Which ocean lies to the east of Canada? to the west? to the north? **2.** What is the name of the large bay that extends far into the interior of northern Canada? **3.** Which bodies of water separate Greenland from Canada? **4.** Which of the Great Lakes are in both Canada and the United States? **5.** Find the St. Lawrence River on your map. Which of the Great Lakes is its source? Into what body of water does it empty? In what direction does it flow? **6.** Which one of the United States lies on Canada's northwest border? **7.** In what part of Canada do we find the highest mountains? About how high do these mountains rise above sea level? What are they called? **8.** Locate the southernmost point in Canada. What body of water does it touch? What is its latitude? **9.** Find the northernmost point in Canada. In what ocean is it located? What is its latitude? If each degree of latitude is a distance of about 70 miles, how far is this northernmost point from the North Pole?

B. Canada is made up of provinces and territories. **1.** Locate and name the ten provinces and the two territories. **2.** The four smallest provinces, called the Maritime Provinces, are on the Atlantic Coast. Which two are islands? Which is a peninsula? Which borders the state of Maine? Of which is Labrador a part? **3.** The two largest and most populated are on the Great Lakes and the St. Lawrence River. Name them. **4.** The interior provinces in western Canada are called the Prairie Provinces. Find them on the map and give their names. **5.** Which Canadian province is on the Pacific coast? Name the large island that is part of this province. **6.** In what part of Canada do most of the people live? How can you tell from the map? **7.** Which city is the capital of Canada? Where is it located? **8.** Canada's largest city is located on the St. Lawrence River. Name the city. What other important Canadian city is on the St. Lawrence? **9.** Which is the most important Canadian city on Lake Ontario? in the interior of western Canada? on the Pacific coast?

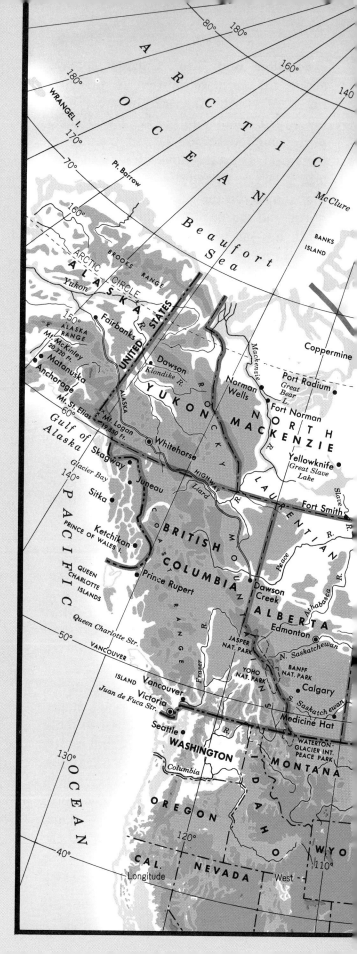

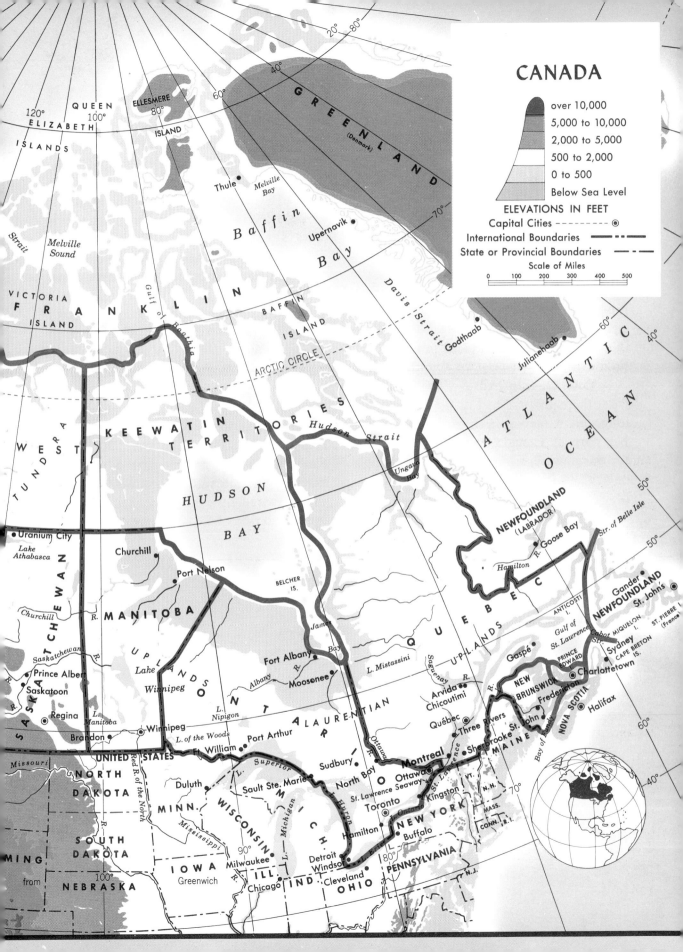

CANADA

over 10,000	
5,000 to 10,000	
2,000 to 5,000	
500 to 2,000	
0 to 500	
Below Sea Level	

ELEVATIONS IN FEET
Capital Cities ---------◉
International Boundaries ━━━━
State or Provincial Boundaries ━━━

Scale of Miles
0   100   200   300   400   500

QUEEN ELIZABETH ISLANDS
ELLESMERE ISLAND
GREENLAND (Denmark)
Strait
Melville Sound
VICTORIA ISLAND
FRANKLIN
Thule
Melville Bay
Baffin Bay
Upernavik
Gulf of Boothia
BAFFIN ISLAND
Davis Strait
ARCTIC CIRCLE
Godthaab
Julianehaab
WEST
TUNDRA
KEEWATIN
TERRITORIES
Hudson Strait
Ungava Bay
ATLANTIC OCEAN
HUDSON BAY
Uranium City
Lake Athabasca
Churchill
Port Nelson
BELCHER IS.
NEWFOUNDLAND (LABRADOR)
R. Goose Bay
Str. of Belle Isle
Hamilton
Churchill R.
SASKATCHEWAN
MANITOBA
UPLANDS
Lake Winnipeg
James Bay
Fort Albany
Moosonee
R.
Albany R.
L. Mistassini
Saguenay R.
QUEBEC
UPLANDS
ANTICOSTI I.
NEWFOUNDLAND
Gander
St. Johns
ST. PIERRE (France)
Saskatchewan R.
Prince Albert
Saskatoon
Winnipeg
L. Nipigon
LAURENTIAN
Gulf of St. Lawrence
Gaspé
PRINCE EDWARD
MIQUELON
Sydney CAPE BRETON IS.
R.
Regina
L. Manitoba
Brandon
Winnipeg
L. of the Woods
Port Arthur
Ft. William
ONTARIO
L. Superior
Sudbury
North Bay
Arvida
Chicoutimi
Québec
Three Rivers
St.
NEW BRUNSWICK
Fredericton
Charlottetown
St. John
NOVA SCOTIA
Halifax
Missouri
NORTH DAKOTA
Red R. of the North
Duluth
MINN.
WISCONSIN
Sault Ste. Marie
MICH.
L. Huron
North Bay
Ottawa
St. Lawrence Seaway
Toronto
Ottawa R.
Kingston
Sherbrooke
MAINE
Bay of Fundy
VT.
N.H.
SOUTH DAKOTA
MING
from
NEBRASKA
IOWA
Greenwich
ILL.
IND.
Milwaukee
Mississippi R.
L. Michigan
Chicago
Detroit
Windsor
Cleveland
OHIO
Hamilton
NEW YORK
Buffalo
PENNSYLVANIA
MASS.
CONN.
R.I.
N.J.
Montreal

Canada's middle west is an extension of the northern part of the plains region found in our country. Near the United States border, spring wheat is grown on the plains. As one travels north on the plain, lakes and pine forests cover the landscape. The plain continues north to the Arctic Ocean, where the land is almost always frozen and no trees can grow. This is the cold northern Polar region.

The Rocky Mountains extend through western Canada. Pine forests cover the western slopes of the mountains. The magnificent scenery here always attracts tourists. Mining, grazing, logging, and farming in the valleys, all find a place in this mountainous landscape.

A Cool Climate. All of Canada lies far from the equator. Most of the country has long, cold winters with short, cool summers. No part of Canada has climate suitable for warm-weather crops. Most of the people live in the southern part of the country. In this area the temperatures are not so extreme.

In the far northern interior, temperatures have been known to drop to 82 degrees below zero during the winter. In the same area, the thermometer sometimes rises to 90 degrees and above in summer. Of course, this does not mean that it is always so cold in winter or always so warm in the summer. It does mean that there is always a marked difference between summer and winter in interior Canada.

The most even temperatures are found along the coast of British Columbia in the west. Winds from over the Pacific help to keep the climate here mild, and the high mountains shelter the coastal area from the cold Arctic air which moves into the interior. Along the west coast, there is a frost-free period of over 200 days. Rains are heavy in this part of Canada, especially in late autumn and winter.

The extremely cold, winter temperatures in the interior of Canada freeze the rivers

Old World Scene. Two-wheeled carts drawn by horses in a little French-Canadian village near Quebec give it the appearance of a town in France.

Upper Town, Quebec. Old houses line the two streets which form the intersection here. Notice that the advertising signs are in English and French.

and lakes for many months of the year. Spring is very late in coming, especially along the eastern coast where the cold Labrador ocean current brings down great cakes of ice to melt near the coasts of the Atlantic Provinces.

It is so cold in the far north of Canada and around the Hudson Bay that people do not live there unless they have to. Fur trappers and people who work for the government are about the only people who come to this part of Canada. They try to spend only part of their time there.

The Canadian People. In spite of its size, Canada has fewer people than our state of New York. Most of the Canadian people live in the larger cities within 100 miles of the United States border.

There are two principal groups of people in Canada—the English-speaking and the French-speaking. The French people settled in Canada first, but the English took control of the land after the French and Indian War. That was a long time ago.

The descendants of the French settlers have kept their language and their Catholic religion. The French-speaking people live mostly in the Province of Quebec and hold fast to their language and customs.

More than half the people in Canada today are English-speaking. Perhaps you have heard Canada called the "Dominion of Canada." This means it is one of the free nations that belongs to the British Commonwealth of Nations. By choice, Canada acknowledges the Queen of England as head of state. It elects its own government, makes its own laws, and is a free and independent country.

Canada has admitted people from many other nations to its land. There are large groups of Germans, Russians, Dutch, Poles, and Ukranians. After World War II, over one million war victims from Europe found new homes in Canada.

Indians and Eskimos together make up only a small part of the total population —about one in every one hundred people. So that the Indian and Eskimo children can be educated, teachers are sent by the government and by Catholic and other missions to the wandering tribes that inhabit northern Canada.

The Canadian people are energetic. In many parts of the country the people enjoy a high standard of living. Some of the rural areas of southern Ontario and Quebec, however, are poor. In these areas it is difficult to make a living, just as it is in certain parts of the United States. Schools, hospitals, and government services in Canada are among the best in the world. Although Canada has a small population compared to many other countries, the value of its trade with other lands is one of the highest in the world.

Facts *to remember*

1. Canada is similar to the United States in that it, too, was once a colony of England. English is its principal language, most of its ancestors came from Europe, and its principles of government, religion, and education are much like ours.

2. The United States and Canada are partners and neighbors, working together for the betterment of North America.

3. Canada, the largest country in the Western Hemisphere, lies to the north of the United States. It consists of ten provinces and two territories. The interior is extremely cold. This country has fewer people than our state of New York. The French settled here first, but the British took control after the French and Indian War.

4. The people are energetic. They have excellent schools, hospitals, and government services. The value of Canada's trade is one of the highest in the world. Nearly all the French-speaking people of Canada are Catholics.

What *have I learned?*

On a separate piece of paper, write each statement, using the word or words from the parenthesis that make it correct.

1. The (United States, Canada, the United States and Canada) built the St. Lawrence Seaway.

2. (Canada, the Soviet Union, the United States) is the largest country in the world.

3. The western border of Canada touches the (Arctic, Atlantic, Pacific) Ocean.

4. The part of Canada that is coldest is near (the Great Lakes, the Arctic Ocean, the West Coast).

5. The greatest number of Canadians are (of English descent, of French descent, Indians).

6. (All, One half, Very few) of the Canadian people speak English.

7. Canada is made up of (twelve, eight, ten) provinces and two territories.

8. (The Laurentian Upland, The Appalachian Highlands, The Central Plain) is a feature of the surface of Canada not found in the United States.

9. The most even temperatures in Canada are found (in the north, in the west, in the east).

10. Recently, (good farmland, mineral wealth, fishing grounds) have been found in the Laurentian Upland.

Facts *to understand*

Answer each of the following questions in a sentence or two.

1. Why is it a blessing that the United States and Canada are such good friends?

2. In what ways are Canada and the United States similar?

3. How would you describe the Canadian people?

4. What kind of climate does Canada have?

5. In what ways does the surface of Canada resemble that of the United States?

6. Why are there two groups of people who speak different languages in Canada?

7. What does the term "Dominion of Canada" mean?

8. List several examples of the energy and good spirit of the people of Canada.

9. Why is the population very small in the northern parts of Canada?

2
Eastern Canada

Open-air Market. Housewives in Quebec make a daily trip to this city market place. Vegetables and fruit produced by local farmers are sold here.

In our study of the United States we divided the states into groups. Because Canada is such a large country, we shall divide it in the same way into groups of provinces and territories. Remember that each province is like a state and has its own capital city.

In this chapter we shall first read about the four Atlantic Provinces. Later in the chapter we shall read about the two provinces whose southern sections lie in the valley of the St. Lawrence River. We shall call them the St. Lawrence Provinces.

part of the province of Newfoundland. This cold, rocky area borders on the Atlantic and is almost uninhabited.

Roadside Devotion. Shrines and Stations of the Cross are found throughout the Quebec countryside. Devout country people pause and say a prayer.

THE ATLANTIC PROVINCES

The four Atlantic Provinces take their name from the Atlantic Ocean. All four of the provinces lie along the Canadian coast of this ocean. They are the island of Newfoundland; the peninsula of Nova Scotia; New Brunswick; and Prince Edward Island. The Atlantic Provinces are small, both in area and in population. They are separated from the rest of Canada by the rocky Laurentian Upland. Travel between the Atlantic Provinces and the interior of Canada is usually by means of the St. Lawrence.

Labrador, on the mainland, is considered

Tourists in Quebec. Visitors find this old city fascinating in many ways. Here old-fashioned carriages are seen lined up outside a city park.

Historic Region. In 1497 John Cabot landed on the mainland of Newfoundland, thus establishing the claim of England to Canada. He was followed by fishermen from Portugal, France, and Spain.

A Relic of Colonial Times. This is Artillerie Street in the old section of Quebec. It was one of the original thoroughfares within the city walls.

Some of the early French settlers made their homes in Acadia. Today, Acadia is called *Nova Scotia,* meaning "New Scotland." When you are older, you will read the poem *Evangeline* by the American poet Longfellow. It tells how the French settlers were driven from Acadia by the English in 1755. About 3,000 Acadians were forced to leave their homes and to settle elsewhere in other New World colonies. Most of them never returned to Acadia.

Although Newfoundland was one of the first English colonies in America, it became a province of Canada only in 1949. For 450 years it had been a separate British colony.

During the American Revolutionary War, many colonists, loyal to the mother country, left New England and settled in the Atlantic Provinces of Canada. Halifax became a British military and naval base before our War of Independence. The city is still an important naval base today.

Population. Most of the people of these four provinces live in small towns. Many came from England, Scotland, and Ireland. The majority of them are English-speaking. Some, however, speak Gaelic, the ancient language of Ireland and Scotland. Even today many Scotsmen in Nova Scotia wear kilts on special occasions. They dance the Highland fling to the music of the bagpipes.

The city populations are not large. Halifax, the capital of Nova Scotia, is the largest city of the Atlantic Provinces. It has a population of 93,300 people — a small city when compared to large cities in the United States. St. John, New Brunswick, is the next largest city with about 86,000 people. St. John's, Newfoundland, has about 80,000 people. Fredericton, the capital of New Brunswick, and Charlottetown, the capital of Prince Edward Island, are very small cities.

Near-by Fishing Banks. The four sea-coast provinces produce nearly half the fish caught each year in Canada. Cod, lobster, halibut, haddock, sardines, and herring are the leading varieties. Oysters are found near Prince Edward Island and New Brunswick. Each spring, a fleet of fishing boats sails from St. John's in Newfoundland to the coast of Labrador. Here they kill large numbers of seals to obtain their valuable skins and blubber.

Off the coasts of Newfoundland and Nova Scotia are the rich fishing banks called the Grand Banks. These same banks are used by New England fishermen. Fish come in great numbers to these shallow waters to feed and are easily caught in nets or by lines.

The irregular coast line of these provinces provides many harbors and coves for trawlers, schooners, and other kinds of fishing boats.

Some of the fish is salted or dried. A larger amount is sent to market frozen, smoked, or canned. Much of it is shipped abroad to countries where fish is needed.

Forests. Almost one half of Canada is covered with forests. Except for Prince Edward Island, the Atlantic Provinces have a large part of their land covered by softwood forests. There are also some patches of hardwoods. Evergreens, such as spruce and balsam, are the chief softwoods. Birch, maple, and oak are among the hardwoods.

Lumbering is carried on in the Atlantic provinces in much the same way as it is in New England. There are many lumber roads in the forests. Tractors haul the logs out, and, where possible, the logs are sent down the streams to sawmills or pulp mills. Some of the logs are used for timber, but most of the lumber is made into wood pulp for paper. Pine trees are cut and sold as Christmas trees in the United States.

Seacoast Industry. A Gaspe Peninsula fisherman and his family are busy cleaning their catch of fish on the banks of the Gulf of St. Lawrence.

Minerals. There are many important mineral deposits in these provinces, but few minerals are mined.

St. John's, Newfoundland. The capital of Newfoundland is an ancient city. Its splendid harbor makes it a center for ocean steamers and fishing boats.

Raising Potatoes. The climate and soil of Prince Edward Island, like those of Maine, are good for potatoes, although other crops do well here also.

Cape Breton Island in Nova Scotia produces about one third of Canada's coal. Mines at Cape Breton extend out from the land under the sea. Because it is expensive to transport coal from Cape Breton Island to the industrial cities along the St. Lawrence River and the Great Lakes, a limited amount is mined. In many cases, these cities find it cheaper to import coal from the United States. The coal fields of Pennsylvania and West Virginia are actually closer to the Canadian cities that use the coal than the mines at Cape Breton Island.

In Newfoundland there are rich veins of high-grade iron ore. Several of the mine tunnels here also extend under the sea just as the coal mines do at Cape Breton. Newfoundland iron ore is sent to blast furnaces in Nova Scotia and Great Britain.

Deposits of lead, zinc, copper, and other minerals are waiting to be developed in the Atlantic provinces.

Farming. There are two good farming areas in the Atlantic Provinces. One is Prince Edward Island, and the other is in the valleys of Nova Scotia.

The climate and soil in this area are much like those of New England. As a result, the crops raised are similar also. Farmers carry on mixed farming. They till the soil to make it serve their needs and purposes. Grains, potatoes, and apples are among the important crops. Livestock ranches and dairy farms are very successful in the moist pasture lands.

Prince Edward Island, the smallest Canadian province, has nearly all its deep, red soil in crops. The island is well known for its potatoes. Many are exported as food or as seed potatoes.

Nova Scotia is best known for fruit growing. The Annapolis Valley is famous for its apple trees. Sea breezes from the Bay of Fundy keep the buds from blossoming too soon in spring. In this way, they escape the danger of being exposed to frosts. Other fruits include cherries, pears, plums, and various berries.

Except for Prince Edward Island and the Annapolis Valley, there is little other good farm land because of the forests, rocky soil, and bogland. As in New England, the settlers here looked mostly to the sea for their livelihood. The soils they found were thin, and the growing season short.

Manufacturing. The chief source of income for the people of these provinces is manufacturing. The industries use the raw materials of the land.

Pulp and paper mills are important in most of the provinces, especially New Brunswick. Nova Scotia has many other industries as well, including cotton and woolen manufacturing. At Halifax and other coastal towns, there are shipyards that build fishing boats, and factories that make nets, lines, and other fishing gear.

Many people are employed in canning, drying, and freezing fish and fish products. New Brunswick has the largest sardine cannery in the world.

An iron and steel mill in Sydney, Cape Breton, makes use of iron ore from Newfoundland and coal from near-by mines.

Vacationland. Every year the Atlantic Provinces welcome a large share of summer tourists from the United States and other countries. They come by boat, air, railroad, and automobile. Beautiful scenery and a cool, pleasant summer make the region an ideal vacationland. Sportsmen find its lakes, rivers, and coast lines a fisherman's paradise. Artists sketch the picturesque rural fishing villages along the coast. Oxen plowing the fields remind tourists of the past.

Ice-free Ports. Halifax is a world port. Ships from many countries dock in its spacious harbor, said to be large enough to hold the whole British fleet. Wheat, wood pulp, farm products, and fish are shipped from Halifax. It is one of Canada's few ice-free ports and usually is busier during the winter than in the summer. Some manufacturing is carried on in the city, and goods are distributed to other parts of the Atlantic Provinces by ship and rail.

St. John, New Brunswick, is another important ice-free port. Strong tides from Bay of Fundy keep the water from freezing. Both ports are busy during the long, winter months especially. That is when the St. Lawrence River freezes over, and ships cannot reach Montreal and other Canadian cities on the Great Lakes.

Gander Airport. All the Atlantic Provinces have airports. Most planes crossing the Atlantic Ocean refuel at Gander, Newfoundland. A look at the globe shows that Gander is on the direct air route between

Industry of the Atlantic Provinces. This is the giant plant of a paper company in eastern Canada. Much of our country's paper comes from this area.

New York City and cities in western Europe. This part of North America is nearest to the British Isles. Goose Bay, Labrador, is another busy international airport. It is used when Gander is closed by bad weather.

Canadian Vacationland. The Laurentian Mountains are famous for beautiful ski trails. These skiers are enjoying a winter holiday at Adele-en-Haut.

THE ST. LAWRENCE PROVINCES

Summer in Quebec Province. These farmers are loading their wagon with freshly-mown hay. As in our country, hay is used as winter feed for animals.

The southern part of Canada's two largest provinces, Quebec and Ontario, lies in the St. Lawrence Valley. More than half of the people of Canada live in this lowland, which extends to the Ontario Peninsula on the Great Lakes. The part of the St. Lawrence Valley in Quebec is known as French Canada, because the first settlers there were French. Their descendants still live in the valley and retain their own language and customs.

The rocky Laurentian Upland rises to the north of this valley. Ridges of the Appalachian Highlands extend from the United States across the border into Quebec. In both of these upland regions the population is sparse.

The St. Lawrence Lowland is the "cradle" of Canada. This river-and-lake route was the ancient trail of the fur traders and the missionaries. Canada had its beginnings on the shores of the St. Lawrence River, Lake Ontario, and Lake Erie. Tourists visit this region to see the distinctive, old-time look of the countryside.

Farming. Some of Canada's richest farmland lies in the St. Lawrence Valley and on the Ontario Peninsula. Good soils cover the nearly-level plain. Rainfall is plentiful, and the growing season is long enough for certain crops.

Farms are located near either rivers or railroads. Farm products can, therefore, be moved easily to market. Most farms are small. They are generally long and narrow. The farmhouses and the barns are located close to the road so that winter snows do not close them in. Beyond the cultivated lands are forests and a few settlements.

French-speaking farmers in the St. Lawrence valley specialize in dairying. The milk is sold in near-by cities. Butter and cheese are made for export. Among the crops grown in the St. Lawrence valley are tobacco, potatoes, oats, wheat, hay, rye, beans, peas, and strawberries.

The Ontario Peninsula, the most southern part of Canada, is wedged in between Lake Huron on one side and Lakes Erie and Ontario on the other. It is the best fruit-growing region of Canada. Fruit orchards produce peaches, apples, pears, grapes, cherries, and plums. Dairying and livestock are also important. Mixed farming is carried on across the Detroit River opposite Detroit, Michigan. Sugar beets, corn, tobacco, truck crops, and hogs are raised.

Mineral Wealth. Rich mineral deposits are found in the provinces of Quebec and Ontario. More than half of the asbestos of the world is mined in Quebec in the region between the St. Lawrence River and Vermont. *Asbestos* is a mineral made up of long, gray fibers. Because it does not burn, it can be made into fireproof shingles and boards for buildings, clothing for firemen, and covering for pipes.

Over three quarters of the world's supply of nickel comes from mines in the Sudbury region of Ontario. Nickel is mixed with iron and chromium to make stainless steel and other alloys.

Iron deposits have been discovered, and mines have been opened in eastern Quebec near the border of Labrador. A railroad was built to carry the ore to a port on the St. Lawrence River. Some of this ore has even been sent to the eastern United States.

Power and Manufacturing. Extending from Quebec City in the St. Lawrence Valley to the city of Windsor at the end of Ontario Peninsula is the most important industrial area of Canada. The province of Quebec produces the largest amount of hydroelectric power in Canada; Ontario has the largest amount of mineral wealth. Ontario carries on one half of Canada's manufacturing, and Quebec accounts for one third of it. There are booming cities and factories along the superhighways throughout these two provinces.

The chief manufactures are food products, clothing, automobiles, machinery, pulp and paper, tobacco, and textiles.

Asbestos Mine. Quebec produces almost half of the world's asbestos supply. The material is used widely in industry because it will not burn.

Canada's Largest City. Montreal, with a population of over one million, is the largest city in Canada. It is the second largest French-speaking city in the world—Paris, France, is the largest. Montreal, an island city located in the St. Lawrence River, is the chief port of Canada. Grain elevators and warehouses line the docks of Montreal's harbor. Wheat, flour, wood pulp, paper, lumber, and furs are shipped from the port. Cotton, sugar, rubber, coffee, tea, and other products are imported.

Montreal is linked to New York City by rail, air, and water. Canada's two transcontinental railroads pass through Montreal. It is also a great airline center. Ocean liners were able to reach this port even before the St. Lawrence Seaway was completed several years ago.

There are many factories, banks, universities, and churches in this thriving city.

Quebec. The early French settlers built a town on top of a steep cliff on the shore of the St. Lawrence River. They called it Quebec. They were all Catholic people. The way of life they adopted in America was much the same as it had been in France. They planned to convert the Indians and give an example of a Christian way of life.

Catholics and others from all over the world now visit the beautiful, old-world city of Quebec. It is very much like visiting a city in France. Many pilgrims visit the shrine at the church of St. Anne de Beaupré, near Quebec.

The city of Quebec, the second largest city in the province of Quebec, is a busy seaport. It is noted especially for the manufacture of paper and aluminum.

In Arvida, north of Quebec city, is the

The Port of Montreal. A dock worker unloads large drums of oil from a freighter. Located on the St. Lawrence, Montreal is Canada's leading port.

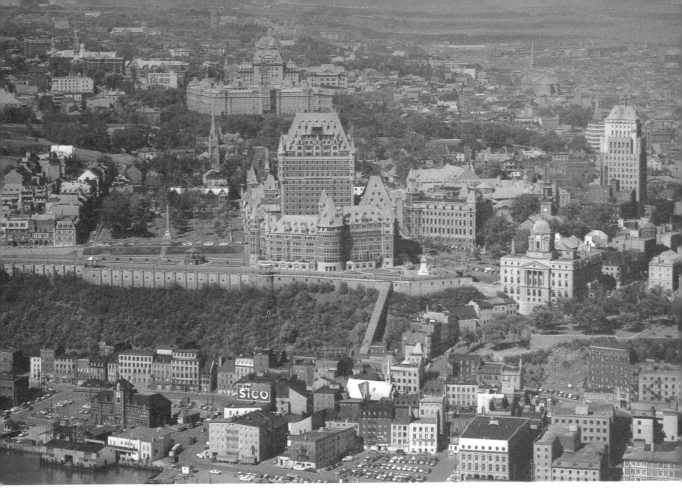

largest aluminum plant in Canada. Hydro-electric power plants on the Saguenay River supply the cheap electricity needed.

Toronto and Hamilton. Toronto, Ontario's capital, is the second largest city in Canada. It is Canada's chief port on the Great Lakes. Toronto has 4000 factories making various products. Transportation vehicles, machinery, chemicals, leather, and wood products are among the leading manufactures. A large amount of freight is handled in the well-equipped port. Wheat from Canada's prairie provinces is re-shipped at this lake port.

South of Toronto is the city of Hamilton, Ontario, noted for its iron and steel mills. Cheap power from Niagara Falls, water transportation on the Great Lakes, and a nearby-by market for goods have helped both cities to prosper.

Eastern Canada **307**

Two-level City. In this air view you can see the two different levels of the city of Quebec. In the center is a famous hotel — the Chateau Frontenac.

Busy Toronto. The capital of Ontario Province is a railroad center and important lake port. Its industries make it one of Canada's busiest cities.

Capital of Canada. Ottawa is the capital city of Canada. It has many magnificent government buildings. As in Washington, D.C., thousands of government workers live in the city of Ottawa.

Ottawa factories make lumber products. Forests are close by. The logs are floated down the river, and waterfalls supply power for the pulp and paper mills. Thus man works with nature, as God intends that he should, to earn a living and make a better life.

Facts *to remember*

1. The four Atlantic Provinces rely upon the St. Lawrence River mostly for their transportation route to the interior of Canada.

2. Although crops similar to those of New England grow on Prince Edward Island and in the valleys of Nova Scotia, the chief income of the people along the Atlantic Ocean is from manufacturing. Fishing is also carried on.

3. Halifax and St. John are important ice-free ports. Good international airports are located at Gander and Goose Bay.

4. The southern parts of Quebec and Ontario, both of which lie in the St. Lawrence Valley, are still inhabited mostly by French-speaking people.

5. Some of Canada's richest farmland is in the St. Lawrence Valley. Dairy products and crops are exported. Quebec and Ontario mine more than one half of the world's supply of asbestos and three fourths of the world's supply of nickel.

6. The province of Quebec produces much hydro-electric power and is the most important area of Canada. Montreal is Canada's largest city and chief port. It is linked to New York City by rail, air, and water. Ottawa is the capital city.

What *have I learned?*

I

On a separate piece of paper, write each statement, using the words or phrases from the parenthesis which make it correct.

1. Labrador is (a manufacturing, a farming, a cold and rocky) area of Newfoundland.

2. Newfoundland (recently became, has always been, will soon become) a province of Canada.

3. (Halifax, St. John, Cape Breton Island) is an important naval base today.

4. The chief source of income for the people of the Atlantic provinces is (fishing, farming, manufacturing).

5. Early Atlantic Province settlers made their living mostly by (fishing, lumbering, farming).

II

In each of the following sentences, the word in capitals makes the sentence either right or wrong. Write all the sentences correctly on a piece of paper. Change wrong words to correct words.

1. Quebec and Ontario are in NORTHERN Canada.

2. French-speaking people in the St. Lawrence Valley specialize in MANUFACTURING.

3. ASBESTOS is used for fireproofing.

4. Three fourths of the world's nickel supply comes from the MONTREAL region.

5. Much FISHING is done in Quebec.

6. TORONTO is the largest city of Canada.

7. The early FRENCH settlers came to Quebec.

8. The capital city of Canada is HAMILTON.

9. Canada's cities are LARGE when compared to those of the United States.

10. HALIFAX is an important refueling airport.

Facts *to understand*

Give reasons for these statements.

1. The region from Quebec City to the city of Windsor is the most important industrial area of Canada.

2. Although the Atlantic Provinces are rich in minerals, little mining is done there.

3. Many crops are raised in the St. Lawrence Valley.

4. Montreal is a large and important city.

5. People from all over the world visit Quebec.

3
Western Canada

Prairie Wheat Fields. The Province of Saskatchewan is the heart of Canada's Wheat Belt. This scene is like one in the Wheat Belts of our country.

When you studied the United States, you learned about the region called the West. The Great Central Plain is partly in this western half of the United States. The Rocky Mountains are located there also. Not so many people live in the western half of the United States as live in the eastern half.

In this chapter you will be studying the western part of Canada. You will find that it is very much like the western part of the United States. The Great Central Plain and the Rocky Mountains extend north into Canada. Just as in the western United States, not so many people live in western Canada as in eastern Canada.

First you will learn about the three Prairie Provinces—Manitoba, Saskatchewan, and Alberta. Then you will learn about the province of British Columbia on the Pacific coast of Canada.

The Prairie Provinces. A *prairie* is a grassy plain. It is a long stretch of almost flat land. The surface of the three Prairie Provinces of Canada is mostly level, with rolling hills here and there. These provinces form part of the Great Central Plain of North America that extends from the Arctic to the Gulf of Mexico. In southwestern Alberta there is a beautiful stretch of the Rocky Mountains. Here the Jasper and the Banff National Parks attract many tourists.

The almost empty plains seem to stretch endlessly to the horizon in these Prairie Provinces. Here are only "wide open

The "Black Gold" of Western Canada. Oil wells near Alberta produce nine tenths of the Canadian oil supply. Oil from this field goes to Vancouver.

spaces." A Saskatchewan wheat farm or an Alberta livestock ranch often spreads across many square miles. The people are used to traveling great distances and working long hours. Most of them live in small communities strung out along the lines of the railroads and highways. Some settlements consist of only a house or two, a cluster of barns, a clump of trees, and a row of grain elevators.

Canadian Bread Basket. Canada raises enough wheat to feed 100 million people. Between Winnipeg, in Manitoba, and Calgary, in Alberta, the world's finest wheat is grown. In a good year, as many as 700 million bushels of wheat are produced in this area. Oats, barley, and potatoes are also raised.

These provinces produce more grain than Canada can consume. The United States does not need these crops, either, because our own spring and winter wheat belts produce more wheat and other grains than we can use. However, many other countries, such as Great Britain, need wheat and buy it from Canada. Exporting wheat and flour is one of Canada's main industries.

Cattle and Sheep Ranges. Beef cattle and sheep graze on the drier parts of the Prairie Provinces. The sheep are raised for both meat and wool. Canadian beef is famous for its high quality.

In the cities of Edmonton, Calgary, and Winnipeg in the Prairie Provinces, and in Montreal in the province of Quebec, there are large meat-packing plants. Canada exports large quantities of beef and lamb to Great Britain and other countries of Europe.

Prairie Cities. Winnipeg, in Manitoba, is the largest city of the plains. Many railroads pass east and west and north and south through the city, making it a "gateway city" across the prairies. It is the leading grain center of Canada and a market for furs from northern Canada. Regina, in Saskatchewan, and Edmonton, in Alberta, are also grain centers.

Since the discovery of oil in the Prairie Provinces, Edmonton has become a leading oil and natural gas center. Nine tenths of Canada's oil comes from the province of Alberta. Pipelines have been laid to carry oil and gas to Vancouver on the Pacific coast and to ports on the Great Lakes. More lines are being laid to carry oil to the cities of eastern Canada, where it is needed.

The Pacific Coast Province. British Columbia is Canada's far-western province. It is a region of mountains, valleys, and high plateaus. These mountains and plateaus extend south into our Pacific Northwest and north into our state of Alaska.

Travel is difficult between the interior of Canada and the Pacific coast. The land is very rugged, and the mountains very high. There are many rushing rivers and large lakes in western Canada. Railroads and highways must use passes through the high mountains. In other places, where there are no natural passes, tunnels must be dug through the mountains.

The most densely populated part of British Columbia is the southwestern section along the Pacific coast. Here many inlets cut the irregular coast line, and large islands lay offshore. Vancouver Island is the largest of these islands. The city of Victoria, the capital of British Columbia, is located on Vancouver Island.

A Mild Climate. This Pacific coastal area has the mildest climate of all Canada. Along the coast, warm winds blow from the Pacific. These warm winds carry much moisture. As they are forced to rise on the western slopes of the high coastal mountains, the warm, moist air is cooled, and heavy rains fall. Rains are plentiful all year round, and are especially heavy in the winter and fall. They help fir and cedar trees to grow straight up to enormous heights. Little snow falls here in winter, and flowers bloom as late as December. The climate in this part of British Columbia is much like that of our Pacific Northwest region.

The Canadian Rockies. One of the most beautiful mountain regions in the world is in British Columbia. The mountains here run along the boundary line between the provinces of British Columbia and Alberta. You can see high, snow-covered peaks above, and glaciers moving down the mountain valleys below.

There are hundreds of blue lakes and swift-flowing streams with waterfalls, surrounded by green forests. Visitors are amazed at the variety of wildlife in the Canadian National Parks. Bear, elk, deer, moose, and caribou live in the safety of the parks, where hunting is not permitted. Bird life is plentiful, and beautifully-colored flowers carpet the valleys and uplands. Thousands of city people are thrilled with the wild beauty of the Canadian Rockies.

Canada's Richest Forests. British Columbia's greatest resource is timber. Enormous stands of Douglas fir, Sitka spruce, red cedar, pine, and hemlock grow in the forests of western Canada. Some giant trees are 300 feet high and as much as ten feet

The Scenic Canadian Rockies. Bow Valley is one of the many attractive regions which bring large numbers of tourists every year to British Columbia.

thick. Forests are everywhere, even within sight of the settled areas. The sale of this valuable wood provides about half the income of the province.

Lumbering is the chief industry of British Columbia. The industry is carried on in much the same way as it is in our states of Washington and Oregon. Thousands of men work in the logging camps and sawmills. When the lumber is cut in a certain area, the camp is moved to another place.

Some trees are cut for pulpwood. Like Quebec and Ontario, British Columbia has many mills where wood pulp and paper are produced. Most of the lumber for construction is exported by way of the Pacific port of Vancouver.

For many, many years, man has used these valuable timber and wood resources. The Canadian government sees to it, however, that the rich forests are not destroyed. New forests are planted where old forests are cut down. Thus man plans to have his descendants enjoy God's gifts found in nature.

Pacific Fisheries. About half of Canada's yearly catch of sea food is obtained in the west coast fisheries. The chief fish caught here is the salmon. Millions of cases of salmon are canned each year and exported to many other countries.

Tuna, herring, halibut, and flounder are caught also. Crabs, clams, and oysters add to the total value of the catch.

Most fishing is done near the coast. Some of the fish is sold fresh, some frozen, and some in cans.

Minerals and Power. British Columbia ranks third among the provinces in the production of minerals. Only Ontario and Quebec are more important. There are rich deposits of lead, zinc, copper, silver, and sulphur. Iron ore, copper, and soft coal are mined on Vancouver Island.

Capital Cities --------- ⊙
International Boundaries ━━━ ━ ┉
State or Provincial Boundaries ━━ ━ ┉
Scale of Miles

0   100   200   300   400   500

ELLESMERE
ISLAND

G R E E N L A N D
(To Denmark)

B a f f i n

B a y

VICTORIA
ISLAND

BAFFIN

ISLAND

CIRCLE

ARCTIC

A T L A N T I C

PITCHBLENDE

FURS

O C E A N

N W E S T   T E R R I T O R I E S

SILVER

RADIOACTIVE
METALS

H U D S O N

B A Y

COPPER

NEWFOUNDLAND
(LABRADOR)

COD

MANITOBA

St. John's

NEWFOUNDLAND

ST.
PIERRE
MIQUELON
I. (To France)

Saskatchewan

R.

SASKATCHEWAN

IRON

L.
Winnipeg
BEET
SUGAR

ONTARIO

Q U E B E C

OYSTERS

PR.
EDWARD
I.

HALIBUT
CAPE BRETON I.

Charlottetown

NEW
BRUNSWICK
Fredericton

GYPSUM

COTTON
COFFEE
SUGAR

Lawrence

R.

G

Regina

Winnipeg

NICKEL

St.

ASBESTOS

A

NOVA SCOTIA

Halifax

COPPER

Québec

L. Superior

Montreal

FISHING
EQUIPMENT

WHEAT
PAPER
WOOL

L. Michigan

L. Huron

Ottawa

Toronto

L. Ontario

HADDOCK

A T L A N T I C

U S T A T E S

L. Erie

O C E A N

British Columbia has an abundance of water power for manufacturing. This hydroelectric power is still largely undeveloped, but more and more is being used each year. Some four hundred miles north of Vancouver city there is a large aluminum refining plant at Kitimat. Here bauxite ore is brought all the way from the island of Jamaica in the Caribbean Sea to be made into aluminum. Much electricity is needed to make this metal. It is furnished by hydroelectric power produced on a branch of Fraser River near Prince Rupert.

Some Farming. Only small, scattered districts of British Columbia are farming areas. The largest of these is the lower valley of the Fraser River. Mixed farming is carried on here. Dairy crops, fruits, and vegetables are raised for the city markets of Vancouver and Victoria. In the interior valleys and plateaus, some sheep and livestock are raised.

Vancouver, Chief Pacific Port. Of all the Canadian cities, only Montreal and Toronto are larger than the city of Vancouver. It is one of Canada's fastest-growing cities. Vancouver, situated on the delta plain of the Fraser River, relies on the farms in the Fraser Valley for food.

Most of Canada's trade with Asia and Australia flows through Vancouver. Lumber, canned salmon, wheat, wool, and minerals are exported.

Facts *to remember*

1. The Canadian Prairie Provinces form part of the Great Central Plain of North America. Canada's tremendous wheat crop is raised on this level land. Beef cattle and sheep graze on the drier stretches of prairie land.

2. Between the interior of Canada and the Pacific coast, travel is difficult because of the rugged Canadian Rockies and many rushing rivers.

3. Timber is British Columbia's greatest resource. In addition, large catches of sea food are taken from along the Pacific coast. Many minerals are mined in this area.

4. The Pacific coastal area has the mildest climate of all Canada. The region of Canadian Rockies is one of the world's most beautiful mountain regions.

5. The chief cities of Western Canada are Edmonton, Calgary, Winnipeg, and Regina in the Prairie Provinces; and Vancouver, a port on the Pacific coast.

What *have I learned?*

Rewrite each sentence, using only the correct word or words in italics.

1. Western Canada is *very much like* or *unlike* Western United States.

2. A prairie is a *level* or *rugged* area.

3. People in the Prairie Provinces live *close together* or *far apart*.

4. Canada raises much *wheat* or *corn*.

5. *Regina* or *Winnipeg* is the largest city of the plains.

6. British Columbia is Canada's *far-eastern* or *far-western* province.

7. Vancouver is an *inland city* or *island*.

8. The climate of Canada's Pacific coastal area is *mild* or *cold*.

9. Canadian National Parks are noted for *large playgrounds* or *wildlife*.

10. British Columbia's greatest resource is *minerals* or *timber*.

Facts *to understand*

Give reasons for these statements.

1. Western Canada is much like Western United States.

2. Travel is difficult between the interior of Canada and the Pacific coast.

3. The Pacific Coast area has the mildest climate of all Canada.

4. Great forests grow in British Columbia.

5. Not much agriculture is carried on in British Columbia.

4

The Canadian Northlands

The northern part of Canada is a vast, empty region. It covers one third of Canada's total area and is still considered a frontier land. Northern Canada is divided into the Yukon Territory and the Northwest Territories of Mackenzie, Keewatin, and Franklin. In this chapter we shall also study Greenland, the largest island in the world. Greenland is not part of Canada.

Surface and Climate. The Canadian Northlands are a varied area of mountains, plateaus with deep canyons, frozen treeless plains, and Arctic Islands. One of these islands, Baffin, is twice the size of Colorado. Others have greater areas than several of our states. The second longest river in North America, the Mackenzie, crosses the Canadian Northlands and empties into the Arctic Ocean.

The Arctic winters are long and cold, but the summers are often quite warm. During the long, summer days, flowers grow in many places, and birds are everywhere. In the winter, because the air is too cold to hold much moisture, there is little snow. The Arctic is not really the land of snow and ice that many people believe it to be. However, the snow that does fall remains almost all year.

The far northern part of the Yukon and Northwest Territories is a treeless lowland called the *tundra*. Only a few small plants grow there during the short summer. The ground on the tundra is frozen to great depths. During the summer months the tundra thaws out at the surface and becomes a vast swamp infested with mosquitoes, flies, and other insects.

Hunting Polar Bears. Arctic Eskimos, dressed in warm clothing, expertly land a large polar bear. The thick fur will be traded or made into clothing.

Indians and Eskimos. The population of the Northern Territories is only about 25,000. About half of these people are Indians and Eskimos. The rest are white trappers, traders, and a few missioners.

Eskimos wander about the far north, in the area bordering the Arctic Ocean, seeking food and clothing. They hunt seal and walrus. From the fatty meat of these animals they obtain oil for lamps. The caribou, a deer-like animal of the tundra, supplies meat for food and hides for clothing. Clothing made from caribou skins is light in weight but very warm. Eskimo women chew the caribou hides until they are soft enough to be sewed into clothing.

Fish is a very important Eskimo food. The Eskimos catch large numbers in Arctic waters. They often have to fish through holes cut in the ice. Eskimos also trap animals for furs. Some are used for clothing; others are sold or traded to white men.

Eskimos are adopting modern ways very rapidly. They are smart people who learn quickly and easily. They now eat canned food and use stoves. Many have given up their small boats, called *kayaks,* and are using motor boats for fishing and hunting.

When they travel overland, they now use private planes as often as dog sleds. They even have hi-fi sets and radios.

Indians live in the northern forests, south of the tundra. They make a living by hunting and trapping. All through the long winter they set their traps and remove any animals they catch. The animals are skinned, and the furs stored until spring. When spring comes, fox, muskrat, mink, and ermine skins are packed into bundles. Some Indians carry the furs in small boats, which they paddle down the streams to the trading posts. Others use motor boats. At the post, they exchange the furs for food, clothing, traps, and money.

Indian and Eskimo Missions. With the first French settlers to Canada came many priests—Jesuits, Franciscans, and others. They set out at once to do missionary work. Many of these priests suffered torture and death from pagan Indians. In time, however, the missions grew and made thousands of native converts.

Some of the tribes were nomads, always on the move from place to place. The missioners settled many of these people in Christian villages. French nuns started schools to educate the Indian girls. Katerine Tekakwitha, the holy Mohawk Indian girl from New York, died in the Christian settlement near Montreal. This Catholic Indian community still exists.

The early missionaries waged a long battle against traders who gave the Indians rum in exchange for furs. Abuse of rum brought sin and lawlessness among the natives. Even government officials at times failed to see the harm the rum traffic was causing. The missionaries, however, never stopped trying to correct this abuse. Catholic missions today bring the good news of salvation to the Indians and the Eskimos of Northern Canada.

Help for the Indians and Eskimos. Canadians have made many very good laws for the benefit of all their people. For example, parents receive an allowance of money for each child in the family. This helps parents with large families. This allowance is paid also, of course, to families of Indians and Eskimos. The government builds schools for Indian children. Traveling schools and bookmobiles follow the Eskimos as they wander in search of food and clothing. The government of Canada is very successful in trying to educate all its people.

A Treasure House of Minerals. Northern Canada has rich mineral resources. The airplane has made it possible to work mines in places which once were hard to reach. Supplies come in by air, and minerals are carried out by air. Machinery and heavy freight come by ship during the warm months when the rivers are open. Airplanes use skis for landing on snow-covered lakes. From June to October, airplanes with floats use the lakes.

The Yukon and the western part of the Northwest Territories are the most highly developed mining regions. Gold, silver, lead, zinc, cadmium, copper, tungsten, and petroleum are obtained in this mineral-rich region. At Port Radium on Great Bear Lake, pitchblende is mined. Pitchblende yields radium and uranium. These two metals are sources of atomic energy.

Gold is mined at Yellowknife on the Great Slave Lake and also near Dawson in Yukon Territory. Dawson is on the Klondike River near the point where it flows into the Yukon. The Alaska Highway joins Dawson with Fairbanks in Alaska.

Oil deposits exist in the valley of the Mackenzie River near the Arctic Circle. During World War II petroleum from this region supplied our air bases in Alaska.

GREENLAND

Greenland is the largest island in the world. Look at the map on pages 6-7 and find Greenland. Most of it lies north of the Arctic Circle, to the northeast of Canada. Greenland is covered by a great ice sheet. In some places the ice covers the surface to a depth of two miles. Huge blocks of ice break off the ice sheet at the coast. They form icebergs, which are carried south by the Labrador Current into the North Atlantic.

Greenland is a part of the Kingdom of Denmark. Denmark is a small country in Europe located between the North Sea and the Baltic Sea. Greenland is about 50 times the size of Denmark. The people of Greenland, however, live only on a narrow part of the south and west coasts of this large country. There are now about 27,000 Greenlanders, more than half of them Eskimos. They live mostly by hunting and fishing.

About 6000 Americans also live on the island. They maintain a large United States Air Force base there. The base is at the city of Thule, on the northwestern coast. American planes fly men and supplies to this northern base to insure the safety of our continent.

The Danish Government encourages the people to live in villages close to the shore. Danish ships bring in supplies. Denmark has always sent missionaries to the island, so

that the people have become Christians. Each village has its own little church. Teachers, doctors, nurses, and other officials come from Denmark to care for the people. Greenlanders are a hardy, strong people who live principally on a diet of meat and fish.

Because the landscape of their country is so drab and colorless, the Greenlanders have a special fondness for color. They paint their houses red, yellow, blue, and many other colors of the rainbow. Women wear bright blouses and colorful knitted caps. Many wear high red boots over their warm fur trousers.

Large deposits of minerals have been located in Greenland. One is called *cryolite,* and Greenland is the only place in the world where this mineral is found. It is used in the process by which aluminum is extracted from its ore. The United States buys large quantities of cryolite from Greenland. Lead and zinc are other important minerals found along the eastern coast. Coal is mined in places along the western coast.

Other minerals are known to exist on this vast island, but it is very difficult to mine them. Only rarely does the temperature rise above freezing in the mining areas, even in summer. It is almost impossible to get a supply of fresh water from the permanently frozen ground. Ice-breaking ships are needed to bring in machinery, men, and supplies.

In spite of their hardships, Greenlanders love their grim island. In the future, men may bring prosperity to this cold land by finding a way to develop its resources.

Facts *to remember*

1. The northern part of Canada is a vast, empty region. Few people live there. Winters are long and cold. Only a few small plants grow on the tundra during the short summers.

2. The second longest river in North America, the Mackenzie, crosses the Canadian Northlands.

3. The Eskimos, who live in the far north, hunt animals for food and clothing. Fish is an important food. They now use motorboats and airplanes.

4. Indians in the northern forests south of the tundra exchange furs for food, clothing, traps, and money. Many Indians were converted to Christianity by zealous missionaries. The holy Mohawk girl, Katerine Tekakwitha, lived in a community of Christian Indians in Canada.

5. Good laws benefit all the Canadian people. The government tries to see that everyone receives a good education.

6. Northern Canada has rich mineral resources. Airplanes make mining possible.

7. Greenland is the largest island in the world. It has a small population. Its many mineral deposits have not been fully developed because of the severe climate and difficult transportation.

What *have I learned?*

I

Copy Column A. Opposite each item from Column A write the item from Column B that best fits it.

Column A	Column B
1. A vast, empty region	tundra
2. An island twice the size of Colorado	Mackenzie
3. The second longest river in North America	government
4. A cold, treeless lowland	Northern Canada
5. Ocean north of Canada	
6. Deer-like animal of the tundra	missionaries
7. Convert the Indians to Christianity	Arctic
8. Make mining possible in the Northlands	airplanes
9. A source of atomic power	Baffin
10. Makes laws to help its people	pitchblende
	caribou

II

On a separate piece of paper, write each statement, using the word or phrase from the parenthesis which makes it correct.

1. The tundra is a (grassy prairie, a highland, a treeless lowland).
2. Indians and Eskimos represent (all, one half, a very small part) of the population of the Canadian Northlands.
3. Small boats used by the Eskimos are called (punts, totems, kayaks).
4. The island of (Greenland, Vancouver, Baffin) is the largest in North America.
5. Indians of the Canadian Northlands gather (gold nuggets, uranium, furs) for trading.
6. Pitchblende is a source of (electrical, steam, atomic) power.
7. Eskimos use the hide of the (caribou, reindeer, buffalo) for clothing.
8. The Yukon Territory is famous for (fertile farmland, mineral deposits, national parks).
9. The island of Greenland comes under the government of (Great Britain, Sweden, Denmark).
10. (Cryolite, Bauxite, Pitchblende) is a mineral found only in Greenland.

Facts *to understand*

Answer each of the following questions in a sentence or two.

1. Why is the northern part of Canada a mostly empty region?
2. How do the Eskimos and Indians of Canada make a living?
3. How have the missionaries helped the Indians?
4. Why are airplanes used in the mining areas?
5. How does the government of Canada help its people?

Unit Six Review

Questions for Discussion and Review

1. In what ways are the United States and Canada similar? 2. What advantages do the people of the Atlantic Provinces have over the people of the Canadian Northlands? 3. Why is there not more manufacturing in Canada? 4. Describe the climate of Canada's Pacific Coast. 5. In what occupations are the people of Canada engaged? 6. Name the provinces of Canada. 7. Name the territories of Canada. 8. Why is the St. Lawrence Valley the most thickly settled area of Canada? 9. Why is the Canadian Northland the least thickly settled area of Canada? 10. How did it come about that Canada is a land of two different languages? 11. What is the modern name for the place once called Acadia? 12. What is it that draws Canadians and New Englanders to fish in the same area? 13. What limits the amount of coal mined on Cape Breton Island? 14. Which section of the United States is similar to the Atlantic Provinces in climate and soil? 15. Why are Gander and Goose Bay ideally suited as fueling stops for airliners? 16. What is the value of nickel in manufacturing? 17. What is the chief crop of the Prairie Provinces? 18. What mineral discovery has led to the growth of the city of Edmonton? 19. How does the climate of Canada's Pacific Coast contribute to its lumbering industry? 20. What resource makes the Canadian Northlands more and more valuable today?

Using the Maps and Globe

1. On an outline map, mark Canada's principal fishing grounds.
2. Sketch a map of Canada, and mark all provinces and territories. Show mountain ranges.
3. Trace the route of the early fur traders and missionaries.
4. On a globe or wall map, indicate the various surface features of Canada.
5. Use a wall map to explain the climate in different parts of Canada.

Using Geography Words

Here is a list of special words that have been used in this Unit. Write a sentence using each to prove you know its meaning in geography.

tundra	*pitchblende*	*prairie*	*gateway city*
kayaks	*province*	*blubber*	*founder*
asbestos			*territories*

Getting Information from Books

Read reference books such as *Compton's Pictured Encyclopedia* for information on the following topics. Prepare to give an oral or written report.

Evangeline

Quebec

Canada's Forests

British Commonwealth
of Nations

Fishing Banks of Canada

Final Test

Write each sentence on your paper, choosing the correct word or words in the parenthesis.

1. (English, Spanish, German) is one of the principal languages of Canada.
2. Most of the Canadian people live in the (eastern, northern, southern) part.
3. (Columbus, Drake, Cabot) gave England a claim to Canada.
4. (Salmon, Seals, Bears) are killed for their skins and blubber.
5. About (one half, one fourth, all) of Canada is covered with forests.
6. The best grain-producing area of Canada is in the (Atlantic, St. Lawrence, Prairie) provinces.
7. (Montreal, Gander, Winnipeg) is nearest to the British Isles.
8. The Province of (Saskatchewan, Quebec, New Brunswick) produces the most hydroelectric power.
9. (Vancouver, Toronto, Montreal) is the largest city of Canada.
10. The capital city of Canada is (Hamilton, Ottawa, Sydney).
11. Canada raises enough (vegetables, wheat, fruit) to feed 100 million people.
12. (Keewatin, Dawson, Vancouver) is an island.
13. The mildest climate of all Canada is in the (west, north, east).
14. Canada's richest forests are located in (British Columbia, Alberta, Prince Edward Island).
15. The province of (Ontario, Nova Scotia, Manitoba) has Canada's greatest mineral resources.
16. Canada is the (largest, second largest, third largest) country in the world.
17. The (Rocky Mountains, Sierra Nevada, Appalachian Highlands) extend through western Canada.
18. Canada is a member of (the Iron Curtain, the British Commonwealth of Nations, the Organization of American States).
19. The Province of Ontario is famous for (mineral deposits, cattle ranches, wheat farms).
20. Newfoundland is one of the (Atlantic, Prairie, St. Lawrence) Provinces.
21. The treeless plain of the Canadian Northlands is called (the uplands, the tundra, the prairie).
22. Saskatchewan is one of the (Prairie, Atlantic, St. Lawrence) Provinces.
23. The chief fish caught in Canada's west coast fisheries is (tuna, cod, salmon).
24. Labrador is part of (Newfoundland, New Brunswick, Nova Scotia).
25. (Toronto, Quebec, Hamilton) is the second largest city in Canada.

Applying Christian Principles.

Write each sentence on your paper, choosing the correct word or words to make it true.

1. The virtue of brotherly love is best practiced by the United States and Canada when **a.** each mines its own minerals **b.** when they work peacefully together **c.** when people live in large cities.
2. Canada can best help the world by **a.** preserving her fishing banks **b.** asking that planes refuel within the United States **c.** exporting fish to countries that need it.
3. The early settlers helped the Indians most by **a.** sowing crops **b.** bringing the Catholic Faith **c.** not letting other countries mine the minerals.
4. Man cooperates with God when he **a.** preserves and replants forests **b.** makes himself rich by pearl-fishing **c.** hires only a few men in his factory.
5. The Canadian Government helps its citizens most when it **a.** tries to interest the Eskimos in eating more vegetables **b.** builds schools for Indian children **c.** asks its people to learn to speak French.
6. Canada's huge wheat crop is best used when it **a.** is stored in elevators **b.** is sent to countries which cannot grow enough wheat **c.** made into cakes and pies.
7. Modern inventions improve the lives of the Eskimos by **a.** helping them provide food for their families **b.** bringing them new movies **c.** giving them more leisure time.
8. Canada's great mineral deposits will be used when **a.** Canada reduces their prices **b.** man discovers the best way to cooperate with God in developing these resources **c.** the Canadian people become more ambitious.
9. The different language and customs of the French-Canadian people should cause us to **a.** be amused at their unusual way of living **b.** distrust them **c.** take a special interest in them as children of God.

Neighbors in Middle America

MEXICO
CENTRAL AMERICA
THE WEST INDIES

**In this Unit
you will learn that:**

1 Middle America is made up of three regions: Mexico, the country just south of the United States; a group of countries between Mexico and South America, called Central America; and the islands of the Caribbean Sea, called the West Indies.

2 Throughout Middle America, many of the people are of Spanish and Indian descent. Together with South America, Middle America is often called Latin America, because of the influence of Spain and Portugal, the two Latin countries which explored and settled most of the entire region.

3 Middle America is close to the equator. Most of the lands here have a climate that is warm to hot. The people usually live in areas of greater elevation, such as mountains or plateaus, because the climate is more bearable at higher altitudes.

4 Farming is the chief occupation throughout Middle America. The climate is suited to the growth of crops such as coffee, pineapples, and sugar which require warm sunny days and a long growing season. Minerals are produced in some areas.

5 Most of the people of Middle America are Catholic by birth. However, there are generally not enough priests, Sisters, or Brothers to do the work of the Church.

Latin America includes those countries of North America lying south of the United States, plus all the countries of South America. *Middle America* is the part of Latin America located on the North American continent, including the islands east of the mainland in the Atlantic Ocean and the Caribbean Sea. This group of islands is known as the West Indies.

The people of Middle America are descended from native Indians and from early European settlers. The early settlers came from the Latin countries of Europe —Spain, France, and Portugal. Spanish remains the chief language. Some people in the West Indies speak French. Nearly all the people of Middle America are Catholics.

Our neighbors in Middle America live differently in some ways from people in the United States and Canada. Their warm climate makes the problem of getting food, clothing, and shelter rather simple. They do not have to plan and save for long, cold winters as people living to the north do. On the other hand, most of the countries of Middle America have not yet developed the industries necessary to use their rich resources.

Let us see how the people of Middle America live and work.

UNITED STATES

MEXICO

Gulf of Mexico

Pacific Ocean

CENTRAL AMERICA

MIDDLE AMERICA

From the southern border of the United States southward, North America tapers gradually to become a very narrow neck of land. This southern part of the continent, together with the islands of the Caribbean, is called Middle America.

Mexico is the largest country in Middle America. Notice its generally mountainous appearance. South of Mexico are the seven small countries of Central America, fitted together on a long, narrow piece of land between the Pacific and the Caribbean. The surface throughout Central America is mostly a lowland, with some highland areas.

To the northeast lies the long island chain of the West Indies, also occupied by several small countries. These islands have both mountainous and lowland surfaces.

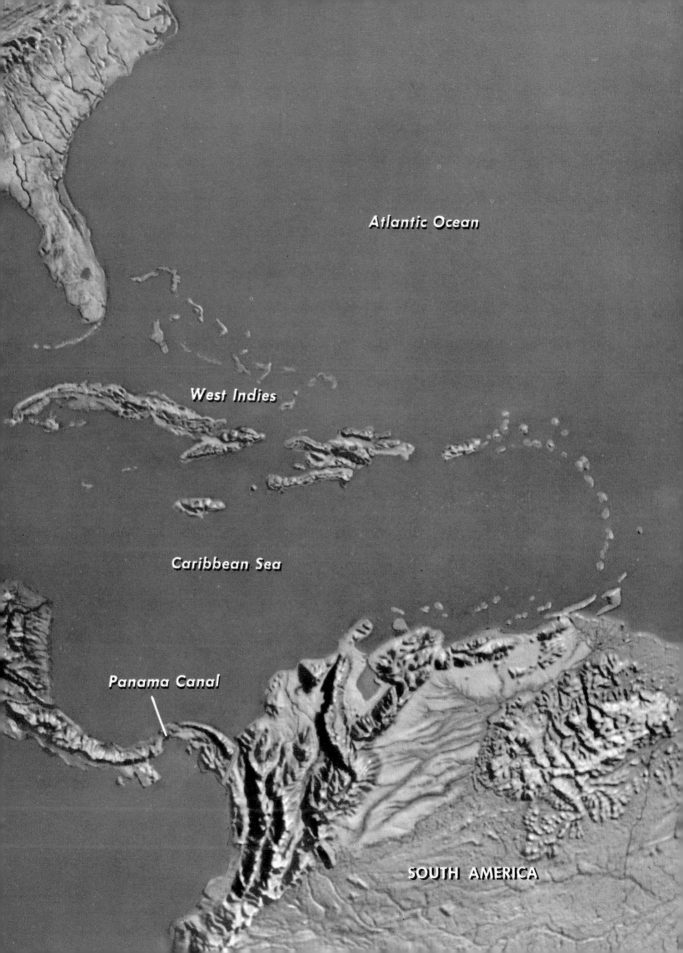

Atlantic Ocean

West Indies

Caribbean Sea

Panama Canal

SOUTH AMERICA

A Mountainous Country. A peasant and his donkey survey the scene in southern Mexico. This is Chilapa, on the central plateau, near Mexico City.

Mexico

Mexico is our nearest Latin American neighbor. Texas, New Mexico, Arizona, and California touch the Mexican border. Highways and railroads from these border states now connect directly with Mexico City. The Pan-American Highway runs from Texas to Mexico City and then on to South America. Airlines connect our large cities with Mexico City in a matter of hours.

Many Americans visit Mexico and get to know the Mexican people. Many Mexicans visit this country. Travel helps people of all nations to live as members of God's great family of nations.

Location and Size. Locate Mexico on the map on page 326. You see a long, wedge-shaped country, very wide in the north and coming almost to a point in the south. Mexico has two large peninsulas—Lower California in the northwest and Yucatan in the southeast.

Mexico's northern border extends from the Gulf of Mexico to the Pacific Ocean. To the north is the United States. To the east lies the Gulf of Mexico; to the west, the Pacific Ocean. The Gulf of California separates the Lower California peninsula from the mainland. To the south are Guatemala and British Honduras.

Mexico is the third largest nation of North America. It is made up of 29 states, two territories, and a federal district which includes the capital, Mexico City.

Surface of Mexico. More than two thirds of Mexico is hilly or mountainous. Narrow lowlands extend along the western and eastern coasts. The interior is a high plateau open to the north, with mountains along the eastern and western edges.

The eastern mountains have volcanoes with giant cones rising more than three miles above sea level. Among them are Mt. Orizaba (18,700 feet) and Popocatepetl (17,887 feet). These peaks can be seen from Mexico City.

Highland and Lowland Climate. Mexico has an "up and down" climate. Look at the map on page 326. Note that Southern Mexico is in the Tropical Zone, while the northern part is close to the Tropical Zone. The coastal lowlands are hot and damp.

For a temperate climate, one must climb. The climate in the southern part of the central plateau is delightful. Days are warm, and nights are cool. Two thirds of Mexico's people live in this high region. Mexico City and other leading cities are located on the plateau.

About half of Mexico is dry. The other half has abundant moisture. The steady winds from the warm Caribbean Sea and the Gulf of Mexico give up their moisture on the cool slopes of the eastern mountains. In crossing these mountains, these winds become dry. The southern and eastern parts of Mexico, therefore, get much rainfall, most of it in the summer. The western interior, especially in the north, has a dry climate.

Few people choose to live on the hot, damp coastal lowlands. Mosquitoes and other insects breed there. They carry disease germs and make conditions difficult in other ways.

Much of northern Mexico is a desert. Parts of western Mexico, including Lower California, have little rain. The northern plateau is an extension of the dry lands in Arizona and New Mexico. Few people live in these parts of Mexico.

Yucatan Peninsula is hot and dry, even though it is on the east coast. There are no mountains for the winds to climb and be cooled, so there is very little rainfall.

The Mexican People. Unless you live in the southwestern part of our country, you probably do not know many Mexican people. Many Americans, especially those who live far from the Mexican border, know very little about the Mexican people. Mexicans speak a different language, either Spanish or Indian.

Most of the Mexican people are of Indian descent. Long before Columbus came, Indians were living in Mexico. The two chief groups were more highly civilized than the Indians who lived in our own country. The Mayas lived on the Yucatan Peninsula. The Aztec lands stretched from the Pacific Ocean to the Gulf of Mexico. The Aztecs were in control of Mexico when the Spanish settlers arrived.

Market Day on the Plaza. Country people from all around the little town of Amecameca come to buy and sell different items in the village square.

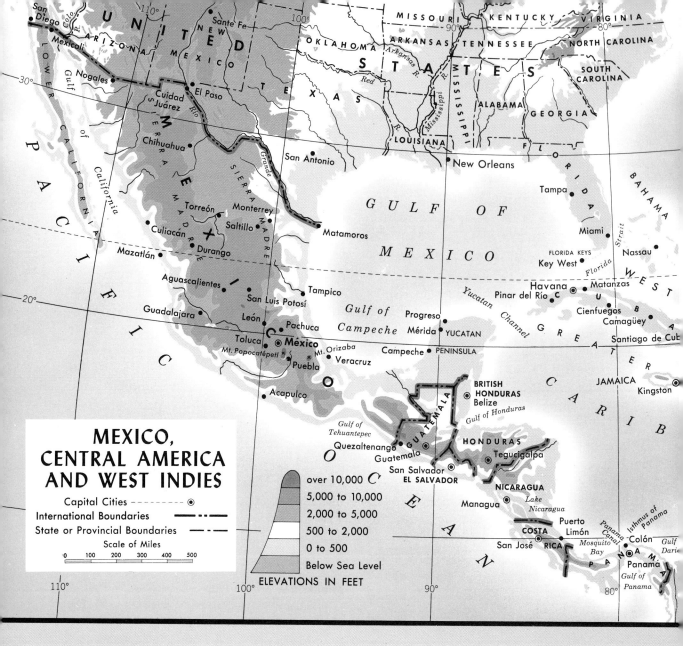

Studying the Map

A. 1. Which river forms part of the boundary between Mexico and the United States? Name the state that borders this river. **2.** Which three of the Western States border Mexico? **3.** Which body of water lies east of Mexico? west of Mexico? Which would be crossed in sailing from Mexico to Florida? **4.** The northern boundary of the Tropical Zone is the Tropic of Cancer. What part of Mexico lies in this zone? **5.** How would you describe the surface of the interior of Mexico? How can you tell? **6.** Name and locate two peninsulas that are part of Mexico.

7. Find Mexico City, the capital and largest city.

B. Central America is made up of six republics and one British possession. **1.** List the six countries and the capital city of each country. What is the name of the British possession? **2.** Locate the Panama Canal on the isthmus of Panama. What bodies of water does it connect? In what direction does it run? **3.** In which zone does Central America lie? What kind of climate would you expect to find in the countries of Central America? **4.** Where are the lowlands of Central America? the highlands? **5.** What body of water lies between Central America and the West Indies?

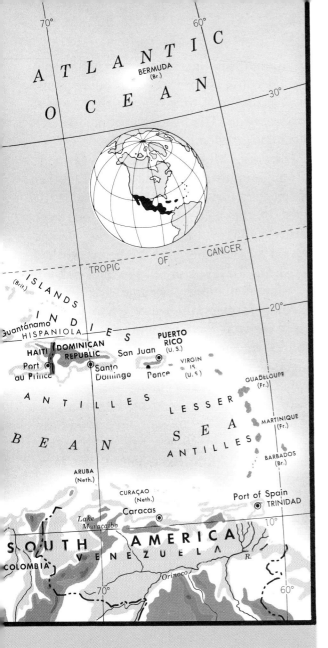

C. The West Indies are a large group of islands lying southeast of the United States. **1.** Name the four largest islands in the group. Which of these islands is divided into two countries? Which is a territory belonging to the United States? **2.** The smaller islands of the West Indies are called the Lesser Antilles. Name an island or islands in this group belonging to the United States. to Britain. to France. **3.** What kind of climate would you expect to find in the West Indies? Why? **4.** Use the scale of miles to measure the distance from Havana, Cuba, to Key West, Florida.

Spanish Conquerors. In 1519 several hundred soldiers under Hernando Cortez landed on the east coast of Mexico. In a short time they conquered the Aztec empire, and the Indians were reduced to slavery. For 300 years the Spaniards ruled the country. They lived on their large estates, while the Indians toiled in the fields or in the deep, dangerous gold and silver mines.

Mexican Independence. Gradually, the Indians and many of the descendants of the Spanish settlers became dissatisfied under the rule of Spain. They were joined by *mestizos,* who were of mixed Indian and Spanish descent. After a series of wars, Mexico gained its independence. For over 100 years, however, the country could not establish a peaceful government. Civil war broke out again and again. Many leaders were unjust, evil, and greedy. Some of them attacked the Catholic Church.

During these troubled years, Mexico and the United States were sometimes enemies. Once they were even at war. Texas, once part of Mexico, revolted and chose to become part of the United States. In recent years, however, the Mexican government has established peace, law, and order. Free Mexico is our good neighbor today and is a respected member of the world family of nations.

The Old and the New. The Mexican people today display both old and new ways of living. In the big cities, Mexicans live much like workers in our cities. In the countryside, colorful laborers, or *peons,* still live as they have lived for the past century or more. They wear wide-brimmed hats called *sombreros.* The man's overcoat is a *serape,* a woolen blanket of many colors.

Today a little more than half of the Mexicans are mestizos, of mixed Indian and Spanish descent. More than one fourth

OUR LADY
OF GUADALUPE

Not far from Mexico City, there is a little church with a very famous shrine. It is the shrine of Our Lady of Guadalupe. Above the altar, in a golden frame, there is a picture of Our Lady like no other picture in the world. It is bright with glowing colors, and is painted on the coarse material of a peasant's cloak. Our Lady herself painted this picture miraculously when she appeared to a poor Mexican peasant 400 years ago.

During the years after her miraculous appearance, while the cloak was displayed over the altar, many other miracles were performed at this Mexican shrine. Cripples were cured, the sick were healed, and sinners returned to God. Crowds of devout people came from near and far.

In 1945, Pope Pius XII named Our Lady of Guadalupe "Empress of the Americas." She is now the Patroness of North and South America, including the United States, Canada, and all of Latin America.

are Indian, and the rest are mostly Spanish.

Many Mexicans are still poor. Some have no schools to go to, so they cannot read or write. The Mexican people like art, music, gay festivals, and flowers.

Farming. Most Mexicans are farmers, although industry is increasing the number of city factory workers. Until recently, most of the land was divided into large farms called *haciendas*. A few people owned all the land, and the peons worked for them. Today, more of the land belongs to a larger number of people.

Many farmers still live very poorly. They use oxen and wooden plows. Their farm houses are small. The walls are made of adobe, and the floor is bare ground. The walls are thick to keep out the heat and cold. Adobe houses have no windows.

Mexico does not have enough good farm land. Much of it is too dry or too steep for farming. More than half of the farm land is planted in corn. Corn was grown by the Indians in Mexico before Columbus came. The climate and soil are not ideal for growing corn, but the Mexicans continue to plant it. They like corn foods.

Farming in the Lowlands. The lowlands in Mexico are along the eastern coast, the western coast, and the Yucatan peninsula.

Along the eastern coast, with the exception of the Yucatan peninsula, there is heavy rainfall and high temperatures. Most of the products of this region are tropical or sub-tropical—sugar cane, rice, tobacco, pineapples, oranges, and lemons. Good coffee is grown on the slopes of the mountains west of Veracruz.

Along the western coastal lowlands we find truck farms in the irrigated river valleys. One of these irrigated valleys is near the mouth of the Colorado River in Lower California. Truck vegetables, cotton, wheat, and alfalfa are grown.

Over half the world's supply of sisal hemp comes from the large plantations of the Yucatan Peninsula. Fibers are removed from the leaves of this plant and dried. The dried hemp is used to make cord and twine. People also use it to make beautiful baskets, carpets, rugs, and hammocks. Sisal hemp and hemp products are exported to many parts of the world.

Farming on the Plateau. The northern part of the Mexican plateau has large areas of level land with mountains rising here and there. The land receives only light rainfall. Desert shrubs abound. One of these desert shrubs is called *guayule*. From it, rubber can be obtained. Cotton, wheat, fruits, and other crops are grown by irrigation along the Rio Grande River.

The northern plateau is also used for grazing land. Cattle, sheep, horses, and goats are raised. The hides are exported, but the meat is used in Mexico.

The southern part of the plateau has more rainfall than the northern part. Irrigation is necessary in some places. Farmers raise corn, beans, peppers, wheat, alfalfa, and other crops. The amount grown on each acre is small. In most cases the land is better suited as grassland for raising cattle, sheep, hogs, horses, and goats.

Products from the Forests. The dense tropical forests in the hot, moist lowlands along the Gulf of Mexico yield many products. Beautiful woods for making furniture come from these jungles. Mahogany and ebony trees are two of these valuable woods.

Some of the trees produce valuable sap, juices, and gums. *Chicle* is made from the sap of the tree that grows wild in southern Mexico. Large quantities of chicle are exported to our country to be used in making chewing gum. Valuable dyes are made from the juices of other trees.

Charcoal is the principal fuel used by the people. It is made from the wood of trees growing on the high slopes of the hills. It is a common sight in some places to see donkeys loaded down with charcoal.

Products from the Mines. Mexico is rich in minerals. Mining is, and has always been, one of the principal industries of this country. The Mexican plateau is rich in copper, gold, silver, lead, and other minerals. Only a small amount of coal is mined. Mexico leads all the other countries of the world in the production of silver. It is a leading Mexican export.

Mexico is rich in petroleum. The center of the petroleum industry is the city of Tampico on the Gulf of Mexico.

Iron ore is found near Durango. Northeast of Durango is the city of Monterrey, only a little more than 100 miles south of the Rio Grande. Monterrey is a growing center of industry and business. Mexico's iron and steel industry is located in Monterrey. There are large smelters and huge

Mexican Handicraft. This highly skilled worker in a silver factory in Mexico City patiently carves a beautiful set of silver ornaments for export.

refineries for various metals. The city is the most important railroad center in northern Mexico.

In southern Mexico, between the Gulf of Tehuantepec and the Gulf of Campeche, is a thriving sulphur mine. Half of this sulphur goes to the United States, and the rest goes to Europe. Sulphur exports bring millions of dollars a year to Mexico.

More Manufacturing. Mexico is rapidly increasing its manufacturing industry. For centuries Mexicans have been making beautiful, useful, and artistic things by hand. Laces, hats, clothing, leather goods, shawls, and blankets made by skillful Mexican hands always have been eagerly bought by United States tourists.

Today, in the cities, big machines in modern factories are beginning to turn out products by mass production. United States businessmen with money and experience have established branch factories in Mexico. They employ many Mexicans. They use Mexican raw materials. Sugar refineries, iron and steel mills, paper, chemicals, cement, and cordage factories have begun making such products as rayon, plywood, fertilizers, electrical equipment, and aluminum.

The largest manufacturing center is in Mexico City and the surrounding area. Other centers are in Monterrey, Guadalajara, Orizaba, and Veracruz. These cities have good means of transportation for bringing in raw materials. They can also ship products easily to other countries. Thus the foreign trade of Mexico has increased. Mexico, like Canada, trades mostly with the United States.

Petroleum Storage Tanks. Minerals are Mexico's chief source of wealth. The oil from this refinery at Salamanca is shipped to Tampico on the coast.

Capital of Mexico. The high altitude of Mexico City gives it a mild climate, in spite of its tropical location. Notice the modern buildings.

Mexico City. The capital city of Mexico is one of the largest cities in the world. It has a population of over four million people. Its streets are jammed with traffic, and its sidewalks are crowded. To the north and east of the city, factory smokestacks stretch out for miles like a forest. The city has grown so rapidly that public services like water, sewerage, and schools must all be expanded.

New buildings of glass and aluminum have been erected to house banks and offices. Schools, hospitals, and roads are also rapidly being built.

Mexico City is the heartland of Mexico. It is leading the way to a better living for an ever-growing population. Much remains to be done in Mexico. Outside the cities many people still live in clay huts. Many are poorly fed and poorly clothed. One out of every five cannot read or write.

Planning, effort, and high ideals help a nation to use wisely the resources with which it has been blessed. To do so, it may need aid from other nations. Nations, like individuals, have the duty to share the good things God has given them. When nations share their blessings, they become stronger, richer, and happier.

With assistance and good will from neighbors like the United States, Mexico is gradually bringing its people to healthier and happier living.

UNITED STATES

PACIFIC

LOWER CALIFORNIA

Gulf of California

COPPER
ZINC
GOLD
LEAD
TUNGSTEN
STEEL
TOBACCO
Torreón
Monterrey
COTTON
San Luis Potosí
Tampico
Aguascalientes
Guadalajara
SILVER
México
Puebla
Veracruz
Acapulco

SIERRA MADRE
MEXICO

GULF OF MEXICO

BAHAMA

GRAND BAHAMA I.
Nassau
ANDROS ISLANDS
Havana
SUGAR
FRUIT
Cienfuegos
Camagüey
Santiago de Cuba
JAMAICA

GREATER

CARIBBEAN

Mérida
YUCATAN
SISAL HEMP
CHICLE
PENINSULA
MAHOGANY
BRITISH
Belize
HONDURAS
Puerto Barrios
GUATEMALA
HONDURAS
Guatemala
Tegucigalpa
San Salvador
EL SALVADOR
NICARAGUA
Managua

OCEAN

COSTA RICA
San José
Panama Canal
Colón
Panamá

Capital Cities - - - - - - - - ◎
International Boundaries ━━━ ━ ━
Scale of Miles
0   100   200   300   400   500

Facts *to remember*

1. Mexico touches our southern border. Highways, railroads, and airplanes connect our border states with Mexico City.

2. Two thirds of Mexico is hilly or mountainous. Leading cities are in the high region, which has a temperate climate. Few people live in the hot, damp coastal lowlands. Much of Mexico lies within the Tropical Zone. About half of the country is very dry.

3. Most of the Mexican people are of Indian descent. They were once ruled by Spaniards.

After many wars, Mexico gained its independence. Leaders often were unjust, evil, greedy, and opposed to the Catholic Church. Many Mexicans are still poor and uneducated.

4. Today, Mexico and the United States are good neighbors.

5. Many Mexicans are farmers. There is not enough good farm land. Tropical and subtropical crops are grown. Over half of the world's supply of sisal hemp comes from the Yucatan Peninsula. Livestock graze on the northern plateau.

6. Dense tropical forests are located along the Gulf of Mexico. Mining is one of the principal

ATLANTIC

OCEAN

BERMUDA
(Br.)

WATLING OR
SAN SALVADOR I.

ISLANDS

INDIES

DOMINICAN
REPUBLIC

Port HAITI
au Prince

San Juan

VIRGIN IS.
(U. S.)

Santo
Domingo

PUERTO
RICO
(U. S.)

GUADELOUPE
(Fr.)

ANTILLES

SEA

MARTINIQUE
(Fr.)

BARBADOS
(Br.)

ARUBA
(Neth.)

CURAÇAO
(Neth.)

LESSER

ANTILLES

Port of Spain

TRINIDAD

COLOMBIA

VENEZUELA

SOUTH AMERICA

1. Mexico touches the *northern* or *southern* border of the United States.

2. Lower California and Yucatan are *islands* or *peninsulas*.

3. Mexico consists mostly of *rugged* or *level* land.

4. When winds climb the cool slopes of the mountains, they become *wet* or *dry*.

5. The *Aztecs* or *Mayas* Indians were in control of Mexico when the Spanish settlers arrived.

6. Today most Mexicans are *poor* or *rich*.

7. *Corn* or *vegetables* is the favorite food of the Mexicans.

8. Mexico and the United States were *always* or *not always* friends.

9. Over half of the world's supply of *lemons* or *sisal hemp* comes from the Yucatan Peninsula.

10. The principal fuel of the Mexicans is *charcoal* or *coal*.

11. Mexico leads the countries of the world in the production of *petroleum* or *silver*.

12. *Sulphur* or *chicle* is used in making chewing gum.

13. *Veracruz* or *Mexico City* is the largest manufacturing center of Mexico City.

14. *Few* or *many* people own the land in Mexico today.

15. Mexico is now *independent* or *under the rule of Spain*.

Facts *to understand*

Give a reason for each of the following statements.

1. Many Mexicans are poor.

2. Mexico was not satisfied with Spanish rule.

3. Farming is difficult in Mexico.

4. Mexico is increasing its manufacturing industry.

5. The United States can help Mexico bring its people to healthier and happier living.

6. It is good for people of one country to travel in another country.

7. Two thirds of the people of Mexico live in the Central Plateau.

8. The Mexican people today display both old and new ways of living.

9. Mexico is still unable to raise enough crops to feed all its people adequately.

10. Many people live in Mexico City and the area that surrounds it.

industries. Mexico is specially rich in silver, petroleum, and sulphur.

7. Manufacturing in Mexico is increasing. Factories are beginning to turn out products by mass production. Foreign trade has increased.

8. Mexico City is one of the largest cities of the world. It is a modern city that is leading the way to a better living for an ever-growing population. Mexico needs the help of the United States.

What *have I learned?*

Rewrite each sentence, selecting the word or words in italics that makes it correct.

2
Central America

Stretching southeastward from Mexico all the way to the continent of South America is a strip of land over 1000 miles long. It is known as Central America and is divided into six independent countries and one British possession. The six independent countries are: Guatemala, El Salvador, Honduras, Nicaragua, Costa Rica, and Panama. British Honduras is a colony of Great Britain. The narrowest part of Central America is the Isthmus of Panama. The Panama Canal, joining the Atlantic Ocean with the Pacific, cuts across this isthmus.

Surface and Climate. There are lowlands along both coasts of Central America. The lowland along the Caribbean Sea is much wider than the lowland along the Pacific Ocean. The interior of Central America between the two lowlands is mountainous.

All of the Central American countries are in the Tropical Zone, or low latitudes. The lowlands are very hot. Rainfall is heavy in most areas, especially in summer.

The People of Central America. Most people live in the highlands, in settlements that are from 2000 to 5000 feet above sea level. The climate in these higher areas is cooler than in the lowlands. Most of the population of these countries is made up of mestizos, who are part Indian and part

Spanish. In Guatemala there are many Indians; in Costa Rica there are many Spanish. Negroes were once brought in to work on the plantations, and many of their descendants have remained.

The largest number of people work at farming. Bananas and coffee are the chief farm exports.

Let us see how the people work and live in the different countries lying between the Caribbean Sea and the Pacific Ocean.

Guatemala. Guatemala has the largest population in Central America. There are about three and one half million people—nearly as many as live in Chicago. Many of them are Indians, living now very much as they did before Columbus discovered America. The rest are mestizos of mixed Spanish and Indian blood.

Guatemala uses its low and high land for different kinds of crops. On the wetter tropical lowlands in the east, bananas, sugar cane, cacao, coconuts, and pineapples grow well. Higher up on the cooler mountain slopes, coffee, corn, potatoes, peas, peppers, and wheat are raised. Coffee is the chief export. On the drier west coast lowlands there are cotton plantations and cattle ranches.

Guatemala is rich in timber and minerals. Ways and means of shipping these products, however, are poor.

Guatemala City, the capital, is a modern city. The market place in Guatemala City is very interesting and colorful. Indian people display pottery, woven textiles, baskets, flowers, fruits, and foods that they have brought here on foot from faraway mountain villages.

The education of all Guatemalan children is required by law. Spanish is the language used throughout the country. Most of the people are Catholics, but the practice of their religion is not strong.

El Salvador. El Salvador, lying along the Pacific coast, is about the same size as Massachusetts. It has over two million people. El Salvador is the smallest but most densely populated of the Central American countries. San Salvador, the capital and largest city, has many modern buildings and excellent railroad and highway connections with other parts of Central America.

Farming is the chief industry, and high-grade coffee is the main export. The coffee tree is cultivated on both large and small farms. Volcanic soils on the Pacific slopes of the northern highlands are good coffee areas. The temperatures are mild, and the yields of the coffee trees are usually high.

Other crops grown in El Salvador are cotton, sugar cane, henequen, and rice. Corn and beans are raised for home use,

Indian Market Place. In most villages of Central America, like this one in Guatemala, the Indians set up a market just outside the village church.

Ball Game in El Salvador. These young boys have fun playing their favorite game — soccer. Beyond the field, smoke pours from a smoldering volcano.

as well as some wheat and cattle. One unusual product is called "balsam of Peru", a juice from a tree that grows nowhere else in the world. It has several uses as a medicine.

Air View of Tegucigalpa. You can see in the distance the mountains in which this capital of Honduras is located. Gold and silver are mined nearby.

As in the other Central American countries, the language and culture of the people is Spanish, and the chief religion Roman Catholic.

Honduras. Honduras, slightly larger than Tennessee, has about two million people. It is a mountainous land bordering on both the Pacific Ocean and the Caribbean Sea. Unlike the other Central American countries, it has no volcanoes.

Bananas form one third of Honduras' exports. As a result, it is often called "The Banana Country." Large plantations on the northeast coast make up Bananaland. The banana plant grows so tall it looks like a tree, but it is a plant. Tiny bananas branch out from a single flower stalk. At first they grow downward, and then point upward as they ripen into a huge bunch, weighing from 50 to 125 pounds. Two men harvest each bunch. Much care must be given to the bananas as they are rushed to market in carefully ventilated vehicles. The United States buys most of the bananas exported from Honduras.

Tegucigalpa, the capital of Honduras, looks like a Spanish city and has an Indian name. Its streets are steep, and its houses have red-tiled roofs. This city has excellent airplane service to other Latin American cities and to the United States.

British Honduras. In the early days, British shippers established a base on what is now called British Honduras. Britain has since claimed this colony of coastal lowlands and interior highlands. The colony has only about 82,000 people. They live in the tropical rain forest producing bananas, sugar cane, and other tropical foods, where the land has been cleared. Some food must be imported.

Forests products are mohagany, cedar, and rosewood used for furniture. They are the chief exports. Other forest products of British Honduras are logwood for dyes and chicle for chewing gum. Belize is the capital city.

Nicaragua. Nicaragua, largest in area of the Central American republics, has the fewest people. Nicaragua has many active volcanoes, and earthquakes occur very often. Managua, the capital of Nicaragua, is a new city of 100,000 people. In 1931 it was completely destroyed by a violent earthquake and fire, but it has since been rebuilt. Breezes from nearby lakes make Managua's climate somewhat mild.

Exports of cotton, coffee, gold, and hardwoods are profitable. The government is now stronger than it was in the past, and living conditions in Nicaragua have improved.

Costa Rica. Most of the people in Costa Rica are of Spanish descent. Disease long ago wiped out most of the Indians. Like Guatemala, Costa Rica has an interior plateau where the climate is temperate. Here most of the people live.

Many Costa Ricans are farmers. They work on coffee plantations. Coffee, bananas, cacao, and cattle are the chief products of Costa Rica. The Caribbean and Pacific coasts of Costa Rica are hot, moist lowlands. Some gold and silver is mined, and a little rubber is produced. Beautiful orchids are taken by air to American florists. Costa Rica has many forests, and lumbering is a growing industry.

San Jose, the capital, has a large airport. Limon is the Atlantic seaport, and Puntarenas is the Pacific seaport of Costa Rica. On his last voyage to America, Columbus landed near the present site of Limon.

Grinding Sugar Cane. In spite of many industrial improvements, some of Nicaragua's farming methods are quite old. Here oxen turn a grinding wheel.

Shrine of the Blessed Virgin. This beautiful public statue is in the center of San Jose, Costa Rica. Public shrines are everywhere in Middle America.

Panama. The country of Panama occupies the narrow isthmus connecting the two American continents. It is shaped like a double curve. Note that one part of it

Air View of Panama City. Capital and chief city of the Republic of Panama, this Pacific port is located near the entrance to the Panama Canal.

extends in an east-and-west direction, so that the Pacific end of the big canal is actually farther east than the Caribbean end.

Panama, smaller in area than West Virginia, has a population of less than one million. The land is rugged. Hills and mountains surround plateaus and river valleys. Dense jungle growth results from the humid air and heavy rainfall.

The chief products of Panama are corn, or *maize,* bananas, cacao, and sugar. Many people work serving the needs of ships of many lands that pass through the Panama Canal. Panama City has fine hotels.

Shrimp and pearl fisheries are found in the Pacific coastal waters. Tropical woods and rubber come from Panama's forests.

The Panama Canal Zone. Through the small country of Panama is a strip of land about 50 miles long and about 10 miles wide. This narrow strip is on both sides of the Panama Canal, which connects the Atlantic Ocean with the Pacific Ocean. The land, governed by the United States, is called the Panama Canal Zone.

Look at the map of the world in your atlas. Note the length of the water route from eastern United States to western United States around the southern tip of South America. The Panama Canal saves ships a detour of almost 10,000 miles. Heavy, bulky goods are carried by big ships from coast to coast. The "water bridge" lifts the ships on the Caribbean side at Colon and lowers them on the Pacific side at Balboa. It is a short route from ocean to ocean.

The canal is open to ships of all nations. They pay a toll, or fee, for using it. Not only fuel, time, and labor are saved, but a dangerous journey is avoided. Without the Panama Canal, ships would have to brave the storms going around Cape Horn at the southern end of South America.

BUILDING THE PANAMA CANAL

The narrow strip of land called the Isthmus of Panama had attracted men of vision for many years. Early Spanish explorers sought a river or some waterway which might cross it. Not finding one, they did the next best thing—they used the isthmus as a short land route between the oceans.

By 1900, however, trade increased between countries so much that a shorter, all-water route was needed between the two oceans. A French company started to build a canal across the narrow isthmus. Unfortunately, they suffered from disease and bad management, and the project was a terrible failure.

In spite of this, the United States soon became interested in a canal across the isthmus. Before starting the huge task, however, the United States was determined to avoid the danger of disease which had ruined the French effort. Major General William Gorgas of the United States Army Medical Corps was made chief sanitation officer and led the battle against disease.

Gorgas knew something the French had not known. It had been discovered that the two diseases which had tragically infected so many of the workers on the French canal effort were malaria and yellow fever, and that these two diseases were passed by the bite of mosquitoes. He knew that the only way to prevent the diseases was to kill the mosquitoes, and destroy their breeding places. Swamps were cleared, lakes and ponds were drained, jungles were cut down, and screens were put on all windows. In two years, there was no more yellow fever, and malaria was no longer a killer. This victory over disease paved the way for the construction of the canal, which began in 1904.

The construction job under Major General George Goethals was enormous. Along the 40-mile stretch, men worked with picks, shovels, drills, and dynamite, clearing a way through jungle and high mountains. Huge steamshovels dumped millions of tons of earth into waiting railway cars, to be removed from the cut. Lock gates were built to allow ships to sail "up" and "down" the water stairways between the high interior lakes and the lower ocean entrances.

After nearly ten years of hard work, the canal was opened. Since 1913, the 50-mile waterway from Atlantic to Pacific has been used by more than 6000 ships a year. The benefits of the canal are open to all nations in peacetime. The tolls they pay are balanced by the ease and convenience which this marvelous waterway brings to world trade.

Facts *to remember*

1. Central America stretches southeastward from Mexico to the continent of South America. It includes the countries of Guatemala, El Salvador, Honduras, Nicaragua, Costa Rica, and Panama, and the colony of British Honduras. All of the Central American countries are in the Tropical Zone, or low latitudes. Lowlands are along the coasts; the interior is mountainous. Most people live in the highlands because the climate there is cooler.
2. Farming is the main occupation. Tropical crops are raised. Coffee and bananas are exported. Central America has areas of dense forests and valuable mineral deposits. Because of poor transportation, little mining and lumbering is done. Shrimp and pearl fisheries are found in the Pacific coastal waters.
3. Guatemala has the largest population of any country in Central America. El Salvador is the most densely populated. Large cities in both of these countries have modern buildings and excellent railroad and highway connections. The language and culture is for the most part Spanish, and the chief religion is Roman Catholic.
4. The Panama Canal divides the country of Panama. This canal connects the Atlantic Ocean and the Pacific Ocean. It is open to all nations. It saves fuel, time, labor, money and lives. The Panama Canal Zone is governed by the United States.
5. Most of the people who live in the rural areas of Central America are very poor.

What *have I learned?*

Copy these statements on another sheet of paper. Identify the country referred to by writing its name to the right of the statement.
1. I have the largest population of any country in Central America.
2. I have no volcanoes, and I am called "The Banana Country."
3. My volcanic soils on the Pacific slopes of the northern highlands are good coffee areas.
4. In 1931 my capital city was completely destroyed by a violent earthquake and fire.
5. A large airport is located at San Jose, my capital.
6. On my drier west coast lowlands, there are cotton plantations and cattle ranches.
7. British shippers established a base on me.
8. I am the most densely populated of the Central American countries.
9. A canal that joins the Atlantic and Pacific was cut through me.
10. I am a mountainous land bordering the Pacific Ocean and the Caribbean Sea.

Facts *to understand*

Answer each of the following questions in a sentence or two.
1. How has the Panama Canal helped all nations?
2. Why do most of the people of Central America live in the highlands?
3. Why do we say these are "independent countries"?
4. How can these countries help the world?
5. Why do we say the people of Central America live differently from the people of the United States and Canada?

3

The West Indies

Trinidad, British West Indies. Columbus discovered this lovely island in 1498. Islanders and tourists enjoy its balmy climate and quiet waters.

When Christopher Columbus discovered the islands in the Caribbean Sea, he thought he had found India, which he had set out to reach. Since then, everyone has called these islands the *West Indies*. The natives are called *West Indians*.

The West Indies curve around the Caribbean Sea, separating it from the Atlantic Ocean. They extend southeast, like huge stepping-stones, from Florida to South America. Most of them are small. Only four have a population of more than one million people.

These islands are really the tops of mountains that begin at the bottom of the ocean. Some, like Cuba and Puerto Rico, were formed when the earth's layers of rock pushed together into folds. Others were formed by underwater volcanic lava that built up from the ocean floor.

Today you will find very few descendants of the Indians on these islands. Nearly all the people of the West Indies are settlers, or descendants of settlers. There are Spanish, English, French, Dutch, Negroes from Africa, and Americans from the United States.

We shall study the islands in groups: the Greater Antilles, the Lesser Antilles, the Bahamas, and Bermuda.

Pirate-proof Harbor. The fortified castle called El Morro once was needed to protect the harbor of Havana from pirates sailing the "Spanish Main."

The Greater Antilles. Four large islands make up the Greater Antilles. They are Cuba, Hispaniola, Jamaica, and Puerto Rico, a self-governing commonwealth of the United States.

Sugar Harvest. Sugar cane is grown on more than three fourths of Cuba's available farm land and is its most important crop. Most sugar is exported.

Cuba. The Republic of Cuba is the largest and most important of the West Indies. Its people are chiefly Spanish. The Spanish language is used for the most part, although many speak English also. Negro laborers come to Cuba from near-by islands to work on the plantations at harvest time.

Most of Cuba is a rolling land. Some low mountains rise in the central, western, and southeastern parts of the island. The fertile limestone soil is well suited for growing tropical crops. Cuba enjoys a warm, even temperature and has plenty of rain.

Sugar cane and tobacco are the two principal crops raised in Cuba. This Caribbean island produces almost half the world's supply of sugar. The sugar is planted on big plantations on the coastal lowlands. It grows rapidly and is harvested during the drier winter season.

The stalks of sugar cane are cut up and crushed at sugar mills. The juice of the stalks is made into raw sugar and molasses. The raw sugar is sent to refineries in the United States and other countries.

Tobacco is Cuba's second important

crop. It grows well in the western and central parts of the island. The sandy soil must be well fertilized. Tobacco raising requires many laborers. Cuban tobacco leaves are the world's finest for making cigars. Cuba has many cigar factories in its capital city of Havana.

Vegetables, pineapples, coffee, and bananas are other crops grown on Cuban farms and plantations. Manganese, chromium, iron ore, and copper are mined in Cuba's eastern mountains.

Habana, or Havana, as we call it, is the capital, largest city, and chief port of Cuba. It has more than half a million people. It is a city of broad boulevards, stately buildings, beautiful homes, and fine suburbs. Many American tourists have visited Havana. Its land-locked harbor handles cargo ships from all over the world. Some manufacturing is done in the city. Santiago de Cuba is the chief port city in the southeastern end of the island.

The Dominican Republic. The second largest island in the West Indies is Hispaniola, which means "Little Spain." It is a mountainous island with many valleys and lowlands. The Dominican Republic occupies the eastern two thirds of the island. Although it is called a republic, there have been many changes in its government in recent years.

The country is not densely populated. The people are chiefly white people of Spanish descent. There are some Negroes. Others are of mixed white and Negro blood.

Farming is the main industry. Sugar, cacao, and coffee are the principal products. Cattle are raised, and the hides are exported.

The capital city, once called Ciudad Trujillo in honor of a strong ruler, was given its old name of Santo Domingo when the ruler was overthrown in 1961.

Port-au-Prince, Haiti. The streets of this old Caribbean city are always crowded with colorfully costumed women, many carrying things on their heads.

Haiti. The western third of the island of Hispaniola is a small country called Haiti.

Haiti is densely populated. Over three million people live on a piece of land about the size of Maryland. Much of the land is very mountainous. Many people live in thatched huts on mountainside farms. Nearly all the people in Haiti are Negroes. Since Haiti was once a French colony, the people still speak French.

Farming is the chief occupation of the people of Haiti. Many raise only what they need for themselves. Coffee, sugar, hemp, and tropical woods are exported. Some manufacturing is carried on.

Port-au-Prince is the capital and chief city. It has few modern buildings.

Many of the people in the hill country and swamps cannot read or write. They are very poor. Beliefs in witch doctors and other customs brought from Africa years ago still exist among them.

Island Port. This is the city of San Juan, capital and major seaport of the island of Puerto Rico. Many new houses and buildings are going up here.

Puerto Rico. Every year thousands of American tourists visit the lovely island of Puerto Rico in the West Indies. They land at the capital city of San Juan.

The island of Puerto Rico is not much bigger than the state of Delaware. Through the interior from east to west runs a range of mountains. They rise about 4000 feet above sea level. A narrow coastal plain extends around the island. Excellent roads twist and turn up and around the green-covered mountains.

The coastal lowlands of Puerto Rico are always warm, with an average temperature of 77 degrees. The mountain temperature is about 10 degrees cooler. Steady winds from the northeast bring much rain to the northern or windward side of the island. There they climb the slopes of the mountains and become cool. The southern coast receives little rainfall. For farming, the land must be irrigated with mountain water.

Farming in Puerto Rico. Only two fifths of Puerto Rico is suited for farming. The Puerto Ricans, however, make good use of every square foot of it. Even so, they must import from the United States over half of all their food. Most of the land is used for raising money crops, or cash crops, to be sold in the United States.

The principal money crops are sugar cane, coffee, tobacco, and pineapples. Sugar cane and pineapple plantations thrive on the flat coastal plains. Tobacco and coffee grow well on the lower mountain slopes. The higher mountain land is wooded, rocky, or bare.

Since 1951 Puerto Rico has been a self-governing commonwealth under the protection of the United States. The people rule themselves. They have their own constitution, and they elect their own governor.

The people of Puerto Rico are American citizens. While they live in Puerto Rico, they have no vote in American elections, and they pay no taxes to the United States. If they move to one of the states, however, they may vote, and they must pay taxes.

Most of the people are of Spanish descent. Others are part Indian, Negro, French, or Italian. Race or color are not considered among the Puerto Ricans. Everyone is accepted, regardless of race, in church, school, work, and play.

Nearly all Puerto Ricans are Catholics. There are not enough priests, Brothers, and Sisters to take care of the work of the Church, however. Many American priests and religious people are now helping to serve the spiritual and bodily needs of the Puerto Rican Catholics.

"OPERATION BOOTSTRAP"

There is an old American saying, that when a person helps himself out of a difficulty, he is "lifting himself by his own bootstraps." The people of Puerto Rico have suffered under a number of difficulties for many years. Today they are helping themselves to overcome these difficulties, and the way they are doing it has been called "Operation Bootstrap."

In Puerto Rico, there are more than 3 million people crowded into a small amount of land. There is no coal or oil for producing power. For many years the people were too poor to eat well, to go to school, or to have a doctor. There were no industries to supply employment, and not enough good farm land to provide crops. The people's houses were little more than huts, in which many persons would occupy one room.

Today, this is changing. Men who were farmers are learning new trades. Experts from the United States have been invited to come and teach the Puerto Ricans how to make things in factories. In eight years, more than 450 new factories have opened, and are prospering. New, inexpensive homes are being built.

Now people come from all over the world to Puerto Rico. They come mostly from other countries that are poor. They want to observe Operation Bootstrap so they can try it out for themselves.

These visitors do not come to enjoy the beauties of a tropical island, the stretches of white sandy beaches, or the ideal Caribbean climate. They see teeming life on busy thoroughfares in San Juan, new factories, modern stores, large office buildings and free hospitals and clinics. They visit schools and universities. They visit the clean, spacious homes of the people.

The people of Puerto Rico, working together for the good of all, are giving an example to the world of how man can overcome the obstacles that are sometimes in his way. By their energy, cooperation, and sacrifice they are "lifting themselves by their own bootstraps."

Building New Homes. One of the first steps in "Operation Bootstrap" has been the construction of adequate homes for all.

Beautiful Caribbean Beach. Vacationers enjoy a stroll on the beach at Caneel Bay on the island of St. John. The Virgin Islands attract many tourists.

The Lesser Antilles. The Lesser Antilles include many islands to the east and southeast of the Greater Antilles. Most of these islands are under British, French, or Dutch rule. Three islands of the group called the Virgin Islands belong to the United States.

The Virgin Islands. The most important thing about the Virgin Islands is their location. They are on the major steamship route between Europe and the Panama Canal. For that special reason, our government bought them from Denmark in 1917. Our Navy uses the good harbor at Charlotte Amalie to protect our shipping in the Panama Canal. The Virgin Islands lie about fifty miles east of Puerto Rico.

Like other Caribbean islands, these islands are really the tops of undersea mountains. Columbus first saw them and named them. There are nine small islands, and many very tinier ones. Three of the largest belong to the United States—St. Croix, St. Thomas, and St. John. The rest belong to Great Britain.

These islands are an ideal vacationland. The climate all the year is warm and pleasant, cooled by steady breezes. The land is a gentle, hilly surface. To preserve the beauty of woodlands and sandy coves, the United States Government maintains the Virgin Islands National Park. Caring for tourists is the chief business on the islands.

Most of the natives are Negroes, descendants of former slaves. On the hill slopes they raise fruits and vegetables. Some are fishermen. Many live in Charlotte Amalie, the capital city, on the island of St. Thomas.

Bay rum, made from bay leaves raised on the island of St. John, is the chief export of the Virgin Islands. Sugar, molasses, and hides are other products. Fish are abundant in the waters around the islands.

The people of the islands owned by the United States are American citizens. They may not vote, however, and they are not taxed. Their governor is appointed by the President of the United States, but the people elect their own lawmakers. Catholics make up about half the population.

Jamaica. Jamaica is a small island with a very dense population. Together with several tiny islands which lie nearby, it was granted its independence in 1962, after many years as a British colony. Most of the population is made up of Negro laborers who raise their own food crops or work on the sugar and banana plantations.

The island of Jamaica is often struck by hurricanes. Each year, more than 100 inches of rain falls on the northeast coast of the island (the side which receives the prevailing winds), while only about 30 inches falls annually on the south coast. Plantations in the southern part of the island require irrigation to produce crops.

Trinidad. Trinidad is another one of the islands known as the Lesser Antilles. It is very close to the mainland of South America. Like Jamaica, Trinidad was for many years a British colony. It was a member of a loose union of British colonies, and its capital city, called Port of Spain, served for many years as the capital of the federation of island-colonies. Since 1962, however, Trinidad and the nearby island of Tobago have been completely independent, and have left the federation.

Trinidad is one of the richest islands in the West Indies. Cacao and sugar are its chief agricultural products. Most of the

Dockside at Barbados. Old sailing ships give the appearance of the past to this sleepy island in the eastern Caribbean. Sugar and rum are exports.

Policeman on Duty. In the Bahamas, it is a common sight to see these native policemen in fancy uniforms. His helmet protects him from the sun.

world's supply of asphalt, used for paving streets and highways, comes from Trinidad. Pitch Lake, many miles in extent, provides

Traffic in Nassau. The modern sports car and the old carriage make a strange contrast. What do you notice different about the way the people drive?

a source of this important material that is so enormous that it will probably never be exhausted.

In addition, Trinidad is very rich in petroleum. With the great demand for oil and oil products, it is likely that Trinidad will long continue to be one of the richest islands in the Caribbean.

The West Indies Federation. In 1956, ten British colonies joined together to form an island federation in the West Indies. The purpose of the federation was to join together in a common union ten small islands of the Lesser Antilles. Just as the fifty states of our country join in a union for the good of all, these island colonies joined in order to govern themselves and conduct their affairs better than they could as separate colonies.

In 1962, however, the strongest of the federation's members, Trinidad and Tobago, achieved their independence and left the union of islands. Eight members of the federation still wish to enjoy the advantages of unity, and with the help of Great Britain they plan to form another West Indies Federation soon. The eight islands

include Antigua, Barbados, Dominica, St. Kitts, Montserrat, and others.

The Bahamas. North of the West Indies lie thousands of small islands called the Bahamas. Some are only reefs or tiny points of rock. The islands belong to Great Britain. Nassau is the capital city, where one fourth of the population lives. Winter tourists come by ship and plane to visit Nassau's famous Paradise Beach.

Diving for sea sponges is the chief industry in the Bahamas. Some fruits and vegetables are grown for winter markets in the United States.

Bermuda. In the Atlantic Ocean, six hundred miles east of North Carolina, is an island group known as Bermuda. It belongs to Great Britain. The mild climate during the winter draws many people to these colorful and lovely shores, with their pink coral beaches. Easter lilies are raised for our

markets. Hamilton is the capital and chief resort city. Ocean liners from the United States and Europe dock at Hamilton, and American and European airlines use its airport. Sportsmen come to Hamilton to boat, fish, and play golf. Bermuda relies on tourists for most of its income.

Bermuda faces the problem of getting good drinking water. There are no streams of any size. People must catch rainwater and store it in tanks and cisterns, which they keep underground. At times, there is a serious shortage when rainfall is light.

The Governor of the Bermudas is appointed by the British monarch. There are no taxes on income or property. Great Brittain has a naval base, and the United States has air bases in the islands.

Facts *to remember*

1. The West Indies curve around the Caribbean Sea, and separate it from the Atlantic Ocean. These islands, which extend from Florida to South America, are tops of mountains. These islands are divided into four groups: The Greater Antilles, the Lesser Antilles, the Bahamas, and Bermuda.

2. The Republic of Cuba is the largest and most important of the West Indies. Cuba has a warm climate and plenty of rain. It is mostly rolling land with fertile soil, where tropical crops are grown. Sugar and tobacco are its chief crops.

3. Puerto Rico is a self-governing commonwealth, under the protection of the United States. We export much food to Puerto Rico since only two fifths of its land is suited to farming. The people are Americans, and nearly all are Catholics.

4. The United States bought three of the largest of the Virgin Islands from Denmark. Our Navy uses the good harbor at Charlotte Amalie to protect our shipping to the Panama Canal. Caring for tourists is the chief business on the islands. Most of the natives are Negroes.

5. Eight small islands, British colonies in the West Indies, form the West Indies Federation. Jamaica is an independent island. Trinidad, once a member of the West Indies Federation, is now independent. Jamaica exports rum, sugar, and other agricultural products; Trinidad produces oil and asphalt.

What *have I learned?*

I

On a separate piece of paper, write each sentence, using the word or words that make it correct.

1. Most of the people of the West Indies are (Negroes, Indians, Americans).
2. (Hispaniola, Haiti, Cuba) is the largest and most important of the West Indies.
3. The chief crop of Cuba is (tobacco, sugar, vegetables).
4. (Lumbering, Fishing, Farming) is the main industry of Hispaniola.
5. Most of the people of Haiti are (wealthy, farmers, factory workers).
6. Puerto Ricans (pay taxes to the United States, are citizens of the United States, raise more food than they need).
7. The Virgin Islands are important because of their (size, location, minerals).

8. Oil has made (Barbados, Jamaica, Trinidad) one of the richest islands of the West Indies.
9. "Operation Bootstrap" is now going on in (Cuba, Puerto Rico, The Virgin Islands).
10. The Greater Antilles include the island of (Cuba, Trinidad, Bermuda).

II

Copy the word or words from Column A. Next to each, write the word or phrase from Column B which best matches it.

Column A	Column B
1. Greater Antilles	Capital of Dominican Republic
2. Ciudad Trujillo	between Europe and the Panama Canal
3. Haiti	sugar and tobacco
4. Virgin Islands	Bahamas
5. Charlotte Amalie	four large islands
6. Puerto Rico	St. Thomas Island
7. Cuba	part of Hispaniola
8. Self-governing island	Federation of the British West Indies
9. Trinidad	large oil resources
10. Nassau	Puerto Rico

Facts *to understand*

Give a reason for each statement.

1. Every year thousands of American tourists visit Puerto Rico.
2. Cuba has many cigar factories in Havana.
3. Puerto Ricans must import food from the United States.
4. The Virgin Islands are important to the United States.
5. The West Indies were named by mistake.
6. Most of the people of Haiti speak the French language.
7. The various islands of the British West Indies united into a federation.
8. Columbus named the islands he discovered in the Caribbean the West Indies.
9. A large number of American missioners are going to Puerto Rico.
10. The Virgin Islands are an ideal vacation spot for tourists.

Unit Seven Review

Questions for Discussion and Review

1. Why do the people of Middle America live differently than we do? **2.** How can the United States help Mexico? **3.** Of what value is the Panama Canal? **4.** Why are tropical crops raised in Middle America? **5.** In what ways have the countries of Middle America helped the United States? **6.** What is the meaning of the term "Latin America"? **7.** Name the countries of Central America. **8.** What is the largest and most important island of the West Indies? **9.** Which of the Virgin Islands belong to the United States? **10.** Throughout Mexico and Central America, where do most of the people live? **11.** What are the islands which make up the Greater Antilles? **12.** Why is the country of Nicaragua subject to frequent earthquakes? **13.** What makes the Pacific slopes of the mountains in El Salvador particularly good for raising coffee? **14.** Which country of Central America has the largest population? **15.** From which country do we get "Balsam of Peru"? **16.** Which is the largest of the Central American republics? **17.** What could be done in Mexico to make better use of the available farm land? **18.** What is the capital of Puerto Rico? **19.** Why do we say that Mexico is a land of "the old and the new"? **20.** In what ways are Mexico's industries expanding and growing?

Using the Maps and Globe

1. Use the scale of miles on the map to find the length of the Panama Canal.
2. Roughly sketch and label the most important islands separating the Caribbean from the Atlantic.
3. On an outline map, mark off the countries of Central America, shade in areas according to rainfall, and show what products come from the various countries by pasting pictures of them on the map.
4. Trace Columbus' route to the Virgin Islands.
5. Use the wall map to explain how the United States can use the West Indies to advantage.

Using Geography Words

Here is a list of special words that have been used in this Unit. Write a sentence using each to prove that you know its meaning in geography.

cacao   maize   mestizos   water bridge
  balsam   serape   peons   sombreros
          guayule   haciendas

Getting Information from Books

Read reference books such as *Compton's Pictured Encyclopedia* for information on the following topics. Prepare to give an oral or written report.

Mexican People   Panama Canal
Hernando Cortez   Guatemala
Our Lady of Guadalupe

Final Test

Write each sentence on your paper, choosing the correct word or words from the parenthesis.
1. The people of (The Bahamas, Puerto Rico, Mexico) are American citizens.
2. The Panama Canal connects the Atlantic Ocean with the (Gulf of Mexico, Caribbean Sea, Pacific Ocean).
3. Most of the people of Central America live in (highlands, lowlands, valleys).
4. The heartland of Mexico is (Mexico City, Monterrey, Orizaba).
5. Charcoal is made from (coal, other minerals, wood).
6. (Lettuce, Apples, Pineapples) is a tropical fruit.
7. All of Middle America lies in the (Intermediate, Polar, Tropical) Zone.
8. Most Mexicans are (Negroes, mestizos, Eskimos).
9. (Rugs, Ashtrays, Woolens) are made from sisal hemp.
10. (Mexico, Guatemala, Cuba) is the third largest nation in North America.
11. Mexico does not have enough (grazing land, good farm land, hemp).
12. (Mahogany, henequen, cotton) is a forest product.
13. (Cortez, Diaz, Columbus) named the Virgin Islands.
14. Diving for sea sponges is the chief industry in (the Bahamas, Mexico, Honduras).
15. Nearly all the people of Middle America are (Protestants, Catholics, heathens).

16. Coffee is an important product in (El Salvador, Trinidad, Cuba).

17. (Mexico, Trinidad, Panama) is not known as an oil-producing land.

18. The capital of Nicaragua is (Managua, Port-au-Prince, Charlotte Amalie).

19. In southern Mexico, (bauxite, coal, sulphur) is an important mineral.

20. A person of mixed Spanish and Indian descent is called a (serape, mestizo, sombrero).

21. (Sugar, cotton, rice) is the main product of the island of Cuba.

22. (Farming, Cattle-raising, Mining) is the chief occupation of the people of Haiti.

23. (Trinidad, El Salvador, Dominican Republic) was a member of the Federation of the British Indies.

24. Hispaniola is made up of two countries—Haiti and (Puerto Rico, Guatemala, Dominican Republic).

25. San Salvador is the capital city of (Nicaragua, Panama, El Salvador).

Applying Christian Principles

Write these sentences on another paper. Choose the ending that makes the sentence correct.

1. When nations share their blessings they **a.** often become poor themselves **b.** become weak **c.** become stronger, richer, and happier.

2. God's great family of nations can be more closely united especially through **a.** good transportation **b.** irrigation **c.** individual wealth.

3. To be a good neighbor to all peoples of the world, a country must **a.** be free **b.** have many minerals **c.** fight.

4. The people of Central America showed real charity when they **a.** sold orchids to the United States **b.** helped to build the Panama Canal **c.** took pearls from oysters.

5. The United States has a duty to **a.** obtain tax from the Puerto Ricans **b.** share her resources **c.** send tourists to Bermuda.

Table 1 · Area and Population

World Summary

	square miles	population
Africa	11,635,000	261,000,000
Antarctica	5,100,000	—
Asia	17,035,000	1,877,500,000
Australia	2,974,581	10,604,000
Europe	3,850,000	484,500,000
North America	9,028,716	273,000,000
South America	6,860,000	148,000,000

Europe

	square miles	population	Catholics
Albania	10,629	1,607,000	92,632
Austria	32,376	7,067,000	6,338,846
Belgium	11,775	9,153,000	8,800,000
Bulgaria	42,796	7,867,000	50,000
Czecho-Slovakia	49,381	13,742,000	8,600,000
Denmark	16,619	4,617,000	26,608
Estonia	17,413	1,196,000	?
Finland	130,165	4,497,000	2,340
France	212,659	46,200,000	38,399,000
Germany, East	41,645	17,241,000	1,858,770
Germany, West	95,931	56,172,000	26,618,935
Greece	51,843	8,389,000	55,000
Hungary	35,918	10,045,000	5,998,000
Iceland	39,758	179,000	806
Ireland	27,136	2,815,000	2,645,820
Italy	116,372	50,463,762	50,211,443
Latvia	24,695	2,094,000	500,000
Lithuania	26,173	2,713,000	?
Luxembourg	999	314,000	313,000
Netherlands	15,800	11,702,229	4,688,300
Norway	125,064	3,614,000	6,891
Poland	120,355	29,965,000	29,200,000
Portugal	35,466	9,146,000	8,300,000
Romania	91,584	18,567,000	1,700,000
Soviet Union	1,914,939	54,000,000	10,000,000*
Spain	195,504	30,559,000	30,293,000
Sweden	173,378	7,542,459	27,500
Switzerland	15,944	5,470,000	2,174,831
United Kingdom	94,511	52,675,094	4,941,415
Yugoslavia	98,766	18,538,150	5,894,032

Asia

	square miles	population	Catholics
Aden	112,000	660,000	300
Afghanistan	250,000	13,000,000	None
Bhutan	18,000	700,000	—
Burma	261,789	21,527,000	186,021
Cambodia	88,780	4,952,000	54,108
Ceylon	25,332	10,167,000	711,436
China	3,760,339	669,000,000	3,000,000
Hong Kong	391	3,178,000	177,279
India	1,221,880	440,316,000	6,148,627
Indonesia	735,865	95,189,000	1,271,095
Iran	628,060	20,678,000	28,093
Iraq	172,000	7,085,000	212,570
Israel	7,993	2,203,300	40,599
Japan	142,688	94,053,000	285,364
Jordan	37,500	1,690,000	46,449
Korea	85,285	32,970,000	486,127
Laos	91,000	1,850,000	24,831
Lebanon	4,000	1,822,000	689,000
Malaysia	130,407	10,019,000	189,941
Nepal	54,362	9,407,000	700
Pakistan	364,737	93,812,000	318,239
Philippines	115,758	28,727,000	21,639,181
Saudi Arabia	870,000	6,500,000	6,000
Soviet Union	6,735,201	163,500,000	10,000,000*
Syria	72,234	4,561,000	166,000
Thailand	200,148	27,181,000	111,893
Turkey	296,500	28,602,000	21,176
Vietnam	127,000	30,616,000	1,300,000
Yemen	75,000	5,000,000	—

Australia and New Zealand

	square miles	population	Catholics
Australia	2,974,581	10,603,936	2,137,373
New Zealand	103,736	2,414,984	346,531

Africa

	square miles	population	Catholics
Algeria	847,500	11,020,000	946,000
Burundi	10,744	2,500,000	1,384,582
Cameroun	166,880	4,500,000	761,727
Central Africa	238,000	1,180,000	144,424
Chad	495,000	2,571,000	75,616
Congo (Brazzaville)	139,000	790,000	266,042
Congo (Leopoldville)	904,757	14,150,000	4,996,354
Dahomey	44,290	2,050,000	240,784
Ethiopia (+Eritrea)	398,350	22,000,000	136,154
Gabon	102,290	410,000	190,899
Ghana	91,843	6,943,000	602,325
Guinea	96,865	3,000,000	22,027
Ivory Coast	127,520	3,300,000	231,529
Kenya	224,960	7,287,000	913,707
Liberia	43,000	2,500,000	12,769
Libya	679,000	1,216,000	37,858
Malagasy	228,000	5,200,000	1,104,486
Mali	450,000	4,100,000	19,197
Mauritania	418,810	1,000,000	2,000
Morocco	172,104	11,925,000	394,556
Niger	490,000	3,000,000	13,200
Nigeria	339,169	35,752,000	1,665,539
Rwanda	10,166	2,500,000	673,435
Senegal	76,000	2,260,000	155,591
Sierra Leone	27,925	2,500,000	22,557
Somali Republic	262,000	2,030,000	3,700
Republic of S. Africa	472,359	16,122,000	885,376
South-West Africa	317,887	534,000	62,999
Sudan	967,000	12,109,000	200,000
Tanganyika	362,688	9,404,000	1,487,705
Togo	20,400	1,480,000	228,821
Tunisia	58,000	4,168,000	70,000
Uganda	93,981	6,845,000	2,005,273
United Arab Republic	386,198	26,570,000	172,69'

Africa—Continued

	square miles	population	Catholics
Upper Volta ..	105,900	4,467,000	137,257
British Territories ..	785,418	10,355,000	2,000,000
Portuguese Territories ..	793,030	11,969,855	1,906,747
Spanish Terrs. .	117,001	286,000	200,000
French Somaliland ..	8,880	81,000	5,080

North America

	square miles	population	Catholics
Bahamas	4,404	106,677	17,692
Bermuda	21	42,640	4,410
British Honduras	8,867	90,343	56,000
Canada	3,851,809	18,238,247	8,230,000
Costa Rica	23,421	1,225,000	1,089,192
Cuba	44,206	6,933,000	5,830,000
Dominican Rep.	19,333	3,098,000	3,036,791
El Salvador ...	8,259	2,501,000	2,454,780
Guatemala	42,042	3,868,000	3,486,390
Haiti	10,714	4,233,000	2,874,363

	square miles	population	Catholics
Honduras	44,482	1,883,000	1,876,205
Jamaica	4,411	1,638,000	600,000
Mexico	758,259	36,091,000	33,984,000
Nicaragua	57,145	1,477,000	1,476,120
Panama	28,576	1,084,000	796,836
Puerto Rico ...	3,435	2,349,000	2,100,000
Trinidad	1,864	859,000	120,000
United States ..	3,628,150	187,000,000	42,876,665

South America

	square miles	population	Catholics
Argentina	1,072,700	20,009,000	17,727,925
Bolivia	416,040	3,462,000	3,345,400
Brazil	3,286,270	70,799,000	64,171,400
British Guiana .	83,000	566,000	83,000
Chile	286,397	7,802,000	6,706,940
Colombia	439,520	14,447,000	14,673,300
Ecuador	116,270	4,455,000	4,105,187
French Guiana .	35,135	31,000	27,129
Paraguay	157,000	1,812,000	1,703,238
Peru	514,059	10,365,000	9,800,000
Surinam	55,400	308,000	37,206
Uruguay	72,172	2,827,000	2,357,000
Venezuela	352,150	7,524,000	6,982,272

Table 2 Populations of Major Cities

City and Country	population
Aachen, *West Germany*	170,000
Aarhus, *Denmark*	118,493
Abadan, *Iran*	283,625
Aberdeen, *Scotland*	185,379
*Abidjan, *Ivory Coast*	125,700
*Accra, *Ghana*	388,231
Adana, *Turkey*	230,024
*Addis Ababa, *Ethiopia*	500,000
Adelaide, *Australia*	587,656
Agra, *India*	375,665
Aguascalientes, *Mexico*	126,222
Ahmedabad, *India*	788,333
Akron, *Ohio*	290,351
Albany, *New York*	129,726
Albuquerque, *New Mexico*	201,189
Aleppo, *Syria*	451,435
Alexandria, *Egypt*	1,600,000
*Algiers, *Algeria*	870,000
Allahabad, *India*	332,295
Allentown, *Pennsylvania*	108,347
Alma-Ata, *USSR*	455,000
Amagaski, *Japan*	405,955
Amarillo, *Texas*	137,969
*Amman, *Jordan*	280,000
Amritsar, *India*	325,747
Amoy, *China*	240,000
*Amsterdam, *Netherlands*	866,342
Anaheim, *California*	104,184
*Ankara, *Turkey*	646,151
Anshan, *China*	400,000
Antwerp, *Belgium*	849,432

City and Country	population
Arad, *Romania*	106,457
Arak, *Iran*	60,000
Archangel, *USSR*	256,000
Arequipa, *Peru*	124,334
Arnheim, *Netherlands*	124,818
Asmara, *Ethipoia*	132,000
Assiut, *Egypt*	400,000
Asunción, *Paraguay*	210,000
Astrakhan, *USSR*	294,000
*Athens, *Greece*	1,852,709
Atlanta, *Georgia*	487,455
Augsburg, *West Germany*	207,050
Auckland, *New Zealand*	448,365
Austin, *Texas*	186,545
Arellaneda, *Argentina*	380,000
*Baghdad (Gr.), *Iraq*	552,047
Baku, *USSR*	968,000
Baltimore, *Maryland*	939,024
*Bamako, *Mali*	105,000
Bandung, *Republic of Indonesia*	1,046,089
Bangalore, *India*	778,977
*Bangkok, *Thailand*	2,318,000
Barcelona, *Spain*	1,800,000
Bari, *Italy*	311,268
Barnaul, *USSR*	320,000
Barquisimeto, *Venezuela*	203,000
Barranquila, *Colombia*	456,000
Basel, *Switzerland*	200,700
Basra, *Iraq*	206,000
Baton Rouge, *Lousiana*	152,419
*Beirut, *Lebanon*	500,000

(*denotes capital city)

Major World Cities—Continued

City and Country	population	City and Country	population
Belem, *Brazil*	402,170	Changchun, *China*	420,000
Belfast, *Northern Ireland*	440,100	Changsha, *China*	700,000
*Belgrade, *Yugoslavia*	700,000	Changteh, *China*	300,000
Belo Horizonte, *Brazil*	693,328	Charleroi, *Belgium*	469,259
Benares, *India*	355,777	Charlotte, *North Carolina*	201,564
*Bengazi, *Libya*	70,533	Chattanooga, *Tennessee*	130,009
Bergen, *Norway*	115,000	Chelyabinsk, *USSR*	688,000
Berkeley, *California*	111,268	Chemnitz, *East Germany*	286,226
*Berlin, *East Germany*	1,084,010	Chengtu, *China*	440,000
Berlin, *West Germany*	2,202,200	Chenteh, *China*	510,000
*Berne, *Switzerland*	161,300	Chicago, *Illinois*	3,550,404
Bielefeld, *West Germany*	175,174	Chihuahua, *Mexico*	149,437
Bilbao, *Spain*	281,000	Chinkiang, *China*	220,000
Birmingham, *Alabama*	340,887	Chittagong, *Pakistan*	364,205
Birmingham, *England*	1,105,651	Christchurch, *New Zealand*	220,510
Bloemfontein, *Rep. of South Africa*	163,000	Chungking, *China*	1,620,000
Bochum, *West Germany*	366,383	Cincinnati, *Ohio*	502,550
*Bogotá, *Colombia*	1,200,000	Ciuj, *Romania*	154,752
Bologna, *Italy*	441,143	Cleveland, *Ohio*	876,050
Bombay, *India*	4,146,191	Cochabama, *Bolivia*	90,037
*Bonn, *West Germany*	145,063	Cologne, *West Germany*	200,000
Boras, *Sweden*	67,016	*Colombo, *Ceylon*	480,000
Bordeaux, *France*	257,946	Columbus, *Ohio*	471,316
Boston (Gr.), *Massachusetts*	2,589,301	*Conakry, *Guinea*	100,000
Bradford, *England*	295,768	Concepción, *Chile*	167,468
Braila, *Romania*	102,491	Constantine, *Algeria*	217,000
*Brasilia, *Brazil*	141,742	Constantsa, *Romania*	100,000
Bratislava, *Czecho-Slovakia*	247,000	*Copenhagen, *Denmark*	960,913
*Brazzaville, *Republic of the Congo*	105,200	Cordoba, *Argentina*	635,000
Bremen, *West Germany*	564,979	Cordoba, *Spain*	178,973
Bremerhaven, *West Germany*	141,800	Corpus Christi, *Texas*	167,690
Bridgeport, *Connecticut*	156,748	Coventry, *England*	305,060
Brisbane, *Australia*	620,121	Croyden, *England*	252,387
Bristol, *England*	436,440	Curitiba, *Brazil*	361,309
Brno, *Czecho-Slovakia*	306,371	Czestochowa, *Poland*	148,000
Brunswick, *West Germany*	245,983	Dacca, *Pakistan*	556,712
*Brussels (Gr.), *Belgium*	1,398,326	Dairen, *China*	1,054,000
Bucaramanga, *Colombia*	200,000	*Dakar, *Senegal*	234,500
*Bucharest, *Romania*	1,236,905	Dallas, *Texas*	679,684
*Budapest (Gr.), *Hungary*	1,850,000	*Damascus, *Syria*	454,603
Buenos Aires, *Argentina*	3,799,200	Davao, *Philippines*	231,833
Buffalo, *New York*	532,759	Dayton, *Ohio*	262,332
Bursa, *Turkey*	153,190	Dearborn, *Michigan*	112,007
Bydgoszcz, *Poland*	231,000	Debrecen, *Hungary*	130,000
Cadiz, *Spain*	107,856	Delhi, *India*	914,790
Cagliari, *Italy*	148,500	Denver, *Colorado*	493,887
*Cairo, *Egypt*	3,100,000	Des Moines,, *Iowa*	208,982
Calcutta, *India*	2,926,498	Detroit (Gr.) *Michigan*	1,670,144
Calgary, *Canada*	279,062	Dniepropetrovsk, *USSR*	658,000
Cali, *Colombia*	600,000	Donetsk, *USSR*	701,000
Callao, *Peru*	131,305	Dortmund, *West Germany*	635,199
Camaguey, *Cuba*	204,254	Douala, *Cameroun*	125,000
Cambridge, *Massachusetts*	107,716	Dresden, *East Germany*	493,515
Camden, *New Jersey*	117,159	*Dublin, *Ireland*	535,488
*Canberra, *Australia*	56,430	Duisberg, *West Germany*	503,851
Canton, *China*	1,650,000	Duluth, *Minnesota*	106,884
Canton, *Ohio*	113,631	Dundee, *Scotland*	182,959
Cap Haitien, *Haiti*	60,000	Dunedin, *New Zealand*	105,003
Cape Town, *Republic of South Africa*	731,484	Durban, *Republic of South Africa*	655,000
*Caracas, *Venezuela*	1,371,875	Düsseldorf, *West Germany*	700,000
Cardiff, *Wales*	251,270	*Edinburgh, *Scotland*	468,378
Cartagena, *Colombia*	180,000	Edmonton, *Canada*	337,568
Casablanca, *Morocco*	960,812	Eindhaven, *Netherlands*	168,858
Catania, *Italy*	361,466	Enschede, *Netherlands*	126,122
Cebu, *Philippines*	259,194	Elizabeth, *New Jersey*	107,698

(*denotes capital city)

City and Country	population
Elizabethville, *Republic of the Congo*	182,638
El Paso, *Texas*	276,687
Erfurt, *East Germany*	186,000
Erie, *Pennsylavnia*	138,440
Erivan, *USSR*	509,000
Essen, *West Germany*	728,578
Evansville, *Indiana*	141,543
Fatshan, *China*	450,000
Fez, *Morocco*	280,000
Flint, *Michigan*	196,940
Florence, *Italy*	438,138
Foochow, *China*	400,000
Fortaleza, *Brazil*	514,818
Fort Wayne, *Indiana*	161,776
Fort Worth, *Texas*	356,268
Frankfort, *West Germany*	671,624
Frederiksberg, *Denmark*	118,993
Freiburg, *West Germany*	139,000
Fresno, *California*	133,929
Fukuoka, *Japan*	647,122
Galatz, *Romania*	102,232
Gary, *Indiana*	178,320
Gdansk (Danzig), *Poland*	286,000
Gelsenkirchen, *West Germany*	389,952
Genoa, *Italy*	775,106
General San Martin, *Argentina*	269,514
Geneva, *Switzerland*	168,900
Ghent, *Belgium*	455,022
Glasgow, *Scotland*	1,054,913
Glendale, *California*	119,442
Gorki, *USSR*	942,000
Gorlovka, *USSR*	293,000
Goteborg, *Sweden*	408,436
Granada, *Spain*	232,054
Grand Rapids, *Michigan*	201,487
Graz, *Austria*	237,041
Greensboro, *North Carolina*	119,574
Groningen, *Netherlands*	146,301
Guadalajara, *Mexico*	737,346
*Guatemala City, *Guatemala*	385,000
Guayaquil, *Ecuador*	403,184
Haarlem, *Netherlands*	169,497
Hagen, *West Germany*	197,036
(The) Hague, *Netherlands*	605,876
Haifa, *Israel*	174,000
Haiphong, *Vietnam*	367,000
Hakodate, *Japan*	243,183
Halifax, *Canada*	92,511
Halle, *East Germany*	278,700
Halsingborg, *Sweden*	77,006
Hamadan, *Iran*	100,000
Hamburg, *West Germany*	1,836,958
Hamilton, *Canada*	273,991
Hamma, *Syria*	173,000
Hammond, *Indiana*	111,698
Hangchow, *China*	600,000
Hankow, *China*	800,000
Hanoi, *Vietnam*	638,000
Hanover, *West Germany*	576,185
Harbin, *China*	760,000
Hartford, *Connecticut*	177,397
*Havana, *Cuba*	1,158,203
(Le) Havre, *France*	165,000
Heidelberg, *West Germany*	127,651
*Helsinki, *Finland*	464,100

City and Country	population
Hiroshima, *Japan*	431,336
Hobart, *Australia*	115,887
Holguin, *Cuba*	226,644
Homs, *Syria*	293,500
Hong Kong (Br.), *China*	3,100,000
Honolulu, *Hawaii*	294,194
Houston, *Texas*	938,219
Howrah, *India*	433,630
Hue, *Vietnam*	104,500
Hyerabad, *India*	1,166,860
Ibadan, *Nigeria*	600,000
Iloilo, *Philippines*	150,976
Inchon, *Korea*	402,000
Indianapolis, *Indiana*	476,258
Indore, *India*	310,859
Innsbruck, *Austria*	100,699
Irkutsk, *USSR*	365,000
Isfahan, *Iran*	255,000
Istanbul, *Turkey*	2,000,000
Ivanavo, *USSR*	332,000
Izmir, *Turkey*	370,923
Jackson, *Mississippi*	144,422
Jacksonville, *Florida*	201,030
*Jakarta (Batavia), *Republic of Indonesia* .3,317,562
Jedda, *Saudi Arabia*	250,000
Jersey City, *New Jersey*	276,100
*Jerusalem, *Israel*	161,000
Jogjakarta, *Republic of Indonesia* 341,424
Johannesburg, *Republic of South Africa* ..1,096,541
*Kabul, *Afghanistan*	300,000
Kaliningrad *USSR*	202,000
Kanpur (Cawnpore), *India*	705,383
Kansas City, *Kansas*	121,901
Kansas City, *Missouri*	475,539
Kaohsiung, *Taiwan (Formosa)*	438,429
*Karachi, *Pakistan*	1,912,598
Karaganda, *USSR*	398,000
Karlsruhe, *West Germany*	244,000
Kassel, *West Germany*	209,792
*Katmandu, *Nepal*	175,000
Katowice, *Poland*	269,000
Kawasaki, *Japan*	632,975
Kazan, *USSR*	643,000
Keelung, *Taiwan (Formosa)*	286,373
Khabarovsk, *USSR*	322,000
Kharkov, *USSR*	930,000
*Khartoum, *Sudan*	93,103
Kiel, *West Germany*	272,000
Kiev, *USSR*	1,102,000
Kingston-upon-Hull, *England*	303,268
Knoxville, *Tennessee*	111,827
Kobe, *Japan*	1,113,977
Kowloon, *China*	675,000
Krasmoyarsk, *USSR* 409,000
Krasnodar, *USSR*	312,000
Krefeld, *West Germany*	210,519
Krivoy Rog, *USSR*	386,000
*Kuala Lumpur, *Malaysia*	316,230
Krakow, *Poland*	479,000
Kuibyshev, *USSR*	806,000
Kure, *Japan*	210,000
Kyoto, *Japan*	1,284,818
*Lagos, *Nigeria*	379,000
Lahore, *Pakistan*	1,296,477
Lanchow, *China*	600,000

(*denotes capital city)

Major World Cities—Continued

City and Country	population
Lansing, *Michigan*	113,058
Lanus, *Argentina*	244,473
*La Paz, *Bolivia*	347,394
La Plata, *Argentina*	410,000
Lattakia, *Syria*	109,216
Lausanne, *Switzerland*	118,900
Leeds, *England*	510,597
Leicester, *England*	273,298
Leipzig, *East Germany*	592,821
Leningrad, *USSR*	3,300,000
Leon, *Mexico*	209,469
*Leopoldville, *Republic of the Congo*	389,547
Liege, *Belgium*	607,117
Lille, *France*	194,616
*Lima, *Peru*	1,262,107
Lincoln, *Nebraska*	128,521
Linz, *Austria*	196,206
*Lisbon, *Portugal*	818,382
Little Rock, *Arkansas*	107,813
Liverpool, *England*	747,490
Ljubljana, *Yugoslavia*	155,000
Lodz, *Poland*	708,000
*Lome, *Togo*	70,000
London, *Canada*	169,564
†London (Gr.), *England*	8,171,902
Long Beach, *California*	344,168
Los Angeles, *California*	2,479,015
Louisville, *Kentucky*	390,639
*Luang Prabang, *Laos*	45,000
Lübeck, *West Germany*	233,320
Lucknow, *India*	496,861
Ludwigshafen, *West Germany*	167,440
Lugansk, *USSR*	274,000
*Luxembourg, *Luxembourg*	80,000
Lvov (Lwow), *USSR*	410,000
Lyons, *France*	553,039
Macao (Port.), *China*	187,772
Macon, *Georgia*	122,876
Madison, *Wisconsin*	126,700
Madras, *India*	1,725,216
*Madrid, *Spain*	2,000,000
Madura, *India*	361,781
Magdeburg, *East Germany*	260,618
Magnitogorsk, *USSR*	311,000
Makassar, *Republic of Indonesia*	603,767
Makeyevka, *USSR*	358,000
Malaga, *Spain*	350,000
Malang, *Republic of Indonesia*	374,554
Malmo, *Sweden*	235,370
*Managua, *Nicaragua*	176,569
Manchester, *England*	661,041
Mandalay, *Burma*	186,000
Manila (Gr.), *Philippines*	3,006,627
Mannheim, *West Germany*	312,000
Mansura, *Egypt*	146,700
Maracaibo, *Venezuela*	456,000
Mar del Plata, *Argentina*	270,000
Marianao, *Cuba*	229,576
Marrakech, *Morocco*	241,900
Marseille, *France*	661,492
Mecca, *Saudi Arabia*	300,000
Medan, *Republic of Indonesia*	532,129
Medellin, *Colombia*	650,000
Meknes, *Morocco*	177,128
Melbourne (Gr.), *Australia*	1,907,366

City and Country	population
Memphis, *Tennessee*	497,524
Merida, *Mexico*	170,513
Meshed, *Iran*	242,000
Messina, *Italy*	251,423
Mexicali, *Mexico*	171,648
Mexico City (Gr.), *Mexico*	4,829,402
Miami, *Florida*	291,688
Milan, *Italy*	1,580,978
Milwaukee, *Wisconsin*	741,324
Minneapolis, *Minnesota*	482,782
Minsk, *USSR*	509,000
Miskole, *Hungary*	175,000
Mobile, *Alabama*	202,779
*Mogadishu, *Somali Republic*	86,643
Molotov (Perm), *USSR*	628,000
*Monrovia, *Liberia*	53,000
Monterrey, *Mexico*	596,993
*Montivideo, *Uruguay*	922,885
Montgomery, *Alabama*	134,393
Montreal, *Canada*	1,191,062
*Moscow, *USSR*	5,032,000
Mosul, *Iraq*	340,541
Moulmein, *Burma*	103,000
Mukden (Shenyang), *China*	2,290,000
Mülheim (Ruhr), *West Germany*	186,114
München-Gladbach, *West Germany*	153,543
Munich, *West Germany*	1,102,914
Murcia, *Spain*	243,000
Murmansk, *USSR*	226,000
Nagasaki, *Japan*	344,153
Nagoya, *Japan*	1,591,935
Nagpur, *India*	449,099
*Nairobi, *Kenya*	186,000
Nanking, *China*	1,113,972
Nantes, *France*	222,790
Naples, *Italy*	1,179,608
Nashville, *Tennessee*	170,874
Natal, *Brazil*	162,537
Newark, *New Jersey*	405,220
New Bedford, *Massachusetts*	102,477
Newcastle, *Australia*	208,905
Newcastle, *England*	269,389
*New Delhi, *India*	2,000,000
New Haven, *Connecticut*	152,048
New Orleans, *Louisiana*	627,525
New York City, *New York*	7,781,984
Niagara Falls, *New York*	102,394
Nice, *France*	244,360
*Nicosia, *Cyprus*	82,000
Nijmegen, *Netherlands*	131,593
Nikolayev, *USSR*	224,000
Ningpo, *China*	300,000
Niteroi, *Brazil*	245,467
Nizhni Tagil, *USSR*	338,000
Norfolk, *Virginia*	304,869
Nottingham, *England*	311,645
Novosibersk, *USSR*	887,000
Nuremburg, *West Germany*	461,319
Oakland, *California*	367,548
Oberhausen, *West Germany*	259,000
Odense, *Denmark*	105,915
Odessa, *USSR*	667,000
Ogomosho, *Nigeria*	139,000
Oklahoma City, *Oklahoma*	324,253
Omaha, *Nebraska*	301,598

(*denotes capital city)

Major World Cities—Continued

City and Country	population
Omdurman, *Sudan*	132,619
Omsk, *USSR*	579,000
Oporto, *Portugal*	310,475
Oran, *Algeria*	430,000
Osaka (Gr.), *Japan*	3,011,563
Oshogobo, *Nigeria*	122,000
*Oslo, *Norway*	461,591
Ostrava, *Czecho-Slovakia*	199,902
*Ottawa, *Canada*	429,750
Oxford, *England*	106,124
Palembang, *Republic of Indonesia*	723,000
Palermo, *Italy*	587,063
Palma, *Spain*	140,000
*Panama City, *Panama*	200,000
*Paris (Gr.), *France*	2,850,189
Pasadena, *California*	116,407
Paterson, *New Jersey*	143,663
Patna, *India*	362,817
Patras, *Greece*	95,364
Pecs, *Hungary*	115,000
*Peiping, *China*	4,140,000
Penang, *Republic of Malaysia*	234,930
Penza, *USSR*	605,000
Peoria, *Ilinois*	103,162
Perth, *Australia*	419,755
Peshawar, *Pakistan*	218,691
Philadelphia, *Pennsylvania*	2,002,512
*Phnom-Penh, *Cambodia*	550,000
Phoenix, *Arizona*	439,170
Pilsen (Plzen), *Czecho-Slovakia*	134,273
Piovdiv, *Bulgaria*	162,518
Piraeus, *Greece*	183,877
Pittsburgh, *Pennsylvania*	604,332
Plymouth, *England*	204,279
Ploesti, *Romania*	114,560
Poona, *India*	480,982
Port Said, *Egypt*	240,000
*Port-au-Prince, *Haiti*	200,000
Portland, *Oregon*	372,676
Porto Alegre, *Brazil*	641,473
Portsmouth, *England*	215,198
Poznan, *Poland*	408,000
*Prague, *Czecho-Slovakia*	988,949
*Pretoria, *Republic of South Africa*	420,000
Providence, *Rhode Island*	207,498
Puebla, *Mexico*	287,952
Puntarenas, *Costa Rica*	49,870
Pusan, *Korea*	1,162,614
Pyongyang, *Korea*	285,965
Quebec, *Canada*	357,568
*Quezon City, *Philippines*	394,374
*Quito, *Ecuador*	277,270
*Rabat, *Morocco*	224,901
Ramat Gan, *Israel*	82,000
*Rangoon, *Burma*	740,000
Rawalpindi, *Pakistan*	340,175
Reading, *Pennsylvania*	98,177
Recife, *Brazil*	797,234
Regina, *Canada*	112,141
Resht, *Iran*	109,491
Richmond, *Virginia*	219,954
*Reykjavik, *Iceland*	76,000
*Riga, *Latvia*	605,000
Rio de Janeiro, *Brazil*	3,307,613
*Riyadh, *Saudi Arabia*	280,000

City and Country	population
Rochester, *New York*	318,611
Rockford, *Illinois*	128,075
*Rome, *Italy*	2,160,773
Rosario, *Argentina*	761,300
Rostock, *East Germany*	155,351
Rostov-on-Don, *USSR*	597,000
Rotterdam, *Netherlands*	729,744
Sacramento, *California*	191,667
*Saigon, *Vietnam*	1,800,000
*Salisbury, *South Rhodesia*	260,800
Salonika (Thessaloniki), *Greece*	373,635
Salt Lake City, *Utah*	189,454
Salvador, *Brazil*	655,735
Salzburg, *Austria*	106,897
*Sana, *Yemen*	75,000
San Antonio, *Texas*	587,718
San Diego, *California*	573,224
San Francisco, *California*	740,316
San Jose, *California*	204,196
San Jose, *Costa Rica*	144,454
San Luis Potosi, *Mexico*	159,640
*San Salvador, *El Salvador*	203,000
Santa Ana, *El Salvador*	109,711
Santa Clara, *Cuba*	144,630
Santa Fe, *Argentina*	275,000
*Santiago, *Chile*	1,914,539
Santiago de Cuba, *Cuba*	166,565
Santo Domingo, *Dominican Republic*	367,053
Santos, *Brazil*	265,735
São Paulo, *Brazil*	3,850,000
Sapporo, *Japan*	523,829
Sarajevo, *Yugoslavia*	395,000
Saratov, *USSR*	581,000
Saskatoon, *Canada*	95,526
Savannah, *Georgia*	149,245
Scranton, *Pennsylvania*	111,443
Seattle, *Washington*	557,087
Semarang, *Republic of Indonesia*	520,565
Sendai, *Japan*	425,272
*Seoul, *Korea*	2,444,883
Seville, *Spain*	500,000
Sfax, *Tunisia*	65,635
Shanghai, *China*	7,100,000
Sheffield, *England*	493,954
Sherbrooke, *Canada*	66,554
Shiraz, *Iran*	171,000
Shizouka, *Japan*	328,819
Sian, *China*	1,500,000
Siangtan, *China*	300,000
Singapore, *Republic of Malaysia*	1,665,400
Shreveport, *Louisiana*	164,372
Skopje, *Yugoslavia*	167,000
*Sofia, *Bulgaria*	725,756
Solingen, *West Germany*	177,175
Somerville, *Massachusetts*	94,697
Soochow, *China*	260,000
South Bend, *Indiana*	132,445
Spokane, *Washington*	181,608
Springfield, *Massachusetts*	174,463
Srinagar, *India*	207,787
Stalingrad, *USSR*	680,000
Stalino, *USSR*	1,050,000
Stalinsk, *USSR*	377,000
Stavanger, *Norway*	53,000
St. Etienne, *France*	181,730

(*denotes capital city)

Major World Cities—Continued

City and Country	population
St. John, *Canada*	95,563
St. Johns, *Canada*	90,838
St. Louis, *Missouri*	750,026
St. Paul, *Minnesota*	313,411
St. Petersburg, *Florida*	181,298
*Stockholm (Gr.), *Sweden*	1,125,000
Stoke-on-Trent, *England*	265,506
Strasbourg, *France*	200,921
Stuttgart, *West Germany*	648,639
Subotica, *Yugoslavia*	118,000
Sucre, *Bolivia*	60,092
Suez, *Egypt*	156,300
Surabaya, *Republic of Indonesia*	1,310,631
Surakarta, *Republic of Indonesia*	445,305
Sverdlovsk, *USSR*	777,000
Swansea, *Wales*	166,740
Sydney (Gr.), *Australia*	2,181,211
Syracuse, *New York*	216,038
Szczecin (Stettin), *Poland*	269,000
Szeged, *Hungary*	136,752
Tabriz, *Iran*	290,000
Tacoma, *Washington*	147,979
Taegu, *Korea*	678,277
Taichung, *Taiwan (Formosa)*	286,058
Tainan, *Taiwan (Formosa)*	324,147
*Taipei, *Taiwan (Formosa)*	947,922
Taiyuan, *China*	500,000
Tallin, *Estonia*	280,000
Tampa, *Florida*	274,970
Tampere, *Finland*	127,300
Tampico, *Mexico*	122,197
*Tananarive, *Malagasy*	240,000
Tangier, *Morocco*	141,926
Tanta, *Egypt*	175,000
Tashkent, *USSR*	911,000
*Tegucigalpa, *Honduras*	125,000
*Tehran, *Iran*	2,000,000
Tel Aviv-Jaffa, *Israel*	383,000
Tetuan, *Morocco*	101,155
Three Rivers, *Canada*	53,477
Tientsin, *China*	3,100,000
Tiflis, *USSR*	694,000
Tilburg, *Netherlands*	138,546
Timisoara, *Romania*	142,251
*Tirana, *Albania*	59,887
*Tokyo (Gr.), *Japan*	10,115,795
Toledo, *Ohio*	318,003
Tomsk, *USSR*	249,000
Topeka, *Kansas*	119,484
Toronto, *Canada*	1,824,481
Torreon, *Mexico*	179,955
Toulouse, *France*	268,863
Tourane, *Vietnam*	110,500
Trenton, *New Jersey*	114,167
Trieste, *Italy*	273,390
Tripoli, *Lebanon*	100,000
*Tripoli, *Libya*	170,000
Tsinan, *China*	472,279
Trondheim, *Norway*	59,000
Tsingtao, *China*	850,508
Tucson, *Arizona*	212,892
Tucuman, *Argentina*	251,000
Tula, *USSR*	345,000

City and Country	population
Tulsa, *Oklahoma*	261,685
*Tunis, *Tunisia*	680,000
Turin, *Italy*	1,019,230
Turku, *Finland*	127,400
Ufa, *USSR*	546,000
*Ulan Bator, *Mongolian Republic*	150,000
Upsala, *Sweden*	79,292
Utica, *New York*	100,410
Utrecht, *Netherlands*	256,332
*Vaduz, *Liechtenstein*	3,300
Valencia, *Spain*	544,306
Valencia, *Venezuela*	161,443
Valparaiso, *Chile*	261,684
Vancouver, *Canada*	790,165
Varna, *Bulgaria*	119,769
Vasteras, *Sweden*	79,210
Venice, *Italy*	336,184
Veracruz, *Mexico*	144,232
Verdun, *Canada*	78,317
Verona, *Italy*	221,138
Vicente Lopez, *Argentina*	149,958
Victoria, *Canada*	154,152
*Vientiane, *Laos*	138,000
*Vienna, *Austria*	1,670,000
Vilnyus, *Lithuania*	235,000
Vinh, *Vietnam*	150,000
Vladivostok, *USSR*	283,000
Volvograd, *USSR*	591,000
Voronezh, *USSR*	454,000
*Warsaw, *Poland*	1,136,000
*Washington, *District of Columbia*	763,956
Waterbury, *Connecticut*	107,130
*Wellington, *New Zealand*	249,138
Wenchow, *China*	631,276
Wichita, *Kansas*	254,698
Wichita Falls, *Texas*	101,724
Wiesbaden, *West Germany*	258,700
Wilmington, *Delaware*	95,827
Windsor, *Canada*	114,367
Winnipeg, *Canada*	475,989
Winston-Salem, *North Carolina*	111,135
Worcester, *Massachusetts*	186,587
Wroclaw, *Poland*	429,000
Wuhan, *China*	1,800,000
Wuppertal, *West Germany*	420,000
Yanchow, *China*	250,000
*Yaoundé, *Cameroun*	60,000
Yarmouth, *England*	65,000
Yaroslavl, *USSR*	406,000
Yawata, *Japan*	332,163
Yokahama, *Japan*	1,375,710
Yokosuka, *Japan*	287,000
Yonkers, *New York*	190,634
Youngstown, *Ohio*	166,689
Zagreb, *Yugoslavia*	470,000
Zahle, *Lebanon*	40,000
Zamboanga, *Philippines*	131,411
Zaporozhe, *USSR*	435,000
Zaragoza, *Spain*	301,000
Zhadanov, *USSR*	284,000
Zurich, *Switzerland*	428,000
Zwickau, *East Germany*	129,394

(*denotes capital city)

Alabama

*Montgomery	134,393
Birmingham	340,887
Mobile	202,779

Alaska

*Juneau	6,797

Arizona

*Phoenix	439,170
Tucson	212,892

Arkansas

*Little Rock	107,813

California

*Sacramento	191,667
Los Angeles	2,479,015
San Francisco	740,316
San Diego	573,224
Oakland	367,548
Long Beach	344,168
San Jose	204,196
Fresno	133,929
Glendale	119,442
Pasadena	116,407
Berkeley	111,268
East Los Angeles	104,270
Anaheim	104,184
Torrance	100,991
Santa Ana	100,350
San Bernardino	91,922
Burbank	90,155
Stockton	86,321
Riverside	84,332
Garden Grove	84,238
Downey	82,505
Santa Monica	82,249
Arden Arcade	73,352
Hayward	72,700
Richmond	71,854
Compton	71,812

Colorado

*Denver	493,887
Pueblo	91,181

Connecticut

*Hartford	162,178
Bridgeport	156,748
New Haven	152,048
Waterbury	107,130
Stamford	92,173
New Britain	82,201

Delaware

*Dover	7,250
Wilmington	95,827

Florida

*Tallahassee	48,174
Miami	291,688
Tampa	274,970
Jacksonville	201,030
St. Petersburg	181,298
Orlando	88,135
Fort Lauderdale	83,648

Georgia

*Atlanta	487,455
Savannah	149,245
Macon	122,876
Columbus	116,779
Augusta	70,626

Hawaii

*Honolulu	294,194

Idaho

*Boise	34,481

Illinois

*Springfield	83,271
Chicago	3,550,404
Rockford	128,075
Peoria	103,162
Evanston	79,283
Decatur	78,004

Indiana

*Indianapolis	476,258
Gary	178,320
Fort Wayne	161,776
Evansville	141,543
South Bend	132,445
Hammond	111,698

Iowa

*Des Moines	208,982
Cedar Rapids	92,035
Sioux City	89,159
Davenport	88,981
Waterloo	71,755

Kansas

*Topeka	119,484
Wichita	254,698
Kansas City	121,901

Kentucky

*Frankfort	18,365
Louisville	390,639

Louisiana

*Baton Rouge	152,419
New Orleans	627,525
Shreveport	164,372

Maine

*Augusta	21,680
Portland	72,566

Maryland

*Annapolis	23,385
Baltimore	939,024
Dundalk	82,428

Massachusetts

*Boston	2,589,301
Worcester	186,587
Springfield	174,463
Cambridge	107,716
New Bedford	102,477
Fall River	99,942
Somerville	94,697
Lynn	94,478
Newton	92,384
Lowell	92,107
Quincy	87,409
Lawrence	70,933

Michigan

*Lansing	113,058
Detroit	1,670,144
Grand Rapids	201,487
Flint	196,940
Dearborn	112,007
Saginaw	98,265
Warren	89,246
Pontiac	82,233
Kalamazoo	82,089
Royal Oak	80,612
St. Clair Shores	76,657

Minnesota

*St. Paul	313,411
Minneapolis	482,872
Duluth	106,884

Mississippi

*Jackson	144,422

Missouri

*Jefferson City	28,228
St. Louis	750,026
Kansas City	475,539
Springfield	95,865
St. Joseph	79,673

Montana

*Helena	20,227

Nebraska

*Lincoln	128,521
Omaha	301,598

Nevada

*Carson City	5,163

New Hampshire

*Concord	28,991
Manchester	88,282

New Jersey

*Trenton	114,167
Newark	405,220
Jersey City	276,101
Paterson	143,663
Camden	117,159
Elizabeth	107,698
Clifton	82,084
Woodbridge	78,846
East Orange	77,259
Bayonne	74,215

New Mexico

*Santa Fe	33,394
Albuquerque	201,189

New York

*Albany	129,726
New York	7,781,984
Buffalo	532,759
Rochester	318,611
Syracuse	216,038
Yonkers	190,634
Niagara Falls	102,394
Utica	100,410
Tonawanda	83,771
Schenectady	81,682
New Rochelle	78,812
Mt. Vernon	76,010

North Carolina

*Raleigh	93,931
Charlotte	201,564
Greensboro	119,574
Winston-Salem	111,135
Durham	78,302

North Dakota

*Bismark	27,670

*indicates state capital

Ohio		
*Columbus	471,316
Cleveland	876,050
Cincinnati	502,550
Toledo	318,003
Akron	290,351
Dayton	262,332
Youngstown	166,689
Canton	113,631
Parma	82,845
Springfield	82,723

Oklahoma
*Oklahoma City	324,253
Tulsa	261,685

Oregon
*Salem	49,142
Portland	372,076

Pennsylvania
*Harrisburg	79,697
Philadelphia	2,002,512
Pittsburgh	604,332
Erie	138,440
Scranton	111,443

Allentown	108,347
Reading	98,177
Upper Derby	93,158
Bethlehem	75,408

Rhode Island
*Providence	207,498
Pawtucket	81,001

South Carolina
*Columbia	97,443
Charleston	75,940

South Dakota
*Pierre	10,088

Tennessee
*Nashville	170,874
Memphis	497,524
Chatanooga	130,009
Knoxville	111,827

Texas
*Austin	186,545
Houston	938,319

Dallas	679,684
San Antonio	587,718
Fort Worth	356,268
El Paso	276,687
Corpus Christi	167,690
Amarillo	137,969
Lubbock	128,691
Beaumont	119,175
Wichita Falls	101,724
Waco	97,808
Abilene	90,368
Odessa	80,338

Utah
*Salt Lake City	189,454
Ogden	70,197

Vermont
*Montpelier	8,782

Virginia
*Richmond	219,958
Norfolk	304,869
Arlington Co.	163,401
Portsmouth	144,773
Newport News	113,662

Roanoke	97,110
Alexandria	91,013
Hampton	89,258

Washington
*Olympia	18,273
Seattle	557,087
Spokane	181,608
Tacoma	147,979

West Virginia
*Charleston	85,796
Huntington	83,627

Wisconsin
*Madison	126,706
Milwaukee	741,324
Racine	89,144

Wyoming
*Cheyenne	43,505

District of Columbia
*Washington	763,956

Table 4 Populations of States

States	Total Population	Catholic Population	States	Total Population	Catholic Population
Alabama	3,266,740	116,441	Montana	674,767	153,800
Alaska	226,167	35,775	Nebraska	1,411,330	264,305
Arizona	1,302,161	306,691	Nevada	285,278	52,073
Arkansas	1,786,272	46,677	New Hampshire	606,921	225,417
California	15,717,204	3,544,436	New Jersey	6,066,782	2,504,187
Colorado	1,753,947	327,841	New Mexico	951,023	359,703
Connecticut	2,535,234	1,167,967	New York	16,782,304	5,986,819
Delaware	446,292	99,481	North Carolina	4,556,155	45,437
District of Columbia	763,956	306,863	North Dakota	632,446	161,507
Florida	4,951,560	521,109	Ohio	9,706,397	2,101,223
Georgia	3,943,116	64,063	Oklahoma	2,328,284	101,323
Hawaii	632,772	200,000	Oregon	1,768,687	214,191
Idaho	667,191	44,730	Pennsylvania	11,319,366	3,491,387
Illinois	10,081,158	3,033,434	Rhode Island	859,488	521,353
Indiana	4,662,498	649,062	South Carolina	2,382,594	35,536
Iowa	2,757,537	464,444	South Dakota	680,514	131,111
Kansas	2,178,611	289,545	Tennessee	3,567,089	79,220
Kentucky	3,038,156	309,538	Texas	9,597,677	1,933,385
Louisiana	3,257,022	1,111,998	Utah	890,627	46,032
Maine	979,265	266,855	Vermont	389,881	123,309
Maryland	3,100,689	448,182	Virginia	3,966,949	212,947
Massachusetts	5,148,578	2,664,210	Washington	2,853,214	358,206
Michigan	7,823,195	2,022,516	West Virginia	1,860,421	109,373
Minnesota	3,413,864	899,987	Wisconsin	3,951,777	1,319,244
Mississippi	2,178,141	65,516	Wyoming	330,066	48,500
Missouri	4,319,813	719,938			

*indicates state capital

Table 5 Exports and Imports

EUROPE

CHIEF EXPORTS	← country →	CHIEF IMPORTS
Iron and steel products, textiles, coal, flax	Belgium	Wool, cotton, wheat, meats, metal goods
Tobacco, eggs, barley, corn, silk, attar of roses	Bulgaria	Textiles, machinery, metals, paper
Dairy products, pork, fish	Denmark	Textiles, mineral oils, coffee, oil cake, automobiles
Wood pulp, paper, timber, butter	Finland	Machinery, foods, cotton, textiles
Cotton, woolen, and silk textiles, wine, iron and steel products	France	Wool, cotton, wheat, pearls, precious stones, machinery, wines, coffee, meats, fruits
Iron and steel goods, machinery, chemicals, coal and coke, textiles, paper	Germany	Meats, wheat, cotton, wool, timber, iron ore, oilseeds
Tobacco, currants, wine, raisins	Greece	Wheat and other foods, textiles
Cereals, cattle, hogs, hides	Hungary	Foods, textiles, mineral oils, machinery
Cattle, pork, dairy products, eggs, horses	Irish Republic	Foods, coal, machinery, iron and steel products
Silk, textiles, rice, hemp, automobiles, chemicals, fruits	Italy	Cotton, wheat, coffee, wood, petroleum products, iron and steel products
Meats, dairy products, sugar, textiles, machinery	Netherlands	Timber, cereals, coffee, coal, mineral oils, chemicals
Fish, wood products, aluminum	Norway	Foods, automobiles, machinery
Wood products, coal, metals, meats, eggs	Poland	Cotton, chemicals, metals
Fish, wine, cork	Portugal	Fish, wheat, sugar, cotton, iron and steel
Corn, barley, wheat, petroleum products, timber	Romania	Textiles, metals, machinery
Wheat, wood products, petroleum products, furs	Russia (USSR)	Cotton, wool, machinery, tea, rubber
Fruits, olive oil, wines, cork, lead	Spain	Cotton, machinery, fertilizers, automobiles, corn
Wood products, meats, iron ore, metal goods	Sweden	Coal, iron and steel, copper, foods
Textiles, cheese, watches, clocks, machinery	Switzerland	Foods, silk, cotton, wool, iron and steel, coal
Textiles, iron and steel products, machinery, coal	United Kingdom	Foods, wool, cotton, rubber, petroleum products, metals, wood products
Livestock, eggs, fruits, wood	Yugoslavia	Textiles, coffee, rice, machinery

Exports and Imports—Continued

ASIA

CHIEF EXPORTS	← country →	CHIEF IMPORTS
Tea, rubber, copra, coconut oil	Ceylon	Rice, textiles, coal, petroleum products
Bean cake, beans, silk, coal, eggs, millet, tea, cotton	China	Sugar, rice, cotton, petroleum products, silver, coal, paper
Wheat, tea, rice, oilseeds, cotton, jute, gunny cloth	India	Cotton manufactures, machinery, sugar, iron and steel products
Rice, rubber, coal, zinc, fish	Indochina	Textiles, machinery, foods
Rubber, sugar, tobacco, petroleum products	Indonesia	Textiles, rice, iron and steel products
Dates, hides	Iraq	Textiles, iron and steel products
Raw silk, textiles, coal, glass, metals, tea, sugar, drugs	Japan	Cotton, wood, oil cake, wool, iron and steel products, mineral oils
Rubber, tin, rice, copra	Malaya	Rice, coal, foods, iron and steel goods
Oil, rugs, fruits, cotton	Iran	Textiles, sugar, tea, metals, automobiles
Fruits, nuts, silks, hides	Israel	Textiles, foods, machinery
Copra, sugar, tobacco, manila hemp	Philippine Islands	Textiles, machinery
Rice, tin, rubber, teak, tungsten	Thailand	Foods, textiles, metal products
Rugs, hides	Syria	Textiles, hardware
Fruits, tobacco, rugs	Turkey	Cotton, textiles, metals, coffee, tea, sugar

AFRICA

CHIEF EXPORTS	country	CHIEF IMPORTS
Wines, sheep, wheat, fruits, nuts, wool	Algeria	Textiles, sugar, coffee, petroleum products
Cobalt, gold, diamonds, uranium ore, rubber, palm nuts, ivory	Congo (Leopoldville)	Petroleum products, textiles, clothing, machinery
Cotton, cotton seeds, cottonseed cake, onions	Egypt	Tobacco, timber, flour, automobiles, coal
Hides, meat, gold, vanilla	Malagasy	Textiles, iron and steel goods
Wheat, barley, hides, skins	Morocco	Textiles, machinery, hardware, tea, sugar, candles, spirits
Olives, hides	Tunisia	Textiles, metal products
gold, diamonds, wool, hides and skins	South Africa	Textiles, clothing, timber products, machinery

AUSTRALIA

CHIEF EXPORTS	country	CHIEF IMPORTS
Wool, wheat, flour, butter, meats, sugar, lead	Australia	Textiles, petroleum products, automobiles, machinery, iron and steel products
Dairy products, wool, meats	New Zealand	Textiles, iron and steel products, machinery

SOUTH AMERICA

CHIEF EXPORTS	← country →	CHIEF IMPORTS
Corn, wheat, linseed oil, wool, meats, hides, quebracho extract	Argentina	Oils and fats, textiles, iron and steel products, timber, machinery
Tin, silver, lead, copper, rubber	Bolivia	Wheat, textiles, petroleum products
Coffee, oranges, hides, rubber, yerba maté	Brazil	Machinery, petroleum products, automobiles
Copper, nitrate, iodine, wool, oats, barley, wheat	Chile	Machinery, petroleum products, automobiles, iron and steel goods
Coffee, bananas, hides, platinum, petroleum	Colombia	Foodstuffs, textiles, iron and steel products, automobiles
Coffee, cacao, bananas, rice, balsa wood	Ecuador	Foods, textiles, machinery
Oranges, yerba maté, timber, hides, tobacco, beef, quebracho extract	Paraguay	Textiles, machinery
Cotton, sugar, vanadium, petroleum, hides, copper	Peru	Foods, textiles, machinery
Meats, hides, wool, linseed oil	Uruguay	Textiles, machinery, lumber, petroleum products
Petroleum, coffee, cacao, iron ore, sugar, gold	Venezuela	Iron and steel products, foods, textiles

NORTH AMERICA

CHIEF EXPORTS	← country →	CHIEF IMPORTS
Wheat, wood pulp, paper, wood, manufactured products, fish, iron	Canada	Sugar, coffee, rubber, tea, cotton, mineral oils, machinery, textiles
Coffee, bananas, cacao	Costa Rica	Textiles, iron and steel products, foods
Sugar, tobacco, molasses	Cuba	Foodstuffs, machinery, various manufactured articles
Sugar, coffee, cacao, tobacco	Dominican Republic	Textiles, iron and steel goods, foods
Coffee, sugar, henequen	El Salvador	Textiles, machinery, iron and steel goods
Coffee, bananas	Guatemala	Textiles, iron and steel products, foods
Coffee, cotton, wood	Haiti	Textiles, iron and steel products
Bananas, sugar	Honduras	Iron and steel products, foods
Petroleum, silver, lead, zinc, coffee	Mexico	Machinery, textiles, iron and steel products
Bananas, mahogany, coffee, sugar	Nicaragua	Textiles, foodstuffs, machinery
Bananas, cacao, hides, cabinet woods	Panama	Foods, textiles, machinery
Cotton, mineral oils, wheat, iron and steel products, lumber, machinery	United States	Sugar, raw silk, wood, spices, tin, coffee, tea, rubber, wood pulp, paper

Table 6
The Planets and the Solar System

Distance from Sun
(in miles)

Planet	Greatest	Least
Mercury	43,355,000	28,566,000
Venus	67,653,000	66,738,000
Earth	94,452,000	91,342,000
Mars	154,760,000	128,330,000
Jupiter	506,710,000	459,940,000
Saturn	935,570,000	836,700,000
Uranus	1,866,800,000	1,698,800,000
Neptune	2,817,400,000	2,769,600,000
Pluto	4,300,000,000	2,750,000,000

Distance from Earth
(millions of miles)

	Greatest	Least
Mercury	136	50
Venus	161	25
Earth	—	—
Mars	248	35
Jupiter	600	367
Saturn	1028	744
Uranus	1960	1606
Neptune	2910	2677
Pluto	3600	3200

Table 7
Size and Time

World Dimensions

Population of the Earth	3,060,800,000 people
Diameter of the Earth	8,000 miles (approx.)
Circumference of the Earth	25,000 miles (approx.)
Area of the Earth	197,000,000 square miles
Land Area of the Earth	56,000,000 square miles U.S. 6% of land area
Water Area of the Earth	141,000,000 square miles
Highest Altitude of Land, Mt. Everest, Asia	29,002 feet
Lowest Altitude of Land, Dead Sea, Palestine	1,292 feet
Greatest Depth of Ocean, off Philippine Islands, Pacific Ocean	34,218 feet

Size and Time—Continued

Oceans and Areas

Arctic Ocean	5,541,000
Atlantic Ocean	31,529,000
Pacific Ocean	63,985,000
Indian Ocean	28,357,000

Mountains and Heights

Asia, Mt. Everest, Nepal-Tibet	29,002
South America, Mt. Aconcagua, Argentina	23,081
North America, Mt. McKinley, Alaska	20,269
Africa, Mt. Kilimanjaro, Tanganyika	19,565
Europe, Mt. Elborus, Caucasus	18,481
Antarctica, Mt. Markham	15,100
United States, Mt. Whitney, California	14,495
Australia, Mt. Kosciusko, New South Wales	7,328

Islands and Areas

Greenland, Arctic Region	837,000
Papua (New Guinea) East Indies	342,232
Madagascar, Indian Ocean	228,707
Borneo, East Indies	282,416
Baffin, Arctic Region	231,000

Rivers and Lengths

miles

Nile, Africa	4,000	Amur, Asia	2,900	Hwang, Asia	2,700
Amazon, South America	3,900	Lena, Asia	2,860	Mekong, Asia	2,600
Yangtze, Asia	3,100	Yenisei, Asia	2,800	Mackenzie, Canada	2,500
Congo, Africa	2,900	Missouri, United States	2,723	Mississippi, United States	2,470

Standard Time Differences

At 12 o'clock noon U.S. Eastern Standard Time (New York City), the standard time in foreign cities is as follows:

		Bogotá	12:00 NOON
		Bombay	10:30 P.M.
		Budapest	6:00 P.M.
		Buenos Aires	2:00 P.M.
		Calcutta	10:30 P.M.
		Cape Town	7:00 P.M.
Athens	7:00 P.M.	Caracas	12:30 P.M.
Baghdad	8:00 P.M.	Geneva	6:00 P.M.
Belfast	5:00 P.M.	Halifax	1:00 P.M.
Berlin	6:00 P.M.	Havana	12:00 NOON

Honolulu	7:00 A.M.*
Hongkong	1:00 A.M.*
London	5:00 P.M.
Mexico City	11:00 A.M.
Moscow	8:00 P.M.
Paris	6:00 P.M.
Rome	6:00 P.M.
Tokyo	2:00 A.M.*
Warsaw	6:00 P.M.
Winnipeg	11:00 A.M.

*next day

Index and Pronunciation

Credits

The full color global relief photographs, reproduced on the pages listed below, were photographed for the exclusive use of WILLIAM H. SADLIER, INC., in their textbooks and related publications. The photographs are of the six-foot geophysical relief globe, photographed by special arrangement with GEO-PHYSICAL MAPS, INC., copyright 1956, New York. The global photography was done by CARU STUDIOS.

Global relief photographs: cover, 2-3, 30-31, 102-103, 154-155, 214-215, 290-291, 322-323

The maps reproduced on the pages listed were made by the following *cartographers:*

GENERAL DRAFTING CO., INC., 6-7, 18-19, 20, 21, 35, 44, 57, 62-63, 74-75, 106-107, 144-145, 158-159, 180-181, 218-219, 252-253, 270-271, 272-273, 282, 294-295, 312-313, 326-327, 332-333

CARU STUDIOS, title, 4, 5, 9, 12, 14, 17, 24 (top, bottom), 160, 224, 231

CHARLES W. NORTH STUDIOS, 194-195

The illustrations reproduced on the pages listed were made by the following *artists:*

GENERAL DRAFTING, 45

NICK EGGENHOFFER, 164

CHARLES W. NORTH STUDIOS, 14, 26-27, 36, 67, 85, 111, 112, 121, 163, 208, 221, 222

H. B. VESTAL, title, ii, iii, vi-vii, 1, 29, 101, 153, 213, 289, 321

The *photographs* reproduced on the pages listed were obtained from the following sources:

CHARLES PHELPS CUSHING, 5, 15 (center, Ruth Block), 16 (Sawders), 94, 105 (Hoit), 110 (Sawders), 115, 116 (Sawders), 121 (bottom), 132

A. DEVANEY, 11, 13, 23 (C. M. Abbot), 32 (Winston Pote), 38 (bottom), 48 (bottom), 54 (right, David Lawlor), 59 (top, bottom), 69, 88, 93 (top), 95 (top), 96 (top), 108, 120, 131 (David W. Corson), 148, 149 (bottom), 157 (J. C. Allen), 164 (top), 169 (bottom), 183 (J. C. Allen), 184, 188, 197 (bottom), 200, 201 (top), 204 (bottom), 256 (bottom), 261, 277 (Josef Scaylea), 281 (top), 284 (top), 292, 302 (George Hunter), 303 (top, G. Hunter), 305 (G. Hunter), 307 (top, G. Hunter), 310 (G. Hunter), 338 (top, H. Lanks)

FREE LANCE PHOTOGRAPHERS GUILD, 43 (Griffin), 47 (top), 55 (bottom), 79 (top), 82, 127 (Ramsey), 162, 167, 169 (top), 172, 186, 189 (DePalmer), 199 (L. Duncan), 207 (Ellis-Sawyer), 223 (B. and I. Spring), 227, 230 (top, R. Bigby), 231 (bottom, Willinger), 236 (W. Eymann), 238 (F. H. Ragsdale), 239, 242-243 (bottom, Otto Done), 244 (P. and E. Jenkins), 247 (A. Ragsdale), 254-255 (McKinney), 257 (left, Don Knight), 257 (right, Jeff Thomson), 259 (B. and I. Spring), 262 (John H. Atkinson Jr.), 263 (top B. and I. Spring), 266 (bottom)

EWING GALLOWAY, 48 (top), 49, 53 (top), 57, 58, 64, 72, 73, 77, 80, 84 (top), 85, 87, 89, 92, 93 (bottom), 96 (bottom), 97, 128, 137, 140, 165 (top), 187, 196, 198 (top), 220 (bottom), 232, 240, 244, 281 (bottom), 286, 297, 300, 316, 338 (bottom, Lanks), 339

PHILIP D. GENDREAU, 14 (top), 15 (top, bottom), 22, 26, 33, 37, 40, 41, 42 (bottom, Julius Fanta), 46 (H. Angell), 53 (bottom), 54 (left), 60, 61, 65, 70 (bottom, Julius Fanta), 81, 84, 95 (bottom), 104, 109, 117 (McManigal), 125, 129, 136, 156, 161, 165 (bottom), 168, 173, 177, 179 (Angell), 180, 192, 197 (top), 217 (bottom), 220, 228 (McManigal), 229, 235, 237, 241 (bottom), 242 (left), 249 (top), 256 (top), 257 (bottom), 260 (George Cox), 293 (Lanks), 299 (top), 301 (top, Lanks), 303 (bottom), 304, 311, 324 (Lanks), 325 (Lanks), 336 (top), 337

MONKMEYER PRESS PHOTO SERVICE, 268 (Ted Bank), 279 (Deller), 285 (Pat Miller), 296 (Lanks)

PIX, INC., 309 (Karsh)

RELIGIOUS NEWS SERVICE, 205 (top, middle, bottom)

SHOSTAL PRESS AGENCY, 8, 25, 38 (top), 42 (top), 47 (bottom), 50, 51, 52, 55 (top), 70 (top), 71, 74, 78, 79 (bottom), 83, 91, 94 (bottom, J. Zehrt), 98, 114, 118, 119, 122 (Leahey), 123, 126, 130 (top, bottom), 135 (top), 138, 139, 141, 142, 146, 147, 149 (top), 166, 174 (top, bottom), 176, 178, 182-183 (4), 190, 191, 194, 195, 198 (bottom), 201 (top), 202 (bottom), 203, 204 (top), 206 (top, bottom), 216, 217 (top), 226, 230 (bottom), 231, 233, 241 (top), 242 (top, Ray Manley), 243 (top), 246, 248 (top), (bottom, Al Christman), 250, 251, 263 (top), 264 (R. Atkeson), 265 (Josef Scaylea), 266 (top), 269, 272, 274, 275, 276, 280, 283, 284 (bottom, Hal Strong), 285 (top, Rupert Leach), 299 (bottom, Fanta), 301 (bottom), 306, 307 (bottom), 315 (J. Barnell), 317 (Martin Helfer), 318 (Martin Helfer), 330, 331, 334 (D. Forbert), 335 (D. Forbert), 336 (bottom, R. and W. Rosine), 341, 342 (top), 342 (bottom, J. Barnell), 343, 344, 345, 346 (Manley), 347, 348, 349 (R. Sole)

Set in Linotype Times Roman by Primar Typographers, Inc.
Art and layout design by Charles W. North Studios
Format by F. Sadlier Dinger
Printed by Polygraphic Company of America, Incorporated
Bound by Van Rees Book Binding Corporation, and John F. Cuneo Company
Published by William H. Sadlier, Inc., New York and Chicago

World
ATLAS

The New Catholic Geography Series

ATLAS
OF
THE WORLD

The pages of maps in this atlas cover the entire world. They have been brought together so that you can turn to them whenever you need a good map. The detailed maps are here for reference and they should be used constantly for obtaining all kinds of geographic information.

The maps employ different colors to indicate different political sub-divisions such as states and countries. Other symbols are used to show such features as mountains, large bodies of water, rivers, capital cities, etc. The relative size and importance of cities are indicated by the size of the type used to name them. A scale of miles is given with many of the maps so that the distance between places can be accurately measured. Parallels and meridians are indicated to help you locate places with respect to the equator and the prime meridian.

Get into the habit of consulting your atlas frequently. It will help you gain a better understanding of the way geography influences people's lives in our country and in other lands. Use the maps to make comparisons and to help you solve geographic problems. The atlas should be used as a reference in just the same way as you use your dictionary or an encyclopedia.

PUBLISHED BY

W. H. Sadlier, Inc.

Printed in the United States of America

COPYRIGHT BY C. S. HAMMOND & CO. MCMLXV

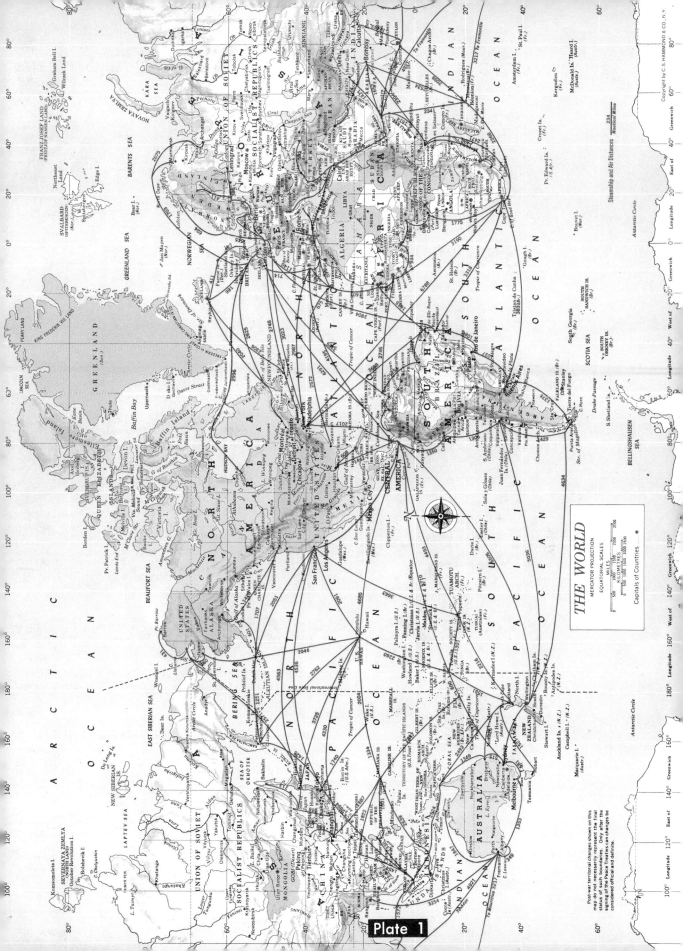

THE WORLD

MERCATOR PROJECTION
EQUATORIAL SCALES
MILES
KILOMETRES
Capitals of Countries............ *

Steamship and Air Distances

234 Nautical Miles

Post-war territorial changes shown on this
map do not necessarily represent the final
status of such boundaries. Only after the
signing of the Peace Treaties can changes be
considered official and definite.

Copyright by C. S. HAMMOND & CO., N.Y.

Plate 1

Plate 2

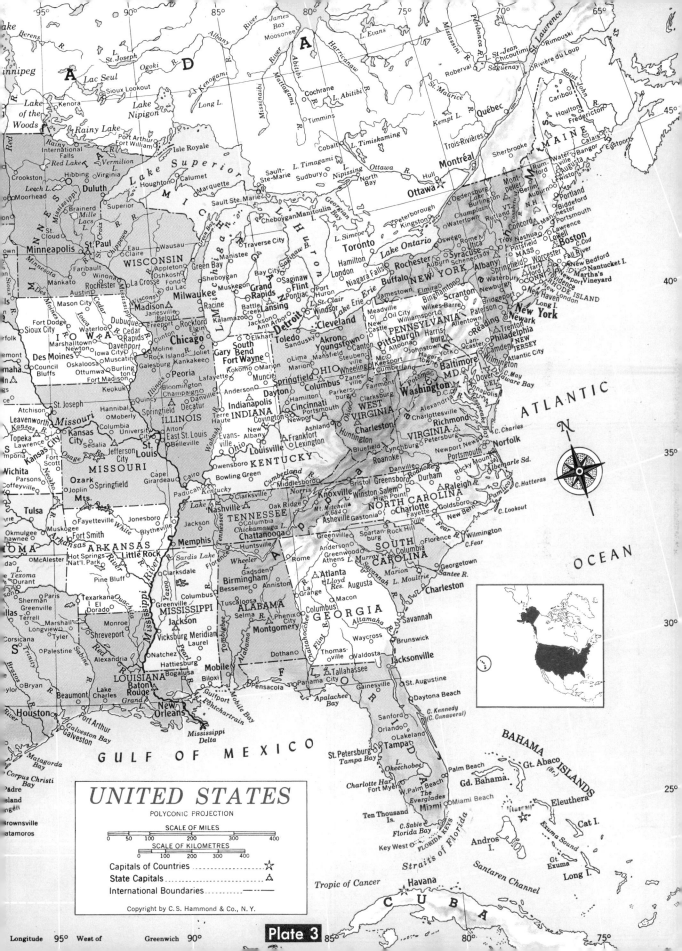

UNITED STATES

POLYCONIC PROJECTION

SCALE OF MILES

| 0 | 50 | 100 | 200 | 300 | 400 |

SCALE OF KILOMETRES

| 0 | 100 | 200 | 300 | 400 |

Capitals of Countries .... ☆

State Capitals .... △

International Boundaries .... —

Copyright by C.S. Hammond & Co., N.Y.

Plate 3

Longitude 95° West of Greenwich 90°

Plate 4

Plate 6

UNITED STATES
Southeastern and South Central Section

POLYCONIC PROJECTION

SCALE OF MILES

0   50   100   150   200   250

National Capital ⊛
State and Provincial Capitals ⊙
International Boundaries
State and Provincial Boundaries
Canals

Copyright by C. S. HAMMOND & Co., N.Y.

Plate 7

Plate 8

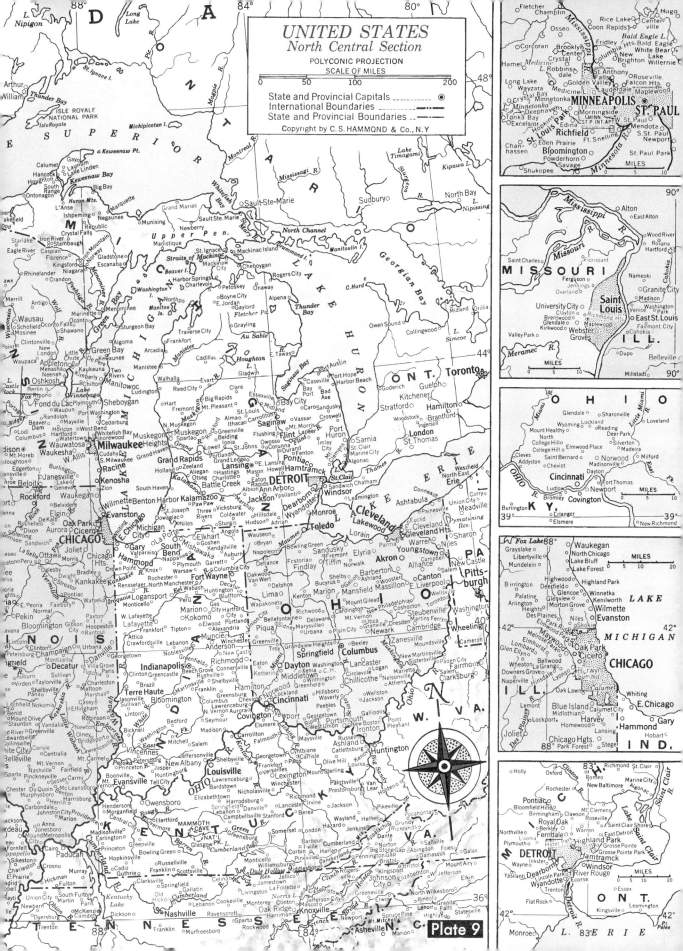

UNITED STATES
Western Section

POLYCONIC PROJECTION
SCALE OF MILES

0 50 100   200   300

State and Provincial Capitals .... ⌂
International Boundaries —— —— ——
State and Provincial Boundaries — · — · —

Copyright by C.S. HAMMOND & Co., N.Y.

Plate 10

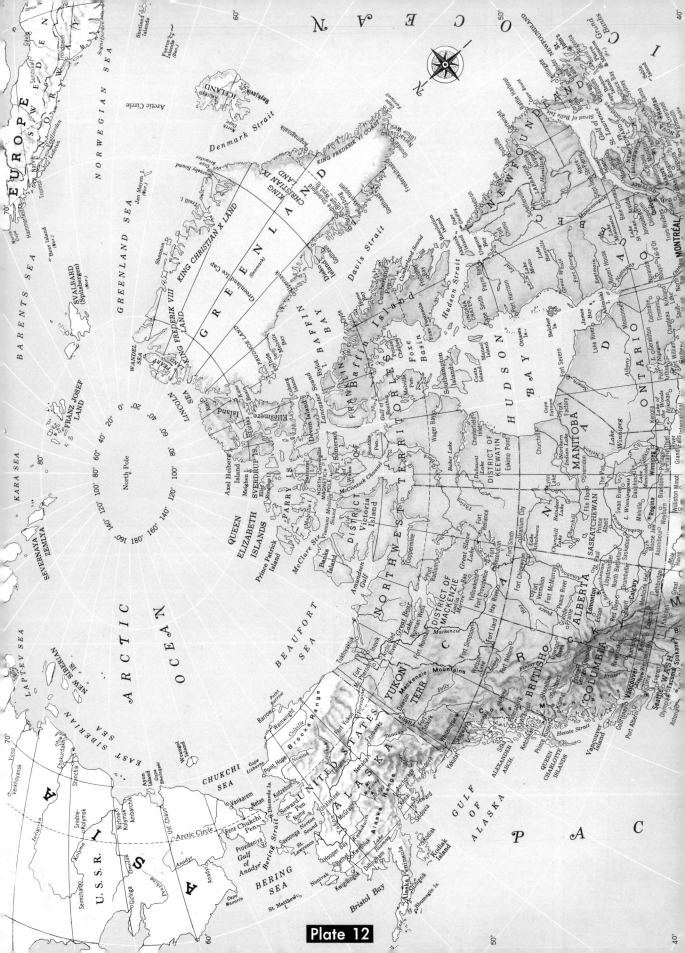

Plate 12

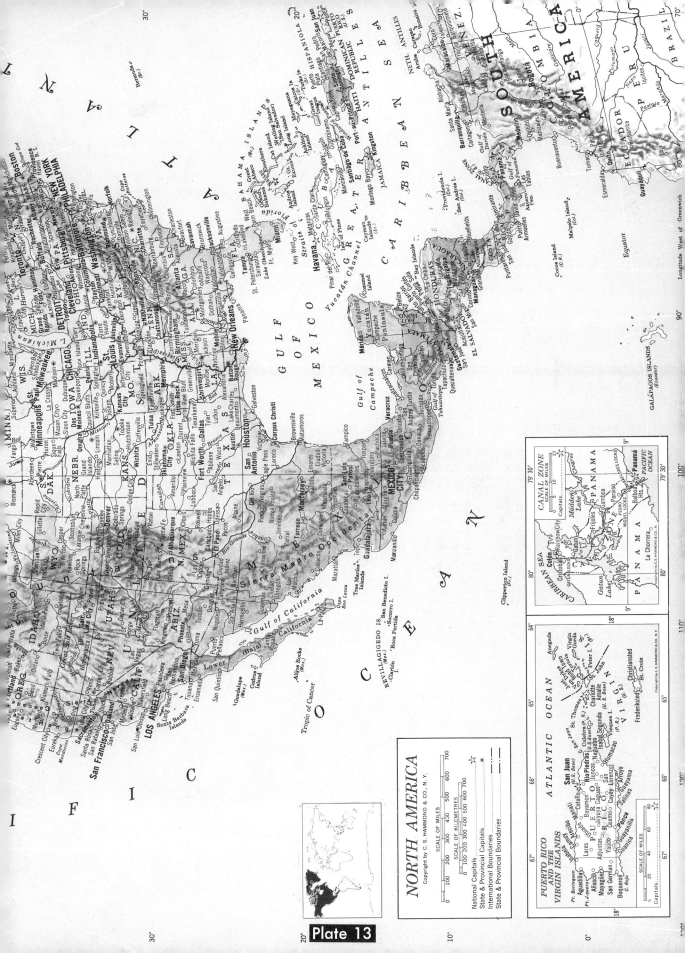

NORTH AMERICA

Copyright by C. S. HAMMOND & CO., N.Y.

SCALE OF MILES
100 200 300 400 500 600 700

SCALE OF KILOMETRES
0 100 200 300 400 500 600 700

National Capitals .... ⊛
State & Provincial Capitals .... ⊙
International Boundaries .... ‒·‒·‒
State & Provincial Boundaries ...... ‒‒‒‒

CANAL ZONE
SCALE OF MILES
0   5   10
Capitals........ ⊛

PUERTO RICO AND THE VIRGIN ISLANDS
SCALE OF MILES
0   20   40   60   80
Capitals........ ⊛

Plate 13

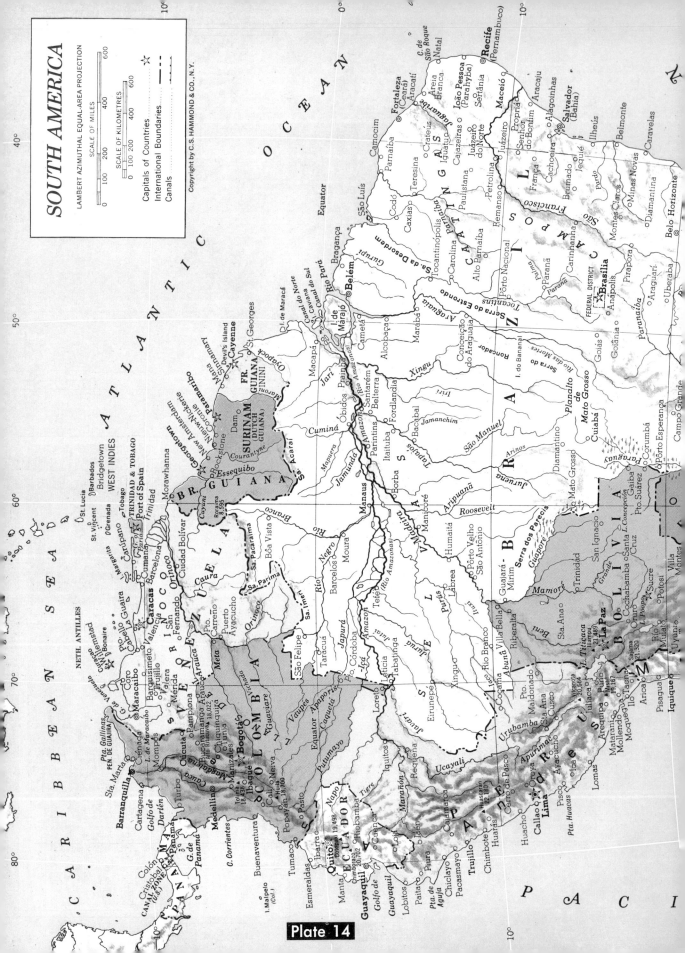

SOUTH AMERICA

LAMBERT AZIMUTHAL EQUAL-AREA PROJECTION

SCALE OF MILES
0   100   200   400   600

SCALE OF KILOMETRES
0   100   200   400   600

Capitals of Countries ✸
International Boundaries ------
Canals ─·─·─

Copyright by C.S. HAMMOND & CO., N.Y.

Plate 14

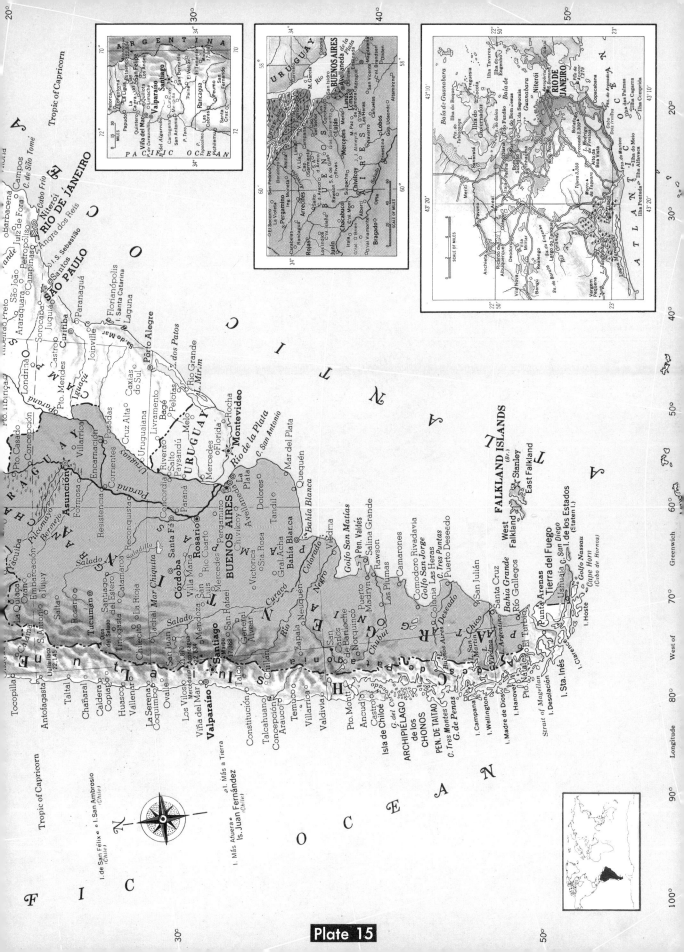

Plate 15

COMMUNISM
IN EUROPE
◼ U.S.S.R.
▢ Other Communist Countries

Plate 16

Longitude West of Greenwich   Longitude East of Greenwich

BARENTS SEA

North Cape
Vadsö
Kolguev I.
Naryan Mar
Vorkuta
Salekhard
(Obdorsk)
Usa
Ob
Surgut
Ob
80°

Tana
Pechenga
(Petsamo)
Murmansk
KANIN PEN.
Chebaskaya Bay
Berezovo
70°
Khanty-Mansisk
Tobolsk
Irtish

L. Inari
Kirovsk
KOLA PEN.
Mezen Bay
Mezen
Ust Tsilma
Pechora
60°
Krasnouralsk
Nizhni Tagil
Kirovgrad
Sverdlovsk
Tyumen
Tobol

Torne
Muonio
Kandalaksha
White Sea
Archangel
Mezen
Berezniki
Kama
Izhevsk
Sarapul
Zlatoust
Troitsk
Kustanai

Tornio
paranda
Oulu
Kem
Onega
Northern Dvina
Syktyvkar
Kotlas
Kirov (Vyatka)
Kotelnich
Perm (Molotov)
Chelyabinsk
Kurgan

FINLAND
L. Oulu
Onega
Nyandoma
Veliki Ustyug
Magnitogorsk
50°

Vaasa
Kuopio
Joensuu
L. Onega
Petrozavodsk
Vologda
Kazan
Kuibyshev
Ufa
Belaya
Orenburg (Chkalov)

Tampere
Sortavala
L. Ladoga
Vyborg
Rybinsk Res.
Cherepovets
Rybinsk (Shcherbakov)
Kostroma
Ivanovo
Balakhna
Gorki (Nizhni Novgorod)
Volga
Ulyanovsk
Kuibyshev (Samara)
Uralsk
Aktyubinsk

Turku Helsinki (Helsingfors)
Hangö
Kotka
LENINGRAD
Kalinin (Tver)
Yaroslavl
Volga
Dzerzhinsk
Res.
Temir
Chelkar

Gulf of Finland
Narva
Kingisepp
L. Ilmen
MOSCOW (Moskva)
Orekhovo-Zuevo
Oka
Penza
Saratov
Engels
Emba

Tallinn (Revel)
Tartu
L. Peipus
Pskov
Velikie Luki
Kaluga
Tula
Michurinsk
Tambov
UNION OF SOVIET FEDERATED SOCIALIST REPUBLICS

Hiiumaa (Dagö)
Pärnu
ESTONIAN S.S.R.
WHITE
Smolensk
Orel
Volga
Kara-Bogaz-Gol

G. of Riga
Cēsis
Rēzekne
Bigosovo
RUSSIAN
Bryansk
Voronezh
Don
Volgograd (Stalingrad)
Guryev

Riga
LATVIAN S.S.R.
Jelgava
Šiauliai
Daugavpils
Vitebsk
Gomel
Kursk
CASPIAN SEA

LITHUANIAN S.S.R.
Panevėžys
S.S.R.
Millerovo
Tsimlyansk Res.
Volga
Fort Shevchenko

Kaunas
Vilna
Negoreloye
Minsk
Bobruisk
Kiev
Poltava
Kharkov
Lugansk
Shakhty
Astrakhan

Kaliningrad
(R.S.F.S.R.)
Grodno
Stolbtsy
Kremenchug
Dneprodzerzhinsk
Kramatorsk
Donets
Don

Białystok
Pinsk
Rovno
Zhitomir
Kirovograd
Dnepropetrovsk
Zaporozhe
Makeevka
Donetsk
Rostov
Elista

POLAND
Brest
Bug
Lublin
Shepetovka
UKRAINIAN
Krivoi Rog
Dnieper
Taganrog
Zhdanov

WARSAW
Wisla
Lvov
Ivano-Frankovsk
Vinnitsa
S.S.R.
Nikolaev
Kherson
Sea of Azov
Krasnodar
Armavir
Pyatigorsk
Grozny
Makhachkala

Przemyśl
Kraków
Mukachevo
Chernovtsy
Dnestr
Tiraspol
Bendery
Odessa
Kerch
Novorossisk
Maikop
Kislovodsk
Karachaevsk
Ordzhonikidze
Caucasus
Krasnovodsk

HUNGARY
Satu Mare
Oradea
Cluj
Arad
MOLDAVIAN
Iaşi
Roman
Kishinev
Belgorod-Dnestrovski
CRIMEAN PEN.
Simferopol
Tuapse
Sochi
Sukhumi
Kutaisi
GEORGIAN S.S.R.
Tbilisi
ARMENIAN S.S.R.
AZERBAIDZHAN S.S.R.
Baku

Budapest
Debrecen
Timişoara
Sibiu
Braşov
Prut
Sulina
Sevastopol
Yalta
Batumi
Leninakan
Eriyan
Nakhichevan
40°

Szeged
Arad
RUMANIA
Ploieşti
Brăila
Galaţi
BLACK SEA
Trabzon
Erzurum
Dzhulfa
Araxes

Craiova
Bucharest
Constanţa
Sinop
Samsun
Kızılırmak
IRAN
30°

Belgrade
Danube
Iron Gate
Pleven
Ruse
Varna
Burgas
ISTANBUL (Constantinople)
Ereğli
Sivas

Niš
Sofia
Plovdiv
Stara Zagora
BULGARIA
Edirne (Adrianople)
Bosporus
Üsküdar (Skutari)
Sea of Marmara
Bursa
Eskişehir
Ankara (Angora)
Konya
Kayseri
Maraş

Skopje
Rhodope
Tekirdağ
Dardanelles
İzmir (Smyrna)
Manisa
Afyon
Tarsus
Adana
Aleppo

Bitola
GREECE
Kavalla
Salonika
Lesbos
Chios
TURKEY
Konya
Mersin (İçel)
Antakya
SYRIA

Ioánnina
Larisa
Vólos
Euboea
Chalcis
Samos
Antalya
El Ladhiqiya

Trikkala
Lamía
ATHENS
Piraeus
Rhodes
Nicosia
Larnaca

Patras
Corinth
Kalamai
Canea
Candia
CYPRUS

C. Matapan
Crete
AEGEAN SEA
40°
50°

Plate 17

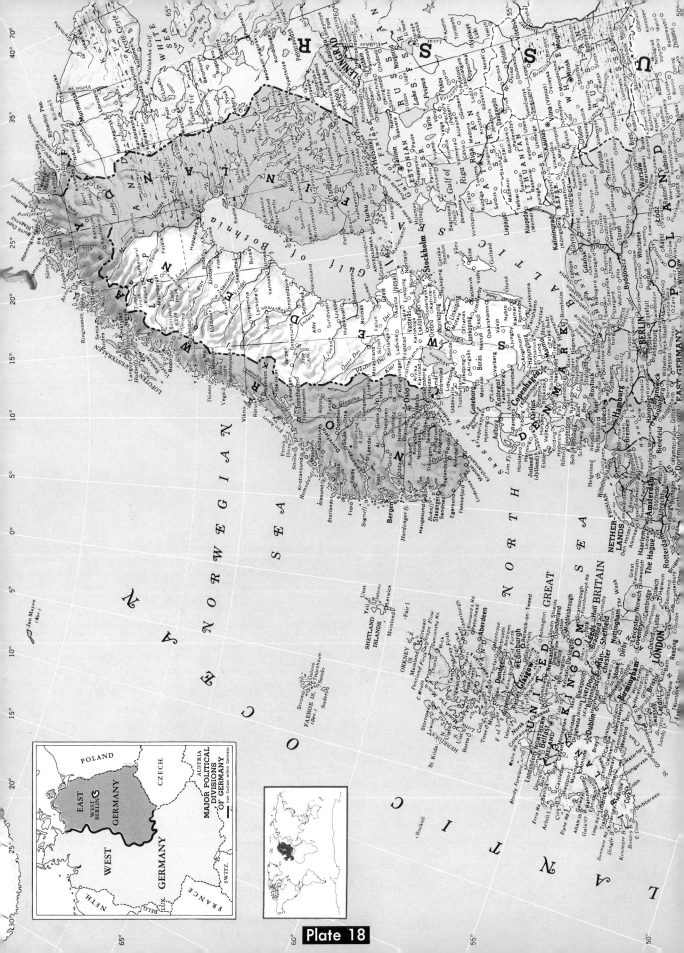

Plate 18

WESTERN and
CENTRAL EUROPE

CONIC PROJECTION

SCALE OF MILES

SCALE OF KILOMETRES

National Capitals..........✳
Administrative Centers.....◉
International Boundaries....
Internal Boundaries........
Canals.....................

Copyright by C. S. HAMMOND & CO., N.Y.

Plate 19

BALKAN STATES

CONIC PROJECTION

SCALE OF MILES
0 25 50 100 150 200 250

SCALE OF KILOMETRES
0 60 120 180 240 300

Capitals of Countries ⊛ Canals
International Boundaries

Longitude East of Greenwich

Plate 20

Copyright by C.S. HAMMOND & Co., N.Y.

2535

Plate 22

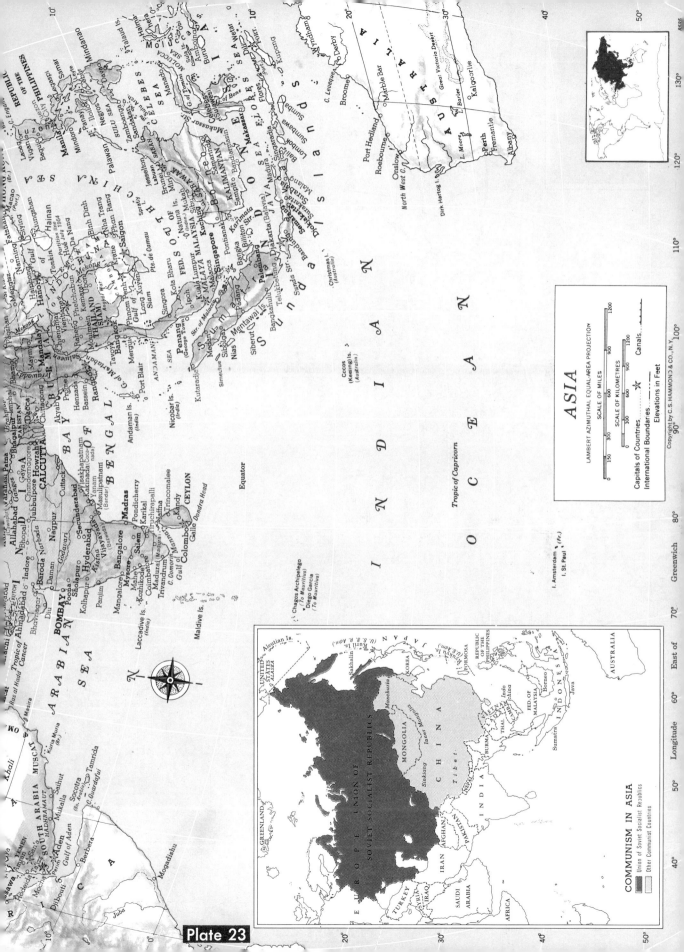

ASIA

LAMBERT AZIMUTHAL EQUAL-AREA PROJECTION

SCALE OF MILES

0   150   300   600   900   1200

SCALE OF KILOMETRES

0   300   600   900   1200

Capitals of Countries........ ✪

International Boundaries.....

Elevations in Feet

Copyright by C. S. HAMMOND & CO., N.Y.

COMMUNISM IN ASIA

■ Union of Soviet Socialist Republics

□ Other Communist Countries

Plate 23

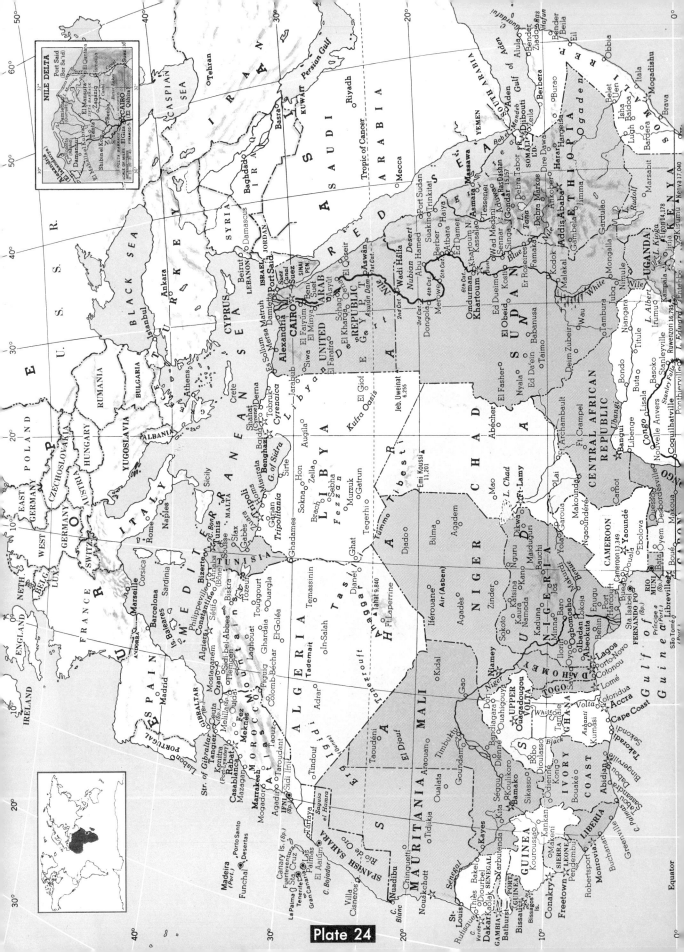

Plate 24

Plate 25

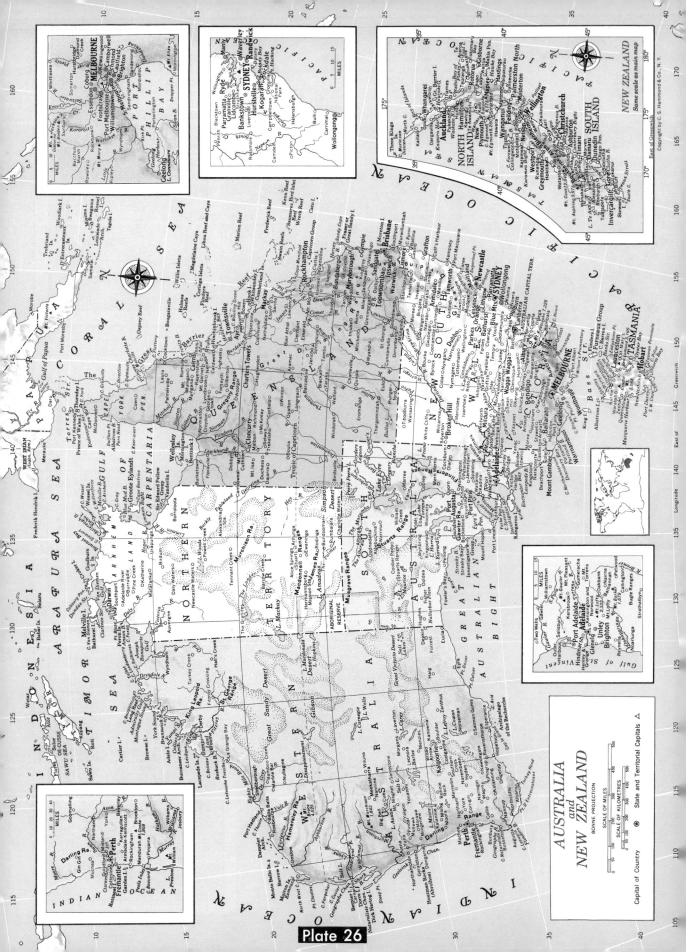

AUSTRALIA
and
NEW ZEALAND

BONNE PROJECTION

SCALE OF MILES

SCALE OF KILOMETRES

⊛ Capital of Country   ▲ State and Territorial Capitals

Plate 26

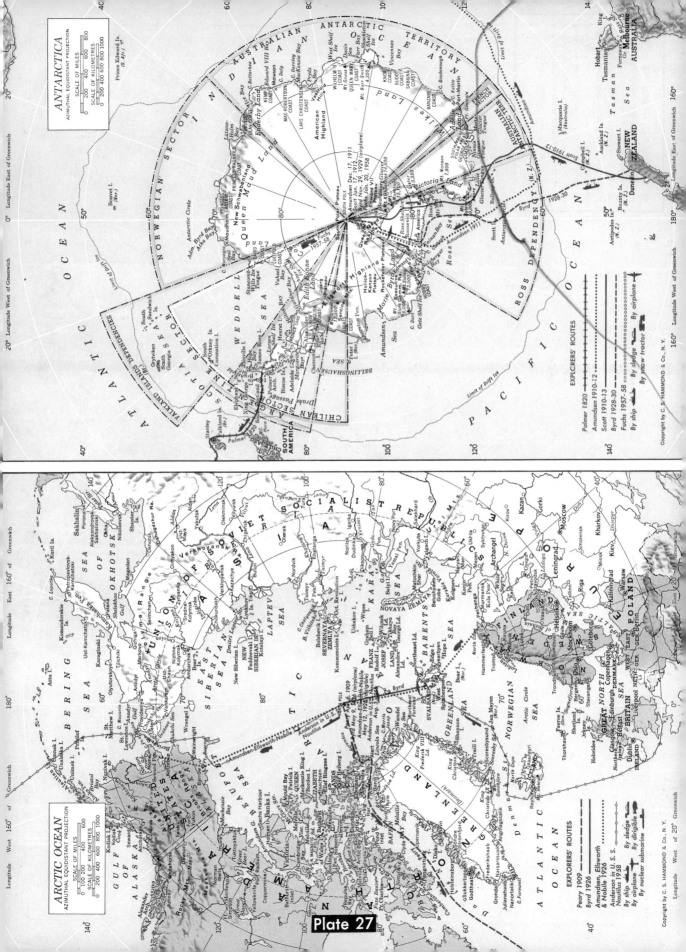

Plate 27

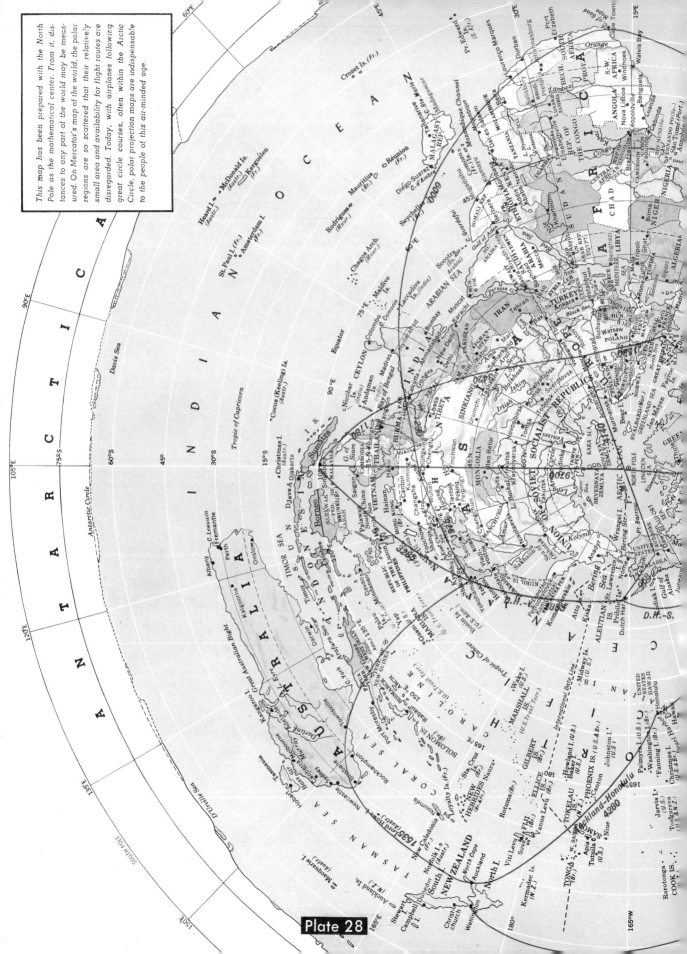

Plate 28

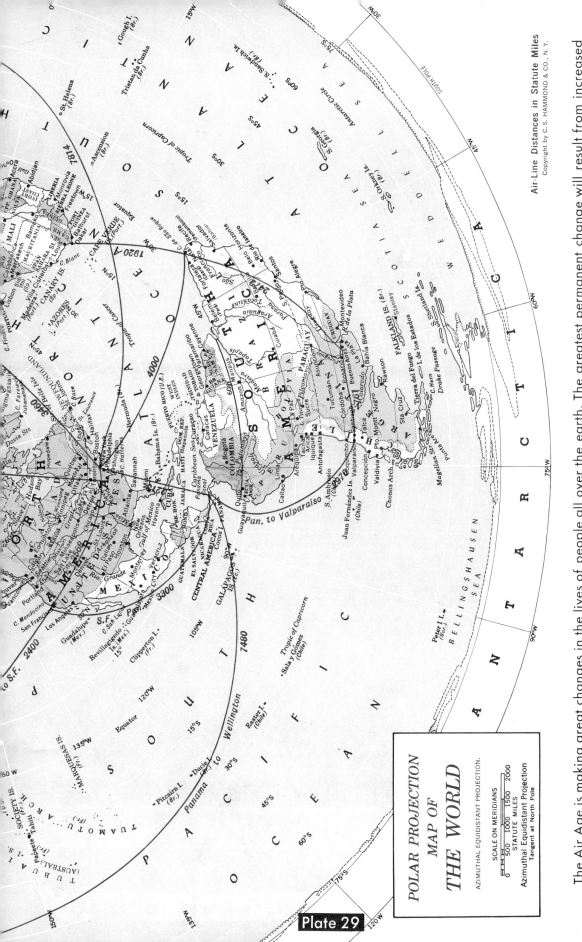

POLAR PROJECTION
MAP OF
THE WORLD

AZIMUTHAL EQUIDISTANT PROJECTION.

SCALE ON MERIDIANS

0 500 1000 1500 2000
STATUTE MILES

Azimuthal Equidistant Projection
Tangent at North Pole

Plate 29

Air-Line Distances in Statute Miles

The Air Age is making great changes in the lives of people all over the earth. The greatest permanent change will result from increased use of the air for transportation. The airplane is free to move in any direction. This has made possible new routes of travel that will save thousands of miles over the old routes that crossed the Atlantic, Pacific, and Indian oceans. In flying from our country to parts of Europe and Asia, for example, the shortest routes cross the North Polar Region. This map shows why these routes are shorter, and so it is useful in mapping great circle routes. Any straight line drawn through the North Pole on this map projection represents a great circle route. A straight line drawn between two places on any other map projection would not indicate the shortest route.

THE NEW CATHOLIC GEOGRAPHY SERIES